The Hundred Languages of Children

The Hundred Languages of Children

THE REGGIO EMILIA EXPERIENCE IN TRANSFORMATION

Third Edition

CAROLYN EDWARDS,
LELLA GANDINI, and
GEORGE FORMAN, *Editors*

In collaboration with REGGIO CHILDREN
and Innovations in Early Education: The International Reggio Exchange

 PRAEGER

AN IMPRINT OF ABC-CLIO, LLC.
Santa Barbara, California • Denver, Colorado • Oxford, England

Library of Congress Cataloging-in-Publication Data

The hundred languages of children : the Reggio Emilia experience in transformation / Carolyn Edwards, Lella Gandini, George Forman Editors. — 3rd ed.
        p. cm.
    Includes bibliographical references and index.
    ISBN 978-0-313-35961-3 (hardback) — ISBN 978-0-313-35981-1 (pbk. : alk. paper) — ISBN 978-0-313-35962-0 (ebook)
    1. Early childhood education—Italy—Reggio Emilia.   2. Early childhood education—United States—Case studies.   3. Reggio Emilia approach (Early childhood education)   I. Edwards, Carolyn P.   II. Gandini, Lella. III. Forman, George E., 1942–   IV. Title: One hundred languages of children.
    LB1139.3.I8H85   2011
    372.210945'43—dc23

                                                                    2011042170

ISBN: 978-0-313-35961-3 (cloth)
        978-0-313-35981-1 (paper)
EISBN: 978-0-313-35962-0

16 15 14   4 5

This book is also available on the World Wide Web as an eBook.
Visit www.abc-clio.com for details.

Praeger
An Imprint of ABC-CLIO, LLC

ABC-CLIO, LLC
130 Cremona Drive, P.O. Box 1911
Santa Barbara, California 93116-1911

This book is printed on acid-free paper ∞
Manufactured in the United States of America

Contents

Part IV: The Idea of the Hundred Languages of Children and Its Evolution

Part V: Conclusion

Acknowledgments

We would like first to acknowledge our positive dialogue with the chapter authors, who contributed so many valuable ideas to this volume. Our dialogue has been going on for more than 20 years, since the preparation of the first edition, and surely illustrates how the Reggio Emilia experience is an evolving one, not a static model with a codified set of theories and practices. We remember that for Loris Malaguzzi, it was especially difficult to commit his thoughts to paper, as they were always undergoing continuous change in his efforts to define and win respect for the culture of children and the role of educators, and to his memory, this book is dedicated.

Each of the contributing authors carries on Malaguzzi's intellectual legacy and contributes to building progressive educational systems for young children. Many of our contributing authors are part of three interlocking organizations described in this book: Reggio Children; Municipal Preschools and Infant-Toddler Centers; and Istituzione of the Municipality of Reggio Emilia. We appreciate that these organizations have entrusted to us the responsibility of bringing together into one integrated English-language collection, ideas about the extraordinary developments in the small city of Reggio Emilia, which now belong to the world of education beyond Italy. We especially thank Amelia Gambetti, Annamaria Mucchi, and Paola Ricco for facilitating the complicated arrangements and communications involved in a cross-national and cross-language collaboration; without their kind dedication, this book could not have been accomplished. We also thank Reggio Children for permission to reprint many quotations from Reggio Children publications that appear throughout this book. We recognize the copyright of the

Preschools and Infant-Toddler Centers–Istituzione of the Municipality of Reggio Emilia and the copyright of Reggio Children for designated photos and line drawings graciously provided. No artwork in this book should be reproduced without explicit written permission of the volume editors or the copyright holders.

In accomplishing this task, we also recognize the precious collaboration of our European and American authors. Our debt is deep to *Innovations in Early Education: The International Reggio Exchange,* journal of the North American Reggio Emilia Alliance, edited by Judith Kaminsky, coedited by Lella Gandini, and published by Wayne State University in Detroit, Michigan. *Innovations* was a critical source of published interviews that several contributing authors drew on in providing new or updated chapters for this edition. *Innovations* graciously provided us with permission to reprint many excerpts or reuse material in adapted form; these sources are cited with author, title, and publication information in endnotes and references. Likewise, we acknowledge Taylor and Francis Books UK for permission to reprint selected short quotations from books by Vea Vecchi, Carlina Rinaldi, and Gunilla Dahlberg. We thank Children in Scotland for permission to reprint the Preface by Jerome Bruner that appeared in *Children in Europe—Celebrating 40 Years of Reggio Emilia,* March 2004. We appreciate that the Hawkins Centers of Learning and the University Press of Colorado provided permission to adapt and reprint material by David Hawkins.

We also wish to acknowledge our heartfelt appreciation to the colleagues and graduate students who shared photographs, reviewed drafts, added sections, or otherwise contributed to this book: Jennifer Strange and JoAnn Ford, Webster University and Maplewood-Richmond Heights Early Childhood Center, Missouri; Margie Cooper, Inspired Practices in Early Education, Roswell, Georgia; Ellen Hall, Boulder Journey School, Boulder, Colorado; Cathy Carotta, Jill Dibbern-Manhart, and Kris Mixan, Lied Center for Childhood Deafness, Omaha, Nebraska; Laura Friedman, educator from Maine; Mary Ellin Logue, University of Maine, Orono; Keely Cline, East Tennessee State University; Amy Colgrove, Jennifer Gerdes, Traci Kutaka, Sandie Plata-Potter, Charli Raben, Lixin Ren, Sai Sato Mumm, Yinjing Shen, Xiaoqing Tu, and Ann Watt, University of Nebraska–Lincoln; and many others too numerous to mention who have influenced our thinking and expanded our knowledge of the Reggio experience. Carolyn Edwards extends her particular thanks to the University of Nebraska–Lincoln and the UNL Instructional Design Center for essential help in supporting her work on this book.

We feel deep gratitude and love for our respective three families for their sustaining support and encouragement.

Finally, we deeply and respectfully thank the educators, parents, and children who allowed our contributing authors to tell their stories and share their photographs and drawings. It is for them, and the children coming after them, that this book was written.

About the Contributors

Simona Bonilauri, *Pedagogista,* Instituzione Preschools and Infant-Toddler Centers of the Municipality of Reggio Emilia

Jerome Bruner, Research Professor of Psychology and Senior Research Fellow, New York University School of Law, and honorary citizen of Reggio Emilia

Paola Cagliari, *Pedagogista* and Director, Municipal Infant-Toddler Centers and Preschools, Reggio Emilia

Margie Cooper, President, Inspired Practices in Early Education, Inc., Roswell, Georgia

Gunilla Dahlberg, Professor of Early Childhood Education, Stockholm University, Sweden

Graziano Delrio, Mayor, Reggio Emilia

Carolyn Edwards, Willa Cather Professor, Psychology and Child, Youth, and Family Studies, University of Nebraska–Lincoln

Tiziana Filippini, *Pedagogista,* Instituzione Preschools and Infant-Toddler Centers of the Municipality of Reggio Emilia

George Forman, Professor Emeritus of Education, University of Massachusetts–Amherst, and President, Videatives, Inc.

Brenda Fyfe, Professor and Dean of Education, Webster University, St. Louis, Missouri

Amelia Gambetti, Consultant, Liaison for Consultancy to Schools and Co-chair International Network, Reggio Children

Lella Gandini, Occasional professor, visiting scholar, and US Liaison for the Dissemination of the Reggio Emilia Approach, Reggio Children

Howard Gardner, Hobbs Professor of Cognition and Education, Harvard University

Elena Giacopini, *Pedagogista,* Instituzione Preschools and Infant-Toddler Centers of the Municipality of Reggio Emilia

Claudia Giudici, *Pedagogista,* President, Istituzione Preschools and Infant-Toddler Centers of the Municipality of Reggio Emilia

David Hawkins (deceased), Professor, University of Colorado–Boulder

Loris Malaguzzi (deceased), philosopher and founding director, Preschools and Infant-Toddler Centers of the Municipality of Reggio Emilia

Deanna Margini, *Pedagogista,* Instituzione Preschools and Infant-Toddler Centers of the Municipality of Reggio Emilia

Peter Moss, Professor of Early Childhood Provision, Thomas Coram Research Unit, Institute of Education, University of London

Sandra Piccinini, *Pedagogista,* former President, Istituzione Preschools and Infant-Toddler Centers of the Municipality of Reggio Emilia

Carlina Rinaldi, *Pedagogista* and President, Reggio Children, and President, Foundation Reggio Children–Loris Malaguzzi Center

Laura Rubizzi, Teacher, Instituzione Preschools and Infant-Toddler Centers of the Municipality of Reggio Emilia

Ivana Soncini, Psychologist, Instituzione Preschools and Infant-Toddler Centers of the Municipality of Reggio Emilia

Sergio Spaggiari, former Director, Municipal Infant-Toddler Centers and Preschools, Reggio Emilia

Vea Vecchi, *Atelierista*, and Consultant for Publications and Exhibits, Reggio Children

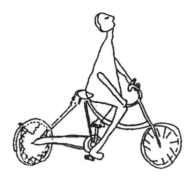

Foreword

Howard Gardner

A mid the multitude of books about education issued these days, few stand out. This book that you hold in your hands does. An integrated set of essays on a unique approach to early childhood education, *The Hundred Languages of Children* documents the remarkable set of schools that have evolved over almost 50 years in Reggio Emilia in northern Italy. At the same time, the book constitutes a profound meditation on the nature of early human nature and the ways in which it can be guided and stimulated in different cultural milieus. Anyone with an interest in the education of children should read it; few who do so will remain unaffected by the experience.

In the opening pages of this book, you will read the remarkable story of how Loris Malaguzzi, an intellectually oriented young Italian teacher, became interested in the building of a new school directly after World War II and how a momentary infatuation with this new construction turned into a lifelong love affair with young pupils. Without question, Malaguzzi (as he is universally called) is the guiding genius of Reggio—the thinker whose name deserves to be uttered in the same breath as his heroes Froebel, Montessori, Dewey, and Piaget. But far more so than most other educational thinkers, Malaguzzi dedicated his life to the establishment of an educational community: a remarkable group of teachers of various stripes and specialties who have worked together for years, even decades, with parents, community members, and thousands of children, to set up a system that works.

The Reggio system can be described succinctly as follows: it is a collection of schools for young children in which each child's intellectual, emotional, social, and moral potentials are carefully cultivated and guided. The principal educational vehicle involves youngsters in long-term engrossing projects, which are carried out in a beautiful, healthy, love-filled setting. Dewey wrote about progressive education for decades, but his school lasted a scant 4 years. In sharp contrast, it is the Reggio community, more so than the philosophy or method, that constitutes Malaguzzi's central achievement. Nowhere else in the world is there such a seamless and symbiotic relationship between a school's progressive philosophy and its practices.

Words are necessarily the prime medium in a book. The writers have done a splendid job of recreating the special atmosphere of Reggio, and the various photos and diagrams presented here add the essential visual element to the portrait. The various exhibitions about Reggio that have been mounted have helped to convey its special flavor, and there are now several film and video treatments as well. Of course, there is no substitute for a visit to Reggio Emilia, and without a doubt, the publication of this book will increase traffic to the lush and civilized Emilia Romagna area. Yet even for those who are quite familiar with the Reggio scene, this book provides a wealth of additional information. As one who had the privilege of visiting in Reggio several years ago, and has remained in touch ever since, I can say that I learned something on nearly every page of this gritty volume.

In reading *The Hundred Languages of Children,* I was struck—or struck anew—by many messages, of which I shall mention just a few. So much has been written about progressive methods in education, but so rarely are the ideals of progressive education actually realized. Perhaps one reason why is that one needs a team that is willing to work together for decades in the service of a set of energizing ideas; the team needs to evolve procedures for attaining an education of quality while still encouraging growth for all who participate. So much has been written about the powers of the young mind, and yet so rarely can they be seen in full action. In Reggio, the teachers know how to listen to children, how to allow them to take the initiative, yet how to guide them in productive ways. There is no fetish made about achieving adult standards, yet the dedication exemplified by the community ensures that work of quality will result. The effect comes about because of the infinite care taken with respect to every aspect of existence, whether it be the decision to constitute groups of two compared with three children, the choice of brush or color, or the receptivity to surprises and to surprise. Reggio successfully challenges so many false dichotomies—art versus science, individual versus community, child versus adult, enjoyment versus study, nuclear family versus extended family; by achieving a unique harmony that spans these contrasts, it reconfigures our sclerotic categorical systems.

As an American educator, I cannot help but be struck by certain paradoxes. In America, we pride ourselves on being focused on children, yet we do not pay sufficient attention to what they are actually expressing. We call for cooperative learning among children, yet we have rarely sustained cooperation at the level of teacher and administrator. We call for artistic works, but we rarely fashion environments that can truly support and inspire them. We call for parental involvement but are loathe to share ownership, responsibility, and credit with parents. We recognize the need for community, but we so often crystallize immediately into interest groups. We hail the discovery method, but we do not have the confidence to allow children to follow their own noses and hunches. We call for debate but often spurn it; we call for listening but prefer to talk; we are affluent but do not safeguard those resources that can allow us to remain so and to foster the affluence of others. Reggio is so instructive in these respects. Where we are often intent to invoke slogans, the educators in Reggio work tirelessly to solve many of these fundamental—and fundamentally difficult—issues.

It is tempting to romanticize Reggio Emilia. It looks so beautiful, it works so well. That would be a mistake. It is clear from the essays in this book that Reggio has struggled much in the past and that, indeed, conflict can never be absent from the achievements of any dynamic entity. The relationships to the Catholic Church have not been easy; the political struggles at the municipal, provincial, and national levels never cease; and even the wonderful start achieved by the youngsters is threatened and perhaps undermined by a secondary and tertiary educational system that is far less innovative. Reggio is distinguished less by the fact that it has found permanent solutions to these problems—because, of course, it has not—than by the fact that it recognizes such dilemmas unblinkingly and continues to attempt to deal with them seriously and imaginatively.

No matter how ideal an educational model or system, it is always rooted in local conditions. One could no more transport the Diana School of Reggio to New England than one could transport John Dewey's New England schoolhouse to the fields of Emilia Romagna. But just as we can now have "museums without walls" that allow us to observe artwork from all over our world, so, too, we can now have "schoolhouses without walls" that allow us to observe educational practices as they have developed around the globe.

I have had the privilege of visiting centers of early childhood education in many lands and have learned much from what I have observed in these diverse setting. Like other educational tourists, I have been impressed by the stimulating children's museums in the big cities of the United States, the noncompetitive classroom environments in Scandinavia, the supportive and sensitive training of artistic skills in China, the well-orchestrated engagement of joint problem-solving activity in Japan, and the sincere efforts now underway in many lands to develop sensitivity to diverse ethnic and racial groups in young children. In its own way, each of these educational environments has to struggle with and find its own comfortable point of repose between the desires of the individual and the needs for the group; the training of skills and the cultivation of creativity; the respect for the family and the involvement in a wider community; attention to cognitive growth and concern with matters of temperament, feelings, and spirit.

There are many ways to mediate among these human impulses and strains. To my mind, no place in the contemporary world has succeeded so splendidly as the schools of Reggio Emilia. When the American magazine *Newsweek,* in typically understated fashion, chose "The Ten Best Schools in the World" in December 1991, it was entirely fitting that Reggio Emilia was its nominee in the Early Childhood category. Reggio epitomizes for me an education that is effective and humane; its students undergo a sustained apprenticeship in humanity, one that may last a lifetime.

Thanks to the efforts of Carolyn Edwards, Lella Gandini, and George Forman, this remarkable educational enterprise can now become better known within—and more effectively emulated by—the community of concerned citizens of our troubled world.

Preface: Reggio: A City of Courtesy, Curiosity, and Imagination

Jerome Bruner

The proportions of small cities have their own appeal; they are neither confusingly large nor suffocatingly small. They favor imagination, energy, community spirit. When I came to visit Reggio Emilia, invited to see the most famous nursery schools in the world, I was expecting the latest "small town" miracle. But I wasn't prepared for what I found. In fact, I had heard of Reggio many years before, in the 1970s. Then, as professor of development at Oxford University (the proverbial Yankee at Oxford), I was head of a research program for the improvement of nursery schools in England and sifted Europe in the search for good examples. Even the brief visit to the excellent Italian nursery schools of the time had not prepared me for Reggio, however. It was not only the fact that the early childhood services were better than anything I had ever seen before. I had been expecting something of this kind, and I had also heard their praises sung many times in international congresses on early childhood. What struck me in Reggio Emilia was seeing how imagination was cultivated there, reinforcing at the same time the children's sense of the possible. It was the expression of something profoundly rooted in the city itself, something very Reggiano.

Because in Reggio, one is given to meeting a rare form of courtesy, a precious form of reciprocal respect. Maybe this kind of courtesy is easier to manage in a small city; maybe it is a reflection of Reggio's preeminence in the area of social services. Whatever the origin, however, it is a quality that is intrinsic to the place. I would like to try and explain myself.

Cultivating imagination is the first thing, but it isn't enough to read fairy tales. It is imagination that saves us all from the obvious and the banal, from the ordinary aspects of life. Imagination transforms facts into conjecture. Even a shadow cast onto the floor is not only a shadow: it is a mystery. Try drawing one, and you will realize.

One day, in a Reggio municipal nursery school, I was observing some 4-year-old children and a teacher who were projecting shadows and making efforts to draw them. The concentration was absolute, but even more surprising was the freedom of exchange in expressing their imaginative ideas about what was making the shadows so odd, why they got smaller and swelled up or, as one child asked: "How does a shadow get to be upside down?" The teacher behaved as respectfully as if she had been dealing with Nobel Prize winners. Everyone was thinking out loud: "What do you mean by upside down?" asked another child. Here we were not dealing with individual imaginations working separately. We were collectively involved in what is probably the most human thing about human beings, what psychologists and primate experts now like to call "intersubjectivity," which means arriving at a mutual understanding of what others have in mind. It is probably the extreme flowering of our evolution as humanoids, without which our human culture could not have developed, and without which all our intentional attempts at teaching something would fail.

To cultivate it requires an atmosphere of reciprocal respect and support, the type of respect that distinguishes schools that achieve success—like the municipal preschools of Reggio Emilia.

Part I

Starting Points

Invece il cento c'è

Il bambino
è fatto di cento.
Il bambino ha
cento lingue
cento mani
cento pensieri
cento modi di pensare
di giocare e di parlare
cento sempre cento
modi di ascoltare
di stupire di amare
cento allegrie
per cantare e capire
cento mondi
da scoprire
cento mondi
da inventare
cento mondi
da sognare.
Il bambino ha
cento lingue
(e poi cento cento cento)
ma gliene rubano novantanove.
La scuola e la cultura
gli separano la testa dal corpo.
Gli dicono:
di pensare senza mani
di fare senza testa
di ascoltare e di non parlare
di capire senza allegrie
di amare e di stupirsi
solo a Pasqua e a Natale.
Gli dicono:
di scoprire il mondo che già c'è
e di cento
gliene rubano novantanove.
Gli dicono:
che il gioco e il lavoro
la realtà e la fantasia
la scienza e l'immaginazione
il cielo e la terra
la ragione e il sogno
sono cose
che non stanno insieme.

Gli dicono insomma
che il cento non c'è.
Il bambino dice:
invece il cento c'è.

Loris Malaguzzi

2

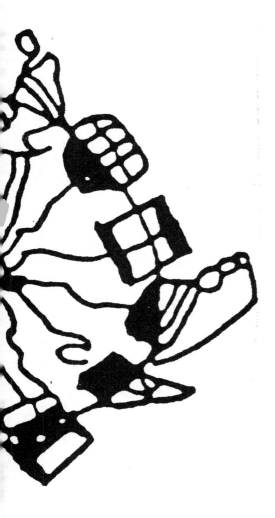

No Way. The Hundred is There.

The child
is made of one hundred.
The child has
a hundred languages
a hundred hands
a hundred thoughts
a hundred ways of thinking
of playing, of speaking.
A hundred always a hundred
ways of listening
of marveling, of loving
a hundred joys
for singing and understanding
a hundred worlds
to discover
a hundred worlds
to invent
a hundred worlds
to dream.
The child has
a hundred languages
(and a hundred hundred hundred more)
but they steal ninety-nine.
The school and the culture
separate the head from the body.
They tell the child:
to think without hands
to do without head
to listen and not to speak
to understand without joy
to love and to marvel
only at Easter and Christmas.
They tell the child:
to discover the world already there
and of the hundred
they steal ninety-nine.
They tell the child:
that work and play
reality and fantasy
science and imagination
sky and earth
reason and dream
are things
that do not belong together.

And thus they tell the child
that the hundred is not there.
The child says:
No way. The hundred *is* there.
　　　　　　　　　—Loris Malaguzzi
(translated by Lella Gandini)

3

Chapter 1

Introduction:
Background and Starting Points

Carolyn Edwards, Lella Gandini, and George Forman

Reggio Emilia is a small city in northern Italy that shines with a bright light for what it has accomplished and what it stands for in the field of education. For the past 50 years, educators, working together with parents and citizens, have built a public system of child care and education long recognized as a center of innovation in Europe and now widely recognized as a point of reference and a resource and inspiration to educators around the world (Edwards & Rinaldi, 2009; Mantovani, 2001, 2007; New, 2003; Organization for Economic Cooperation and Development [OECD], 2006; OECD Review Team Italy, 2001). Programs combine the concepts of social services and education. Children from all socioeconomic and educational backgrounds attend, with children with disabilities receiving first priority and full mainstreaming following Italian national law. More than 14% of the city budget goes to support this early childhood system, which at present includes more than 30 municipal infant-toddler centers and preschools and many other "affiliated" preschools and services for children aged under 6 years.

Map of Italy with indication of the city of Reggio Emilia.

THE REGGIO EMILIA EXPERIENCE

Over the past 50 years, this system has evolved its own distinctive and innovative set of philosophical and pedagogical assumptions, methods of school organization, and principles of environmental design that, taken as a unified whole, we are calling "the Reggio Emilia experience." The Reggio Emilia experience fosters children's intellectual development through a systematic focus on symbolic representation. Young children are encouraged to explore their environment and express themselves through multiple paths and all their "languages," including the expressive, communicative, symbolic, cognitive, ethical, metaphorical, logical, imaginative, and relational (Reggio Children, 2010, p. 4). Children experiment and develop competencies in using spoken language, gestures, drawing, painting, building, clay and wire sculpture, shadow play, collage, dramatic play, music, and emerging writing, to name but a few. Contrary to some orientations to skilled performance by young children, the Reggio teachers emphasize achievement in personal expression and reflection on one's own patterns of thinking. Instead of an early push to read, for example, teachers support a competent ability to communicate with others through speech and other means, so that one can make a contribution to the group. Instead of long hours of practice at a skill, the emphasis is placed on establishing a meaningful and emotional relation to the subject matter—the content of the project. The emphasis falls more on making meaning by inventing symbols in many media rather than translating print, math notation, or a music score into spoken words, correctly executed algorithms, or a violin performance. Children "write" in many ways, including movement, painting, sculpture, and computer animations. Although in Reggio there is emphasis on technical abilities to control these media, this is done not for the sake of adultlike performance in observational drawing or playing a music composition but rather to give the children a number of ways to make their own thinking visible.

Furthermore, from the beginning in Reggio, there has been an explicit recognition of the partnership among parents, educators, and children; classrooms are organized to support a highly collaborative, problem-solving approach to learning. Other important features are the use of small groups in project learning, the teacher–child continuity (two co-teachers work with the same class group for 3 years), and the community-based management method of governance. In Reggio Emilia, education is seen as a communal activity and as sharing of culture through

After an outing to a local cave, the children represent the drama of their experience: hats with headlights, low passages, protruding stalactites and stalagmites, surprise puddles, and even a friendly bat (from "The Hundred Languages of Children" exhibit catalog, 1996).

One of the main squares in Reggio Emilia.

joint exploration between children and adults who together open topics to specu-
lation and discussion. The approach provides us with new ways to think about
the nature of the child as learner, the role of the teacher, school organization and
management, the design and use of physical environments, and curriculum planning that guides experiences of joint, open-ended discovery and problem solving.
Because of all these features, the Reggio Emilia experience is important and exciting to educators around the world.

A DISTINCTIVE CITY AND REGION

The Reggio Emilia experience of childhood education is founded on a distinctive, coherent, evolving set of assumptions and perspectives drawn from four
important intellectual traditions: European and American strands of progressive
education, Piagetian constructivist and Vygotskian sociohistorical psycholo-
gies, Italian postwar left-reform politics, and European postmodern philosophy.
These are blended together with elements of past and present history and culture,
such as the strong regional traditions of participatory democracy—that is, citizen alliances for solidarity and cooperation. A word frequently heard in discussions among Reggio educators is *civile* ("civil"), and the child is understood to

Children's drawing of the central (oldest) part of Reggio Emilia.

have rights to civility, civilization, and civic conscience (see Chapter 3, by David Hawkins, this volume).

Reggio Emilia is known throughout Italy as one of its most livable cities (Bohlen, 1995), with characteristically low unemployment and crime, high prosperity, honest and effective local government institutions, and ample, high-quality social services. The Emilia Romagna Region, in which the city is located, has a very high level of "civic community," that is, citizens bound together by horizontal relations of social solidarity, reciprocity, and cooperation, as opposed to vertical relations of authority and dependency (Putnam, 1993). Robert Putnam collected data revealing that among the 20 regions of Italy, Emilia Romagna has the highest levels of citizen responsibility and basic trust in local institutions and officeholders (as evidenced by high voter turnout, newspaper readership, and membership in clubs and associations). Popular concepts of participatory democracy assert that people can and should speak out "as protagonists" on behalf of themselves and their group, on the basis of their own experience, and at their own level of consciousness. Citizens revere their traditions of mass organization and people across social class lines coming together to solve social problems by means of political parties and economic cooperatives (agricultural, marketing, credit, labor, producer, and consumer unions and cooperatives). These collectivist tendencies are not of recent origin but rather trace back to the craft guilds and communal republics of the medieval 14th century; they are a strong source of identity and pride for the people of the Emilia Romagna Region in general, and the city of Reggio Emilia in particular. Clearly, ideas about participatory democracy and civic community are fundamental to what the educators in Reggio Emilia feel about their educational vision and mission (Edwards, 1995). It is important to understand at the outset, therefore, a bit about how it fits into the larger context of Italian early childhood education.

THE WIDER CONTEXT OF ITALIAN EARLY CHILDHOOD EDUCATION

Susanna Mantovani of the University of Milan is one of the foremost authorities on Italian early childhood education. She has devoted years of experience to national leadership roles, as well as to providing pragmatic and theoretical expertise in her own home area in the Lombardy Region. From her perspective, *pedagogy* can be seen as the general framework within which we think about education, growing out of both its particular cultural context and of cross-fertilization with outside forces, paradigms, and practices (Mantovani, 2007). The pedagogy of early childhood education in Italy, she believes, is currently oriented about certain basic ideas (pp. 116–117). All of these themes are discussed throughout this book, thus indicating the great extent to which the educators in Reggio have been part of, and contributed to, the emergence and clarification of big ideas in the Italian early childhood field:

- A holistic and constructivist approach to understanding children and their development
- The idea of multiple intelligences (*hundred languages* in Reggio Emilia)
- The importance of design and aesthetics of the physical environment
- Attention to participation and engagement of families, citizens, and policy makers
- Attention to inclusion and integration, with respect to all aspects of diversity
- Striving for universal access to educational and care services for all children and families

Mantovani (2007) also summarizes the intellectual trends that dominate contemporary conversations among Italian early childhood experts. Key phrases recur over and over in their discussions about pedagogy. Every one of these key Italian themes intersects with the concepts of education explicated by Reggio educators throughout this book:

- "Pedagogy of well-being" *(pedagogia del benessere)*—a pedagogy of physical and emotional well-being or being deeply at ease in the education and care setting
- "Pedagogy of good taste" *(pedagogia del gusto)*—a pedagogy in which the quality and aesthetics of materials, furnishings, and images (their "taste" or "flavor") help the child appreciate, love, and respect the environment
- "Pedagogy of relations" *(pedagogia delle relazione)*—a pedagogy in which interpersonal and social relationships are seen as a means of enhancing autonomy, belonging, and individual and group learning
- "Pedagogy of continuity" *(pedagogia della continuità)*—the very high degree of continuity; involving continuity of child and teacher groupings over multiple years and a connected curriculum *(progettazione* in Reggio Emilia)
- "Pedagogy of participation" *(pedagogia della participazione)*—the framework of close home–school relationships and participation of parents and citizens in the governance of schools
- "Pedagogy of documentation" *(pedagogia della documentazione)*—documenting what children are and the process of what they do, allowing children and adults to reread past experiences, to renew memories, and to rethink
- "Cultural pedagogy" *(pedagogia culturale)*—the consciousness of the cultural nature of ideas and practices concerning children and education

THE INSPIRATION OF THE EXHIBIT

This book takes it name, *The Hundred Languages of Children,* from the continuously updated traveling exhibition that has been telling the story of the Reggio educational experience since 1981. The exhibit was originally conceived by Loris Malaguzzi and his closest coworkers as a visual documentary on their work in progress and its effects on children. The exhibit has been on tour in North America since 1987, and its most recent version, "The Wonder of Learning: The Hundred Languages of Children," began touring in 2008. "The Wonder of Learning" is a beautiful and intriguing display that narrates an educational story and weaves together experiences, reflections, debates, theoretical premises, and the social and ethical ideals of many generations of teachers, children, and parents. It describes and illustrates—or, as they like to say, makes visible—the philosophy and pedagogy of the Reggio Emilia experience, through photographs depicting moments of teaching and learning; explanatory scripts and panels (many containing texts of children's words); samples of the processes of children's paintings, drawings, collages, and constructions; and audiovisual materials (Cooper, 2008; Gambetti, 2008).

As a medium of communication, the exhibit serves as a tool for professional development and as support to occasions such as meetings, conferences, and workshops, where people meet face-to-face and are able to open themselves in a full, intense, and focused way to the story that the Reggio Emilia educators want to tell. Created by the Reggio educators to inform both public and professional audiences, the exhibit in several ways exemplifies the very essence of the educational approach.

First of all, the exhibit uses **multiplicity,** as opposed to simplicity, to make its points. It plunges the visitor into a form of learning that is multileveled and multimodal. Looking at the large, highly detailed panels, densely embedded with words, images, and artifacts, the mind and senses are overwhelmed with information and impressions coming in on several channels all at once. This gives visitors the immediate and tangible experience of learning through "one hundred languages." As Malaguzzi put it in the catalog, the exhibit creates "a place of uninterrupted condensation of hundreds of subjective and objective experiences" where "we hope to obtain an exciting flux of emotions, but also of images, interactions, and meanings more consonant with even deeply hidden reality" (Reggio Children, 1987, pp. 22–23).

A second quality of the exhibit is its **circularity.** Wandering at will through the exhibit, visitors find themselves on a circular path as they retrace their steps and return repeatedly to favorite sections, panels, or themes, each time with deeper understanding. In just this way, education in Reggio Emilia is anything but linear; it is, instead, an open-ended spiral. Young children are not marched or hurried sequentially from one activity to the next but instead are encouraged to repeat key experiences, observe and reobserve, consider and reconsider, represent and rerepresent.

Third, the exhibit shows the value of **visibility.** As a form of communication, it grew directly out of what Reggio Emilia educators call *documentation.* Early in their history (see the interview with Loris Malaguzzi, Chapter 2 of this volume), the educators realized that systematically documenting the process and results of their work with children would simultaneously serve children, parents, and educators. Documentation provides the children and the adults with a concrete and visible "memory" of what they have said and done to serve as a jumping-off point for the next steps in learning. It provides parents and the public with detailed information about what happens in the schools, as a means of eliciting their reactions and support. Finally, it provides the educators with a tool for research and a key to continuous improvement and renewal. This bold insight led to the development of documentation into a professional art form in Reggio Emilia involving myriad products, including panels, books, slide presentations, and CD/ DVDs to record children's learning experiences.

Fourth, the exhibit demonstrates the value of **collectivity.** It was authored and designed not individually but rather collectively. Loris Malaguzzi, founder and for many years director of the Reggio Emilia system of municipal early childhood education, first led the task of preparing the exhibit, but many administrators, teachers, and others from throughout the city contributed time, labor, ideas, and the results of recording project work in their classrooms (demonstrating the quality of results coming from group effort). Reggio educators believe that reciprocity, exchange, and dialogue lie at the heart of successful education.

Fifth, the exhibit places a value on incompleteness, or **open-endedness.** It never reaches a state in which the Reggio educators say, "Now, it is finished; let's not think about any more changes." Instead, it undergoes transformations and emerges in one after another of separate versions or editions. The first opened in 1981 and began to travel in Europe under the name "L'occhio se salta il muro" ("When the Eye Jumps Over the Wall"). The title became "I cento linguaggi dei bambini" ("The Hundred Languages of Children") for later editions and then "The Wonder of Learning: The Hundred Languages of Children" for the completely revised 2008 North American version. We have noticed some changes across the various editions of the exhibits. For example, compared with the earlier exhibits, "The Wonder of Learning" allows viewers to witness more of the process of teaching, through the fuller explanations on the panels and also the accompanying DVDs that viewers can watch. Also, to supplement the documentation of long-term projects, "The Wonder of Learning" contains one-page summaries of micro-stories printed on separate pages in a portfolio that can be browsed or purchased for later study. Indeed, visiting the exhibit has changed from an experience of standing up and reading the signage to include sitting down and studying the data as well. These changes do not reflect fundamental changes in the philosophy of teaching but rather efforts to improve the exhibit as a means of communication and invitation to dialogue and further study.

In just such a way, the educational work in Reggio Emilia never becomes set and routine but instead is always undergoing reexamination and experimentation. For this reason, the Reggio educators refuse to use the term *model* when talking about their approach and instead speak of "our project" and "our experience."

Finally, the exhibit demonstrates the value of **courage.** At the time the first exhibit was prepared in 1981, Vea Vecchi says she felt like a pioneer—proud and excited to be part of a brave little band inventing new teaching practices and an unusual and beautiful way to present them (Vecchi, 2010, p. 170). Returning in 2008 to undertake the major revisions for "The Wonder of Learning," she became part of a large working committee deliberately composed to be diverse and interdisciplinary. She found that arriving at consensus and creating all of the components of this complex new exhibit required a new and different kind of intellectual courage, because they were without the guiding presence of the brilliant Loris Malaguzzi (1920–1994) to reassure them about their choices and decisions. In her mind, the changing nature of the exhibit preparation traced the evolution of the Reggio experience—from obscure pioneers working with a founding leader to an established system carrying the weight of responsibility in fellowship with a new generation.

THE NEED FOR THIS BOOK

The exhibit does not accomplish everything, however. Unlike a book, it cannot be taken home for study and reflection. It cannot answer all of our questions about the

Loris Malaguzzi, Sergio Spaggiari, and Carlina Rinaldi receive the first copies of the first edition of this book from Lella Gandini.

history and philosophy of the program; curriculum, planning, and teacher behavior; work with parents, including those whose children have "special rights"; and the administrative organization and structure. Thus, the need for this book was born. It allows for a more extended and analytic treatment of the Reggio Emilia approach in all of its aspects, and it provides a forum for both Italians and North Americans to tell what they know about the Reggio Emilia approach.

The first edition, published in 1993, was intended to be a starting point, and it succeeded in initiating discussions, introducing readers to the fundamental points of the Reggio Emilia approach, and describing first steps in using and adapting it in this country. There was such an upsurge of American interest and deepening of reflection that a second edition was published in 1998 to describe the increased sophistication in adaptations and interpretations to the American context, as well as for our Italian colleagues to respond to the intervening years of contact and dialogue with Americans.

Since the publication of the second edition, more than a decade has passed, and it has been a hugely transformative period for the city of Reggio Emilia, for its early childhood services, and for the organization of its national and international outreach. Reggio educators' work has been extremely influential, and many publications have described Reggio-inspired experiments and innovations in various cultural and educational contexts. At the same time, the educational undertaking in the city of Reggio has constantly evolved. Like many communities in the world during this period in history, Reggio Emilia is a city undergoing rapid social change, with increasing population; many more languages, races, and backgrounds; and increasing political controversy arising among the citizens—all of these changes calling forth new civic and political responses to promote solidarity and sustainability. Furthermore, an influx of a new generation of educators, as an older generation retires and the system expands, has introduced new issues in professional development and mentoring. Finally, intense desires to engage in sustained and reciprocal research, exchange, and dialogue with educators of all kinds, in Italy and beyond, has led to a concentrated international focus. In the course of all this transformation, the city is moving away from consolidated traditions toward those that are new and unfamiliar.

Considering that the educators in Reggio Emilia continue to evolve their theories and practices, and also taking into account the expanding web of contacts and exchanges with educators from many countries, the time has arrived for a new and updated third edition of this book—one that focuses on the educational processes and changes. Here we show how the Reggio experience is organic and dynamic and how it is responsive to historical forces and changing societal needs, such as the increasing diversity of the population and the influx of a new generation of educators. As Howard Gardner told George Forman in a 2010 interview, the educators' concerns 30 years ago were focused mainly on the schools. As society changed economically and demographically, the focus expanded to include the schools and the politics of the community, including interactions with the private sector, foundations, and educational institutions. Today, the Reggio Emilia approach focuses on those aspects, as well as Reggio's relation to the wider world.

As the reader will see, although the Reggio experience has become internationally known, it has not become simply a slogan or formula, a recipe or commercial commodity, or a fad or fashion. It has not (indeed, cannot) be thought of as any kind of quick fix, because quick fixes never work in education, and moreover, programs and models from overseas can never be transplanted wholesale from one cultural context to another without extensive change and adaptation. Instead, what we have seen and learned in Reggio Emilia has become a source of energy and inspiration, as we wrestle with our own continuing problems of public school reform and uneven quality, poor coordination, and lack of access and affordability of other kinds of early childhood services. The discourse about the Reggio Emilia experience has entered our pool of common referents and become a source of powerful terms (such as *visibility, context, pedagogical documentation, projected curriculum, image of the child, education as relationship, revisiting, cognitive knots,* and *participation*), as we develop our own shared vocabulary and set of exemplars for talking and arguing in ever more productive ways about theory and practice in education.

Loris Malaguzzi, George Forman, Tiziana Filippini, and Carolyn Edwards during the visit at the University of Massachusetts in Amherst, on the occasion of the inauguration of the exhibit "The Hundred Languages of Children."

THE AUTHORS AND THEIR CHAPTERS

The Editors' Perspectives

The editors originally worked together on the exhibit and conference "The Hundred Languages of Children," held at the University of Massachusetts in Amherst in December 1988. It was during and immediately after this conference that Carolyn Edwards proposed we collaborate to edit a book about the municipal preprimary schools of Reggio Emilia—the first book of its kind. We felt that we had complementary strengths that would yield a useful and significant book. Carolyn Edwards, who also helped host the 1993 exhibit in Lexington, Kentucky, has an extensive background in cultural anthropology and social development and for many years directed the early childhood laboratory school at the University of Massachusetts before moving to the University of Kentucky and then the University of Nebraska–Lincoln, where she focuses on early childhood development and education. Lella Gandini, liaison and bridge to the Italian culture and its people, has consulted to many early childhood systems in Italy, North America, and throughout the world. She has a strong background in art education as well as child development and education. George Forman has studied constructivism from the beginning of the Piagetian movement in the late 1960s and, after retiring from the University of Massachusetts, founded Videatives Inc., producing digital video clips to help educators "see what children know." The three of us had the fortunate opportunity to observe and study these schools during many trips to Reggio Emilia: Lella since1976, Carolyn since 1983, and George since 1985.

The Flow of Chapter Topics

This third edition presents an introduction of the Reggio Emilia experience for both new and returning readers who wish to understand the theoretical foundations and practical strategies of today. Because so many books describe the ways in which the Reggio experience has been taken up in other countries, this book instead focuses on the evolving work taking place in Reggio Emilia. Most of the chapters are written by the Reggio educators. Howard Gardner and Jerome Bruner, distinguished psychologists whose reflections in the opening pages and chapters invite the reader into this book, are frequent and honored guests in Reggio Emilia.

Part I, "Starting Points," begins with a poem by Loris Malaguzzi, founder of the municipal early childhood system in Reggio Emilia. Next, we provide necessary background on the Reggio experience and set the early childhood system in Reggio in the Italian context. That introduction is followed by an interview with Loris Malaguzzi by Lella Gandini. It was welcoming that Malaguzzi took our first edition as an opportunity to write his first comprehensive review of his life's work and the history of the municipal early childhood system in Reggio Emilia. The remaining chapters in this section convey important aspects of what may be distinctive about the context and the early childhood system of Reggio Emilia, and how its leaders are seeking to preserve the strong civic community and commitment to quality of life in the face of significant transformations in political, economic, and demographic conditions.

Part II, "Teaching and Learning through Relationships," explains the system of parent and citizen participation and provides richly detailed information, with many anecdotes and illustrations, of how the teachers and pedagogical coordinators work together to guarantee the quality of the early childhood services for all children.

Part III, "Documentation as an Integrated Process of Observing, Reflecting, and Communicating," presents a detailed analysis of pedagogical documentation and the "pedagogy of listening." Documentation is arguably the single most important educational strategy to emerge from the Reggio Emilia experience, and this section offers an international dialogue on the theory and practice of pedagogical documentation.

Part IV, "The Idea of the Hundred Languages of Children and Its Evolution," describes this concept and its evolution. In recent years, Reggio educators have clarified how they use the word *languages* as a metaphor for the different ways humans express themselves and as a wider view of the extraordinary competence of children. The section explores concepts of "beauty as a way of knowing" and how these ideas drive the work of the *atelierista* ("studio teacher"), the design of space and the environment, and the use of digital technology that affords innovative means to support children's learning and the professional development of teachers. This section concludes with the story of the Loris Malaguzzi International Center, opened in three major phases in 2006, 2009, and 2011. The International Center stands as the physical embodiment of Reggio's progressive vision for the future. Through it, Reggio Children is seeking to accomplish progressive ideals of defending and promoting the rights and potential of all children.

Part V offers our final reflections and thoughts on new questions and directions, as well as a list of guiding principles for teacher–child interaction, as a condensation and synthesis that may be helpful to readers.

THE HISTORICAL CONTEXT OF THE REGGIO EXPERIENCE

As we begin to turn to the experience of children and adults in Reggio Emilia, we need to place this experience in perspective to inquire into the context that made it possible for this educational approach to come together. Doing so will help us better understand those factors that are common to other educational programs in Italy, those that pertain to the Emilia Romagna Region, and those that are unique products of the dedication and vision of the educators of Reggio Emilia.

Historically, early education in Italy has been caught in the tangled web of relations between Church and State. The enormous power conflicts between the centuries-old Catholic Church and the young Italian state (formed only in 1860) have affected many modern outcomes, including early childhood education.

Around 1820 in the northern and central parts of Italy, charitable institutions began to emerge. These were offshoots of a concern for the poor, emerging throughout Europe at that time, with the intention of improving the lives of the urban populace, reducing crime, and forming better citizens (Cambi & Ulivieri, 1988). For young children, there came into being institutions that were, to some extent, forerunners of the two major public early education programs currently offered in Italy: the infant-toddler centers (*asili nido*, or "safe nests"), serving infants aged 4 months to 3 years, and preprimary schools (*scuole dell'infanzia*, or "schools of infancy"), serving children 3 to 6 years old.

The Infant-Toddler Centers (*Asili Nido*)

The early forerunners to the modern infant-toddler centers were creches (*presepi*) for breast-fed or newly weaned infants of working mothers. Industrialists set these up at their factories. For example, in Pinerolo, Piedmont, one was started in the silk mill, where the cradles were rocked by the mill's hydraulic engine. Other similar institutions were promoted by the public administrations of the small, separate states that shared the Italian peninsula before unification. Still others resulted from initiatives by private benefactors (Della Peruta, 1980).

After the unification of the Italian state, these institutions continued to develop, but with difficulties. It was only toward the beginning of the 20th century that some of the private initiatives began to be supported by public funding, mostly municipal. The idea was to move away from charitable assistance, dispensed only by private means, toward programs combining prevention and assistance and funded by both private and public sectors. For example, next to creches or shelters for infants, there would be a center for dispensing medical instruction and help to mothers with the goal of educating them on child care and diminishing infant mortality. All these initiatives eventually culminated in 1925 in passage of a national law, the Protection and Assistance of Infancy, which provided for the National Organization for Maternity and Infancy. This organization, called ONMI, was to expand and organize infant centers under the Ministry of the Interior.

The Fascist regime, which had taken over Italy in 1922, took upon itself all the merits of this innovation, while still trying to keep alive the connection with private, philanthropic support. ONMI centers adopted a medical–hygienic model of child care, which was the prevailing trend of the time, and took up the Fascist ideology of motherhood, which in turn was tied to the regime's policy of population growth. Rosalyn Saltz visited ONMI centers in Rome in 1975 and subsequently remarked:

> Psycho-social aspects of an infant's development are assumed to be adequately served if the psychological atmosphere of the center is not harsh, if children are not in obvious distress and if caregivers appear to be reasonably fond of children. (Saltz, 1976, p. 130)

The ONMI organization remained in place with some ideological changes for 50 years, even through the social upheavals of the 1960s and early 1970s. In December 1971, however, major national legislation to institute a new kind of infant–toddler center was finally passed, drawing on the strong support of labor unions and the women's movement. In December 1975, the 604 ONMI centers all over Italy were officially transferred to city administrations (Lucchini, 1980).

A 1971 law (Law 1044) instituted social and educational services for children aged under 3 years, with the twin goals of insuring adequate assistance to families and facilitating women's entry into the workplace. Law 1044 further stated that families were to apply for services and make partial financial contributions, but the assistance was a matter of public (as opposed to purely private) interest. During the 1970s and 1980s, as employment opportunities for women increased throughout Italy, infant–toddler services began to be seen by many as a right of every working family. In fact, in locations where the services developed particularly well, they further came to be seen as a quality benefit for children in addition to a service to parents (Mantovani, 2001).

Law 1044 made the 20 regional governments of Italy responsible for carrying out the legislation and gave municipal governments the task of establishing standards and regulations, making requests for funds, and constructing and organizing the infant-toddler centers. Inevitably, the network of centers developed in an uneven way across the regions of Italy, influenced by political choices, views about women's roles, financial resources, and norms of administrative effectiveness. Similarly, the law's interpretation and implementation has also varied across municipalities. For example, cities differ in how they have set fee scales and prioritized admission criteria based on maternal employment, family income, and presence of extended family support. By 1986, 1,904 infant-toddler centers had been built, serving some 99,000 children (about 6% of Italian children under age 3), with the lowest percentage (0.7%) in the Campania Region of southern Italy, and the highest (20%) in Emilia Romagna. In the municipality of Reggio Emilia (where the first infant-toddler center was opened in 1970, in advance of Law 1044), the number of children under 3 who were served reached 30%. In the decades that followed, periods of financial slowdown or crisis affected the economies of Europe, with budget deficits, unemployment, and lower rates of growth. In the face of diminished financial and political capital to spend on behalf of children, the European Community began to assess the adequacy and accessibility of services for children and government and workplace policies supporting families (Ghedini, 2001).

Likewise in Italy, budget crises led to a reassessment of services for children under age 3 years. Starting at the end of 1983, infant-toddler services were no longer qualified as "services of public interest" but instead were classified as "services of individual demand," with the assumption that part of the cost would be paid by consumers (Fortunati, 2007). Committed educators and policy makers became concerned that despite research pointing to the benefits of quality child care for both children and families, the trend was once again for the responsibility for children's care and education to be put on the shoulders of mothers—mothers who were now also likely to be wage earners. Although responsible administrations tried to protect their infant-toddler services (indeed, some municipalities even continued to add some new centers), the debate created new awareness about parents' variety of needs in a time of social transformation and the necessity for rationalizing all public expenditures. Building on the knowledge and experience gained in the past, educators and administrators found ways to offer new types of services. Starting in the mid-1980s, especially in regions such as Tuscany, Lombardy, Emilia Romagna, and Umbria, two types of services began to be offered to provide new kinds of flexibility and participation: (1) *spazio bambini*, "children's spaces," serving children aged 18–36 months for a maximum of 5 hours per day, and (2) *centri per bambini e genitori*, or parent–child programs, where parents and children come together with a professional facilitator (Musatti & Picchio, 2010).

Reggio Emilia joined this trend toward new services and opened its first two public–private cooperatives in 1987. In the 1990s, parents formed the Agora

Association to self-manage a classroom of infants and toddlers at a municipal preschool, and such "affiliated services" continue to expand in the city (Piccinini & Giudici, Chapter 5, this volume).

The Preschools (*Scuole dell'Infanzia*)

The contemporary preschools serving children aged 3 to 6 years also have deep roots in the 19th century. One institution, devoted to children aged 2 to 6 years old and considered outstanding was founded by Abbot Ferrante Aporti, in 1831, in the city of Cremona. Teaching and learning were important there, and play was often replaced by crafts for little boys and domestic activities for little girls (Della Peruta, 1980). After 1867, the influence of Froebel's Kindergarten started to take root. At the beginning of the 20th century, as Italy became industrialized and the Socialist Party, with its progressive agenda, emerged and grew, the needs of working women and the care and education of children came into focus. Progressive educators became involved in early childhood education. Pistillo (1989) describes the years around 1904 to 1913 as particularly fertile for early childhood education. During this period, a national law established a teacher training school to prepare teachers of young children. The sisters, Rosa and Carolina Agazzi developed a new philosophy and method of early education. Maria Montessori founded her first Children's House in Rome.

However, the Italian Ministry of Education did not directly assist the growth of preprimary education, and although initiative remained in the private sector, it became increasingly controlled by the Roman Catholic Church. After 1922, the Fascist regime dismissed Montessori education and promoted only those school reforms compatible with Church monopoly and control. The Agazzi method, favored by the Catholic Church, was proclaimed the official state method for the education of young children. In 1933, at the height of Fascism, more than 60% of preprimary schools were run by religious orders (Olmstead & Weikart, 1994).

By the postwar period, however, after all of the years under Fascism, people were ready for change. In 1945 and 1946, for a short period right after the Second World War, people took many initiatives into their own hands. The national government was undergoing reorganization. It was in this period that, in localities with a strong tradition of local initiative, there arose spontaneous attempts to establish parent-run schools, such as that Loris Malaguzzi (Chapter 2) describes so vividly for Reggio Emilia.

Loris Malaguzzi, founder of the system of public early childhood education in Reggio Emilia, was born on February 23, 1920, in Correggio in the Emilia Romagna Region of northern Italy (Gandini, 2007). He moved with his family to the nearby city of Reggio Emilia in 1923, when his father assumed a post as railway stationmaster. He married in 1944 and had one son, Antonio, who became an architect. As a young man in wartime Italy, Malaguzzi taught elementary school in Sologno, a village in the Apennines (1939–1941), and both elementary and middle school in Reggio Emilia (1942–1947). In the meanwhile, he completed an educational degree from the University of Urbino (1946) and threw his energies into supporting the parent-run preschool movement that sprang up just after the Second World War. In his interview with Lella Gandini (Chapter 2), Malaguzzi tells the vivid story of how he first heard about and became involved in the establishment of the first cooperative school in the town of Villa Cella, just outside Reggio, and then led the system of municipal infant-toddler centers and preschools until his death on January 30, 1994.

The Birth of Public Early Childhood Education.   By the 1950s, many educators and parents in Italy had become aware of the critical need for more and better early childhood education. They also knew that the dominant Christian Democratic Party had no intention of changing the status of early childhood education. New ideas about education were entering Italy: the "popular school" movement coming from France; the newly translated writings of progressive educators such as Celestin Freinet and John Dewey. A feverish debate fed people's determination to change education at all levels. In 1951, the Movement of Cooperative Education (MCE) was formed. This organization of elementary teachers had the goal of applying the techniques of Freinet; they achieved cooperation through an Italian style of critical debate. The leader of the MCE was a charismatic educator named Bruno Ciari, who was invited by the left-wing administration of Bologna to organize and direct their city school system. Indeed, it was only in cities with left-wing administrations that progressive municipal early childhood systems were established in the 1960s and 1970s. In cities in which the centrist Christian Democratic Party was dominant, the Catholic Church's monopoly on early education tended to prevail.

Ciari (1961) suggested many educational innovations, both in his writings and through the meetings he organized for teachers in Bologna. Like others in the MCE, he was convinced that a more just society could be achieved through the right kind of early childhood education. His books became classics.

The buildup of energy, enthusiasm, and thoughtful concern generated the takeoff of early childhood education in Italy. The debates initiated by Ciari activated people, which in turn helped Ciari formulate many of his key ideas. Loris Malaguzzi participated in these lively debates, and through them, he came to know Ciari. Deeply inspired by Ciari, Malaguzzi (Chapter 2) recalls him as a fabulous friend and as "the most lucid, passionate and acute intelligence in the field of childhood education." The group around Ciari declared the beliefs that education should liberate childhood energy and capacities and promote the harmonious development of the whole child in all areas—communicative, social, affective, and with respect to critical and scientific thinking. Ciari urged educators to develop relationships with families and encourage participatory committees of teachers, parents, and citizens. He argued there should be two rather than one teacher in each classroom and that teachers and staff should work collectively, without hierarchy. He thought children should be grouped by age for part of the day but mix openly during another part, and he wanted to limit the number of children per classroom to 20. Finally, he gave much attention to the physical setting of education (Ciari, 1972).

In 1967, an explosive pamphlet appeared: "Letter to a Teacher," by Lorenzo Milani and the Scuola di Barbiana (1967). This was a passionate but solidly documented denunciation of selectivity and social class discrimination in the national school system. Widely quoted, the "Letter" became a manifesto in the fight for educational reform. In 1968, the student movement erupted; students occupied the universities and demonstrated in the streets. The next year saw mass mobilization of workers; widespread strikes in the cities arose over the national labor contract negotiations. Women's groups became outspoken and led the protests for better social services, schools, and child care. Oftentimes, all of these groups marched together through the streets, putting concerted pressure on the political parties and government (Corsaro & Emiliani, 1992).

The 10-year period from 1968 to 1977 saw the enactment of many key pieces of social legislation. During this same period, women were entering the labor force in ever greater numbers and vigorously pressing their demands. The most important of the new laws were as follows:

1968   Establishment of government-sponsored preschool education
1971   Establishment of maternity leave (12 weeks of paid leave at 80%–100% of earnings and a further 6 months of leave at 30%)
1971   Establishment of government-sponsored *asili nido* (infant-toddler centers)
1975   Institution of a new family law more protective of women's rights
1977   Institution of work parity (equal pay for equal work) between men and women

In this changing social landscape, with its notable legislative accomplishments, educators were rewarded for their vision and responsiveness to new expectations about care and education for young children. The number of municipal preschools grew rapidly until the mid-1980s, and then more slowly during the following years. Altogether, the percentage of the 3- to 6-year-old population served by state (national), municipal, or private schools reached 88.8% in 1988–1989 and 92.7% in 1992–1993 (Becchi, 1995), and 98.1% in 2001 (OECD, 2006).

Although the promise of the 1968 law has been largely fulfilled, in terms of free education becoming available to children aged 3 to 6, there remains unevenness across the regions of Italy in quality and quantity of services for children and in-service training for teachers (Corsaro & Emiliani, 1992; Olmstead & Weikart, 1994; Pistillo, 1989). Furthermore, the quality of education provided varies widely. A number of municipal systems are known for their excellent systems (e.g., Reggio Emilia, Pistoia, Modena, Parma, Milano, Bologna, Genova, Trento, and San Miniato). Private schools based on a strong philosophy and method, such as Montessori or Rudolph Steiner schools, can also be excellent. However, such levels of quality are not typical of the majority of schools, perhaps because the strong, alternative pedagogies do not mix well with traditional methods (based on either family models of nurturant affection or, more often, elementary school methods) that are most familiar.

Trends of innovation have always existed side by side with the traditional methods, however. New ideas have stirred debate—for example, in connection with establishment of national standards of good preschool practice (*Orientamenti,* or "Guidelines," in 1968; *Nuovi Orientamenti,* or "New Guidelines," in 1991; and *Indicazioni,* or "Indications," in 2004) and community-based management in 1974, as well as such gradual developments as the inclusion of children with disabilities and increased integration of families with children from countries outside the European Community. Recently, attention has turned to the system of state-run (national) preschools and what can be done to bring these schools to a consistently high level of quality.

Starting in the mid-1980s, a long period began in which conservative tendencies in Italian politics made it difficult to pass major new laws or policy initiatives, and this had an impact on childhood services (Fortunati, 2007). Nevertheless, despite those obstacles, educators and citizens working together in progressive cities and regions in the north-central regions have continued their experimentation in creating new types of services, methods of evaluating quality, approaches to financing the costs of services, and forms of outreach to increasingly diverse populations.

Teacher Preparation and Professional Development. For most of the time period we have been describing, teachers qualified to be *educatrici* ("educators") for preschools and infant-toddler centers through a traditional pathway of attending special high school programs. Starting as early as the 1980s, however, many educators surpassed those minimal requirements and attended university programs (Nigris, 2007). In 1998, national legislation established new standards for early childhood teachers. The requirement for preschool teachers became a 4-year degree in Scienze della Formazione Primaria, a course of study preparing both preschool and primary teachers. In 1999, the Italian university system was reformed in alignment with European agreements to consist of a 3-year level (*laurea,* roughly equivalent to the North American bachelor's degree) and a 2-year postgraduate level (*aurea magistrale,* roughly equivalent to the North American master's degree). Beginning in 2007, the 4-year course for preschool teachers was extended to 5 years, as at all other levels of teacher preparation. The trend for infant-toddler teachers in most regions of Italy is to require the 3-year course. The goal of the university programs is to offer studies that are multidisciplinary in approach with integrated theory and practice and involving a partnership with schools (Nigris, 2007). One such university program is offered by the University of Modena and Reggio Emilia.

In conclusion, these recent developments offer opportunities to educators throughout the world who seek to know in greater depth and with greater clarity about the Reggio work with young children. They also validate and reward the achievement of the Reggio educators and citizens, for their unique and magnificent combination of commitment and determination, research and experimentation, renewal and openness—all strengthened by years of work in refining skills of communication and documentation. Let us go now to that story and learn of its implications and possibilities.

REFERENCES

Becchi, E. (Ed.). (1995). *Manuale della Scuola del Bambino dei 3 ai 6 anni* [Handbook for the school of the young child, 3 to 6 years of age]. Milan: Franco Angeli.

Bohlen, C. (1995, March 24). Tell these Italians communism doesn't work. *New York Times International.* Available at www.nytimes.com/1995/03/24/world/reggio-emilia-journal -tell-these-italians-communism-doesn-t-work.html.

Cambi, F., & Ulivieri, S. (1988). *Storia dell'infanzia nell'Italia liberale* [Childhood history in liberal Italy]. Florence: La Nuova Italia.

Ciari, B. (1961). *Le nuove tecniche didattiche* [The new teaching techniques]. Rome: Editori Riuniti.

Ciari, B. (1972). *La grande disadattata* [The great maladjusted]. Rome: Editori Riuniti.

Cooper, M. (2008). Anticipation and reflection of the exhibit. *Innovations in Early Education: The International Reggio Exchange, 15*(2), 14–20.

Corsaro, W. A., & Emiliani, F. (1992). Child care, early education, and children's peer culture in Italy. In M. E. Lamb, K. J. Sternberg, C. P. Hwang, & A. G. Broberg (Eds.), *Child care in context* (pp. 81–115). Hillsdale, NJ: Lawrence Erlbaum.

Della Peruta, F. (1980). Alle origini dell'assistenza alla prima infanzia in Italia [At the origins of early childhood assistance in Italy]. In L. Sala La Guardia & E. Lucchini (Eds.), *Asili nido in Italia* [Infant-toddler centers in Italy] (pp. 13–38). Milan: Marzorati.

Edwards, C. P. (1995). Democratic participation in a community of learners: Loris Malaguzzi's philosophy of education as relationship. Invited lecture, Nostalgia del Futuro, symposium honoring the contributions to education of Loris Malaguzzi. University of Milan, Italy. Available at http://digitalcommons.unl.edu/famconfacpub/15.

Edwards, C. P., and Rinaldi, C. (Eds.). (2009). *The diary of Laura: Perspectives on a Reggio Emilia diary.* St. Paul, MN: Redleaf Press.

Fortunati, A. (2007). Italy: Quality. Public policies. In R. S. New & M. Cochran (Eds.), *Early childhood education: An international encyclopedia, Vol. 4: The countries* (pp. 1122–1125, 1150–1154). Westport, CT: Praeger.

Gambetti, A. (2008). *The wonder of learning: The hundred languages of children,* a new exhibit from Reggio Emilia, Italy—North American version. *Innovations in Early Education: The International Reggio Exchange, 15*(2), 1–13.

Gandini, L. (2007). Loris Malaguzzi. Biographical entry in R. S. New & M. Cochran (Eds.), *Early childhood education: An international encyclopedia* (Vol. 2, pp. 497–499). Westport, CT: Praeger.

Ghedini, P. (2001). Change in Italian national policy for children 0–3 years old and their families: Advocacy and responsibility. In L. Gandini & C. P. Edwards (Eds.), *Bambini:*

The Italian approach to infant/toddler care (pp. 38–48). New York: Teachers College Press.

Lucchini, E. (1980). Nasce l'asilo nido di tipo nuovo [The birth of the new type of infant-toddler centers]. In L. Sala La Guardia & E. Lucchini (Eds.), *Asili nido in Italia* [Infant-toddler centers in Italy] (pp. 191–286). Milan: Marzorati.

Mantovani, S. (2001). Infant-toddler centers in Italy today: Tradition and innovation. In L. Gandini & C. P. Edwards (Eds.), *Bambini: The Italian approach to infant/toddler care* (pp. 23–37). New York: Teachers College Press.

Mantovani, S. (2007). Italy: Pedagogy and curriculum. Infant/toddler care. In R. S. New & M. Cochran (Eds.), *Early childhood education: An international encyclopedia, Vol. 4: The countries* (pp. 1113–1118, 1137–1141). Westport, CT: Praeger.

Musatti, T., & Picchio, M. (2010). Early education in Italy: Research and practice. *International Journal of Early Childhood Education, 42,* 141–153. Available at www.springerlink.com/content/124m17l73033nq10.

New, R. S. (2003). Reggio Emilia: New ways to think about schooling. *Educational Leadership, 60*(7), 34–38.

Nigris, E. (2007). Italy: Teacher training. In R. S. New & M. Cochran (Eds.), *Early childhood education: An international encyclopedia, Vol. 4: The countries* (pp. 1145–1150). Westport, CT: Praeger.

OECD Review Team for Italy. (2001). OECD country note: Early childhood education and care policy in Italy. Available at http://www.oecd.org/dataoecd/15/17/33915831.pdf.

Olmstead, P., & Weikart, D. P. (Eds.). (1994). *Families speak: Early childhood care and education in 11 countries.* Ypsilanti, MI: High/Scope Press.

Organization for Economic Cooperation and Development (OECD). (2006). *Starting strong II. Early childhood education and care.* Paris: OECD Publishing.

Pistillo, F. (1989). Preprimary education and care in Italy. In P. Olmstead & D. Weikart (Eds.), *How nations serve young children: Profiles of child care and education in 14 countries* (pp. 151–202). Ypsilanti, MI: High/Scope Press.

Putnam, R. D. (1993). *Making democracy work: Civic traditions in modern Italy.* Princeton, NJ: Princeton University Press.

Reggio Children. (1987/1996/2005). *The hundred languages of children: Narrative of the possible* (exhibit catalog). Reggio Emilia, Italy: Municipal Infant-Toddler Centers and Preschools of Reggio Emilia.

Reggio Children. (2010). *The infant–toddler centers and preschools of Reggio Emilia: Historical notes and general information.* Reggio Emilia, Italy: Municipal Infant-Toddler Centers and Preschools of Reggio Emilia.

Saltz, R. (1976). Infant day care Italian style. In M. L. Hanes, I. J. Gordon, & W. F. Breivogel (Eds.), *Update: The first ten years of life* (pp. 128–144). Gainesville: University of Florida Press.

Scuola di Barbiana. (1967). *Lettera a una Professoressa* [Letter to a teacher]. Florence: Libreria Editrice Fiorentina.

Vecchi, V. (2010). *Art and creativity in Reggio Emilia: Exploring the role and potential of ateliers in early childhood education.* New York: Routledge.

Chapter 2

History, Ideas, and Basic Principles:
An Interview with Loris Malaguzzi

Lella Gandini

WHEN WE GOT THE NEWS

I have the privilege of remembering with images that are still clear. When word got to the city (at the time news traveled slowly and was imprecise, as were our own perceptions, having lost the habit during the war, which was still hot and palpable, through mourning and rubble), I remember my reaction was confused and incredulous. Word had it that at Villa Cella, the people had gotten together to put up a school for the young children; they had pulled out the bricks from the bombed-out houses and had used them to build the walls of the school. Only a few days had passed since the Liberation and everything was still violently topsy-turvy.

I asked my comrades for confirmation. No one was sure. There was no telephone, and Cella seemed lost, geographically.

I felt hesitant, frightened. My logical capabilities, those of a young elementary school teacher overwhelmed by the events, led me to conclude that, if it were true (and how I hoped it were!), more than anomalous or improbable, it was out of this world. . . . A partisan, Avvenire Paterlini, advised me to wait, that maybe someone from Cella would show up. No one did.

That is why I got on my bicycle and rode out to Villa Cella. I got confirmation from a farmer just outside the village; he pointed out the place, a long way ahead. There were piles of sand and of bricks, a wheelbarrow full of hammers, shovels and hoes. Behind a curtain made of rugs to shield them from the sun, two women were hammering the old mortar off the bricks.

The news was true, and the truth was there, for all to see on this sunny spring day, in the uneven but stubborn hammering of these two women. One of them looked up at me and waited; I was a stranger, someone from the city, maybe they could tell from the part in my hair or my low-cut brown shoes. "We're not crazy! If you really want to see, come on Saturday or Sunday, when we're all here. Al fom da boun l'asilo (we're really going to make this school)!"

I went home. My feelings of wonder, and the sense of the extraordinary, were stronger than my happiness. I was an elementary school teacher. I had been teaching for 5 years, and had done 3 years of university. Maybe it was my profession that hampered me. All my little models were laughingly overturned: that building a school would ever occur to the people, women, farm laborers, factory workers, farmers, was in itself traumatic. But that these same people, without a penny to their names, with no technical offices, building permits, site directors, inspectors from the Ministry of Education or the Party, could actually build a school with their own strength, brick by brick, was the second paradox.

Be it trauma or paradox, it was, nevertheless, true, and I liked it. I was excited by the way it all overturned logic and prejudices, the old rules governing pedagogy, culture, how it forced everything back to the beginning. It opened up completely new horizons of thought.

I realized that the impossible was a category to be redefined, including as it did the end of the War, the partisan struggle, the Liberation, the "May spring," renewed consciences, hope itself. I even liked to mock Marx's wisdom. "Man builds his own history but necessarily to his own liking."

My strongest sentiment was that it was all right with me that the idea and the intuition and the realization of the project were all born there, in Cella, in the midst of farmers and factory workers. I sensed that it was a formidable lesson of humanity and culture, which would generate other extraordinary events. All we needed to do was to follow the same path.

My ride back from Cella was festive.

This is merely the beginning of the "People's Nursery School" of Villa Cella.

I had the honor of experiencing the rest of the story, with its difficulty, its petty stubbornness, and its enthusiasm. And it remained an uninterrupted lesson given by men and women whose ideas were still intact, who had understood long before I had that history can be changed, and is changed by taking possession of it, starting with the destiny of the children.

Loris Malaguzzi, quoted in Renzo Barazzoni (2000), *Brick by Brick:
The History of the "XXV Aprile" People's Nursery School
of Villa Cella*, Reggio Emilia, Italy: Reggio Children (English edition),
pp. 13–15. Reprinted with permission from Reggio Children.

PART I: HISTORY

"Good," they say, "If that is true, come work with us."[1]

It all seemed unbelievable: the idea, the school, the inventory consisting of a tank, a few trucks, and horses. They explain everything to me: "We will build the school on our own, working at night and on Sundays. The land has been donated by a farmer; the bricks and beams will be salvaged from bombed houses; the sand will come from the river; the work will be volunteered by all of us."

"And the money to run the school?"

A moment of embarrassment and then they say, "We will find it." Women, men, young people—all farmers and workers, all special people who had survived a hundred war horrors—are dead serious.

Within eight months, the school and our friendship had set down roots. What happened at Villa Cella was but the first spark. Other schools were opened on the outskirts and in the poorest sections of town, all created and run by parents. Finding support for the school, in a devastated town, rich only in mourning and poverty, would be a long and difficult ordeal and would require sacrifices and solidarity now unthinkable. When to the "school of the tank" at Villa Cella seven more were added in the poor areas surrounding the city, started by women with the help of the National Liberation Committee, we understood that the phenomenon was irreversible. Some of the schools would not survive. Most of them, however, would display enough rage and strength to survive for almost 20 years.

Finally, after 7 years of teaching in a middle school, I decided to leave my job. The work with the children had been rewarding, but the state-run school continued to pursue its own course, sticking to its stupid and intolerable indifference toward children, its opportunistic and obsequious attention toward authority, and its self-serving cleverness, pushing prepackaged knowledge. I went to Rome to study psychology at the National Center for Research. When I returned to Reggio Emilia, I started a town-sponsored mental health center for children with difficulties in school for the municipality. Thus, I started two parallel lives, one in the morning at this center and the other in the afternoon and evening in the small, parent-run schools.

The teachers in these small schools had exceptionally high motivation. They were very different one from another, for they had been trained in various Catholic or other private schools, but their thoughts were ample and greedy, and their energy boundless. I joined up with these teachers and started to work with the children, teaching them as we ourselves were learning. Soon we became aware that many of them were in poor health and undernourished. We also learned how alien the standard Italian language was to them, as their families had for generations spoken a local dialect. We asked the parents to help us, but finding ways for all of us to cooperate effectively turned out to be a most demanding task, not for lack of determination but a lack of experience. We were breaking traditional patterns.

A group of children and teachers from the Villa Cella School, 1950.

When we started to work with these courageous parents, we felt both enthusiasm and fear. We knew perfectly well how weak and unprepared we were. We took stock of our resources, not a difficult task. More difficult was the task of increasing those resources. Even more difficult was to predict how we would use them with the children. We were able to imagine the great challenge, but we did not yet know our own capabilities nor those of the children. We informed the mothers that we, just as the children, had much to learn. A simple, liberating thought came to our aid—namely, that things about children and for children are only learned from children. We knew how this was at the same time true and not true. However, we needed that assertion and guiding principle; it gave us strength and turned out to be an essential part of our collective wisdom. It was a preparation for 1963, the year in which the first municipal schools came to life.

The Year 1963: The First City-Run School for Young Children

Gandini: *Will you recall that event for us?*

Malaguzzi: It was a school with two classrooms, large enough for 60 children, and we gave it the name of Robinson, to recall the adventures of the Defoe's hero. You will have heard how the birth of the first school in 1963 established an important landmark. It affirmed for the first time in Italy the people claiming a right to found a secular school for young children—a rightful and necessary break in the monopoly the Catholic Church had hitherto exercised over children's early education. It was a necessary change in a society that was renewing itself and changing deeply and in which citizens and families were increasingly asking for social services and schools for their children. They wanted schools of a new kind: of better quality, free from charitable tendencies, not merely custodial, and not discriminatory in any way.

It was a decisive achievement, although the school was housed in a small wooden building assigned us by the authorities. Indeed, it was difficult to find enough children to participate because of the novelty of a city-run school. Three years later, it burned down one evening. We all ran there, even the mayor, and there we stood watching until only ashes remained. Yet one year later, the school was rebuilt in brick and concrete. We were now involved in a serious endeavor. From these early roots of civic determination and passion, widening to become part of the public consciousness, are the happenings and stories that now I am narrating to you.

From the parent-run schools, we had received the first expert group of teachers. Responsibilities were clear in our minds; many eyes, not all friendly, were watching us. We had to make as few errors as possible; we had to find our cultural identity quickly, make ourselves known, and win trust and respect. I remember that, after a few months, the need to make ourselves known became so strong that we planned a most successful activity. Once a week, we would transport the school to town. Literally we would pack ourselves, the children, and our tools into a truck, and we would teach school and show exhibits in the open air, in the square, in public parks, or under the colonnade of the municipal theater. The children were happy. The people saw; they were surprised, and they asked questions.

We knew that the new situation required continuity but also many breaks with the past. The experiences of the past we sought to preserve were the human warmth and reciprocal help, the sense of doing a job that revealed—through the children and their families—unknown motivation and resources, and an awareness of the values of each project and each choice, for use in putting together entirely different activities. We wanted to recognize the right of each child to be a protagonist and the need to sustain each child's spontaneous curiosity at a high level. We had to preserve our decision to learn from children, from events, and from families, to the full extent of our professional limits, and to maintain a readiness to change points of view, so as never to have too many certainties.

It was a feverish time, a time of adaptation, of continuous adjustment of ideas, of selection of projects, and attempts. Those projects and attempts were expected to produce a great deal and to do well; they were supposed to respond to the combined expectations of children and families and to reflect our competences, which were still in the making. I remember that we really got involved in a project based on Robinson Crusoe. The plan was for all of us together, including the children, to reconstruct the story, the character, and the adventures of our hero. We worked on reading and retelling the story; we used our memory as well as our skills at drawing, painting, clay, and woodworking. We rebuilt the ship, the sea, the island, the cave, and the tools. It was a long and spectacular reconstruction.

The following year, experts by now, we went on to work on a similar reconstruction of the story of Pinocchio. Then, a few years later, we changed gears. I had been at the Rousseau Institute and at the Ecole des Petits (School for Young Children) of Piaget in Geneva. Because we were inspired by Piaget, we opted to work with numbers, mathematics, and perception. We were then, and still are, convinced that it is not an imposition on children or an artificial exercise to work with numbers, quantity, classification, dimensions, forms, measurement, transformation, orientation, conservation, and change, or speed and space, because these explorations belong spontaneously to the everyday experiences of living, playing, negotiating, thinking, and speaking by children. This was an absolutely new challenge in Italy, and our initiative rewarded us. It marked the beginning of an experimental phase that gained breath from examining different psychological theories, looking at different theoretical sources and the research coming from outside our country.

However, in thinking back on that experience, a time during which we were proceeding without clear points of reference, we should also recall our excesses, the incongruity of our expectations, and the weaknesses of our critical and self-critical processes. We were aware that many things in the city, in the country, in politics, in customs, and in terms of needs and expectations were changing. In 1954, the Italian public started watching television. Migrations from the south to the north began, with the consequent abandonment of the countryside. With new work possibilities, women were developing aspirations and demands that were breaking with tradition. The baby boom modified everything, particularly the role and the aims of schools for young children, and led to a powerful, growing demand for social services. Furthermore, the request to place young sons and daughters in preschools was developing into a mass phenomenon.

From all this emerged the need to produce new ideas and to experiment with new educational strategies, in part because the municipal government was increasingly determined to institute more schools to satisfy the emerging needs of children and families. Women's groups, teachers, parents, citizens' councils, and school committees were starting to work along with the municipality to support and contribute to that development.

After much pressure from and battles among the people, in 1967, all the parent-run schools came under the administration of the municipality of Reggio Emilia. We had fought for eight years, from 1960 to 1968. As part of the larger political struggle all over Italy for publicly supported schools for young children as the entitlement of every child aged 3 to 6 years, we had debated the right of the state and the municipalities to establish such schools. In the national parliament confrontation, the secular forces were victorious over the side arguing for Catholic education. Our city was at the forefront: in 1968, there were 12 classes for young children run by the municipality. There would be 24 in 1970, 34 in 1972, 43 in 1973, 54 in 1974, and 58 in 1980, located in 22 school buildings.

Today, when in Italy 88% of the children between ages 3 to 6 years have acquired the right to go to school and parents choose between three types of institutions—national, municipal, and private—it seems appropriate to remember those remote events, humble yet powerful, that took place in the countryside and on the urban periphery, those events from which those in the city drew inspiration to develop an exemplary policy in favor of the child and the family.

The Year 1976: A Hard Year—A Good Year

Gandini: *You said that the education of young children was a virtual monopoly of the Catholic Church. How did Catholic people react to a lay school?*

Malaguzzi: Already by 1970, the scenario had changed. Schools and social services had become inescapable national issues, and the cultural debate around them had become more enlivened and at the same time more civil. I remember that it had not been that way when in 1963 we had organized an Italian-Czech seminar on the subject of play. It had not been that way when in 1968 we sponsored a symposium on the relationship among psychiatry, psychology, and education—considered a dangerous or unknown combination at the time—nor, for that matter, when later we organized a meeting among biologists, neurologists, psychologists, and experts in education to discuss children graphic's expression. The latter meeting, because of its attention to biology and neurology, brought upon us the accusation of having placed too much emphasis on materialism.

Our experience had brought us a long way and had become a reference point for educators in many areas of the country. This was especially true for young teachers who were discovering a profession that up to then had been monopolized by nuns. Around 1965, our schools had gained two fabulous friends. The first was Gianni Rodari, a poet and writer of widely translated stories for children, who dedicated his most famous book, *Grammatica della fantasia* ("The Grammar of Fantasy," 1973/1996), to our city and its children. The second was Bruno Ciari, the most lucid, passionate, and acute intelligence in the field of childhood education. They were indeed stupendous friendships. In 1971, with notable daring, we organized a national meeting for teachers only. We expected 200 participants, but 900 showed up. It was dramatic and exalting, and at the same time, it was an event that allowed us to publish the first work on the subject of early education, *Esperienze per una nuova scuola dell'infanzia* ("Experiences for a New School for Young Children," 1971). After a few months, we published another work, *La gestione sociale nella scuola dell'infanzia* ("Community-based Management in the Preprimary School," 1971). Those two works contained anything that we had put together with the teachers of Reggio Emilia and Modena (where I was also a consultant) with regard to our ideas and experiences.

In 1972, the whole city council, including the Catholic minority, voted in favor of the rules and regulations that we had drafted to govern the schools for young children. After years of polemics, or simply lack of acknowledgment, this event marked the legitimization of 10 years of laborious effort. We celebrated in every school.

In 1975, I was invited to be the keynote speaker at another meeting, organized this time by the regional government of Emilia Romagna, on the rights of children. It could not have come at a better time. I had just returned from a visit to the Institut Rousseau and the Ecole des Petits in Geneva and was fired with admiration for the Piagetian views and with the plans, mentioned earlier, that we soon started to implement.

The year 1976 was a hard, unexpected year. In November, the government speaker for the Catholic establishment, through the government-sponsored radio network, began a defamatory campaign against the city-run schools for young children and especially against our schools. They were attacked as a model of education that was corrupting the children and as a model of a policy of harassment against private, religious schools. After 7 days of this campaign, we felt that we had to react. My decision was to suspend the regular planning activities of teachers and invite the local clergy to come to an open debate inside our schools. This public discussion lasted the better part of 5 months. As the time went by, the harsh opposition became more civil, tempered, and honest; as ideas began to emerge, a reciprocal understanding began to take shape. At the end of this adventure, we were left exhausted with the sense that the anguish had dissipated, and I believe this sense of relief was shared by everyone on both sides. What remained was a feeling of enrichment and humanity.

Reflecting on this event in historical perspective, we can see that this ugly affair arose from the deep uneasiness felt by some Church officials over the loss of their monopoly on education. They were simultaneously being confronted with a decrease in the number of men and women choosing religious vocations, resulting in the increased need for secular teachers and a consequent increased cost of running their schools. Furthermore, the Italian Constitution forbade the use of federal funds to support religious schools; therefore, the Church was attempting to obtain financial support from local government (this would later be granted).

Still another factor, in my view, explaining the attack on our schools was the rapid growth of the cultural influence of our experience. Our work, the seminars, the meetings, and the publications had all contributed to a national recognition of our city-run schools. State schools for young children also existed, alongside of the municipal ones, but their growth was slow and too controlled by the central government. Thus, our program was shining a spotlight on the limitations of the religious schools, which were, with a few exceptions, incapable of going beyond the old and outdated custodial approach to education.

One of the consequences was that a government agency called the National Teaching Center established ties with our group and invited me to participate in its meetings. These ties still endure. Another result was that an important publishing company entrusted me with the direction of a new journal, *Zerosei* ("Zero to Six," 1976–1984) and later *Bambini* ("Children," 1985–present), addressed to educators of young children. I am still involved in this enterprise.

In the end, that painful confrontation of 1976 and its favorable conclusion made us stronger and more aware of what we had built, as well as more eager to go on with it. In the 1980s, we went ahead with our first flight abroad toward Sweden, with the first edition of our exhibit, "When the Eye Jumps Over the Wall," and the beginning of other flights that would take us traveling around the world.

A Professional and Life Choice

Gandini: *It seems that you made a choice to dedicate your life to the education and care of young children. When did you make this life choice?*

Malaguzzi: I could just avoid answering, as others have done before, by saying that when you don't ask me I know, but when you ask me, I do not know the answer anymore. There are some choices that you know are coming upon you only when they are just about to explode. But there are other choices that insinuate themselves into you and become apparent with a kind of obstinate lightness, that seem to have slowly grown within you during the happenings of your life because of a mixing of molecules and thoughts. It must have happened this latter way. But also World War II, or any war, in its tragic absurdity might have been the kind of experience that pushes a person toward the job of educating, as a way to start anew and live and work for the future. This desire strikes a person, as the war finally ends and the symbols of life reappear with violence equal to that of the time of destruction.

I do not know for sure. But I think that is where to look for a beginning. Right after the war, I felt a pact, an alliance, with children, adults, veterans from prison camps, partisans of the Resistance, and the sufferers of a devastated world. Yet all that suffering was pushed away by a day in spring, when ideas and feelings turned toward the future seemed so much stronger than those that called one to halt and focus on the present. It seemed that difficulties did not exist and that there were no insurmountable obstacles to overcome.

It was a powerful experience emerging out of a thick web of emotions and from a complex matrix of knowledge and values promising new creativity of which I was only becoming aware. Since those days, I have often reassessed my position, and yet I have always remained in my niche. I have never regretted my choices or what I gave up for them.

Gandini*: What are your feelings and how do you view your experiences when you recall the history of your program?*

Malaguzzi: Dear Lella, you have to agree that seeing an army tank, six horses, and three trucks generating a school for young children is extraordinary. The fact that the school still exists and continues to function well is the minimum that one could expect from such beginnings. Furthermore, its valuable history confirms that a new educational experience can emerge from the least expected circumstances.

If we continue to review those extraordinary origins, it is because we are still trying to understand the intuitions, the ideas, and the feelings that were there at the start and that have accompanied us ever since. These correspond to what John Dewey called "the foundation of the mind" or Lev Vygotsky considered "the loan of consciousness." Such concepts we have always kept in mind, especially in moments when we have had to make difficult decisions or overcome obstacles. Indeed, the first philosophy learned from these extraordinary events, in the wake of such a war, was to give a human, dignified, *civil* meaning to existence; to be able to make choices with clarity of mind and purpose; and to yearn for the future of mankind.

But the same events granted us something else right away, to which we have always tried to remain faithful. This something came out of requests made by mothers and fathers, whose lives and concerns were focused on their children. They asked nothing less than that this school, which they had built with their own hands, be a different kind of school, a school that could educate their children in a different way from before. It was the women especially who expressed this desire. The equation was simple: if the children had legitimate rights, then they also should have opportunities to develop their intelligence and to be made ready for the success that would not, and should not, escape them. These were the parents' thoughts, expressing a universal aspiration, a declaration against the betrayal of children's potential, and a warning that children had first of all to be taken seriously and believed in. These three concepts could have fitted perfectly in any good book on education. And they suited us just fine. The ideas coming from parents were shared by others who understood their deep implications. If our endeavor has endured for many years, it has been because of this collective wisdom.

PART II: PHILOSOPHY

The Sources of Our Inspiration

Gandini: *What theories and schools of thought do you think influenced the formulation of your approach?*

Malaguzzi: When somebody asks us how we got started, where we came from, what the sources of our inspiration are and so on, we cannot help but recite a long list of names. And when we tell about our humble and at the same time extraordinary origins, and we try to explain that from those origins we have extracted theoretical principles that still support our work, we notice much interest and not a little incredulity. It is curious (but not unjustified) how resilient is the belief that educational ideas and practices can derive only from official models or established theories.

We must, however, state right away that we also emerged out of a complex cultural background. We are immersed in history, surrounded by doctrines, politics,

Children and teachers take preschool into a public square for citizens to observe.

economic forces, scientific change, and human dramas; there is always in progress a difficult negotiation for survival. For this reason, we have had to struggle and occasionally correct and modify our direction, but so far destiny has spared us from shameful compromise or betrayal. It is important for pedagogy not to be the prisoner of too much certainty but instead to be aware of both the relativity of its powers and the difficulties of translating its ideals into practice. Piaget has already warned us that the errors and ills of pedagogy come from a lack of balance between scientific data and social application.

Preparing ourselves was difficult. We looked for readings; we traveled to capture ideas and suggestions from the few but precious innovative experiences of other cities; we organized seminars with friends and the most vigorous and innovative figures on the national education scene; we attempted experiments; we started exchanges with Swiss and French colleagues. The first of these groups (Swiss) gravitated around the area of active education and Piagetian tendencies, and the second (French) was influenced by the cooperative education of Freinet, who thought that students should work in groups and be encouraged to learn from their mistakes, and others who invented a very strange school: every three years, this French school would move to a new location, where the reconstruction of old, abandoned farmhouses would be the basis of the educational work with the children. So it was that we proceeded, and gradually things began to come together in a coherent pattern.

The Education of Children in the 1960s

Gandini: *We know that in the 1960s there emerged in Italy a new consciousness regarding the education of young children. What was the cultural scenario that accompanied it?*

Malaguzzi: In the 1960s, issues surrounding schools for young children were at the center of fiery political debates. The need for them was undeniable, but the main debate was whether schools should exist as a social service. More substantive pedagogical considerations remained on the back burner. In reality, on the entire subject of education, Italy was far behind. For 20 years under Fascism, the study of the social sciences had been suppressed and European and American theories and experiences excluded. That kind of isolation was disappearing in the 1960s. The works of John Dewey, Henri Wallon, Edward Claparede, Ovide Decroly, Anton Makarenko, Lev Vygotsky, and later also Erik Erikson and Urie Bronfenbrenner were becoming known. Furthermore, we were reading *The New Education* by Pierre Bovet and Adolfe Ferriere and learning about the teaching techniques of Celestin Freinet in France, the progressive educational experiment of the Dalton School in New York, and the research of Piaget and colleagues in Geneva.

This literature, with its strong messages, guided our choices; and our determination to continue gave impetus to the flow of our experiences. We avoided the paralysis that had stalled leftist political theorists for more than a decade in a debate regarding the relationship between content and method in education. For us, that debate was meaningless because it did not take into account differences that were part of our society and ignored the fact that active education involves an inherent alliance between content and method. Also strengthening our belief in active education was our awareness of the pluralism of the families, children, and teachers becoming ever more involved in our joint project. This awareness was making us more respectful of different political positions. We were becoming freer of intolerance and prejudice.

Looking back, it seems to me that this choice toward respect gave strength to our autonomy as we elaborated our educational project and helped us to resist many contrasting pressures.

The Italian tradition relied on Rosa Agazzi and Maria Montessori, two important figures from the beginning of the century. Montessori was first praised and then relegated to the sidelines by the Fascist regime because of her scientific approach to pedagogy. Agazzi was adopted as a model because her pedagogy was closer to the view of the child in Catholicism. I still believe that the writings of Montessori and Agazzi should be meditated on to move beyond them.

Meanwhile, in practice, the Roman Catholic Church had almost a monopoly on preschool education, concentrating its efforts on helping needy children and offering custodial services rather than responding to the social and cultural changes. The typical classroom contained 40 to 50 children, entrusted to one nun with no teaching degree and no salary. The situation speaks for itself through the numbers:

in 1960, only about one-third of young children were in preschool, where they were taught by 22,917 teachers, of whom 20,330 were nuns.

More About the Sources of Inspiration

Gandini: *You have mentioned a first wave of sources that influenced you. Can you tell us more about other sources that have been important to you?*

Malaguzzi: In the 1970s, we listened to a second wave of scholars, including psychologists Wilfred Carr, David Shaffer, Kenneth Kaye, Jerome Kagan, and Howard Gardner, philosopher David Hawkins, and theoreticians Serge Moscovici, Charles Morris, Gregory Bateson, Heinz Von Foerster, and Francisco Varela, plus those who work in the field of dynamic neuroscience. The network of the sources of our inspiration spans several generations and reflects the choices and selections that we have made over time. From these sources, we have received ideas both long lasting and not-so-long lasting— topics for discussion, reasons to find connections, discordances with cultural changes, occasions for debating, and stimuli to confirm and expand on practices and values. Overall, we have gained a sense of the versatility of theory and research.

But talk about education (including the education of young children) cannot be confined to its literature. Such talk, which is also political, must continuously address major social changes and transformations in the economy, sciences, arts, and human relationships and customs. All of these larger forces influence how human beings— even young children—"read" and deal with the realities of life. They determine the emergence, on both general and local levels, of new methods of educational content and practice, as well as new problems and soul-searching questions.

In Search of an Educational Approach for the Littlest Children

Gandini: *In Italy, group care of very young children (4 months to 3 years of age) in a collective environment has developed in a very successful way. How did it begin in Reggio Emilia?*

Malaguzzi: In Reggio Emilia, the first infant-toddler center (*asilo nido*) for children under 3 years of age came to life 1 year before the promulgation of the 1971 national law instituting this type of service. This law was a victory for Italian women after 10 years of struggle. The new institution was an attempt to meet the joint needs of women, choosing both motherhood and work, and children, growing up in the nuclear family.

Proponents of infant-toddler centers had to deal with the polemic raised by the rediscovered writings of John Bowlby and Rene Spitz, who right after World War II studied the damage resulting from the separation of the mother–child pair. Furthermore, they had to address the resistance of the Catholic world, which feared risks and pathologies in a breakdown of the family. It was a very delicate question. Our experience with children aged 3 to 6 years was a useful point of reference but at the same time not a complete answer. Rather than thinking in terms of custodial care, we argued that their education demanded professional expertise, strategies of care, and environments that were appropriate and unique to their developmental level.

We had many fears, and they were reasonable ones. The fears, however, helped us; we worked cautiously with the very young teachers and with the parents themselves. Parents and teachers learned to handle with great gentleness the children's transition from a focused attachment on parents and home to a shared attachment that included the adults and objects of the infant-toddler center.

It all went much better than expected. We had the great good fortune to be able to plan the environment of the first center with an excellent architect. The children understood sooner than expected that their adventure in life could flow between two agreeable and comfortable places, home and the center. In both, they could express their previously overlooked desire to be mature with peers and to find in them points of reference, understanding, surprises, affective ties, and merriment that could dispel shadows and uneasiness.

For us, the children, and the families, the possibility opened up of a long and continuous period of living together, from the infant-toddler center through the preprimary school, that is, 5 or 6 years of reciprocal trust and work. This time, we discovered, was a precious resource, capable of making synergistic potentials flow among educators, children, and families.

Today, in my city, about 40% of eligible children are served by our municipal infant-toddler centers, and about 10% to 20% more would be if there were space. What have we learned from this experience? Twenty years of work have convinced us that even the youngest children are social beings. They are predisposed; they possess from birth a readiness to make significant ties with other caretakers beside their parents (who do not thereby lose their special responsibilities and prerogatives).

The obvious benefit that the children obtain from interactive play with peers is a most reassuring aspect of the group experience, the potential of which has wide implications not as yet appreciated. In consequence, we agree with the American psychologists (e.g., Ellen Hock, Urie Bronfenbrenner) that it is not so important whether the mother chooses the role of homemaker or working mother, but rather it is the fulfillment and satisfaction she feels in her choice and the support she receives from her family, the child care center, and, at least minimally, the surrounding culture. The quality of the relationship between parent and child becomes more important than the sheer quantity of time they spend together.

PART III: BASIC PRINCIPLES

The Structural Combination of Educational Choices and Organization

Gandini: *What kind of organization helped you to realize the innovative ideas in your schools for young children?*

Malaguzzi: We think of a school for young children as an integral living organism, as a place of shared lives and relationships among many adults and many children. We think of school as a sort of construction in motion, continuously adjusting itself. Certainly we have to adjust our system from time to time while the organism travels on its life course, just as those pirate ships were once compelled to repair their sails, all the while keeping on their course at sea.

It has also always been important to us that our living system of schooling expands toward the world of the families, with their right to know and to participate. It then expands toward the city, with its own life, its own patterns of development, its own institutions, as we have asked the city to adopt the children as bearers and beneficiaries of their own specific rights.

Is It Possible to Create an Amiable School?

Gandini: *A visit to your schools always gives a sense of discovery and serenity. What are the ingredients that create such an atmosphere and level of positive tension?*

Malaguzzi: I believe that our schools show the attempt that has been made to integrate the educational program with the organization of work and the environment, so as to allow for maximum movement, interdependence, and interaction. The school is an inexhaustible and dynamic organism: it has its difficulties, controversies, joys, and capacities to handle external disturbances. What counts is that there be agreement about what direction the school should go and that all forms of artifice and hypocrisy be kept at bay. Our objective, which we will always pursue, is to create an amiable environment where children, families, and teachers feel at ease.

To start, then, with the environment: there is the entrance hall, which informs and documents and which anticipates the form and organization of the school. This leads into the dining hall, with the kitchen well in view. The entrance hall leads into the central space, or *piazza,* the place of encounters, friendships, games, and other activities that complete those of the classrooms. The classrooms and utility rooms are placed at a distance from but connected to the central area. Each classroom is divided into two contiguous rooms, picking up one of the few practical suggestions by Piaget. His idea was to allow children either to be with teachers or stay alone; but we use the two spaces in many ways. In addition to the classrooms, we have established the *atelier,* the school studio and laboratory, as a place for manipulating or experimenting with separate or combined visual languages, either in isolation or in combination with the verbal ones. We have also the *mini-ateliers,* next to each classroom, which allow for extended project work. We have a room for music and an archive, where we have placed many useful objects both large and small, noncommercial, made by teachers and parents. Throughout the school, the walls are used as spaces for both temporary and permanent exhibits about what the children and teachers have created: our walls speak and document.

Learning together is a positive way to work on the early skills of literacy, as in trying to decide how to spell words while typing.

The teachers work in co-teaching pairs in each classroom, and they plan with other colleagues and the families. All the staff members of the school meet once a week to discuss and broaden their ideas, and they participate together in in-service training. We have a team of *pedagogisti* to facilitate interpersonal connection and consider both the overall ideas and the details. The families meet by themselves or with the teachers, in individual meetings, group meetings, or whole school meetings. Families have formed an Advisory Council for each school that meets two or three times a month. The city, the countryside, and the nearby mountains serve us as additional teaching sites.

Thus we have put together a mechanism combining places, roles, and functions that each have their own timing but that can be interchanged with one another to generate ideas and actions. All this works within a network of cooperation and interactions that produces for the adults, but above all for the children, a feeling of belonging in a world that is alive, welcoming, and authentic.

For an Education Based on Inter-Relationships

Gandini: *How do you create and sustain interaction, relationship, and cooperation among all parties connected with the schools?*

Malaguzzi: In our system, we know it is essential to focus on children and be child-centered, but we do not feel that is enough. We consider teachers and families as also central to the education of children. We therefore choose to place all three components at the center of our interest.

Our goal is to build an amiable school, where children, teachers, and families all feel at home. Such a school requires careful thinking and planning concerning procedures, motivations, and interests. It must embody ways of getting along together, of intensifying relationships among the three central protagonists, of assuring fullness of attention to the problems of educating, and of activating participation and research. These are the most effective tools for all those concerned—children, teachers, and parents—to become more united and aware of each other's contribution. They are the most effective tools to use to feel good about cooperating and to produce, in harmony, a higher level of results.

Anyone who starts a program thinks about actions that will transform existing situations into new, desired ones. In our approach, then, to proceed, we make plans and reflections connected with the cognitive, affective, and symbolic realm; we refine communication skills; we are active in exploring and creating along with many other participants, while remaining open to change. In this manner, although the goals are shared all along, the most valuable aspect is still interpersonal satisfaction.

Even when the structure we have in mind (the centrality of children, teachers, and families), reveals flaws and difficulties, and the participation shows different levels of intensity, the stimulating atmosphere of the school provides a sense of positive receptiveness to all concerned. That happens because the school invites an exchange of ideas, it has an open and democratic style, and it tends to open minds.

The aspects of isolation, indifference, and violence that are more and more a part of contemporary social life are so opposite to our approach that they make us even more determined to proceed. The families feel the same way; the alienating aspects of modern life become a reason to be even more eager and open to our offers.

All this contributes to structure an education based on relationship and participation. On the practical level, we must continuously maintain and re-invent our network of communication and encounters. We have meetings with families to discuss curriculum. We ask for their cooperation in organizing activities, setting up the space, and preparing the welcoming of new children. We distribute to each child the telephone numbers and addresses of all the other children and their teachers. We promote visits, including snacks among the children at their homes and visits to parents' workplaces. We organize excursions with parents, for example, to swimming and gymnastics. We work with parents in building furnishings and toys. We meet with them to discuss our projects and our research, and we meet to organize dinners and celebrations in the school.

This type of approach with parents reveals much about philosophy and basic values. These include the interactive and constructivist aspects, the intensity of relationships, the spirit of cooperation, and individual and collective effort in doing research. We appreciate different contexts, pay careful attention to individual cognitive activity within social interactions, and establish affective ties. As we learn two-way processes of communication, we acquire wider awareness of political choices regarding infancy, encourage mutual adaptation among children and adults, and promote growth of adult educational competencies. We have truly left behind a vision of the child as egocentric, focused only on cognition and physical objects, and as one whose feelings and affectivity are underestimated and belittled.

Relationship and Learning

Gandini: *In what particular way do you see children's learning take place within the context of the rich relationships that you describe?*

Malaguzzi: In my view, relationships and learning coincide within an active process of education. They come together through the expectations and skills of children, the professional competence of adults, and, more generally, the educational process.

We must embody in our practice, therefore, reflections on a delicate and decisive point, as follows: *what children learn does not follow as an automatic result from what is taught. Rather, it is in large part due to the children's own doing, as a consequence of their activities and own resources.*

It is necessary to think about the knowledge and skills that children construct independently of and prior to schooling. This knowledge base does not belong to the "prehistory" mentioned by Vygotsky (as if it were a separate experience) but to the children's social development in process. In any context, children do not wait to pose questions to themselves and form strategies of thought, principles, or feelings. Always and everywhere, children take an active role in the construction and acquisition of learning and understanding. To learn is a satisfying experience, but also, as the American psychologist Nelson Goodman tells us, to understand is desire, drama, and conquest. So it is that in many situations, especially when one sets up challenges, children show us that they know how to walk along the path to understanding. Once children are helped to perceive themselves as authors or inventors, once they are helped to discover the pleasure of inquiry, their motivation and interest explode. They come to expect discrepancies and surprises. As educators, we have to recognize their tension, partly because, with a minimum of introspection, we find the same within ourselves (unless the vital appeal of novelty and puzzlement has faded or died). The age of childhood, more than the ages that follow, is characterized by such expectations. To disappoint them deprives children of possibilities that no exhortation can arouse in later years.

Yet in so praising the child, we do not intend to return to the naivety of the 1970s, when discovery of the child's active role in structuring events and the two-way causality in child–adult interaction resulted in a strange devaluation of the role of the adult. Nor do we wish to overvalue the child's control of this interaction. In reality, the two-way direction of interaction is a difficult principle to miss. We imagine the interaction as a ping-pong match. (Do you remember the badminton game between two boys, splendidly recounted by the great Gestalt psychologist Max Wertheimer [1945] in *Productive Thinking*?) For the game to continue, the skills of the adult and child need appropriate adjustments, which allow the growth through learning of the skills of the child.

All of these considerations remind us that the way we get along with children influences what motivates them and what they learn. Their environment must be set up to interface the cognitive realm with the realm of relationship and affectivity. Thus, there also should be connection between development and learning, between the different symbolic languages, between thought and action, and between individual and interpersonal autonomies. Value should be placed on contexts, communicative processes, and the construction of a wide network of reciprocal exchanges among children and between children and adults.

Yet what is most central to success is to adhere to a clear and open theoretical conception that guarantees coherence in our choices, practical applications, and continuing professional growth.

The Widening of Communication Networks

Gandini: *You have described in great detail the importance of relationships in your approach. But is your approach based only on relationship?*

Malaguzzi: No, of course not. Relationship is the primary connecting dimension of our system, however, understood not merely as a warm, protective envelope but rather as a dynamic conjunction of forces and elements interacting toward a common purpose. The strength of our system lies in the ways we make explicit and then intensify the necessary conditions for relations and interaction. We seek to support those social exchanges that better ensure the flow of expectations, conflicts, cooperation, choices, and the explicit unfolding of problems tied to the cognitive, affective, and expressive realms.

Among the goals of our approach is to reinforce each child's sense of identity through a recognition that comes from peers and adults, so much so that each one would feel enough sense of belonging and self-confidence to participate in the activities of the school. In this way, we promote in children the widening of communication networks and mastery and appreciation of language in all its levels and contextual uses. As a result, children discover how communication enhances the autonomy of the individual and the peer group. The group forms a special entity tied together through exchange and conversation, reliant on its own ways of thinking, communicating, and acting.

The approach based on relationship best reveals how a classroom is composed of independent individuals as well as subgroups and alliances with different affinities and skills. The communicative landscape becomes variegated; we notice children who communicate less than others. The teachers—participant observers—respond to what they see by asking questions, initiating face-to-face exchanges, redirecting activities, and modifying the way or the intensity of their interaction with particular children. Small-group activities, involving two to four children, are modules of maximum desirability and communicative efficacy. They are the type of classroom organization most favorable to education based on relationship. They facilitate fruitful conflicts, investigations, and activities connected to what each child has previously said as well as self-regulatory accommodations.

It might help to look at this in systemic terms. The system of relationship in our schools is simultaneously real and symbolic. In this system, each person has a formal role-relationship with the others. Adult and child roles are complementary: they ask questions of one another, they listen, and they answer.

As a result of these relationships, the children in our schools have the unusual privilege of learning through their communications and concrete experiences. I'm saying that the system of relationships has in and of itself a virtually autonomous capacity to educate. It is not just some kind of giant security blanket (the "transitional object" of David Winnicott). Nor is it some kind of flying carpet to take the children to magical places. Rather, it is a permanent living presence always on the scene, required all the more when progress becomes difficult.

What Is Needed to Make an Alliance Succeed

Gandini: *One of the many questions that come up when talking about your program is how you succeed in enlisting and maintaining the participation of families at such a high level.*

Malaguzzi: That is one of the first questions we are usually asked. Let me answer without reference to philosophy, sociology, and ethics. Family participation requires many things, but most of all, it demands of teachers a multitude of adjustments. Teachers must possess a habit of questioning their certainties; a growth of sensitivity, awareness, and availability; the assuming of a critical style of research and continually updated knowledge of children; an enriched evaluation of parental roles; and skills to talk, listen, and learn from parents.

Responding to all of these demands calls forth a constant questioning in teachers of their teaching. Teachers must leave behind an isolated, silent mode of working that leaves no traces. Instead, they must discover ways to communicate and document the children's evolving experiences at school. They must prepare a steady flow of quality information targeted to parents but appreciated also by children and teachers. This flow of documentation, we believe, introduces parents to a quality of knowing that changes their expectations tangibly. They reexamine their assumptions about their parenting roles and their views about the experience their children are living and take a new and more inquisitive approach toward the whole school experience.

With regard to the children, the flow of documentation creates a second, and equally pleasing, scenario. They become even more curious, interested, and confident as they contemplate the meaning of what they have achieved. They learn that their parents feel at home in the school, at ease with the teachers, and informed

Children experimenting at the water table while constructing a fountain, as part of "The Amusement Park for Birds" project.

about what has happened and is about to happen. We know we have built a solid friendship when children readily accept either parent saying, "This evening I am going to school to talk with the teachers" or "I am going to the meeting of the Advisory Council," or when parents help prepare school excursions and celebrations.

Finally, it is important for parents and children to realize how much work teachers do together. They must see how often teachers meet to discuss things, sometimes serenely and other times raising their voices. They must see how teachers cooperate on research projects and other initiatives, how they document their work with patience and care, how skillfully they wield their cameras and video cameras, with what kindness they hide their worries, join children's play, and take responsibility. All of this represents for the children a range of models that make a deep impression. They see a world where people truly help one another.

PART IV: TEACHERS

The Collegial Work of Teachers

Gandini: *In your schools, there seems to be no hierarchy among teachers. Is this really the case?*

Malaguzzi: Co-teaching, and, in a more general sense, collegial work, represents for us a deliberate break from the traditional professional and cultural solitude and isolation of teachers. This isolation has been rationalized in the name of academic freedom, wrongly understood. Its results, certainly, has been to impoverish and desiccate teachers' potential and resources and make it difficult or impossible for them to achieve quality.

I remember, however, that the archetype, one teacher per classroom, was so strongly rooted when we began our work that our proposal of co-teaching pairs, which should have been seen as a welcome liberation from excessive stress, did not at first find ready acceptance among teachers. The ones who did accept it, however, soon discovered the evident advantages, and this cleared up the uncertainty. The work in pairs, and then among pairs, produced tremendous advantages, both educationally and psychologically, for adults as well as for children. Furthermore, the co-teaching pairs constituted the first building block of the bridge that was taking us toward community-based management and partnership with parents.

Community-based management has always been an important part of our history and a supporting beam of our work. At times, it has been a decisive force for revitalization, unification, or cultural education. At other times, it has played a key mediating role with the town administration and political institutions. It has always been essential in strengthening our position.

One regret that has remained constant over the years—shared also by the children—has been our inability to offer a significant number of male teachers. Until a few years ago, Italian law forbade males to teach preprimary children—an immensely stupid law that we openly transgressed, ignoring the warnings and reprimands from the Ministry of Education. Now this prohibition has been lifted, yet other reasons still make it difficult to hire male teachers in the schools for young children. To make matters worse, in Italy as in several other European countries, there are fewer women today choosing to become teachers of young children. Those who do tend to leave this type of job easily for something else. The reasons for this phenomenon are many and should be studied carefully. But the results are clear in terms of the costs, paid by children, in loss of dignity for schools, teachers, and the entire culture.

Formation and Re-Formation of Teachers

Gandini: *How do you now go about supporting teacher development in your schools?*

Malaguzzi: We have no alternatives but continuous professional development. As the intelligence becomes stronger through use, so the teachers' role, knowledge, profession, and competence become stronger through direct application. Teachers—like children and everyone else—feel the need to grow in their competences; they want to transform experiences into thoughts, thoughts into reflections, the reflections into new thoughts and new actions. They also feel a need to make predictions, to try things out, and then interpret them. The act of interpretation is most important. Teachers must learn to interpret ongoing process rather than wait to evaluate results. In the same way, their role as educators must include understanding children as producers, not as consumers. They must learn to teach nothing to children except what they can learn by themselves. Furthermore, they must be aware of the perceptions the children form of the adults and their actions. To enter into relationships with the children that are simultaneously productive, amiable, and exciting, teachers must be aware of the risk in expressing judgments too quickly. They must enter the time frame of children, whose interests emerge only in the course of activity or negotiations arising from that activity. They must realize how listening to children is both necessary and expedient. They must know that experiences should be as numerous as the keys of a piano and that each calls forth infinite acts of intelligence when children are offered an infinite variety of things to choose from. Furthermore, teachers must be aware that practice cannot be separated from objectives or values and that professional growth comes partly through individual effort but in a much richer way through discussion with colleagues, parents, and experts. Finally, they need to know that it is possible to engage in the challenge of longitudinal observations and small research projects concerning the development or experiences of children. Indeed, education without research or innovation is education without interest.

Already this is no small demand! However, it is not possible even to begin if teachers do not have a basic knowledge about various content areas of teaching in order to transform this knowledge into 100 languages and 100 dialogues with children. We have at present limited means to prepare teachers as we would like, but we try to look within ourselves and find inspiration from the things we do.

The *Atelier* as a Place of Provocation

Gandini: *How did the idea and the establishment of the* atelier *work into your educational project?*

Malaguzzi: I will not hide from you how much hope we invested in the introduction of the *atelier.* We knew it would be impossible to ask for anything more. Yet if we could have done so, we would have gone further still by creating a new type of school typology with a new school made entirely of laboratories similar to the *atelier.* We would have constructed a new type of school made of spaces where the hands of children could be active for "messing about" (in the sense that David Hawkins would tell us better, later). With no possibility of boredom, hands and minds would engage each other with great, liberating merriment in the way ordained by biology and evolution.

Although we did not come close to achieving those impossible ideals, the *atelier* has always repaid us. It has, as desired, proved to be subversive—generating complexity and new tools for thought. It has allowed rich combinations and creative possibilities among the different (symbolic) languages of children. The *atelier* has protected us not only from the long-winded speeches and didactic theories of our time (just about the only preparation received by young teachers!) but also from the behaviorist beliefs of the surrounding culture, reducing the human mind to some kind of "container" to be filled.

The *atelier* has met other needs, as well. One of the most urgent problems was how to achieve effective communication with the parents. We wanted to always keep them informed about the goings-on in the schools, and at the same time to establish a system of communication that would document the work being done with the children. We wanted to show parents how the children thought and expressed themselves, what they produced and invented with their hands and their intelligence, how they played and joked with one another, how they discussed hypotheses, how their logic functioned. We wanted the parents to see that their children had richer resources and more skills than generally realized. We wanted the parents to understand how much value we placed in their children. In return, then, we felt it would be fair to ask parents to help us and be on our side.

The *atelier,* a space rich in materials, tools, and people with professional competencies, has contributed much to our work on documentation. This work has strongly informed—little by little—our way of being with the children. It has also, in a rather beautiful way, obliged us to refine our methods of observation and recording so that the processes of children's learning became the basis of our dialogue with parents. Finally, our work in the *atelier* has provided us with archives that are now a treasure trove of children's work and teachers' knowledge and research. Let me underline, however, that the *atelier* was never intended to be a sort of secluded, privileged space, as if there and only there the languages of expressive art could be produced.

It was, instead, a place where children's different languages could be explored by them and studied by us in a favorable and calm atmosphere. We and they could experiment with alternative modalities, techniques, instruments, and materials; explore themes chosen by children or suggested by us; perhaps work on large frescoes in a group; perhaps prepare a poster on which one makes a concise statement through words and illustrations; perhaps even master small projects on a reduced scale, stealing skills from architects! What was important was to help the children find their own styles of exchanging with friends both one's talents and one's discoveries.

But the *atelier* was most of all a place for research, and we expect that it will continue and increase. We have studied everything—from the affinities and oppositions of different forms and colors, to the complex aims of narrative and argumentation; from the transition of images from words to signs and vice versa; from the way children have been contaminated by exposure to mass media, to sex differences in symbolic and expressive preferences. We have always found it a privilege to be able to encounter the fascinating multiple games that can be played with images: turning a poppy into a spot, a light, a bird in flight, a lighted ghost, a handful of red petals within a field of green and yellow wheat. So positive and confirming were our experiences that they eventually led us to expand the use of the *atelier* into the centers for the youngest children in the infant-toddler centers.

Genesis and Meanings of Creativity

Gandini: *The creative behavior and creative production by children has been an elusive theme, about which pages and pages have been written. What is your own view on the subject?*

Malaguzzi: We were all very weak and unprepared in the 1950s when the theme of creativity, just landed from the United States, crossed our path. I remember the eagerness with which we read the theories of J. P. Guilford and Paul Torrance. I also remember how later on those theories could be reread and reinterpreted thought the perspectives of Bruner, Piaget, the Cognitivists, the neo-Freudians, Kurt Lewin, last of the Gestalt psychologists, and the humanistic psychologists Carl Rogers and Abraham Maslow.

It was a difficult but exciting period; we felt that those proposals had great vigor and potential. The work on creativity seemed disruptive to many (almost too many) things, for example, the philosophical dimension of man and life and the productivity of thought. These proposals went so far as to suggest complicity with the unconscious, chance, and the emotions—with feelings and so on. Yet despite their brilliant attractiveness, we have to say frankly that after many years of work, the progress of our own experience, plus our observation and study of children and adults, has suggested to us much caution and reflection.

As we have chosen to work with children, we can say that they are the best evaluators and the most sensitive judges of the values and usefulness of creativity. This comes about because they have the privilege of not being excessively attached to their own ideas, which they construct and reinvent continuously. They are apt to explore, make discoveries, change their points of view, and fall in love with forms and meanings that transform themselves.

Therefore, as we do not consider creativity sacred, we do not consider it as extraordinary but rather as likely to emerge from daily experience. This view is now shared by many. We can sum up our beliefs as follows:

1. Creativity should not be considered a separate mental faculty but a characteristic of our way of thinking, knowing, and making choices.
2. Creativity seems to emerge from multiple experiences, coupled with a well-supported development of personal resources, including a sense of freedom to venture beyond the known.
3. Creativity seems to express itself through cognitive, affective, and imaginative processes. These come together and support the skills for predicting and arriving at unexpected solutions.

4. The most favorable situation for creativity seems to be interpersonal exchange, with negotiation of conflicts and comparison of ideas and actions being the decisive elements.
5. Creativity seems to find its power when adults are less tied to prescriptive teaching methods but instead become observers and interpreters of problematic situations.
6. Creativity seems to be favored or disfavored according to the expectations on the part of teachers, schools, families, and communities as well as society at large, according to the ways children perceive those expectations.
7. Creativity becomes more visible when adults try to be more attentive to the cognitive processes of children than to the results they achieve in various fields of doing and understanding.
8. The more teachers are convinced that intellectual and expressive activities have both multiplying and unifying possibilities, the more creativity favors friendly exchanges with imagination and fantasy.
9. Creativity requires that the *school of knowing* find connections with the *school of expressing,* opening the doors—this is our slogan—to the hundred languages of children.

Starting from these ideas, we have been trying to understand how they should be revised, yet without letting the myths of spontaneity, which often accompany the myths of creativity, mislead us. We are convinced that between basic intellectual capacities and creativity, a theme preferred by American research, there is not opposition but rather complementarity. The spirit of play can also pervade the formation and construction of thought.

Often when people come to us and observe our children, they ask us which magic spell we have used. We answer that their surprise equals our surprise. Creativity? It is always difficult to notice when it is dressed in everyday clothing and has the ability to appear and disappear suddenly. Our task, regarding creativity, is to help children to climb their own mountains, as high as possible. No one can do more. We are restrained by our awareness that people's expectations about creativity should not weigh on the school. An excessive widening of its functions and powers would give the school an exclusive role that it cannot have.

PART V: IMAGES OF CHILDHOOD

Sweeping Childhood Under the Rug

Gandini: *The predicament of childhood today is the subject of much writing. What are your views on this?*

Malaguzzi: The dramatic contradictions that characterize the education of children are constantly on my mind. I am speaking about what we know of children versus what we do not know, as well as what we know but fail to do with them and for them. But the problem is wider still, for it involves the human race and the waste of its intelligence and humanity. In its organization, in its choices, in its ways to come into relation with learning and knowledge, the educational system badly represents the nature and the potential of human capability.

All people—and I mean scholars, researchers, and teachers, who in any place have set themselves to study children seriously—have ended up by discovering not so much the limits and weaknesses of children but rather their surprising and extraordinary strengths and capabilities linked with an inexhaustible need for expression and realization.

But the results of those learned inquires, describing new aspects of development and opening endless possibilities for practical application and ethical and philosophical consideration, have not been sufficiently seized on by educators. Instead, during this delay, metaphors and images reemerge, portraying childhood in one of two extreme ways: as blank, powerless, and entirely shaped by adults, or, on the other hand, autonomously capable of gaining control of the adult world. We have not correctly legitimized a culture of childhood, and the consequences are seen in all our social, economic, and political choices and investments. It is a typical, frightening example of offence and betrayal of human resources.

Specific instances are clearly visible in Europe and the rest of the Western world. We see budgetary cuts, lack of policy and planning, a general lowering of prestige for those who teach or study children, with consequent loss of young people from the profession and an increase in child abuse. We can speak of all of this bad news for children, without even mentioning the disasters of war and epidemics that still ravage our planet and conscience.

It is a painful story. John Dewey confronted this same situation earlier in the century and was inspired to urge a method of education combining pragmatic philosophy, new psychological knowledge, and—on the teaching side—mastery of content with inquiring, creative experiences for children. He envisioned all this, also seeking a new relation between educational and sociocultural research. This last aspect, I believe, is part of the unfinished business of the democratic process but represents the genuine cultural achievement that childhood and coming generations have a right to expect. As Dewey said, "human institutions ought to be judged by their educational influence, and by the measure of their capacity to extend the knowledge and competence of man."

I know all this could take place in such a moment as the present, when science, history, and the public conscience appear unanimous in recognizing the child as endowed with the virtues, resources, and intrinsic rights that we mentioned earlier. But a child so endowed paradoxically explodes in the hands of his creators; such a child becomes too overwhelming for philosophy, science, education, and political economy. The incapacity of societies to respond to such a child would seem to cast doubt on the nobility of our motives regarding children.

Others, too, have sometimes masked their true selfish interests, perhaps even from themselves. Queen Elizabeth (Horace Walpole tells us in his *Anecdotes of Painting,* 1762–1771) was a great collector, yet there is no proof that she admired or loved the art of painting. What is absolutely certain is that she loved, with passion, the paintings that portrayed her!

The Differences Among Children

Gandini: *One aspect that the visitors of your schools find puzzling is how you can respond to children's different capabilities and needs when you give such importance to social relationships and group work.*

Malaguzzi: We certainly recognize differences in the makeup of children side by side with differences that can be reduced or widened by the favorable or unfavorable influences of the environment. But children have—this is my conviction—a common gift, namely, the potential and competencies that I described earlier. We hold this to be true for children who are born in any culture in any place on our planet. Yet recognizing the universality of children's potential opens up new questions with which so far we in Reggio Emilia have had little familiarity but which the multicultural events of our time press upon us with urgency.

I would be very cautious concerning differences in cognitive style and strategies. People are too quick to attribute them to one season of life, especially when looking at infants, whose minds undergo many rapid reorganizations and changes in development. The styles we observe are an objective fact about individuals. Beyond that, however, they also reflect the historical and cultural context.

A child discovers the size of his shadow.

The wider the range of possibilities we offer children, the more intense will be their motivations and the richer their experiences. We must widen the range of topics and goals, the types of situations we offer and their degree of structure, the kinds and combinations of resources and materials, and the possible interactions with things, peers, and adults. Moreover, widening the range of possibilities for children also has consequences for others. It renders teachers more attentive and aware, and makes them more capable of observing and interpreting children's gestures and speech. Teachers thereby become more responsive to children's feedback, take more control over their own expressive feedback to children (correcting excessive monotony or excitement), and make their interventions with children more personal. All of this will make it easier for teachers to pause and make self-evaluations.

The more we distance ourselves from quick and temporary solutions, from responding to individual differences in a hurried way, the wider will be the range of hypotheses open to us. The more we resist the temptation to classify children, the more we become able to change our plans and make different possibilities available. This does not eliminate the responsibility or usefulness of noting differences among children. Let us take them into account, let us keep an eye on them. But let us always exercise caution and learn to observe and evaluate better without assigning levels or grades. Let me add that in reading the specialized literature on evaluation, I have not found the factor of time to be treated correctly. Ferdinando Pessoa (1986) says that the measure of the clock is false. It is certainly false concerning the time of children—for situations in which true teaching and learning take place, for the subjective experience of childhood. One has to respect the time of maturation, of development, of the tools of doing and understanding, of the full, slow, extravagant, lucid and ever-changing emergence of children's capacities; it is a measure of cultural and biological wisdom.

If nature has commanded that of all the animals, infancy shall last longest in human beings—infinitely long, says Tolstoy—it is because nature knows how many rivers there are to cross and paths to retrace. Nature provides time for mistakes to be corrected (by both children and adults), for prejudices to be overcome, and for children to catch their breath and restore their image of themselves, peers, parents, teachers, and the world. If today we find ourselves in an era in which the time and rhythm of machines and profits dominate those of human beings, then we want to know where psychology, education, and culture stand.

PART VI: THEORIES OF LEARNING

The Construction of Meanings

Gandini: *One debate in education that seems never to be settled concerns the role of the adult in children's learning. What are your thoughts about this?*

Malaguzzi: I would not want to minimize the determining role of adults in providing children with semantic structures—systems of meaning that allow minds to communicate. But at the same time, I would like to emphasize children's own participation: they are autonomously capable of making meaning from their daily life experiences through mental acts involving planning, coordination of ideas, and abstraction. Remember, meanings are never static, univocal, or final; they are always generative of other meanings. The central act of adults, therefore, is to activate, especially indirectly, the meaning-making competencies of children as a basis of all learning. They must try to capture the right moments, and then find the right approaches, for bringing together, into a fruitful dialogue, their meanings and interpretations with those of the children.

Our Piaget

Gandini: *You have mentioned Piaget's influence on your work, and at the same time, you have mentioned that your views differ from his on various points. Can you tell us more about this influence and the differences?*

Malaguzzi: Our sense of gratitude toward Piaget remains intact. If Jean Jacques Rousseau invented a revolutionary conception of childhood without ever dealing with children, by observing and talking to children over a long period of time, Piaget was the first to give them an identity based on close analysis of their development.

Howard Gardner describes Piaget as the first to take children seriously; David Hawkins describes him as the one who dramatized children splendidly; and Jerome Bruner credits Piaget with demonstrating that those internal principles of logic guiding children are the same principles as those that guide scientists in their inquiries. In fact, in Reggio we know that children can use creativity as a tool for inquiring, ordering, and even transgressing the given schemes of meaning (which Piaget attributed also to the very young in the last years of his life). They can also use creativity as a tool for their own progress in the worlds of necessity and possibility.

With a simple-minded greed, we educators have tried too often to extract from Piaget's psychology things that he did not consider at all usable in education. He would wonder what use teachers could possibly have for his theories of stages, conservation of matter, and so on. In fact, the richest potentiality of Piagetian thought lies in the domain of epistemology, as seen in his major opus, *Biology and Knowledge* (1971, University of Chicago Press). Nevertheless, many suggestions can be taken directly or indirectly from his works to reflect and elaborate upon the meaning of education.

Barbel Inhelder, Piaget's most devoted disciple, told friends after the death of the maestro: "Write freely about his work, make corrections, try to render his thought more specific; still, it will not be easy for you to overturn the underlying structure of his ingenious theories." We in Reggio have tried to do this. Our interest in him increased once we understood that his concern was with epistemology and that his main goal was to trace the genesis of universal invariant structures. Piaget sacrificed many things to that audacious research; yet he also managed to open other paths of research, such as the study of moral judgment, that he did not pursue, as if a fever was burning in him to simultaneously explore many directions. Some of these paths were later rediscovered after they had been casually abandoned.

Now we can see clearly how Piaget's constructivism isolates the child. As a result, we look critically at these aspects: the undervaluation of the adult's role in promoting cognitive development; the marginal attention to social interaction and to memory (as opposed to inference); the distance interposed between thought and language (Vygotsky criticized this, and Piaget [1962] responded); the lockstep linearity of development in constructivism; the way that cognitive, affective, and moral development are treated as separate, parallel tracks; the overemphasis on structured stages, egocentrism, and classificatory skills; the lack of recognition for partial competencies; the overwhelming importance given to logic-mathematical thought; and the overuse of paradigms from the biological and physical sciences. After making all of these criticisms, however, we must go on to note that many constructivists today have turned their attention to the role of social interaction in cognitive development.

The Dilemma of Learning and Teaching

Gandini: *Learning and teaching do not always go together, but in your program, you have found ways to help children construct their learning. How did you balance this equation?*

Malaguzzi: After all we have said about children, we have to discuss more fully the role that children assume in the construction of self and knowledge, and the help they get in these matters from adults. It is obvious that between learning and teaching, we honor the first. It is not that we ostracize teaching, but we tell it, "Stand aside for a while and leave room for learning, observe carefully what children do, and then, if you have understood well, perhaps teaching will be different from before."

Piaget in *To Understand Is to Invent* (1974) warned us that a decision must be made whether to teach schemes and structures directly or to present the child with rich problem-solving situations in which the active child learns them in the course of exploration. The objective of education is to increase possibilities for the child to invent and discover. Words should not be used as a shortcut to knowledge. Like Piaget, we agree that the aim of teaching is to provide conditions for learning.

Sometimes discussions about education treat teaching and learning as almost synonymous. In reality, the conditions and goals of the one who teaches are not identical to the conditions and goals of the one who learns. If teaching is monodirectional and rigidly structured according to some "science," it becomes intolerable, prejudicial, and damaging to the dignity of both teacher and learner. But even when teachers assume themselves to be democratic, their behavior still is too often dominated by undemocratic teaching strategies. These include directives, ritualized procedures, systems of evaluation (which Benjamin Bloom believed should properly be guiding models of education), and rigid cognitive curriculum packages, complete with ready-made scripts and reinforcement contingencies. All of these strategies provide a professional justification for waste and suffering and at the same time create the illusion of an impressive system that reassures adults at an unthinking level. Official adoption is easy. By the time the shortcomings of such a package or system do emerge, it is already too late and the damage is done.

To conclude, learning is the key factor on which a new way of teaching should be based, becoming a complementary resource to the child and offering multiple options, suggestive ideas, and sources of support. Learning and teaching should not stand on opposite banks and just watch the river flow by; instead, they should embark together on a journey down the water. Through an active, reciprocal exchange, teaching can strengthen learning how to learn.

Our Vygotsky

Gandini: *You have mentioned the importance of the teacher's being able to capture the delicate moment in which the child is ready to take a step toward learning. Could you elaborate on that?*

Malaguzzi: At this point, the intervention of Vygotsky, our own Vygotsky, becomes indispensable for clarifying this and other points raised in the previous paragraphs. Vygotsky reminds us how thought and language operate together to form ideas and make a plan for action, and then for executing, controlling, describing, and discussing that action. This is a precious insight for education.

But upon penetrating the adult–child relationship, and thus returning to the theme of teaching and learning, the Russian psychologist (1978) tells us about the advantages of the *zone of proximal development,* which is the distance between the levels of capacities expressed by children and their levels of potential development, attainable with the help of adults or more advanced contemporaries.

The matter is somewhat ambiguous. Can one give competence to someone who does not have it? The very suggestion seems to readmit the old ghosts of teaching that we tried to chase away. But we can dispel any risk of returning to traditional teaching by holding to our principle of *circularity* (a term not seen in Vygotsky's writings). Put more simply, we seek a situation in which the child is about to see what the adult already sees. The gap is small between what each one sees, the task of closing it appears feasible, and the child's skills and disposition create an expectation and readiness to make the jump. In such a situation, the adult can and must lend to the children his or her judgment and knowledge. But it is a loan with a condition—namely, that the child will repay.

It is useless to assert that the readiness of children is too hard to observe. It can indeed be seen! We need to be prepared to see it, for we tend to notice only those things that we expect. But also we should not be in a hurry. We tend all too often today to become slaves of the clock, an instrument that falsifies the natural and subjective time of children and adults.

Vygotsky's suggestion maintains its value and legitimates broad interventions by teachers. For our part in Reggio, Vygotsky's approach is in tune with the way we see the dilemma of teaching and learning and the ecological way one can reach knowledge.

PART VII: FROM THEORY TO PRACTICE

A Profession That Does Not Think Small

Gandini: *How have you gone about putting into practice the many ideas and inspirations that you have either generated or encountered?*

Malaguzzi: The effect of theories can be inspiring and onerous at the same time. This is especially so when it is time to roll up our sleeves and proceed with educational practice. The first fear is to lose the capacity or the ability to connect the theories with the objective problems of daily work, which in turn are generally complicated by administrative, legal, or cultural realities.

But there are further fears, such as those of getting lost in a blind empiricism that can lead to a break with the connections to the necessary theoretical, ideal, and ethical principles; being troubled by the challenge of new theories and approaches that can bring into question your own training and choices; and, last but not least, missing out on the promise that the schools provide as best as possible for all the children as well as meet the expectations and needs of their families. These fears are unavoidable because in our task we cannot be satisfied with approximate results and because our choice was to set up a school with a critical and reforming function. We did not want to be only sad caretakers.

Our theories come from different fields and we meditate on them as well as on the events that take place in our very hands. But a unifying theory of education

Loris Malaguzzi pauses to tie a child's shoe while visiting the Diana Preschool.

that sums up all the phenomena of educating does not (and never will) exist. However, we do indeed have a solid core in our approach in Reggio Emilia that comes directly from the theories and experiences of active education and finds realization in particular images of the child, teacher, school, family, and community. Together these produce a culture and society that connect, actively and creatively, both individual and social growth.

And still Ferriere, Dewey, Vygotsky, Bruner, Piaget, Bronfenbrenner, and Hawkins are very much present for us, along with the latest suggestions from Kaye on the tutorial role of the adult, Shaffer on the relationship between language and social interaction, Serge Moscovici and Gabriel Mugny on the genesis of representation and the importance of the interpersonal cognitive constructions, and Gardner on the forms of intelligence and open minds. In the same way, we look to the sociolinguistic work on how adults and children jointly construct contexts of meaning, as well as to cognitive research founded on constructivist, symbolic-interactionist, and social-constructivist perspectives. Altogether, this literature counteracts the behaviorist theories that reduce the creative and protagonist force of human action to simple, unreadable behavior.

The Success of a Theory Comes Out in the Practice

Gandini: *But how, concretely, do all these theories connect with what goes on in the schools?*

Malaguzzi: It is well known how we all proceed as if we had one or more theories. The same happens for teachers: whether they know it or not, they think and act according to personal theories. The point is how those personal theories are connected with the education of children, with relationships within the school, and with the organization of work. In general, when colleagues work closely together and share common problems, this facilitates the alignment of behaviors and a modification of personal theories. We have always tried to encourage this.

When we start speaking about the theory and practice of education, we can go on and on. I agree with Wilfred Carr (1986) when he says that it is good to avoid discussing theories too much because the risk is to deprive them of their practical aspect. In truth, a theory is legitimate only if it deals with problems that emerge from the practice of education and that can be solved by educators. The task of theory is to help teachers understand better the nature of their problems. This way, practice becomes a necessary means for the success of theory. In this vein, taking this thought even further, David Hawkins (1966) writes, "the personal knowledge of practitioners was significantly deeper than anything embedded in the beliefs and writings of the academically learned" (p. 3). Therefore, the teacher must be treated not as an object of study but as an interpreter of educational phenomena.

This validation of the practical work of the teacher is the only rich "textbook" on which we can count to aid us in developing our educational reflections. Moreover, the work of the teachers, when not abandoned to itself, when not left without the support of institutions and alliances with colleagues and families, is capable not only of producing daily educational experiences but also of becoming subject and object of critical scrutiny.

Getting from Research to Action

Gandini: *You said that teachers should also be researchers. How do you promote this?*

Malaguzzi: To learn and relearn together with the children is our line of work. We proceed in such a way that the children are not shaped by experience but are the ones who give shape to it. There are two ways in which we can look into children's learning process and find clues for supporting it: one is the way children enter into an activity and develop their strategies of thought and action; the other is the way in which the objects involved are transformed. Adults and children go about their learning differently: they use different procedures, honor different principles, make different conjectures, and follow different footprints.

Our teachers do research, either on their own or with their colleagues, to produce strategies that favor children's work or can be utilized by them. They go from research into action (and vice versa). When all the teachers in the school are in agreement, the projects, strategies, and styles of work become intertwined, and the school becomes a truly different school. Some of our teachers proceed in this research with more intentionality and better methods than others; the records and documentaries that result from their endeavors are significant beyond the immediate needs for action and become common objects of study, at times with so much substance as to become of interest to a wider audience. As a result, these teachers feel, and help others to feel, more motivation to grow and attain a much higher level of professionalism. In the process, our teachers realize that they must avoid the temptation of expecting children to give them back what they already know, but that instead they must retain the same sense of wonder that children live through in their discoveries.

This whole approach causes children to be better known by their teachers. Therefore, they feel more open to challenge, more able to work with their peers in unusual situations, and more persistent, because they realize that what they have in mind can be tried out. Children know that in pursuing their goals, they can make their own choices, and that is both freeing and revitalizing. It is, indeed, what we had promised the children, their families, and ourselves.

Our way of working makes possible the choice among different modes of interaction. Small groups of children work simultaneously and can be found all around the school setting, organized so as to facilitate social, cognitive, verbal, and symbolic constructions. Our children in fact have many choices: they have places where they can be alone, in a small number, in a large group, with the teachers or without them, in the *atelier,* in the *mini-atelier,* in the large *piazza,* or, if the weather is good, in the outside courtyard, rich with small and large play structures. But the choice to work in a small group, where they explore together, pleases both them and us. Because of that, the classroom is transformed into one large space with market stalls, each one with its own children and its own projects and activities. This arrangement permits good observations and organically developing research about cooperative learning and the bartering and marketing of ideas.

We like this arrangement of our school. We live in the tradition of a city with its squares and porticoes, which provide an irreplaceable model for meetings, negotiations, and dialogues of various human encounters; moreover, the central square of our city transforms itself twice a week into the hundred stalls of the market. This market has the same function as the *forum,* of which Bruner (1986) wrote, and whose echo resounds in our schools.

No Planning, Much Reconnaissance

Gandini: *People often ask what kind of curricular planning, if any, you have in Reggio Emilia.*

Malaguzzi: No, our schools have not had, nor do they have, a planned curriculum with units and subunits (lesson plans), as the behaviorists would like. These would push our schools toward teaching without learning; we would humiliate the schools and the children by entrusting them to forms, dittos, and handbooks of which publishers are generous distributors.

Instead, every year each school delineates a series of related projects, some short-range and some long. These themes serve as the main structural supports, but then it is up to the children, the course of events, and the teachers to determine whether the building turns out to be a hut on stilts or an apartment house or whatever.

But, of course, infant-toddler centers and preschools do not start off each school year at square one. They have standing behind them a patrimony of talent, knowledge, experiments, research, documentation, and examples showing successes and failures. The teachers follow the children, not plans. The

Loris Malaguzzi and Giovanni Piazza, *atelierista,* working together on the project "The Amusement Park for Birds."

goals are important and will not be lost from sight, but more important are the why and the how of reaching them.

"Reconnaissance" is a strong word in our vocabulary. Our schools start off with a reconnaissance flight over all the human, environmental, technical, and cultural resources. Then more reconnaissance missions will be made to get a full overview of the situation: within and among schools, to families and Advisory Councils, to the pedagogical team, and to the town administration and elected officials. Also, teachers do reconnaissance trips through workshops, seminars, and meetings with experts in various fields.

What educators acquire by discussing, proposing, and launching new ideas is not only a set of professional tools but also a work ethic that gives more value to being part of a group and to having interpersonal solidarity, while at the same time strengthening intellectual autonomy. The support resulting from an *itinerant reconnaissance education* gives us great strength and help. Its task is to startle and push us along new roads. There is not a better evaluation of our work than this.

If the Curricula Are Found in the Children

Gandini: *Children are the ones who shape their school experience rather than being shaped by them. How does this principle influence your choices about what experiences to offer to children?*

Malaguzzi: If the school for young children has to be preparatory and provide continuity with the elementary school, then we as educators are already prisoners of a model that ends up as a funnel. I think, moreover, that the funnel is a detestable object, and it is not much appreciated by children either. Its purpose is to narrow down what is big into what is small. This choking device is against nature. If you put it upside down, it serves no purpose.

Suffice it to say that the school for young children has to respond to the children: it should be a giant rodeo where they learn how to ride 100 horses, real or imaginary. How to approach a horse, how to stroke it, and how to stay close to it are all aspects of an art that can be learned. If there are rules, children will learn them. If they fall off, they will get back on. If special skills are called for, they will watch their more expert contemporaries carefully, and they will even discuss the problem or ask to borrow the adults' experience.

It is true that we do not have planning and curricula. It is not true that we rely on improvisation, which is an enviable skill. We do not rely on chance either, because we are convinced that what we do not yet know can to some extent be anticipated. What we do know is that to be with children is to work one-third with certainty and two-thirds with uncertainty and the new. The one-third that is certain makes us understand and try to understand. We want to study whether learning has its own flux, time, and place; how learning can be organized and encouraged; how situations favorable to learning can be prepared; which skills and cognitive schemas are worth bolstering; how to advance words, graphics, logical thought, body language, symbolic languages, fantasy, narrative, and argumentation; how to play; how to pretend; how friendships form and dissipate; how individual and group identities develop; and how differences and similarities emerge.

All this wisdom does not compensate for what we do not know. But not knowing is the condition that makes us continue to search; in this regard, we are in the same situation as the children. We can be sure that the children are ready to help us. They can help by offering us ideas, suggestions, problems, questions, clues, and paths to follow; and the more they trust us and see us as a resource, the more they give us help. All these offerings, merged with what we ourselves bring to the situation, make a handsome capital of resources.

In the past few years, we have undertaken many inquiries: how children aged 5 years approach the computer; the differences between graphics by boys and girls; the symbolic meanings of drawings; the constructive capacities of logical-organizational thought (which led to a documentary now revisited with George Forman); the acquisition of reading and writing in a communicative context; the forms of thought used in learning about measurement and numbers; cooperative learning through play (in collaboration with Carolyn Edwards, Lella Gandini, and John Nimmo); and the behavior of infants aged 2 years in partially structured situations. The results of these studies guide us in the formulation of flexible projects. But there is another reason for experimenting and documenting—namely, the necessity to reveal in full light the image of a competent child. This, in turn, bolsters our position against detractors and the mystification of official programs and practices.

In our documentaries, archives, and exhibits, which now tour the world, there is this entire story. It is a history of grownups, projects, curricula that are emerging, but above all, children.

PART VIII: PERTINENT EXPECTATIONS

What Makes a Good Project?

Gandini: *Many teachers also ask about the outstanding project work of children in Reggio Emilia. In your view, Loris, what elements contribute to making a good project?*[2]

Malaguzzi: We use projects because relying on the capacities and resources of children expresses our philosophical view. Either a school is capable of continually transforming itself in response to children, or the school becomes something that goes around and around, remaining in the same spot.

In trying to make a good project, one has to have, above all, a pertinent expectation, shaped in advance, an expectation also felt by the children. This expectation helps the adults in terms of their attentiveness, choices, methods of intervention, and what they do concerning the relationships among participants.

Gandini: *Could you speak about the choice of projects to undertake? Are they often based on something that is already part of their ongoing experience?*

Malaguzzi: Yes. Sometimes we pursue something that already belongs to them, but other times we follow something new. The teachers need only to observe and listen to the children, as they continuously suggest to us what interests them, and what they would like to explore in a deeper way. It is good when the adults' own interests coincide with those of the children, so they can move easily to support children's motivation and pleasure.

A good project has a few essential elements. First, it must produce or trigger an initial motivation to warm up the children. Each project has a sort of prologue phase, in which information and ideas are offered and shared within the group. These will be used later to help the children to expand their intentions along with the adults' intentions, suggesting a final objective.

Gandini: *A discussion at the beginning, to gather the memories, thoughts, and desires of the children, is a very effective way to start.*

Malaguzzi: Yes, because it helps the adults to make predictions and hypotheses about what could happen next. Some of these expectations will not come to pass, but others will come alive during the journey taken with the children in the course of the project. And it is not only the adults who form expectations and hypotheses; also those of children—who can use their capacities to make predictions—are needed to organize the work. The strong motivation with which the children embark will help them to feel comfortable as they go down many different paths, abandoning some, trying others. To this task, they will bring different kinds of intelligences and attitudes and produce an extraordinary blooming of ideas, and also (through their negotiation) a convergence in which ideas become sharper and more selected. They feel free to do so because they are not afraid of mistakes or of demolishing their own ideas. The project's objective serves as a permanent beacon always present. It gives the children enormous energy, because they know where they must arrive.

All through the project, adults should intervene as little as possible. Instead, they should set up situations and make choices that facilitate the work of children. The adults have to continually revisit what has been happening, discuss the findings among themselves, and use what they learn to decide how and how much to enter into the action to keep the children's motivation high.

There are many scientific theories about motivation, but I think teachers can learn a great deal about it by working with children. Some children enter the game right away and do not need warming up. Others warm up during the first activities. Others warm up only when something challenges their ideas within the great market of exchanges.

From Discussion to Graphic Representation

Gandini: *The prologue of discussion among children is often followed by having them do a graphic representation, which in turn is followed by another* *discussion, and so on. How do you see one mode of expression influencing the other, and vice versa?*

Malaguzzi: The verbal discussion is certainly the coordinating fulcrum of negotiations within the group—I mean here the small group—and it makes working together possible. Those children who are weaker in their language abilities may have some difficulty entering this great game in an active way, and therefore, we have to be very attentive to them. We must also be attentive to blocks on communication and give consideration to children's feelings, as, for example, when one child feels he or she does not belong with the others in the group.

Words are so powerful because they are not only the couriers of ideas but also allow for their negotiation and transformation. The question of transferring words into graphic representation is not simple because it involves making strong selections. Sometimes they will need to pause to clarify ideas before putting them down on paper and making them visible to others.

Putting ideas into the form of graphic representation allows the children to understand that their actions can communicate. This is an extraordinary discovery because it helps them realize that to communicate, their graphic must be understandable to others. In our view, graphic representation can be a tool of communication much simpler and clearer than words.

Gandini: *I like very much what you are saying, which explains why children feel a need to put their thoughts in a drawing on paper. I saw your teachers often use this process as a basis for next conversations with the children, asking them to explain what they drew and why. Or invite children to do the same with friends in a pair or in a group.*

Malaguzzi: This is a procedure that we always follow. When children are asked to proceed this way, they and the observing adults are able to revisit what has been happening. The adults should become scribes for the children and take notes that capture the details of what the children say and do. They can use the notes to talk again with the children and tell them, "Today, you have done this work, and you arrived here. Tomorrow morning, this is where we will start."

Gandini: *Could you tell us more about the power of graphics expression?*

Malaguzzi: The use of graphic expression comes from the need to bring clarity. There is also the fact that the child intuitively becomes aware about what this new code can produce from now on. As they go from one symbolic language to another, the children find that each transformation generates something new. This complicates the situation and advances them. As they construct their ideas, they also construct the symbols and a plurality of codes. Therefore, when they draw, they are not only making a graphic intervention but are also selecting ideas and getting rid of excessive, superfluous, or misleading ones. They have to reestablish and clarify the frames or contours of the problem. With each step, the child goes further and higher, as a spaceship with several stages, each pushing the rocket deeper into space.

Another reason that children like to pass through graphic expression is that they feel it as something that consolidates solidarity of thought, of action, of perspectives with other children. I could say that graphic expression serves more as a tie that favors collaborative capacities, so that the game of learning among children allows for discoveries to continue, following one after another.

Gandini: *Clearly you think it is valuable when children go back and forth between representational means or different symbolic languages. Does going from one symbolic system to another help the children to communicate? Is it satisfying to them and to others around them?*

Malaguzzi: To me, a symbol is a word or image that stands for something else. I think this can be our working definition; it is the nucleus that selects and holds secondary aspects. Symbols have profound relations with emotions, feelings, with many things that cannot be quantified through observation.

Gandini: *And when we speak of symbolic language?*

Malaguzzi: Since we are speaking of schools, we are referring to the ways in which symbols are used by children to acquire culture, grow, and communicate. I do not want to limit the domain of symbolic languages only to reading, writing, and numbers. Symbols are used as well by musicians, storytellers, and others.

Gandini: *When you speak of different languages used by children, you say that children rewrite concepts using different means. They rewrite both their emotions and/or what they have perceived intellectually. Therefore, their growth of knowledge is served by making several passages from one symbolic language to another.*

Malaguzzi: Through symbols, the child learns an economical means of expression. The child learns a way to keep the concepts at hand ready to be transferred to another situation or context. Children have an amazing ability to relate to several symbolic languages at the same time. Children are able to watch television, play with a doll or train, leaf through a book, go away from the room, come back, and still reconstruct what was going on with extraordinary logic and precision.

To Be in a Group Is a Situation of Great Privilege

Gandini: *Thinking about cooperation among children, what does it mean for a small group to work together?*

Malaguzzi: In such a time as this, with a society and culture that tend to isolate, to give young children the possibility of being together for several years and working closely together is like an emergency life raft. Their relationships are really something new and different from the close relationships that are inside the family or the usual peer relationships in traditional schools. These new cooperative relationships among young children have not yet been sufficiently studied in terms of their educational potential. They offer children the opportunity to realize that their ideas are different and that they hold a unique point of view. At the same time, children realize that the world is multiple and that other children can be discovered through a negotiation of ideas. Instead of interacting only through feelings and sense of friendship, they discover how satisfying it is to exchange ideas and thereby transform their environment.

Loris Malaguzzi speaking at the University of Massachusetts, Amherst, on the occasion of the opening of the exhibit "The Hundred Languages of Children." Lella Gandini is the translator.

However, the differences in development should not be too great. There ought to be a right distance that is capable of producing the exchanges and the negotiations but at the same time not produce excessive disequilibrium. Therefore, it is better, as we have learned through experiences that have been made in many places, that children be discrepant in developmental level but that their differences not be too much.

Children come to realize that through negotiations, their clashes with others can be muted. Children are willing to change their ideas, especially if the pressure to do so comes from peers rather than adults. As they work and play together, sometimes there are moments when their goal really is to establish a good relationship. They find pleasure in being in a group. Even when they disagree, they may keep it to themselves.

Gandini: *You are saying that young children can realize that others hold different points of view, even delay until an appropriate moment the act of expressing and confronting these differences?*

Malaguzzi: When we see young children cooperating, we notice a sort of ethic: they do everything they can to keep the situation stable and ongoing. Some children have more advanced capacities than others. When one such child makes a suggestion or proposal, the others accept it more willingly than if it had come from an adult. Many of them learn the relativity of their own point of view and how to represent their ideas in a delicate way. They say, "I think," or "In my view," or "I do not know if my ideas are right for everybody."

Of course, conflicts also exist. Clashes of principles and ideas can be very rich but do not necessarily need to be expressed through a direct confrontation. Sometimes children feel the disparity of their views but hold back to maintain the harmony of the group functioning. Later, the contrasting point of view can emerge. Cognitive conflicts are not to be always expressed through confrontation, but may be resolved through an act of love, a peaceful, serene act of acceptance. Sociable emotions have a strong role to play in this complex development.

All of this helps explain why it is so important to record and transcribe the conversations of children. Adults should train themselves to become more sensitive to the layers of meaning in these recorded texts. To find clarity and dispel the fog yields a great deal of information about the thoughts of children. Through careful interpretation, one learns that children continually attempt to draw connections among things and thereby grow and learn.

Therefore, for children to be in a group is a situation of great privilege, as if inside a great, transformative laboratory.

CONCLUSION

Gandini: *We are at the end of our conversation; you have offered much food for thought but not spoiled our appetite for learning more. We are eager to have other opportunities for exchanges with you and the wonderfully competent and warm people who work side by side with you. The host of bright and hopeful ideas and experiences you have been bringing to children in Reggio Emilia now travels far beyond the confines of your city.*

Malaguzzi: This experience and my account of it have no leave-taking. My words instead carry a greeting to our American friends who, like us, are interested in helping children to hold their heads high, friends moreover toward whom we are culturally indebted.

If at the end any message is still needed, it is a message of reflection. I do not know how the world of adults really is. I know that the rich, adult world hides many things, while the poor one knows neither how nor what to hide. One of the things that it hides with the most rigor and callousness is the condition of children. I will refrain from detailing the data about death and desperation. I know that my account is a luxury; it is a privilege because the children of whom I speak live in the rich world.

But also in this world, deception continues, at times cynical and violent, at times more subtle and sophisticated, laced with hypocrisy and illiberal theories. Deception infiltrates even the institutions of early education. The continuing motivation for our work has in fact been an attempt to oppose, albeit with modest

A child peeking around the corner at a teacher playing music in the new Nilde Iotti Infant-Toddler Center.

means, this deception and to liberate hopes for a new human culture of childhood. It is a motive that finds its origin in a powerful nostalgia for the future and for mankind.

And now, if you will indulge a weakness on my part, I propose a toast to Benjamin, the youngest child of Howard Gardner and Ellen Winner. Gardner (1989) tells of his trip to China in his book, *To Open Minds,* which I have just finished reading, and not without emotion. Why Benjamin? Because with the key that he earnestly tries to insert in a lock, he can in a way stand for all the children of whom we have been talking. Let us come closer, observe his action, and join in his adventure. It is his, and our, hope.

NOTES

1. Most of this interview took place over the course of 3 years from 1989 to 1991, but the last section took place in 1992 when we were documenting "The Amusement Park for Birds" project with George Forman. It was difficult for Loris Malaguzzi to be pleased with seeing his ideas written on paper. His thoughts were in continuous lucid progression in

search of a deeper respect for the culture of childhood and wider definition of the role of the teacher, as he reflected on the thousands of experiences of his schools for children. Many times during those years, he would call me and tell me to ditch the piece of a transcription I had sent him to review, because he wanted to start over. So I did that each time he asked. But the dialogue with him continued, making it possible for this project to occur. In fact, in 1991, as I was awaiting a promised conclusion, instead I was surprised to receive, from the hands of Carlina Rinaldi, who had come to the United States, a further series of pieces, accompanied by an outline of how he wanted to fold them into the interview. I did the translation, in cooperation with editing by Lester Little and Carolyn Edwards. Lella Gandini, 2011.

2. This portion of the interview took place in April 1992, while Lella Gandini and George Forman observed and participated in the project "The Amusement Park for Birds." Loris Malaguzzi liked the interview but did not edit the transcription as he had done for the others.

REFERENCES

Barazzoni, R. (2000). *Brick by brick: The history of the "XXV Aprile" people's nursery school of Villa Cella* (J. Costa, Trans.). Reggio Emilia, Italy: Reggio Children.

Bruner, J. (1986). *Actual minds, possible worlds.* Cambridge, MA: Harvard University Press.

Carr, W. (1986). *Becoming critical: Education, knowledge, and action research.* Philadelphia, PA: Falmer Press.

Gardner, H. (1989). *To open minds: Chinese clues to the dilemma of contemporary education.* New York: Basic Books.

Hawkins, D. (1966). Learning the unteachable. In L. Shulman & E. Keislar (Eds.), *Learning by discovery: A critical appraisal* (pp. 3–12). Chicago: Rand McNally.

Malaguzzi, L. (1971). *Esperienza per una nuova scuola dell' infanzia.* Rome: Editori Riuniti.

Malaguzzi, L. (1971). *La gestione sociale nella scuola dell'infanzia.* Rome: Editori Riuniti.

Pessoa, F. (1986). *Il libro del inquietudine.* Milano: Feltrinelli.

Piaget, J. (1962). *Comments on Vygotsky's critical remarks.* Cambridge, MA: MIT Press.

Piaget, J. (1971). *Biology and knowledge.* Chicago: University of Chicago Press.

Piaget, J. (1974). *To understand is to invent.* New York: Grossman.

Rodari, Gianni. (1996). *The grammar of fantasy: An introduction to the art of inventing stories* (translated and with an introduction by Jack Zipes). New York: Teachers and Writers Collaborative. (Originally published as *Grammatica della fantasia* by Giulio Einaudi Editore, Torino, Italy, 1973.)

Vygotsky, L. S. (1978). *Mind in society: The development of higher psychological processes.* Cambridge, MA: Harvard University Press.

Wertheimer, M. (1945). *Productive thinking.* New York: Harper and Row.

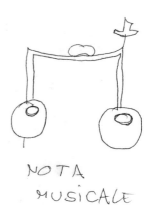

NOTA
MUSICALE

Chapter 3

Malaguzzi's Story, Other Stories, and Respect for Children

David Hawkins

David Hawkins (1913–2002) was a distinguished professor of philosophy at the University of Colorado at Boulder and one of the influential academics who helped shape American progressive school reform during the 1960s, a turbulent but exciting period of educational debate and innovation. He and his wife, Frances, herself a noted expert on early childhood education, founded the Mountain View Center for Environmental Education to promote active intellectual exploration and science education for elementary schools. Hawkins received many honors during his life and influenced other thinkers in education theory, drawing on his broad knowledge of political and social theory, economics, mathematics, physics, biology, and philosophy.

The introductory notes to this chapter were prepared with Carolyn Edwards by Ellen Hall, a founding board member of Hawkins Centers of Learning, which houses the Hawkins's archives, including many of David and Frances Hawkins's writings and photographs, in Boulder, Colorado. The body of the chapter is adapted from Hawkins's Foreword to the second edition of this volume, integrated with passages from a keynote speech he gave in June 1998 in Boulder, Colorado, and his Afterword (slightly edited by Hall and Edwards) published in Frances Hawkins's (1997) autobiography, *Journey with Children: The Autobiography of a Teacher,* with permission of the University Press of Colorado and Hawkins Centers of Learning.

Two concepts are fundamental to Hawkins's philosophy of learning (Hawkins, 1974). The first is the importance of teachers as learners, engaging in a process of inquiry, encountering the world with the same curiosity, interest, wonder, and amazement as the children they teach. The second, strongly connected to the first, stresses the value of learning environments filled with "everyday" materials, gathered and made available to children and adults to initiate and support their explorations and investigations, materials with which the children, to quote Hawkins, can "mess about."

Hawkins inspired many important thinkers, including Loris Malaguzzi. The two men were introduced by Lella Gandini in 1988, and thereafter, Hawkins visited Reggio Emilia on two occasions, the first in 1990 as a participant in an international conference and the second in 1992 to visit the schools. These visits, a true "meeting of minds," made a strong impression on Malaguzzi and the Reggio teachers (Gandini, 2008). It is due to this mutuality and spread of ideas that the following sample of Hawkins's thought is included in this volume.

AN EXTRAORDINARY STORY, AND A MEETING

The extraordinary story told by Loris Malaguzzi, in his interview with Lella Gandini, has reminded me, David Hawkins, of my first meeting with him. That was at the great Reggio Emilia conference of March 1990, when he spoke so incisively on the conference theme, the Potentials and Rights of Children. His story has reminded me also of other stories that have been told, or could be told, from

Children keep watch over a checkers match between Loris Malaguzzi and David Hawkins at La Villetta Preschool.

different times and places. All speak of successful efforts to create new patterns of educational practice that can at least begin to match the manifold talents of young children. Most of these other successes have been limited in scale and often, sadly, in duration. Yet brought together, they spin a golden thread through many decades of adult neglect and preoccupation with other matters. Although education is among the oldest and most vital parts of human praxis, the successes typically have been supported only through a minority tradition, ignored by mainstream society, even by the mainstream of scientific curiosity and research. That this should be true is a paradox. Such a brilliant exception as the case of Reggio Emilia should therefore bring with it much joy.

OTHER STORIES: DEVELOPMENTS IN PROGRESSIVE EDUCATION IN EUROPE AND AMERICA

I think it is worth reminding ourselves of a few of those other stories. Malaguzzi refers in passing to some of them, mainly to the theorists. Let me mention others. In the field of education, as in many others, good theory—I boldly say—has come mostly as a harvest, a reflection of successful practice. Harvested from past practice, theory in turn can, then, bring new practical guidance. An outstanding example of this twofold relation was the part played by John Dewey.

In Dewey's time, almost a century ago, a minority tradition of excellent practice in childhood education already existed in the United States. That tradition had evolved, in turn, from the experience of the Froebel Kindergartens. My own mother received a basic part of her education in a Froebel Kindergarten during the 1870s, when the number of such schools in the United States grew by two or three orders of magnitude. Strong women teachers had been supported by Froebel's basic insight into the learning process but had outgrown the quaint rigidity of his pioneering "system." (Something similar was true later of Montessori's influence.) The pioneering teachers involved in this development were looking for new theoretical recognition and guidance. They found it in John Dewey, already a deeply perceptive philosopher and psychologist. But first they had to educate him—a pupil of profound aptitude! Dewey's own practice was that of a university lecturer, deeply reflective but dry as dust except to those who already shared something of his spirit and insight. Although many contemporaries were profoundly moved by his clarity of understanding, his influence has largely been lost in my country as part of the attrition of childhood education. I am happy that this great educational philosopher is still alive and well in Italy. Looking further back, Froebel linked himself theoretically to the philosopher Georg W. F. Hegel; for practice and commitment, he associated himself with his mentor, Johann Pestalozzi, of Zurich—far north of Reggio Emilia. More than two centuries ago, in 1798, Pestalozzi rescued children tragically orphaned in the wake of Napoleon's armies, and thus developed deep insight concerning the nurturance of their lives and talents.

Coming forward again in time, one sees that the fruition of this long development has been irregular. Its practical influences have also grown in Canada and in Continental Europe, developing differently in Germany and the low countries (Belgium and the Netherlands) and in France and Scandinavia. In the United States, it was once powerful but has largely been co-opted by the schools, in which the original progressive idea of "Kindergarten," or "children's garden," for the most part, survives in name only. This whole international story needs to be rescued.

Here I shall only add a note about Great Britain, where its major developments had a history similar in some ways to that of the United States, starting also from 19th-century small beginnings under such influences as those of Froebel and, later, of Dewey and the McMillan sisters, Margaret and Rachel. Whereas in the United States, this evolution suffered from neglect or rejection after World War II, in England it flourished. In some regions, a large proportion of the Infant Schools (ages 5 to 7+) were radically transformed, as were smaller proportions of Junior Schools (ages 7 to 11+). Visitors to some of those good classrooms could find much to delight in and reflect on. Political ideologues, more recently, have suppressed or ignored these forward steps. But the new ways of learning and teaching have not been wholly reversed. They are successful, they persist, and one still can learn from them.

I mention this British phase of our joint history because it attracted great attention from many of us in the United States, suffering from the loss of our own best traditions. The result was a fashion, a seeking to emulate the "English Infant School." This was a kind of emulation that ignored a long history of development, a well-rooted tree that could not simply be put in an airplane and transported. We have our own strong traditions, and we need to rescue them.

CIVILITY: SERIOUS MEMBERSHIP IN THE COMMUNITY

Historically, we Americans were created as a new society with immigrants increasingly from various parts of the world, and we had the slogan, "life, liberty, and the pursuit of happiness," but we never seem to have had a slogan, "and serious membership in the community." The notion of "community" is in some ways opposed to that of individual liberty. I am feeling critical of our much-valued traditions, which are valuable in many ways, but when it comes to the ability to get together to make plans for the future, we are sometimes not so good at that. We call it politics, and many of us try to avoid it.

The contrast between Italian and American notions of community has lingered with me ever since my visits to Reggio Emilia, and I want to talk about the history that we share with northern Italy since the end of World War II. Two things have been happening, one of which is a gradually decreasing real wage averaged over the whole society, and the other is women's liberation. The combination of those two not only invited more women to enter professional, business, and workaday life but also made it necessary. In Italy, these trends were met—especially in the north—by discussions among people that brought about the kind of concern for child care that did develop there. In the United States, the effect was quite different, in the sense that we made no plans for the care of young children beyond the home, although there were going to be many, many cases of children who needed to be cared for, and quite inadequate child care was often the only thing available.

This is a pretty deep contrast. If you look at the history of Italy, you see they have had a long, long period of time in which to learn this kind of *communitarian* existence. Let me bring up another word that we use rather glibly: *civility.* "Let us be civil"—normally that means, "let us be polite."

But what *civil* really means, if you go back in history, is that people who belong to tribes—or not to tribes, but to clans—used to live rather separated from each other as hunter-gatherers or as early farmers, but then they began to congregate together in places called *cities.* The Latin word for city is *civis,* and from that word, we get *civility* and lots of other words, such as *civic, citizen,* and *civilization.* The different clans had to learn how to live with each other, and they had to practice it for a long time before civility became a social reality. And so I think we see a deep difference between those parts of the world like Emilia Romagna, Italy, with permanent, deeply rooted settlements since ancient times and our own much more scattered, much more diverse, much more mobile society.

Civility, then, means the ability to get together; it doesn't mean to be polite. You don't have to be always polite when you get together, but you do have to congregate, you do want to exchange things, you do want to form common ideas.[1]

AMERICAN PARALLELS: LEARNING THROUGH PROJECTS

After this circuit of history, I come back to the fascinating history of Reggio Emilia and the other Italian communities in which childhood education has similarly evolved and prospered. We who labor in this particular vineyard of early childhood education have much to learn from the history of Reggio and its still-evolving practice. An evolution with such communal support is an achievement that Americans, in particular, will carefully study. But it can be a great mistake for us, as it was in the case of our desire to emulate the English Infant Schools, to think that we can somehow just import the Reggio experience. By reputation, we are prone to look for the quick fix. Such an attitude would deprecate the very achievement it professes to admire. Among many other institutional and cultural differences, we in the United States do not know such solidarity, such sustaining communality, reshaping itself in the ways Malaguzzi describes, demanding better education for children. Our social landscape is different, and so must our battles be.

Although many of us still lack acquaintance with the obvious profusion of Reggio practice, I hazard the opinion that we—we being the United States, Britain, and elsewhere—have contributions both to receive and to give. I shall mention

David and Frances Hawkins.

particularly the practice of developing "project work" for children's inquiry and invention. It is similar to a strategy that we saw well developed, years ago, in California. My wife, Frances Hawkins (1997), taught there and contributed to that strategy, often a great advance over dreary daily "lessons."[2]

When based in part on the interests some children revealed in play and discussion, such projects could enlist their commitment and enthusiasm. Yet fundamental questions remained open about the degree to which such enthusiasms might support, or merely mask, the more hidden and less developed talents of other children. To recognize and encourage these less articulate ones, on their diverse trajectories of learning, remains a constant challenge.

Such questions and challenges, we learned, must always permeate our intellectual curiosity about the earliest years of learning. We came to see the need to evolve a style of classroom practice that would support a greater simultaneous diversity of work than our project methods, even at their best, could easily maintain. Out of this more pluralistic and richer ambiance, ideas and inventions could, at times (although not often), be shared by all. Out of this sharing, projects did indeed sometimes evolve, with great vitality. But the definition and duration of these projects was always a dependent and restricted variable.

I mention this specific topic—projects—because as I read the very open and charming reflections of Loris Malaguzzi, I thought not only of the wider history of childhood education, but also about the details, the debate, the problems, that must have been involved at every step along the way, as Reggio Emilia educators went about confronting traditional Italian educational practice. I have tried to suggest, as an example, that the etiology and uses of "project work" may still be in that problematic state. For our own benefit, we need to know more of the debate, the retrospective valuations, the successive approximations. We need to join in the debate!

In the meantime, it is quite enough that we salute the achievement and devotion revealed in this remarkable story of a devoted teacher-theorist and a devoted community.

MOVING FROM JUST LOVING CHILDREN TO RESPECTING THEM

Let me end with a comment on the notion of respect for children, because that was so fundamental to Malaguzzi's philosophy, as well as to mine.

A proper and serious study of childhood would raise questions, I think, about one tendency widespread among us. In a novel of fantasy, *Where the Blue Begins,* by Christopher Morley (1922), a group of children decide to send one of their number, magically grown up, as a spy, or emissary, to the world of adults. I have suggested, in the same spirit, that we adults need to send emissaries, or messengers, to the estate of childhood. But that may meet only half the need; we too easily learn only what we are prepared to accept. Being repelled, on our mission, by the typical formality and sterility of our institutional treatment of children, many of us react by seeking and advocating patterns of association that are arranged for easy two-way communication, warm and loving. If that is half the story, it is a half that needs redefinition when the other half is told.

Long before the American psychologist Bruno Bettleheim wrote his well-known book *Love Is Not Enough* (1950) on the treatment of emotionally disturbed children, Immanuel Kant, the great German ethical philosopher, had given profound support to the proposition that, in human affairs and generally, love is not enough. The more magic gift is not love, but *respect* for others as ends in themselves, as actual and potential artisans of their own learnings and doings, of their own lives, and thus uniquely contributing, in turn, to their learnings and doings.

Respect for the young is not a passive, hands-off attitude. It invites our own offering of resources. It moves us toward the furtherance of their lives and thus, even, at times, toward remonstrance or intervention. Respect resembles love in its implicit aim of furtherance, but love without respect can blind and bind. Love is private and unbidden, whereas respect is implicit in all moral relations with others.

To have respect for children is more than recognizing their potentialities in the abstract, it is also to seek out and value their accomplishments—however small these may appear by the normal standards of adults. But if we follow this track of thinking, one thing stands out. We must provide for children those kinds of environments that elicit their interests and talents and that deepen their engagement in practice and thought. An environment of "loving adults" who are themselves alienated from the world around them is an educational vacuum. Adults involved in the world of man and nature must bring that world with them to children, bounded and made safe to be sure, but not thereby losing its richness and promise of novelty.

NOTES

1. See Carolyn Edwards (1995) for further discussion of notions of civil community in Malaguzzi's philosophy of education as relationship.

2. The *project approach,* and related *emergent curriculum,* are well known to early childhood educators through the work of Lilian Katz and Sylvia Chard (1989), as well as Betty Jones and John Nimmo (1994).

REFERENCES

Bettleheim, B. (1950). *Love is not enough: The treatment of emotionally disturbed children.* Glencoe, IL: Free Press.

Edwards, C. P. (1995). Democratic participation in a community of learners: Loris Malaguzzi's philosophy of education as relationship. Invited lecture, Nostalgia del Futuro, symposium honoring the contributions to education of Loris Malaguzzi. University of Milan, Italy. Available at http://digitalcommons.unl.edu/famconfacpub/15.

Gandini, L. (2008). Meeting of minds: Malaguzzi and Hawkins. In L. Gandini, S. Etheredge, & L. Hill (Eds.), *Insights and inspirations from Reggio Emilia* (pp. 36–37). Worcester, MA: Davis.

Hawkins, D. (1974). *The informed vision: Essays on learning and human nature.* New York: Agathon Press.

Hawkins, F. P. (1997). *Journey with children: The autobiography of a teacher.* Boulder: University Press of Colorado.

Jones, E., & Nimmo, J. (1994). *Emergent curriculum.* Washington, DC: National Association for the Education of Young Children.

Katz, L. G., & Chard, S. C. (1989). *Engaging children's minds: The project approach.* Norwood, NJ: Ablex.

Morley, C. (1922). *Where the blue begins.* Garden City, NY: Doubleday Press.

Chapter 4

Our Responsibility toward Young Children and toward Their Community

Graziano Delrio

Graziano Delrio has been mayor of Reggio Emilia since 2004. He is by profession an endocrinologist, and he holds an appointment as professor at the University of Modena and Reggio Emilia. A loving husband and father, he has said, "It is not easy to be a father of nine, but it has taught me not to judge others and to be compassionate, as I think back upon how inadequate I was when I had my first child at age 23." During his two terms as mayor, he has focused on community and people. The first term was characterized by the idea of "Reggio Emilia, a collective good; for a serene, safe, and united town." His second term, during a period of global economic crisis, has been based on the concept of "Strong community, safe future" and focused on the

An earlier version of the first part of this chapter was given at the Sixth Annual Conference of the North American Reggio Emilia Alliance in Chicago, June 2010 (published in *Innovations in Early Education: The International Reggio Exchange, 17*[4], 1–5), published by Wayne State College of Education in Detroit, Michigan. The second part is based on a written interview with Lella Gandini in 2009. Reprinted with permission.

issues of education, knowledge, and innovation as the basis for a more international development of the city of Reggio Emilia.

Today, we are focusing on an issue that is important to us: our responsibility toward young children. For us, this means a discussion about children's rights to citizenship. We refer to children as citizens, as harbingers of rights regarding cities. We believe that we adults hold three kinds of obligation to them: what we call civil liability, ethical liability, and political liability.

For us, *civil liability* refers to children's right to education and to equal opportunities, which means the removal of all obstacles to the development of human beings.

Article 3 of the Italian Constitution states: *All citizens have equal social dignity and are equal before the law, without distinction of sex, race, language, religion, and political opinions, personal and social conditions. It is the duty of the Republic to remove these obstacles of an economic or social nature, which constrain the freedom and equality of citizens, thereby impeding the full development of the human person and the effective participation of all workers in the political, economic and social organization of the country.*

This statement is similar to what Thomas Jefferson wrote in the Declaration of Independence in 1776: *We hold these truths to be self-evident, that all men are created equal, that they are endowed by their Creator with certain unalienable Rights, which among these are Life, Liberty and the pursuit of Happiness.*

We in Reggio Emilia believe that we should manage our cities with the objective of building an equal community, acting for the common good of citizens to guarantee equal dignity and equal rights. We assert the right of children to education from birth, even though the Italian school system does not recognize the right to education for children in preschool. In many Italian regions, the provision of early childhood services is still limited, especially for children from birth to 3 years old.

In Reggio Emilia, we are working hard to satisfy the highest number of families' service demands. Especially in this period of economic crisis, school administrators and politicians must be committed to the process of meeting these demands. Preschool services often become the weak link in the chain because this is a service that families often give up if one of the parents loses his or her job. However, this deprives children of their right to education and relationships with friends in school. Because of this, our municipal administration prefers to support families affected by the economic crisis by reducing the fees for early childhood services, which we normally use to manage the costs of the services.

Our responsibility toward children goes beyond the construction of buildings. It concerns the quality of education we offer to our children and our families, the quality of tools and resources, and, in particular, the richness of the approach. We are not generating schools for wealthy people. The Reggio Emilia approach is possible where there is nothing, provided there is respect, listening, and time. This

Majestic stone lions watch over a small square in Reggio Emilia.

is even more important in Italy than in the United States, where quality in education has extended into primary and secondary education. Jerome Bruner said, "Today, Reggio Emilia needs to find a way to generalize the most of what the city has done until now, to influence their educational system on all levels." Last year, we opened a primary school at the Loris Malaguzzi International Center, and we will continue to invest in schools because we believe that every child, every boy and girl, has the right to quality in education.

Our second responsibility toward children concerns *ethical liability*. Ethical liability toward children means that you recognize their dignity as citizens, as bearers of rights related to the city. The child is, therefore, a competent citizen. He or she is competent in assuming responsibility for the city. I often quote this statement by John Adams, the second president of the United States: "Public happiness exists when citizens can take part responsibly for public good and public life. Everywhere, there are men, women, children, whether old or young, rich or poor, tall or short, wise or foolish . . . everyone is highly motivated by a desire of being seen, heard, considered, approved and respected by the people around him and known by him."

In this period of our history, the idea of citizenship has had a strong influence on the identity of the infant-toddler centers and preschools—the sense of belonging, the willingness to take care of one another, the wish to participate, and the desire to be an active part of a process of change toward greater prosperity for the world community. The infant-toddler centers and preschools are places of living together between generations. They are public common spaces where the multitudes aim to become a community of people growing together with a strong sense of the future, a strong idea of participation, of living together, of taking care, one for others. We believe that caring generates care; attention generates attention; a child receiving trust will trust. Taking care of the other people and of the common space is an expression of a sense of affiliation to a community. The school expresses the society through which it is generated, but school is also able to generate a new society. A school that takes care generates a mutual sense of care.

In an interview in 2007 in the *Harvard Business Review,* Howard Gardner said,

My favorite example of an ethical community is a small city called Reggio Emilia in northern Italy. Aside from providing high-quality services and cultural benefits to its citizens, the city provides excellent infant and toddler centers and preschools. Children feel cared for by the community. So, when they grow up, they return this regard by caring for others. They become good workers and good citizens. (Fryer, 2007)

We understand that the purpose of education is not related only to *you* but it is also related to *us*—to the community, to the other people. What drives us to do what we do in Reggio Emilia? We do what we do because we trust. We have confidence in the beauty and the uniqueness of the human person.

Our third responsibility relates to *political liability,* and I will focus, particularly, on intercultural coexistence. Our responsibility toward children is also political. Long after the United States, Europe is now experiencing the migratory phenomenon, which is the subject of a great deal of public opinion in our countries. The reality of immigration is difficult for families and children. Global problems immediately become local problems that cities cannot solve. Reggio Emilia is the only Italian city belonging to the Intercultural Cities Network, which includes one city from every European Union country that has good practices related to intercultural coexistence. I believe that they chose us because of the work that has been done with immigrant children and families in the municipal infant-toddler centers and preschools.

Today, when the *zeitgeist* (the spirit of the times, the mood of an era) tells us that difference is a problem, our society can choose between two kinds of relationships: bonding or bridging. We can stay within the group creating bonds that knit the group together, reinforcing a sense of belonging. Or we can stimulate openness to the other, to the different, thereby gaining knowledge and stimulating curiosity toward the others along a path of enrichment and positive change. This is the bridging approach, a multiconnection, which multiplies knowledge. The bridging approach is exemplified in the drawing by the children from Reggio that is posted on the website of the North American Reggio Emilia Alliance (NAREA).

Children appreciate and are stimulated by diversity. Children are our teachers in their belief that difference is not a problem but a gift. Gardner believes that "children have the cosmopolitism gene and the skill of embracing differences." We all know as well that mothers from different countries have the same fears, the same worries, and the same hopes concerning their children. The key to the future of our children and of our community lies in the attention to the multiple intelligences, to the hundred languages, to intercultural coexistence, and to multi-disciplinarity.

In the municipal infant-toddler centers and preschools in Reggio Emilia, the openness to other cultures has been a community experience. Carola and Marcelo Suárez-Orozco, of New York University, have told us that "Understanding of the community, which is experienced by the families of foreign origins through the preschool, so open to paying attention to the development of the future for our children, is to be seen as an extraordinary experience of intercultural coexistence and of citizenship, a true experience of collective understanding of the common good."

The cultural environment that we wish for our children is the one that states that the other is not a problem but rather, an opportunity. The other is a "fascinating companion for a voyage down the sparkling stream of life" (Joseph Conrad, 1907/1997, p. 116). We have an ethical responsibility toward children to create that cultural environment together with the children. We don't want to forget what John Stuart Mill said in the essay *On Liberty*: "Each is the proper guardian of his own health, whether bodily, or mental and spiritual. Mankind are greater gainers by suffering each other to live as seems good to themselves, than by compelling each to live as seems good to the rest" (Mill, 1869, p. 13).

* * *

Lella Gandini: *You have spoken about the many new immigrants in your city. What should be done to invite the participation of the large variety of new citizens present in Reggio Emilia?*

Mayor Delrio: You are right to speak about "large variety." To a large variety should correspond a large variety of approaches, and it is the direction in which we are moving with different ways and processes. The diversity present in Reggio Emilia is anthropological, social, and cultural. The only place to start is from the Italian Constitution, which establishes fundamental rights in a democracy based on the principles of equality, solidarity, and freedom. On this basis, our city of Reggio Emilia established its own style starting from the rights and the duties, from shared rules and respect of living together, from reciprocity and cooperation. The more this becomes a common patrimony, the easier it is to live together. Reggio Emilia wants to be an open city, intercultural, where the "other" is a welcome companion with whom to do a journey together.

One of the most visible sources of diversity at this point is the one of the country of origin, especially for the immigrants of the first generation. With regard to the families with children, our system of preschools is an exceptional door

Mothers gather in the park in the center of the city.

for immigrants to become part of the community. The children grasp the society in a very original way, and they are a great engine. They expect a society that is open and welcoming, and they perceive that we do not have any other destiny than knowing one another, living together, and not being against but instead in favor of someone or something. The approach of the schools of Reggio puts into practice in a total way the "hundred languages" and makes it a way to create a connection among different generations and backgrounds that are present in the schools. An immigrant mother who participates in the life of the school becomes a Reggio mother because her heart responds not only to her own child but also to the environment in which she lives. She becomes completely inserted, at ease, and curious about the city.

Gandini: *Your administration has made it a priority to create pedestrian-only spaces in the city that invite people to linger, sit, rest, and enjoy the squares and fountains of Reggio Emilia. Why is that important?*

Delrio: What you see today, correctly appreciated by our citizens, is the result of a long and intentional, dedicated and impassioned, work of research and analysis inspired by a guiding principle: to make possible for the community—for the people—to reclaim their own space, that is, the public space. It is not easy to return space to people. For many years, our city had moved in the opposite direction, toward the privatization of spaces and toward letting go of public spaces—at times only considering them a source of money and rendering them private, at other times letting spaces become marginal, in fact, "nonplaces" with no identity, filled with parked cars, garbage containers, or signage.

We have started to work with an idea of a city as a community that places the people at its center. My idea of a city is a "convivial" city—a city for living together and occupying the spaces in a cordial way. The work we have done has been quite intense, and we have had to overcome much resistance and deeply rooted bad habits. We had to change the way we used different places, and we had to give them more quality and value. Many people offered rich suggestions and proposals, including private owners, shopkeepers, and merchants. We have found ways for children, elders, the handicapped, and other vulnerable people to walk easily and securely and find their direction easily. We want spaces to be intuitive, without obstacles, and invite people to sit and rest, maybe enjoy the shade, maybe even have handy a café, and why not a bench from which music emanates?

The best satisfaction for me has been to see that once these spaces were improved after the reconstruction, the people immediately started to live in them just naturally, as if these spaces had always been that way. I am always moved by the joy of the children in front of the renewed fountain near the municipal theater. At the end of the process, when we see a beautiful space, reconquered and well lived in, it might seem that it was something simple and obvious, but instead, it was not that way at all. It is like a poem, the more beautiful and essential it is, the more thought and hard work that went into writing it.

Gandini: *How do you see the development of the education that attracts so many people from all over the world to your city?*

Delrio: As both the mayor and a citizen of Reggio Emilia, I am very proud of our early education system, outstanding in quality. I am also proud of the people who bring it forward, who are the heart of it, and who have the task to prepare new generations to be just as motivated and impassioned as they are.

I am convinced about the choice I made, even if it aroused some disapproval, to shine so much light on this system, saying, "Pay attention. This is our first priority." I did this because people tend to become habituated and not notice anymore the best things we have, as if they were obvious, and this risks abandoning them. Our educational system, so much a part of the identity of this city and now known throughout the world, stands open to differences, dialogue, and exchange, in an ongoing process that still holds great potential. Such relationships, I believe, could be more intense regarding all our institutions of knowledge, from public school to university. Indeed, for that very reason, we have begun to create a shared context in which to work. This initiative has been given the name of Officina Educativa ("Educational Forum") and could involve as many as possible of all the agencies dedicated to education in our city. The Educational Forum should enlarge the acquisition of knowledge at all the levels, along with the community as if it were a shared life, in close relationship with the community.

I would argue that our educational system is our city's most important resource, which can in turn generate economic development for example in tourism, publishing, research, architecture, design, and cultural initiatives that will all have at their center children with their hundred languages. Certainly, the Malaguzzi International Center, Reggio Children, and our system of infant-toddler centers and preschools have a destiny to continue to search, to dialogue, and never to stop. It is the spirit in which the approach was born; it is the safe harbor that Loris Malaguzzi wanted all of us to reach. Therefore, I believe all those skilled and impassioned people must continue to study, to stay curious, and to look forward, while remaining immersed in our reality so that this approach will continue to be so special and enrich the humanity of us all.

REFERENCES

Conrad, J. (1907). *The secret agent.* Online at Project Gutenberg Etext 1997, agent10.txt.

Fryer, B. (Ed.). (2007, March). The ethical mind: A conversation with Howard Gardner. *Harvard Business Review,* pp. 1–5.

Mill, J. S. (1869). *On liberty.* London: Longman, Roberts & Green.

Chapter 5

Reggio Emilia: A Transforming City

Sandra Piccinini and Claudia Giudici

The city represents a natural and human stage where the actors are all the citizens: women and men, young and old, who participate day by day in the changing of the urban landscape. A stage of events, markets, religious and civic celebrations, conferences and meetings, commerce and music. (Piccinini, 2002, p. 13)

A long and adventurous journey links early childhood education to the city of Reggio Emilia. It has been an extraordinary adventure of primarily women, but also men, who have worked with intelligence and passion, day after day, and made it possible. It has been an experience that has been renewed over time because of the awareness of societal changes and new scientific learning about children. The experience continues today, sometimes challenging and sometimes difficult, but it is one that has given joy and learning to many children, promises great hope for the future, and produces a continuous dialogue between the children and the city.

This chapter derives from interviews conducted and translated by Lella Gandini with Claudia Giudici in 2010, as well as from the publications in the references, compiled and brought up to date by the editors.

Our history is one of hard work and joy, of conflicts and continuous discussion. Howard Gardner has observed, "There cannot be absence of conflicts in a dynamic entity," and certainly this is the case with use. For example, the relationship with the Catholic Church was not easy, especially at the beginning (see Loris Malaguzzi, Chapter 2, this volume). Political conflicts between the majority and minority representatives at the municipal level have been challenging, and they continue today.

Reggio Emilia was founded by the Romans in the second century B.C. and was the birthplace of the Italian national flag in 1797. The people of Reggio Emilia have always had a strongly independent character. In the 20th century, the citizens of Reggio Emilia played an important role in the Resistance movement against Fascism and the Nazi occupation, for which the city received Italy's highest national honor with a medal for military valor. Many memorials in the town commemorate this period in the city's history.

Reggio Emilia is located in the Po Valley in northern Italy, now one of the most industrialized parts of Europe. But until 50 years ago, this area was mainly an agricultural society. Because it is now a highly industrialized city (primarily the fashion industry and transformation of agricultural products), Reggio Emilia is linked to the new high-speed railway system in Italy. Reggio Emilia is appreciated for its cuisine, and its most important agricultural products are known all over the world: a very fine cheese, Parmigiano Reggiano, and a sparkling wine, Lambrusco.

Like many cities in the world during the current phase of history, Reggio Emilia is a city in transformation, a city that is changing rapidly. In the course of this evolution, the city is moving away from consolidated traditions toward those that are new and unfamiliar. It is possible to see the signs of this change in the landscape and architecture of the city, yet the social changes are of even more importance, although not as visible.

A RAPIDLY GROWING CITY

Reggio Emilia is a growing city and includes more children, elderly people, and immigrants than ever before. In 1991, there were 133,000 inhabitants in the city, and in 2009, there were 167,000. The growth in the past 20 years has exceeded 35,000 people. The main reasons for this significant growth are, first, an increase in life expectancy in Italy and throughout Europe; second, an increase in birth rate unique to Reggio Emilia compared with neighboring cities; and third, significant growth in immigration due to an economy that attracts manpower from southern Italy and many countries outside Europe.

Let us examine these factors in depth. An increased life expectancy in Europe means that the number of elderly people is increasing throughout the continent, where the average life span is 81 years for women and 75 years for men. In Italy,

Reggio Emilia is a forward-looking city, with many new inhabitants as well as new construction.

life expectancy is 83 for women and 77 for men. The increased life expectancy means that in our city, there are many elders. Twenty-six percent of the population is over 60 years old and 16% is under 18 years old.

The increase in the birth rate in Reggio Emilia began in 1986. At one time, Reggio was one of the cities with the lowest birth rates in northern Italy. In fact, Italy is a country known for its low birth rate. Fertility rates in Italy declined from 2.67 in 1965, to 1.22 in 1994, to 1.19 in 1998 (Organization for Economic Cooperation and Development Review Team for Italy, 2001). That trend was nationwide, including in Reggio Emilia, where the number of children born decreased steadily throughout the 1970s and the first half of the 1980s. However, the birth rate is once again on the rise, and currently the birth rate is again approaching that of the 1970s. In 2008, approximately 1,900 children were born in Reggio Emilia, exceeding the already high number born in 2007. This makes for a younger city. In 2009, about 6% of the population in the city was aged 0 to 5 years old, which is a little higher than for the rest of the Emilia Romagna Region.

The increase in population in Reggio Emilia, as throughout Europe, is primarily due to immigration. In Reggio Emilia, 14% of the population in 2009 was not

Italian, a proportion much higher than in the surrounding province. By and large, immigrants are younger than the rest of the population, and they constitute a large percentage of the children. In 2008, 29% of the children born in Reggio Emilia did not hold Italian citizenship. Yet much assimilation is occurring in the city. Almost one-third of marriages today are mixed, with at least one parent who is non-Italian. The most common countries of origin of residents in Reggio Emilia, besides Italy, include Albania, Morocco, China, Ghana, Ukraine, Tunisia, Egypt, Nigeria, Romania, and many others as well. The most common countries of origin of the young children in the municipal infant-toddler centers and preschools are Nigeria, Morocco, Ghana, Albania, and Tunisia.

NEW INSTITUTIONS FOR A TRANSFORMING CITY

The city is taking some major risks in facing these changes. There is a great deal of concern about the decisions that have to be made. Is this concern rooted in fear, a fear of losing what we already have? A city like Reggio Emilia with a healthy economy and vibrant social system could become conservative and complacent. We believe that our task is to fight against any movement toward conservatism. Now more than ever, it is fitting to recognize and affirm the infant-toddler centers and preschools as public places in which families construct important social and cultural relations. The schools foster integration and solidarity and reduce isolation. Parental participation represents a civic commitment through which they construct citizenship, and this process stabilizes and strengthens social cohesion.

The University of Modena and Reggio Emilia

First of all, we must make a greater cultural investment in our individual citizens. We feel that a citizenry with a higher cultural and educational level will be better able to face the complexity of a more diverse society. Historically in Reggio, good public services and a dynamic economy (1 business for every 12 people) have supported a system of social cohesion and development. Unemployment in Reggio Emilia is low. However, Reggio is facing new challenges not only because of the high level of immigration but also because less than 10% of our residents have an advanced university degree.

In an effort to be responsive to this new reality, Reggio Emilia has become the site of the University of Modena and Reggio Emilia, which has been supported by the local economic community. This university serves the citizens of both cities and includes faculties in Agriculture, Arts and Humanities, Biosciences, Business and Economics, Communication, Education, Engineering, Law, Mathematics and the Natural Sciences, Medicine, and Pharmacy.

The Loris Malaguzzi International Center

In many ways, a new city of Reggio Emilia now exists. This new Reggio will become more visible in the next few years through the transformation of places that will become symbols of this change. The main transformations will be north of the city where large industries were traditionally located. The municipality of Reggio Emilia bought an old factory in this area to create a "house of dance." The municipality also bought the old cheese warehouse of Locatelli to create the Loris Malaguzzi International Center. Many cities in the world are currently converting abandoned industrial spaces for other uses. Reggio Emilia is trying to pursue a cultural use for such spaces, so that culture becomes "productive." The places of work of the past century are transformed into the places of work of today, with an emphasis on being able to do and think together.

For our city and for our schools, the Malaguzzi International Center is a choice that favors quality and sustainability. Indeed, the quality of each is directly related to that of the others. The quality of the International Center infuses strength into the services for children through the cultural and research opportunities and international exchanges that it offers. Quality serves as a safeguard, defense, and source of security and expansion for our system. For example, when in 1991 *Newsweek* magazine recognized the Diana Preschool as "the best preschool in the world," this helped us stave off a political attempt to reduce the importance of the municipal services for children. We have always cultivated an international dimension to the educational dialogue in Reggio Emilia, and today the International Center gives that international dialogue yet more value and power and invigorates the educational system of our city.

Furthermore, the quality of the infant-toddler centers and preschools gives strength reciprocally to Reggio Children and the International Center. The centers and schools provide the matrix—the "DNA"—that makes it possible for their influence to project beyond early childhood, beyond schooling, even beyond the city. This gives rise to the culture of childhood that lends credibility to the International Center and that provides visitors to Reggio with tangible reason to hope for a different kind of school.

REDEFINING THE CITY'S COMMITMENT TO ITS YOUNGEST CITIZENS

Because of the high level of immigration, Reggio Emilia is experiencing an encounter between different cultures for the first time in its history. We are concerned that some of the long-time residents of Reggio are reacting to this encounter with fear, the fear of change, the fear of losing a familiar standard of living. We are also aware that when people feel excluded from the community, the risk of conflict arises. For this reason, we are striving to create educational services for all of the children of our community—a purpose strongly supported by Mayor Graziano Delrio. Already during the administration of the prior mayor, Antonella Spaggiari, response to the transforming population had begun. Mayor Spaggiari thought that to avoid a sense of fear developing in the community, it was important to intensify a transparent dialogue with families. She organized many meetings with them, which took place in the infant-toddler centers and preschools, on the topic of changing families and workforce in Reggio Emilia.

We are working constantly on how to maintain strong citizen participation in the city of Reggio Emilia. In the midst of these great changes, it is necessary to redefine our agreements with our citizens, because we cannot take our shared values for granted. This challenge has been faced by North American society for some time. Yet we realize that there are no predetermined recipes that work for every place and time. Each community must be able to find its own way in relation with others, through the exchange of experiences.

How is it possible to maintain participation in a city in evolution? If change is to result in innovation and renewal is the desired result, then the forms of participation must change over time. During the 1970s, 1980s, and 1990s, the families and children of the municipal infant-toddler centers and preschools established effective strategies for participation in the education of young children and the government of their city. Can these positive forces continue? We believe they can, and we have renewed parent and citizen participation in the schools through a network of advisory councils and Intercouncil.

In Reggio Emilia, 41% of infants and toddlers from birth to 3 years old (1,830 children) participate in early care and education, which is one of the highest percentages in Italy, and 90% of Reggio children aged 3 to 6 years attend preschool (4,783 children). What types of services are best for a city in evolution? Over the years, early childhood services have contributed to cultural growth in our community. Today, in a multiethnic society, these services must take on new and delicate tasks. They must give value to differences and not fear them and offer opportunities to all without exclusion. More facilities must be provided so no one is excluded from attending.

To invest in early childhood at this time of structural crisis in the world economy signifies our resolve to build solid economic, cultural, and social foundations for the future. The wisdom of such investment is demonstrated by numerous national and international studies. We affirm education as a right, rather than some generic need or interest. In view of this affirmation, which emanates from historical experience, the city administration of Reggio Emilia has over time built an integrated public system of services for children aged 0 to six. The services include city-run and cooperative infant-toddler centers, as well as city-run, national, cooperative, and FISM (Federazione Italiana Scuole Materne—Roman Catholic) preschools. Moreover, the city administration has chosen to make education a strategic mission of the city—the key to economic, social, and cultural development.

This integrated public system interprets "public" via agreements that oblige the various institutions to be inclusive in specific ways, for example, in criteria for admission regarding gender, sexual orientation, and ethnic, religious, cultural, and social origin. The agreements also involve shared parameters of quality that are constructed by the community and subject to authority of the city representatives and the participation of families (through the Intercouncil). The system integrates different competencies and responsibilities from the city and surrounding areas. Through collaboration, synergy is created that responds to children's rights to education and increases the quality of the infant-toddler centers and preschools through the exchange of knowledge and experience.

Historically, services for young children have involved a multiplicity of organizations. Our city has instead chosen to create an integrated public system that sustains the engagement of different institutions, tied together by mutual agreements. Such a pluralist, sustainable, and socially participatory choice has made it possible to respond to the demand of diverse viewpoints. Through dialogue and interchange, and by investing private, municipal, and national funds, we have been able to increase quantity, quality, and access to services. We have also been able to reconcile competing views of the role of infant-toddler centers and preschools in creating a culture of childhood and promoting social welfare. The integrated public system of the city of Reggio Emilia, founded on the principle of children's right to education, has flourished on the basis of shared convictions that we maintain are still essential today. These convictions are the source of values for choices to make now and in the future. These values include the following:

- *The complementary rights of children, families, and teachers.* The existence and quality of services depend on attitudes of cooperation directed toward achieving maximum well-being for all involved.
- *The role of the municipality.* This aspect is a guarantee of the quality of the system, which manifests itself in the production of collective "know how," the patrimony of the community and source of research and innovation.
- *Educational organization.* The collegial presence of various adult figures in the services, along with the participation of families, guarantees the social aspect of the quality of education.
- *Flexibility to respond to the needs of children and families.* The schedule of the services is flexible to respond to families' different needs. However, this flexibility is regulated by the right of children and adults to become and to be a group, preserving enough shared time for a community to emerge that knows how to learn together. Community is an objective and a value for children of all ages, beginning from the earliest months of life.

New services for children and families are important to the quality of life. The Ray of Light Atelier is part of the Loris Malaguzzi International Center.

THE ISTITUZIONE

In 2003, a public–private system was created to provide education for all of the children in our community. This system is the Istituzione Scuole e Nidi d'Infanzia of the Municipality of Reggio Emilia and is the product of a collaborative partnership to oversee the educational services from birth to 6 years of age. An Istituzione is one possible way under Italian law to run public services, and our particular Istituzione in Reggio is the first to manage schools.

We believe the Istituzione is the best form of organization to guarantee autonomy and budgetary responsibility for this new entity. Although the municipal government has diverse responsibilities, the Istituzione is exclusively dedicated to services for children from birth to 6 years. Today, the entire wide array of services providing early childhood education and care are organized through the Istituzione, which is charged with the long-term goal to ensure that no child is excluded from the use of these services. To reach this goal, it is necessary for the leadership of the municipality to be aware of the changing nature of the city, to be knowledgeable about the people who live in the community, and to realize how these aspects of our city contribute to the evolution of our culture and our society in Reggio Emilia. We believe that understanding our history is also essential to understanding our present and our future. The municipal government has the responsibility to attend to our new citizens and the city's new economic reality. We must continually search for new strategies that are relevant for children and families to maintain the level of participation in community life that has been a strong characteristic of our history as a city.

The Istituzione is the reference body for the more than 80 schools serving more than 6,000 children (Istituzione, 2010).

Municipal Infant-Toddler Centers and Preschools

The Istituzione directly manages 21 preschools (serving children aged 3–6 years) and 13 infant-toddler centers (serving children birth to 3 years; Istituzione, 2010). All 21 preschools and 9 of the infant-toddler centers are full-time (8:00 a.m. to 4:00 p.m.). Most also offer afternoon extended time (to 6:20 p.m.) and morning early opening (from 7:30 a.m.), reserved for children whose families, for work reasons, show documented need. Three of the municipal infant-toddler centers are part time only (8:00 a.m. to 1:00 p.m.). The school year extends from September 1 to June 30, with services closed for 2 weeks at Christmas and 1 week at Easter. During July, there are special summer sessions in preschools and infant-toddler centers for the families who make a special request.

Cooperative Centers

The Istituzione also oversees about 15 affiliated cooperatives, and the number is growing, which is the result of new initiatives in business incubation and parent management. The first public–private cooperative ventures in Reggio were founded in 1986. In the 1990s, these early cooperatives were joined by cooperatives of young women coming from experiences in business incubation. Reggio Children offered a course for young Italian women, which gave them new job opportunities in the field of education. At that same time, interesting experiences in parent management began.

Cooperative early childhood programs have been emerging since the late 1980s and 1990s in Reggio Emilia as one solution for expanding access to high-quality services for young children, especially services for children under age 3 (Gandini & Kaminsky, 2007). Fifteen affiliated programs are part of the Istituzione, managed by different social cooperatives, (e.g., Coopselios, Pantarei, Sila, and Totem). The programs may be full-time or part-time, but in general, their annual calendar is also September through June. A cooperative is a legitimate, formal organization that is recognized by law. Agreements regulate the relations between the cooperatives and the Istituzione and define the requirements and characteristics considered essential for quality services, such as the school calendar; staff qualifications; the teacher/child ratio; monthly fees paid by families; and family participation. The municipality of Reggio Emilia contributes some partial funding to the cooperatives but does not manage them financially. Professional development is scheduled into the teachers' work week and is organized both within the cooperative centers and also together with educators from the municipal infant-toddler centers and preschools. Opportunities for exchange between the cooperatives and municipal centers continue to be strengthened through organization of a network that functions ever more strongly as an integrated system. Study tours to Reggio Emilia regularly include visits to the cooperative centers as possibilities for observation.

For many years, the rising cost of public early childhood education and care has been a source of national concern, while at the same time, there have been increasing family requests for high-quality care for children under 3 years of age. In some Italian cities, the percentage of children who can find a place in infant-toddler centers is as high as 25% (as in Emilia Romagna in 2007/2008), but the disparity between the north and south of the Italian peninsula is extreme, and the total percentage of children under 3 who are served in Italy is about 10% (Istituzione, 2010).

This is the Italian landscape. In Reggio Emilia, a city that has maintained a progressive local administration, a city that is well known internationally for the quality of early childhood education, a city that has a strong traditional basis of cooperation and volunteer work, there has always been strong interest in new social developments and transformations. Recently, there has been an effort to look for new ways to support and give opportunities to young people's creative potentials.

IN CONCLUSION

Certainly, it is challenging, in a city that has built such a large system of services and with such a rigorous organization, to maintain all of the places currently available in the network, without any lessening of quality, while also guaranteeing research and professional development and, if possible, responding to unspoken need. The difficult times before us call for the creation of an Agreement for Education that commits all parties involved, including teachers and staff, parents, administrators, the institutions, and the international networks.[1] Such an agreement ideally would safeguard values and strengthen services for future generations. Sustainability means not only preserving financial resources but also nourishing the existing cultural patrimony so that it may remain the heritage of future generations.

NOTE

1. On September 29, 2011, the Foundation Reggio Children—Loris Malaguzzi Center was established, with the mission of promoting an education that has in international exchange, research, and participation its own elements of quality, for everyone in Reggio Emilia and the world.

REFERENCES

Gambetti, A. (2002). The evolution of the municipality of Reggio Emilia: An interview with Sandra Piccinini. *Innovations in Early Education: The International Reggio Exchange, 9*(3), 1–3.

Gandini, L., & Kaminsky, J., (2007). Cooperative early childhood education services in Reggio Emilia: An innovative solution for a complex society. *Innovations in Early Education: The International Reggio Exchange, 14*(1), 1–13.

Istituzione Scuole e Nidi d'Infanzia, Municipal Infant-Toddler Centers and Preschools of Reggio Emilia. (2010). Documents: (1) *Infant-toddler centers enrollment school year 2009–2010 for children born in 2007, 2008, 2009;* (2) *Preschools for children enrollment school year 2009–2010 for children born in 2006, 2005, 2004.* (3) *Historical notes and general information;* (4) *Scuole e Nidi d'Infanzia Istituzione del Comune di Reggio Emilia: Bilancio Sociale 2008.*

Organization for Economic Cooperation and Development Review Team for Italy. (2001). OECD country note: Early childhood education and care policy in Italy. Available at http://www.oecd.org/dataoecd/15/17/33915831.pdf.

Piccinini, S. (2002). A city, its theater, the children: An ongoing dialogue. In V. Vecchi (Ed.), *Theater curtain: The ring of transformations* (pp. 12–15). Reggio Emilia, Italy: Reggio Children.

Piccinini, S. (2005). Projecting toward the future of a changing world with respectful consideration of the past. *Innovations in Early Education: The International Reggio Exchange, 12*(4), 1–9.

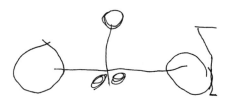

Chapter 6

Micro-Project and Macro-Policy: Learning through Relationships

Peter Moss

LOCAL EXPERIENCE, GLOBAL IMPACT

The city of Reggio Emilia and its network of municipal schools have made an immense contribution to pedagogical thought and practice in early childhood education and care (ECEC). Their pedagogy of relationships and listening, their theory of the hundred languages of childhood, their process of pedagogical documentation, and their innovative roles such as the *atelierista* and the *pedagogista*—all these and more have had great influence well beyond this middling sized city in northern Italy. Many people across the world are working with

I use the term *early childhood education and care* in this chapter because it is now widely used in international work to denote the full range of services for children from birth to 5 or 6 years providing "child care and education." My preference would be *early childhood education,* in which education is understood in its broadest sense as a holistic concept encompassing learning, care, and all aspects of well-being. It is in this sense that early childhood education is understood in countries such as New Zealand that have moved to an integrated early childhood service (Kaga, Bennett, & Moss, 2010) and also, I believe, in Reggio, with its municipal 0–6 service integrated in education.

101

inspiration from the Reggio Emilia experience. In some countries, the influence has been particularly strong; for example, a senior Swedish civil servant, writing about the history of the Swedish preschool, refers to the "new inspirational thinking" that the Reggio Emilia approach has brought to the Swedish preschool (Korpi, 2007). In similar vein, *Starting Strong II,* the final report of the review of early childhood education and care in 20 countries, conducted by the Organization for Economic Cooperation and Development (OECD, 2006), gives a high profile to the pedagogical work in Reggio Emilia and acknowledges its global impact:

> The influence of Reggio Emilia, which now has networks in 13 countries, is also growing, particularly in milieus that are open to experimentation, research and reflection on democratic practice in education. The Reggio pre-schools are strongly influenced by their social and historical context (the aftermath of fascism in Italy) and are concerned "to maintain a vision of children who can think and act for themselves" (Dahlberg *et al.*, 1999). Reggio opposes, in the name of young children and their freedom, dominant educational discourses, such as seeing ECEC services as places to produce pre-defined outcomes that have not been discussed with staff and parents or that ignore the interests, experience and choices of young children. Its adoption of a "pedagogy of listening" respects the efforts of children to make meaning of their experience, and contests an increasingly dominant notion of education as transmission and reproduction, or as preparation for school. (Rinaldi, 2006, p. 64)

But in this chapter, I want to explore a further reason why Reggio Emilia is of wider significance, beyond the inspirational quality of its pedagogical work. I want to argue that Reggio Emilia is a critical case of democratic experimentalism, by which I mean a willingness of a community to engage in collective innovative practice to explore the possibilities of new perspectives and new ways of working. I want also to consider whether the case of Reggio Emilia might offer insights into the possibility of a new relationship in education between national and local and between coherence and diversity, a relationship between municipal micro-projects and national macro-policy based on a strong value given to participatory democracy and pedagogical experimentation.

THE SITUATION TODAY: MORE SERVICES, MORE STANDARDIZATION

In many circles today, early childhood education and care has caught the eye of politicians and policy makers. In 2002 at the Barcelona Summit, the European Union set targets of providing child care by 2010 to at least 90% of children aged between 3 years and the mandatory school age, and at least 33% of children under 3 years. Indeed, growth in ECEC is now a global trend:

> Worldwide access to pre-school facilities has been steadily increasing. Some 139 million children were in ECEC programs in 2006, up from 112 million in 1999. . . . [Enrollment] in 2006 averaged 79% in developed countries and 36% in developing countries. (United Nations Educational, Scientific and Cultural Organisation, 2008, p. 50)

This growth has been driven both by labor-market needs and by a widespread belief (based, I believe, on over-optimistic claims for the impact of early intervention) that ECEC services can solve a wide range of social and economic problems confronting nation-states as they struggle to survive in the increasingly competitive global economy and to reduce the consequences of inequality and social disruption that have followed the resurgence of neo-liberalism since the 1970s. The result has been a highly instrumental and technical approach to ECEC, seeking to discover and apply powerful "human technologies" (Rose, 1999) that will ensure the most effective delivery of predetermined outcomes. The search for "what works" has not been matched by public deliberation on critical questions that should precede such technical solutions, questions such as what is education for. As Gerd Biesta observes:

> A democratic society is precisely one in which the purpose of education is not given but is a constant topic for discussion and deliberation. . . . [T]he current political climate in many Western countries has made it increasingly difficult to have a democratic discussion about the purposes of education. (2007, p. 18)

To which one might add the increasing difficulty of a democratic discussion about the meaning of knowledge and learning, the concept of education itself, and the image of the child, the educator, and the early childhood institution.

This excess of instrumentality and technical practice, supported by the increasing dominance of managerialism, has led to growing numbers of children attending ECEC services and to growing standardization of method and outcome. Fendler describes this process, which privileges *predetermined* outcomes above all else, when she observes that

> Because the developmental goals are specified, there is no theoretical possibility for the subject to have any features or characteristics other than those specified as normal—as defined by their developmental appropriateness. The notion of flexibility, then, may pertain in the course of the interaction. However, there can be no flexibility or variation in the outcome per se. (2001, pp. 133–134)

We may live in an age of hyper-individualism, with a strident rhetoric of "choice" and "diversity." Yet what we actually experience is an unparalleled conformity to universal norms, expressed in the standardizing language of management—quality, excellence, outcomes, assessment, benchmarking, and so on. Despite the world's complexity, multiplicity, and contingency, we end up putting everything we encounter into predefined categories, making the "Other" into the "Same," and everything that does not fit into these categories, which is unfamiliar and not taken for granted, has either to be overcome or is ignored.

REGGIO EMILIA: A LOCAL PROJECT OF DEMOCRATIC EXPERIMENTALISM

It is in this context of standardization and normalization, based on a belief in there being one right answer that science can discover and management deliver, that the local project of Reggio Emilia, and its worldwide appeal, is so important. Because it exemplifies another approach to developing early childhood education—indeed, any education—it is, I believe, a local or micro-project[1] of democratic experimentalism. I hasten to add that the term *democratic experimentalism* is not original. I borrow it from the Brazilian social theorist Roberto Unger who writes that

> The provision of public services must be an innovative collective practice. . . . That can no longer happen in our current understanding of efficiency and production by the mechanical transmission of innovation from the top. It can only happen through the organisation of a collective experimental practice from below. . . . Democracy is not just one more terrain for the institutional innovation that I advocate. It is the most important terrain. (2005a, pp. 179, 182)

Such experimentalism is, for Unger, a feature of "high-energy" democracy, which, by encouraging a high level of organized civic engagement, releases and enhances the creative power of people and "seeks to strengthen our experimental capacities—our ability to try out alternative arrangements among ourselves" (Unger, 2004, p. lxxii). Just as Reggio's pedagogical work starts out from the image of the rich child, so Unger holds up an image of the rich citizen: "the recognition of the genius of ordinary men and women is the core doctrine of democracy" (p. lxxii).

Unger's discussion of democratic experimentalism is part of his wider project of imagining how to reform contemporary societies to empower humanity. How, he asks, can transformative change be brought about in our societies today? He dismisses what he terms two styles of politics, the *revolutionary* with its desire for sudden, violent, and total change, such as the wholesale substitution of one institutional order for another in a national crisis; and the *reformist,* in which marginal and essentially trivial responses are offered to public anxieties, what he describes as a "pessimistic reformism" in which "we are left to humanize the inevitable" (Unger, 1998, p. 20). Instead he argues for "radical" or "revolutionary reform," structural change taken step by step, bringing gradual but cumulative and substantive change: "Reform is radical when it addresses and changes the basic arrangements of a society: its formative structure of institutions and

enacted beliefs. It is reform because it deals with one discrete part of this structure at a time" (Unger, 1998, pp. 18–19). Central to his ideal is the question
"where to?" foregrounding the need for a clear sense of direction: a "program-
matic argument," he proposes, "is a vision of a direction and the next steps"
(Unger, 2005a, p. 164).

Democratic experimentalism should be seen in this wider context, as one
means of contributing to radical reform by the exploration of possible "next
steps" toward a vision of a good life, a vision that provides direction but that
is itself subject to revision; neither means nor ends are fixed, but open to new
perspectives, new understandings, and new relationships. My central argument
is that Reggio Emilia's educational project has been a sustained and important
example of such democratic experimentalism. Indeed, Reggio itself has always
emphasized democracy and experimentation as central values, which have been
expressed through democratic and experimental practices.

Democracy is a form of governance, at all levels. But it is much else besides;
it is a way of living together and relating to others, a way of life and a form of
subjectivity. Reggio Emilia seems to me to provide many examples of the multidi-
mensionality of democracy, in what I would term democratic learning, democratic
decision making, and democratic evaluation (for a fuller discussion of the meanings of democracy and how democracy can be practiced in the early childhood
center, see Moss, 2009). Take, for example, pedagogical documentation, which
Malaguzzi's biographer writes about in these democratic terms:

Children love to climb on the lion sculptures in the city square.

> Behind the practice, I believe, is the ideological and ethical concept of a transparent school and transparent education. . . . A political idea also emerges, which is that what schools do must have public visibility; thus "giving back" to the city what the city has invested in them. . . . Documentation in all its different forms represents an extraordinary tool for dialogue, for exchange, for sharing. For Malaguzzi it means the possibility to discuss and dialogue "everything with everyone." (Hoyuelos, 2004, p. 7)

Carlina Rinaldi (2006) talks about this practice in similar terms: "sharing the documentation means participation in a true act of democracy, sustaining the culture and visibility of childhood, both inside and outside the school: democratic participation, or 'participant democracy,' that is a product of exchange and visibility" (p. 59).

Experimentation, as used here in relation to Reggio Emilia, should not be confused with a particular form of experimental method, which aims for rigorous control of variables and the elimination of alternative hypotheses. Rather, experimentation as a value is understood here to be about bringing something new to life, whether that something is a thought, knowledge, a project, a service, or a tangible product. It expresses a willingness—a desire, in fact—to invent, to think differently, to imagine, and to try out different ways of doing things. It is driven by the desire to go beyond what already exists, to venture into the not yet known, and not to be bound by the given, the familiar, the predetermined, the norm: "experimentation is always that which is in the process of coming about— the new, remarkable, and interesting that replace the appearance of truth and are more demanding than it is" (Deleuze & Guattari, 1994, p. 111). Experimentation is open-ended (avoiding closure), open-minded (welcoming the unexpected), and open-hearted (valuing difference).

The kind of experimentation that marks out Reggio Emilia can be understood as a form of municipal learning, through a collective co-construction of local knowledge based on project work and a "pedagogy of listening and relationships," which also guides the relationships between children and educators in the classrooms of the municipal schools. This pedagogical approach takes the view that for children and adults alike,

> understanding means elaborating an interpretation, what we call an "interpretive theory," that is a theory that gives meaning to the things and events of the world, a theory in the sense of a satisfactory explanation . . . though also provisional. It is something more than simply an idea or a group of ideas; it must be pleasing and convincing, useful and capable of satisfying our intellectual, affective, and also aesthetic needs. That is, it must give us the sense of a wholeness that generates a sense of beauty and satisfaction.
>
> In certain ways, a theory, if possible, must be pleasing to others, too, and it needs to be listened to by others. This makes it possible to transform a world that is intrinsically personal into something shared: my knowledge and my identity are also constructed by the other. Sharing theories is a response to uncertainty and solitude. (Rinaldi, 2006, pp. 113–114)

So experimentation is not directionless. It has a direction, the response to the question "where to?" and it involves working with existing theories (border crossing, as they do enthusiastically in Reggio, over many disciplinary and paradigmatic fields) but also constructing new ones. It is not formulaic, but neither does it lack rigor. Observations, interpretations, and theories are listened to by others and respected, but they are also subject to question, critique, and contestation. Edgar Morin's admonition—to think in context and to think the complex—is heard and followed, creating a "kind of thinking that relinks that which is disjointed and compartmentalized, that respects diversity as it recognizes unity, and that tries to discern interdependencies" (Morin, 1999, p. 130).

Reggio's whole educational project is an example of experimentation that has functioned at several levels. At the municipal level, the city democratically decided to experiment with taking responsibility for the education of its young children and initiating a local educational project to do so, which started with critical questions, notably, "What is our image of the child?" At the level of the school and group, that project has itself valued and fostered educational practice based on the theory and practice of experimentation. The language of experimentation is widely deployed when educators speak about their approach to knowledge and learning. Here, for example, is an *atelierista* writing about the role of the *atelier* in Reggio:

> Because the *atelier* is in contact with the world of art, architecture and design and because the *atelierista* often has sensitive antennae for contemporary issues, it is her task to receive and bring these interesting cultural flows into school, and where possible, rework them in appropriate ways so that they light up areas which can be used for experimentation with children. (Vecchi, 2010, p. 126)

Experimentation need not of course be democratic. Experimentation can, for instance, be undertaken by companies seeking commercial advantage and enhanced profit or by scientists pursuing disciplinary knowledge. Democratic experimentalism is, therefore, a very particular form of experimentation, in which the desire and direction for experimentation comes from collective deliberation and the benefits of experimentation—for example, the local knowledge that has been created—accrue to the common good.

Democratic experimentalism is a choice, a choice that many countries, cities, organizations, and schools today reject or, worse, do not even consider. The results are serious, locking us into an endless round of reproducing, in which the same prescribed means pursue the same known ends, in a repetitive, predictable, and sterile process. Democratic experimentalism values and searches for outcomes but recognizes these can be unexpected and surprising, producing new understandings and meanings; it relishes emotions of wonder, amazement, and excitement. There is a place for predetermined outcomes, but these should be treated with a degree of suspicion, for their capacity to suppress or marginalize what is innovative and original: such outcomes express "our will to truth, which can be thought of in this first instance as a will to certain outcomes, sets communication along present railway tracks as pointed out by Wittgenstein, preventing alternative ways of relating to the world that are open-ended and experimental" (Roy, 2004, p. 302). Democratic experimentalism must learn to walk on two legs!

MICRO AND MACRO

I have argued that Reggio Emilia is an interesting and important example of a local micro-project of democratic experimentalism—or, as in the title of a book about another example of Italian municipal innovation, "The education of young children as a community project" (Fortunati, 2006). The results have been extraordinarily rich and have had widespread appeal. To take just three examples: the role of *ateliers* in early childhood education, applying the theory of the hundred languages of children to learning; the development of pedagogical documentation as a tool for research, evaluation, professional development, planning, and democratic practice; and the many, well-documented examples of complex project work that have given new meaning to the concept of the competent child.

We could leave it at that. But faced with the stifling embrace of managerialism and standardization, I think we should go further and ask: might democratic experimentalism extend beyond the micro-project to become an important part of macro-policy? Or put another way, might the nation-state promote democratic experimentalism and, if so, how? In attempting to answer this question, the case of Reggio Emilia has more limited relevance, because this local project is not the result of, nor has it even been supported by, national government interest and imagination. What Reggio, and other Italian cities and towns that have undertaken similar local projects (and it is always important to remember that Reggio is not an isolated case of municipal experimentation; see, for example, Catarsi, 2004; Corsaro, 2005; Fortunati, 2006; Gandini & Edwards, 2002), have achieved has been in spite of, not because of, the Italian state.

Some writers have proposed the idea of a state that adopts a role of promoting experimentation. For example, Unger refers to democratic experimentalism as more than just ad hoc local projects that, occasionally and by their own exertions, break free from the constraints of the system, examples of which are always around us. He envisages the possibility of a state that actively encourages experimentation as part of a commitment to high-energy democracy. The state can act in various ways to achieve this end, including "producing new social agents" that can create innovative services; monitoring and helping "to propagate the most successful practices, accelerating the process of experimental winnowing out of what does not work"; and last, and perhaps most surprising in the current climate, by providing directly only "those services which are too innovative, too difficult or too unrewarded by the market to be provided directly"—government itself experimenting (Unger, 2005b, p. 179).

An example of national government support for experimentation was to be found until recently in New Zealand, a country that has transformed its early childhood services in the past 20 years, developing an integrated system based on an integrative concept of "early childhood education," understood as "education in its broadest sense," concerned with the education and care of children, the support of parents, and the sustainability of communities (Meade & Podmore, 2010). An important feature of its 2002 10-year strategy for early childhood education—*Pathways to the Future: Ngā Huarahi Arataki*—was[2] the Centers of Innovation program, providing funding and other resources to enable selected centers to undertake action research related to innovation in teaching and learning, as well as sharing their innovative work and research findings with other services. Selected centers were funded for 3 years to enable teachers to take some release to do research, for professional development and relevant equipment, and to pay a research associate to provide advice and support. Each successive selection of centers focused on particular themes, such as Maori services, integrating Information Communications Technologies into the curriculum, and inclusive education for diverse children and families/*whānau* (including cultural inclusiveness and inclusion of children with special needs and gifted children).

The possibilities for the experimental state, which made the stimulation of micro-projects a central plank of macro-policy, require much further thought, deliberation—and experimentation. We need a national (or even regional) Reggio Emilia, a country or region prepared to explore how experimentation might be actively fostered, documented, and evaluated. This exploration could usefully extend to the question of sustainability. No experiment should run forever, yet too many innovative projects end well before their time, unable to continue to maintain, develop, and deepen their experimental work. Reggio, in running a local educational project for more than 50 years, is the exception rather than the norm, and this prolonged sustainability, with the ability Reggio has shown to create new directions for its work and to border cross into new disciplines and theories, calls for further research.

Such research will need to deploy a variety of methods, including quantitative work to shed light on issues such as access, workforce, and costs; qualitative work—for example, critical cases strategically chosen; and the extensive use as a research tool of pedagogical documentation. It will also need to be clear on the role and use of research in creating knowledge and making evaluations. Democratic experimentalism requires, I believe, a view that respects a wide range of research but treats the findings as local knowledge, always produced in a particular context, always partial, perspectival, and provisional, and always subject to deliberation, dialogue, and interpretation; in other words, no research can or should absolve citizens of responsibility for thinking and meaning making. Like the Danish urban researcher Bent Flyvbjerg, I am arguing for the adoption of a "phronetic model of social science" whose purpose is to contribute to society's practical rationality by elucidating where we are, where we want to go, and what is desirable according to different sets of values and interests . . . [and] to society's capacity for value-rational deliberation and action . . . [through] a combination of concrete empirical analyses and practical philosophical-ethical considerations. (Flyvbjerg, 2006, p. 42)

Our democratic deliberations about early childhood education and care need also to engage with some important ethical and political issues that arise from the active pursuit of experimentation, along with accompanying democratic decentralization. How, for example, to accommodate the likely variation in the capacity and willingness of different communities and institutions to experiment? You cannot insist on experimentation by central dictate; rather you have to create conditions that enable those who wish to experiment. But what about those who don't? Are they to be left to follow some sort of standardized educational "program," while some of their neighbors get on with pursuing their experimentation? Or are there ways in which their weaker experimental potential can be nurtured?

What limits should be placed on experimentation, if any? What proposed directions would be deemed ethically or politically unacceptable by the wider society and its democratic institutions? Suppose an extremist administration, of whatever kind, gained control of a municipality and said it wished to experiment with educational theories and practices. Where would the line be drawn and by whom?

Then there is the question of the relationship between diversity and coherence—between what I have termed micro-projects and macro-policy. What would all municipalities and centers have in common in a state that espoused democratic experimentation? What would national citizenship mean in relation to education? The broad picture can be discerned of a state creating an educational framework that establishes certain common values, goals, entitlements, and structures to which all municipalities and centers or schools in that country are bound but that also leaves considerable scope for local interpretation and local experimentation. An important issue here is the relationship not only between the state and the individual school or center but also between the municipality—the democratically elected local government and political expression of the local community—and the individual school or center. In my view, a democratic education calls for an active role for state, municipality, and school and a mutually supportive relationship. But this requires more attention being paid to the position of the municipality, what its role can and should be in democratic experimentalism, and how that role can be well performed.

Of course, no relationship between diversity and coherence and between different levels can ever reach permanent equilibrium. The relationship will and should always be a tense and unstable one, constantly open to critique, review, and re-creation. The devil, too, is in the detail—what exactly do broad principles mean when applied? Relationships depend on different levels having the capacity and willingness to act democratically, while being supportive and trustful of other players and showing openness to learn.

The relationship, and with it possibilities for micro-projects supported by macro-policy, also depends on a shared understanding of democracy. The English political philosopher John Gray proposes an interesting and important distinction in his discussion of liberalism. He argues that there are two strands in liberal democracy. One strand holds to "the ideal of a rational consensus on the best way of life . . . [in] the pursuit of an ideal form of life" (Gray, 2009, pp. 21–22). This strand seeks and values general laws and principles—"a prescription for a universal regime." The other strand, Gray argues, is a project of coexistence rather than consensus, a recognition of the inevitability of often needing to agree to disagree. It seeks and values multiple ways of life and perspectives living and flourishing together, "a philosophy of liberal pluralism, or modus vivendi" (p. 49).

Tolerance is important in both strands, but in the former, it is toleration of the mistaken, who fail to grasp or assent to a universal ideal; in the latter, it is the toleration of legitimate differences arising from divergent values and perspectives. *Modus vivendi* not only creates a respectful, rather than a patronizing, tolerance of diversity, it is "inimical to fundamentalism of every kind" (Gray, 2009, p. 41). It rejects theories that claim a final and total resolution of the problems that beset us, whether the theory be a religion, a political creed such as communism, or some other theory of everything, such as markets and competition—neo-liberalism. If adopting the value of pluralism that underlies the modus vivendi strand, we adopt, in Gray's words, "a subversive doctrine" that "undermines all claims about the best life for the species" (pp. 40–41).

RATIONAL CONSENSUS OR MODUS VIVENDI FOR EARLY CHILDHOOD EDUCATION AND CARE

It seems to me that these strands of liberalism are apparent today in early childhood education. The former, with its belief in rational consensus, is expressed in the language of "quality services," exercising "best practice," based on universal agreement about means and ends and the possibility (and desirability) of a common perspective, common questions, and agreed-upon correct answers to those questions. The latter, modus vivendi, is expressed in those places, like Reggio Emilia, that have pursued experimental projects, starting from their own values, images, and goals and rejecting the idea of linear progress to predetermined outcomes. The former, we might say, want conformity and predictability, the latter amazement and surprise.

Carlina Rinladi writes about "project work" (*progettazione*) with children in the municipal schools of Reggio Emilia in the following terms:

> [It] evokes the idea of a dynamic process, a journey that involves the uncertainty and chance that always arises in relationships with others. Project work grows in many directions, with no predefined progression, no outcomes decided before the journey

begins. It means being sensitive to the unpredictable results of children's investigation and research. The course of a project can thus be short, medium or long, continuous or discontinuous, and is always open to modifications and changes of direction. (Rinaldi, 2005, p. 19)

It seems to me that this could describe equally well Reggio Emilia's own municipal micro-project on education for young children, itself made up of many micro-projects undertaken by children, educators, and schools, all sharing a strong experimental character. The daunting but exciting prospect is whether and how other communities might be enabled to unleash the creativity and inventiveness that Reggio Emilia released when it decided to embark on its educational project.

NOTES

1. I use the term *project* to define a way of working, which may be applied equally to a municipality or a classroom and which corresponds to the Italian term *progettazione,* much used by Reggio educators. Unlike the term *programmazione* ("program"), with its implications of following a linear course of predetermined stages to reach predefined outcomes, *progettazione* ("project") assumes a more open and enquiring approach, with initial hypotheses, which are open to modifications and changes of direction as the actual work progresses. I see projects as being vehicles for experimentation, whether by municipalities, schools, or groups of children and educators.

2. I use the past tense, *was,* because the government in 2009 announced the termination of the program, as part of a general cost-cutting exercise.

REFERENCES

Biesta, G. (2007). Why "what works" won't work: Evidence-based practice and the democratic deficit in educational research. *Educational Theory, 57*(1), 1–22.

Catarsi, E. (2004). Loris Malaguzzi and the municipal school revolution. *Children in Europe, 6,* 8–9.

Corsaro, W. A. (2005). *I compagni: Understanding children's transitions from preschool to elementary school.* New York: Teachers College Press.

Dahlberg, G., Moss, P., & Pence, A. (1999). *Beyond quality in early childhood education and care: Postmodern perspectives.* London: Falmer Press.

Deleuze, G., & Guattari, F. (1994). *What is philosophy?* (H. Tomlinson & G. Burchill, Trans.). London: Verso.

Fendler, L. (2001). Educating flexible souls: The construction of subjectivity through developmentality and interaction. In K. Hultqvist & G. Dahlberg (Eds.), *Governing the child in the new millennium* (pp. 119–142). London: Routledge Falmer.

Flyvbjerg, B. (2006). Social science that matters. *Foresight Europe* (October 2005–March 2006), 38–42.

Fortunati, A. (2006). *The education of young children as a community project: The experience of San Miniato.* Azzano San Paolo, Italy: Edizioni Junior.

Gandini, L., & Edwards, C. P. (Eds.). (2002). *Bambini: The Italian approach to infant and toddler caregiving.* New York: Teachers College Press.

Gray, J. (2009). *Gray's anatomy: John Gray's selected writings.* London: Allen Lane.

Hoyuelos, A. (2004). A pedagogy of transgression. *Children in Europe, 6,* 6–7.

Kaga, Y., Bennett, J., & Moss, P. (2010). *Caring and learning together: A cross-national study of integration of early childhood care and education within education.* Paris: United Nations Educational, Scientific and Cultural Organization.

Korpi, B. M. (2007). *The politics of pre-school—intentions and decisions underlying the emergence and growth of the Swedish pre-school.* Stockholm: Ministry of Education and Research.

Meade, A., & Podmore, V. (2010). *Caring and learning together: A case study of New Zealand.* Paris: United Nations Educational, Scientific and Cultural Organization. Available at http://unesdoc.unesco.org/images/0018/001872/187234e.pdf.

Morin, E. (1999) *Homeland Earth: A manifesto for the new millennium.* Cresskill, NJ: Hampton Press.

Moss, P. (2009). *There are alternatives! Markets and democratic experimentalism in early childhood education and care.* The Hague: Bernard van Leer Foundation.

Organization for Economic Cooperation and Development (OECD). (2006). *Starting strong II.* Paris: OECD Publishing.

Rinaldi, C. (2005). Is a curriculum necessary? *Children in Europe, 9,* 19.

Rinaldi, C. (2006). *In dialogue with Reggio Emilia: Listening, researching and learning.* London: Routledge.

Rose, N. (1999). *Powers of freedom: Reframing political thought.* Cambridge, England: Cambridge University Press.

Roy, K. (2004). Overcoming nihilism: From communication to Deleuzian expression. *Educational Philosophy and Theory, 36,* 297–312.

Unger, R. M. (1998). *Democracy realized.* London: Verso.

Unger, R. M. (2004). *False necessity: Anti-necessitarian social theory in the service of radical democracy* (2nd ed.). London: Verso.

Unger, R. M. (2005a). *What should the left propose?* London: Verso.

Unger, R. (2005b). The future of the left: James Crabtree interviews Roberto Unger. *Renewal, 13,* 173–184.

United Nations Educational, Scientific and Cultural Organization. (2008). *Overcoming inequality: Why governance matters (Education for All global monitoring report 2009).* Oxford, England: Oxford University Press.

Vecchi, V. (2010). *Art and creativity in Reggio Emilia: Exploring the role and potential of ateliers in early childhood education.* London: Routledge.

Part II

Teaching and Learning through Relationships

Chapter 7

Parent Participation in the Governance of the Schools: An Interview with Sergio Spaggiari

Lella Gandini

Community management is the organizational and cultural form which we use to embrace all those processes of participation, of democracy, of shared responsibility, of examining problems and choices which are part of every institution. (Loris Malaguzzi, quoted in *Charter of the City and Childhood Councils,* 2002, p. 9)

I understand participation in the City and Childhood Council to be an assumption of responsibility . . . which comes from the civic sense of belonging and contributing to a civilized community—collective—society. (Domenico Giannantonio, parent, quoted in *Charter of the City and Childhood Councils,* 2002, p. 9)

This chapter is based on interviews published in Gandini (2009), Gandini and Kaminsky (2007), and Spaggiari (2004) in *Innovations in Early Education: The International Reggio Exchange,* published by Wayne State College of Education in Detroit, Michigan. Integrated and updated by the editors to reflect the most current information. The chapter concludes with public remarks he made at the end of his long service (1995 to 2010) as *pedagogista* and director of Infant-Toddler Centers and Preschools.

For me it's a looking for growth through times of shared reflection, through opportunities for exchange, comparing points of view, taking our reflections further, so that I am closer to my child as a parent, so that we grow together as people. (From minutes of the Anna Frank Preschool Council, quoted in *Charter of the City and Childhood Councils,* 2002, p. 25)

It is a committee where people ask questions. Somebody asks a question, and somebody else answers, giving a long speech, like this! . . . I think it is a kind of Parliament. Yes, yes, a Parliament. (Children, Michelangelo Preschool)

Lella Gandini: *One of the most difficult organizational concepts to understand in the educational approach for young children at Reggio Emilia is that of "social" (or community) participation. Could you describe how this concept came into being?*

Sergio Spaggiari: It is a long story. Let me begin by emphasizing that from the 1970s on, the idea of community participation in education has had official recognition. It has been viewed as a means of fostering innovation, protecting educational institutions against the dangers of excessive bureaucracy, and stimulating cooperation between educators and parents. This participation has evolved in two forms: first, through the system of community-based management (what we call *gestione sociale*) in the infant-toddler centers and preschools run by the city, and, second, through committees in the public schools, with wide representation at every level—primary, middle, and secondary. I am going to speak about the first.

Community-based participation in infant-toddler centers and preschools goes back a long way. We can trace the roots back to the extraordinary educational experiences that developed immediately after the Liberation of Italy in 1945 in certain regions of Italy (Emilia Romagna and Toscana), thanks to the initiative and participation of women's groups, ex-resistance fighters (ex-partisans), unions, and cooperatives—all directly involved in promoting educational and welfare services. These initiatives embraced people across the social spectrum and from the very beginning emphasized the values of cooperation and involvement.

Gandini: *In fact, you could have gone back even further in time in looking for the roots of social participation in education. The "cooperative movement," which you just mentioned, in which people come together to pool and share resources and help one another, has been strong in northern Italy for a very long time.*

The first rural cooperative in Italy started in the Emilia Romagna province in 1883. It was a consumer cooperative, responding to desperate economic times, when people needed to eat but could not pay for food. In the cooperative, all the members had the same rights. Eventually, the cooperative movement took root in all sectors of the economy: workers' cooperatives, consumer cooperatives, shops, and both urban and rural cooperative banks. Italian cooperatives—especially those formed in the Emilia Romagna Region—drew inspiration from progressive ideals. From the beginning, the intent of cooperatives was to create a network of mutual support in situations of severe need, but through time, they had a role in a general material and cultural uplift of the disadvantaged sectors of the population.

The cooperative movement was severely suppressed during the Fascist period but sprang up again after the Second World War in the climate of hope and restoration. New development continued throughout the following decades. Cooperative associations began to offer health care, professional development, and cultural and social services; they have been strong supporters of the early childhood system in Reggio Emilia.

Spaggiari: The first examples of participation were the "school-city" committees, which were specifically formed to administer schools for young children democratically and involved both the people who were connected with the school and those peripheral to it. These organizations were created with the specific purpose of "inventing" a school that would involve parents, teachers, citizens, and neighborhood groups—not only in the running of the school but also in defending the rights of children.

Furthermore, although the most active and vibrant models of participation were begun by municipal administrations led by political progressives and leftists, we should seriously remember that there is also a clear link between these models and traditional Roman Catholic support for the role of the family and the community, as evidenced through the extended network of parochial preschools.

Gandini: *What exactly is the role of community-based management, and how was it developed and formalized?*

Spaggiari: In 1971, the idea of participation was finally formalized with the passage of national laws governing infant-toddler centers. This concept had gradually evolved through the past several decades and finally led to the legal formalization of community-based management. It was in large part the concrete realization of the sustaining slogans of many union and political battles dating back to earlier times. The demand was for the national government to provide social funding, the regional governments to take care of overall planning, and the municipal governments to be responsible for the community-based management.

The experience of community-based administration has shown its true worth in its ability to adapt to new cultural and social situations, for example, the influx of newcomers, the contemporary tendency of parents to view the world in individual rather than political or ideological terms, and the recent influx into our schools of a new wave, or new generation, of teachers, *pedagogisti,* and *atelieristi.*

Gandini: *How does the idea of community-based management fit in with your overall educational approach in Reggio?*

Spaggiari: At this point, the goals of community-based management are an integral part of the content and methods of our educational approach. They are central to the educational experience in the infant-toddler centers and preschools here in Reggio Emilia.

The community-based management in these centers and schools seeks to promote strong interaction and communication among educators, children, parents, and community. Community-based management enhances the worth of an educational approach that has its origins and objectives in the principles of communication and solidarity. The participation of the families is just as essential as is the participation of children and educators.

Obviously, such a three-party system is part of the community at large, which in its turn becomes the fourth component, having it own particular influence and worth.

In short, community-based management is not so much a means of governing as it is a philosophical ideal permeating all the aspects of the entire educational experience.

Seen in this context, participation in general, and community-based management in particular, is central to the educational experience. That is, you cannot separate them from the choices of content and method in infant-toddler centers and preschools. They carry equal importance and weight in the individual growth of all children, particularly in this age group. The years from birth to age 6 years must be seen as a precious resource of human potential, in which a forward-looking society must be prepared to invest responsibly.

Gandini: *In the past 30 years in Italy, there has been a drop in the birth rate, which has brought a change in the structure of young families. What effect has this phenomenon had on participation?*

Spaggiari: As a consequence of this drop in the birth rate, the child is perceived as a rare and precious object. Yet because Italy is also an aging society, a child is considered a disruptive presence, almost an intruder, in a world not in tune with the child's needs and rights. For these reasons, the education of children in this age group presents a most difficult and complex task. The enormous responsibilities of this task cannot be undertaken in isolation by either family or school.

There is a much stronger awareness on the part of parents today that the job of educating a child involves much support and solidarity, much sharing of ideas, many encounters, a plurality of views, and, above all, different competencies. It is precisely because families with only one child feel isolated that they will take the initial step toward meeting and working with others. The types of group support that come from participation and community-based management provide a response to the psychological needs of such families. They facilitate a dialogue between the parent and the child, between educators and parents, between groups of educators and different families, and eventually extending to involve the whole community. The idea of seeking solutions collectively, as it is done in many municipal education programs in Italy, is contrary to the popular notion that families tend to see problems in narrow, private terms.

Gandini: *Of course, the issues and needs of families change over time. I understand that this led to the desire to write a new charter, or constitution, for the organization of community management. The name of the school-based councils was changed from "Advisory Council" to "City and Childhood Councils," and a* *group undertook a series of reflections about the identity and role of the councils. The new charter, published in 2002, begins by stating that any group involved in social management in an educational service must be able to reinvent itself from time to time in relation to new social contexts. In that way, it can re-express its potential and continue to survive with fresh thinking and vitality. Can you tell us about the City and Childhood Councils?*

Spaggiari: In light of the changes you mentioned, the role of the City and Childhood Councils has evolved over time. Besides continuing to support the needs of the city, the main role of the City and Childhood Councils has shifted from administrative concerns (e.g., enrollment, fees) and political choices (e.g., new services or centers) to expressly addressing the needs of families and educators. The City and Childhood Councils have therefore become the initiator and main vehicle of participation in all its complex aspects.

We believe in the idea of children as individuals who bring their rights, their abilities, and their competencies with them into the educational process. But it's not only children who have these things inside them. It is also parents who bring abilities, ideas, knowledge, and competencies. We've always considered the family to be an essential element of the educational process. Many, many schools work without making parents the protagonists and the central figures in the education of their children. Sometimes they even blame the parents, who then feel guilty and inadequate because they aren't able to enter into the educational process. When parents don't participate, I believe it is the responsibility of the school to build itself up in such a way and use all the strategies possible to make itself something that the parents can experience with their children. If the parents are not participating, the first responsibility lies within the school.

Gandini: *Who makes up the City and Childhood Councils?*

Spaggiari: Every three years, the parents, educators, and townspeople elect representatives to the City and Childhood Councils for each infant-toddler center and

---

THE IDENTITY OF THE CITY AND CHILDHOOD COUNCILS TODAY

The parents, educators, and citizens elected onto the Councils have as a reference the sharing of values that delineate the educational project: participation, the assuming of responsibility, openness to relationships and exchanging of opinions, the willingness to risk and contemplate change. . . .

The City and Childhood Councils are elected every three years by public election, carried out through individual and secret ballot on specially

(continued)

designed voting forms. Voting takes place during a public election assembly and during the following day.

All parents and all the staff of the infant-toddler centers and preschools have the right to vote, as do all citizens present at the election assembly. The public election is made visible in the city using specially designed advertisements.

All parents and citizens who volunteer as candidates can be elected. All members of staff, whatever their contract, have the right to membership in the Council at the school where they work.

The election lists, made up of parents, staff, and citizens, one for each classroom, are posted in the information areas of each school and each infant-toddler center and also presented during special meetings with the families.

Each parent and teacher votes for their classroom's list. The kitchen personnel, auxiliary staff, the *atelieristi,* the *pedagogisti,* and people from the community divide themselves between the various lists for the classrooms. Parents with more than one child in a school have the right to vote in each of their children's classrooms.

Voters can express their preference for certain candidates or approve the entire list.

There is no limit to the number of elected candidates.

In the years between elections, the parents whose children have finished school can keep their place on the Council as citizens, and the parents of newly admitted children are able to join the Council by a process of co-option. This takes place by reading a list of names of parents who have volunteered to join the Council during a classroom meeting and which is also made public by posting it in the information area of the Infant-Toddler Centers and Preschools. Although this procedure does not include formal voting, it derives its validity from the fact that it allows the addition of new parents to a democratically elected body.

Each Council is free to choose its own form of organization depending on the aims it intends to pursue. Objectives are decided on in Council meetings and can be delegated to groups of various size and duration; these groups are known as working groups.

Meetings for the Councils or for working groups can be called either by the school staff of the Infant-Toddler Centers and Preschools or by members of the City and Childhood Council in connection with projects and work that has been agreed upon.

—From *Charter of the City and Childhood Councils,* 2002, pp. 48–50.
Reprinted with permission from Reggio Children.

preschool. For each one of these services, there is one City and Childhood Council. The City and Childhood Councils then send representatives to participate in an overarching council called the Intercouncil. On the Intercouncil also sit the Director of Municipal Preschools and Infant-Toddler Centers (formerly myself, now Paola Cagliari), the elected city official in charge of education (the *Assessore*), and representatives of Reggio Children, International Association Friends of Reggio Children, and Istituzione Preschools and Infant-Toddler Centers of the Municipality of Reggio Emilia.

In recent years, more than 75% of the parents have voted in the elections for the City and Childhood Councils. And many have served, those who were most motivated to participate and who made their interest known. For example, in 2008, of 5,909 families using our municipal early childhood services, 756 parents were elected, which means that one of every eight families participated in the running of infant-toddler centers and preschools. In this 2008 election, there were actually 3,058 parents who voted, along with 431 townspeople and 415 staff members—suggesting that there was broad participation in the election process.

The City and Childhood Council in a preschool with an enrollment of 75 children might be composed of 19 parents, 13 school staff, and 7 townspeople. Within each council, a group of volunteers takes care of administration: they draw up agendas and emergency plans, process parental concerns and proposals, and so on. Other members serve on different working groups with specific objectives. For example, they study and implement strategies to maximize parental participation; they organize meetings on special subjects, such as children's sleep problems or the need to repaint the dining hall of the school; they consider activities to facilitate the transition from infant-toddler center to preschool or from preschool to elementary school; and so on. They also coordinate work sessions, monitor implementation, and assess the results of the work done.

Gandini: *In what specific ways do infant-toddler centers and preschools involve parents?*

Spaggiari: First of all, because discussion and decision making are done collectively within each school, parents are highly involved. In addition, widening the field of participation, the educators who participate in community-based management include all types of adults working in the schools—teachers, cooks, aides—all of whom must share the responsibility that stems from being part of a community of educators. The ideas and skills that the families bring to the school and, even more important, the exchange of ideas between parents and teachers favor the construction of a new way of educating and help teachers to view the participation of families not as a threat but as an intrinsic element of collegiality and the integration of different wisdoms.

To achieve this, it is necessary, long before a child ever comes to school, to provide children, parents, and teachers with many opportunities for interaction, as Loris Malaguzzi has suggested (see Chapter 2, this volume). There are many opportunities for participation once the school year has begun:

Parents arriving to pick up their children at the preschool at the Loris Malaguzzi International Center.

1. *Meetings at the individual classroom level.* Classroom teachers meet with parents to discuss such things as the happenings within that particular group of children, the pedagogical and practical directions of the group, examples of activities that have taken place (through slide shows, display of work, and so on), and the assessment of the educational experiences. Preferably, these meetings should take place in the evening or at a time that is convenient to the majority of families. The agenda should be agreed on, and parents should be notified well in advance. This type of meeting should be repeated at least five or six times a year.

2. *Small group meetings.* Teachers meet with a small group of parents from their class. The limited number of participants allows for a closer and more personalized discussion of the needs and problems of specific families and particular children. It is useful for the teacher to hold such meetings until all the families have participated at least once during the year.

3. *Individual parent–teacher conferences.* These are usually requested by a family or suggested by the educators and can either deal with specific problems related to a particular family or child or offer the opportunity for in-depth discussion regarding the development of the personality of the child.

4. *Meetings around a theme.* These meetings are initiated and conducted by parents and educators and are open to all those connected with the center or the school who are interested in discussing or widening their knowledge of a specific subject. Such themes might include the role of the father, children's fears, and so on. The topic in question is debated and analyzed by all the people present, thus providing everybody with the opportunity to exchange ideas and points of view.

5. *Encounters with an expert.* These encounters take the form of a lecture or round-table discussion and might involve many schools. They are tailored to increase everybody's knowledge of problems or issues of common interest—for example, fairytales, children's sexuality, books for young children, children's diet, and so on.

6. *Work sessions.* These are opportunities to contribute in a concrete way to the improvement of the school. Parents and teachers come together to build furnishings and equipment, rearrange the educational space, improve the schoolyard, and maintain classroom materials.

7. *Labs.* In these "learning by doing" meetings, parents and teachers acquire techniques with a strong educational potential, such as working with paper (origami), making puppets, working with the shadow theater, using photographic equipment, and so on. One such example is "the cooking practicum" in which the cook and parents of new children together prepare dishes on the menu that may have been unfamiliar to them.

8. *Holidays and celebrations.* These are group activities in which children, parents, grandparents, friends, and townspeople come together. Sometimes they involve the whole school, sometimes just a particular class. Examples of

celebrated events include children's birthdays, a grandparent's visit, the end of the year, seasonal occurrences, and so on.

9. *Other meeting possibilities.* Trips into town, picnics, excursions, short holidays at the seaside or in the mountains, often at city-owned hostels, are possibilities. One special event is "a day at the school" when a parent spends the whole day in his or her child's class. Other activities involve small groups visiting each others homes, or the whole group spending some time in a specific place—for example, the gym, swimming pool, main city square, or the market.

Gandini: *Over these past 10 or 15 years, what has changed in terms of parent participation?*

Spaggiari: To put it succinctly, what has changed most of all are the reasons and the motives that stimulate parents to participate. In other words, this is a time when the ideologies and grand ideals of the past are in a state of crisis. These ideologies and ideals, together with the trust and conviction that they engendered, have long been the main spring of people's social and public commitment. However, it is clear that nowadays people participate and become involved, even in the

Voting, as drawn by a 5-year-old child. The ballot is also shown, with SI ("yes") crossed out instead of NO. From Diana Preschool, 1999.

field of education, not so much out of idealistic fervor or political conviction but rather out of a desire to seek opportunities for personal growth or for their children's growth, for meaningful experiences and to both give and receive enrichment and help.

At the root of this is a strong call for meaningful reasons for participation, which is linked closely, not just superficially, to a growing desire on the part of people to meet and interact with others, to emerge out of solitude and anonymity, and to experience new feelings of solidarity and reciprocity.

Gandini: *Can you give an example in which parent participation was particularly important in recent years?*

Spaggiari: In the years between 2001 and 2006, Italian national laws and regulations made impossible any new investments and new hiring in the public services and city schools, in Reggio and elsewhere. During this period, our preschools and infant-toddler centers had to be staffed with temporary personnel (teachers, *atelieristi, pedagogisti,* cooks, and auxiliary staff) who had short-term contracts. Previously, when a teacher or a staff member retired, we were to be able to hire, through the usual public employment competition, another qualified person with a stable contract, but not in those years.

Our parents and the City and Childhood Council became very aware and concerned about this situation. By March 2006, our preschools and infant-toddler centers were functioning with 45% temporary staff and a great deal of turnover. By law, the temporary staff had to be moved regularly to different places. This created a great deal of uneasiness for families and educators, because it was difficult to maintain the continuity of relationships that is essential in our system. Teachers, who manage the schools and infant-toddler centers as a collective group, found it difficult to maintain the sense of group and the organization of the work. Furthermore, the didactic planning or *progettazione* could not function well because the temporary teachers did not know how long they would stay and found it difficult to project for the future.

Parents became active in their protest. They collected thousands and thousands of signatures for a petition to the City Governing Council because this form of precarious work was compromising the quality of education. "There is no quality in precariousness" [*Non c'é qualitá nella precarietá*] was their slogan. In June 2006, the parents' representatives participated in the meeting of the Reggio Emilia City Council, presenting their official request that the city government advocate to the national government to modify the laws, at least for the services devoted to young children. As the city government took on this mission, there was a favorable change in the national government, and a financial law was passed that made it possible again to use regular competitions for hiring staff for the early childhood services.

Between 2007 and 2008, we saw the light at the end of the tunnel. We worked hard to make it possible to organize competitions for hiring preschool and infant-toddler center teachers, *pedagogisti, atelieristi,* cooks, and auxiliary staff for all our schools and centers to function well, and we hired many new personnel.

Gandini: *I understand that this is of great importance!*

Spaggiari: I am convinced that an educational experience of this dimension, or any experience that involves profound human dedication, tends to dissipate if it does not regenerate itself. It is indispensable that there is the introduction of new strength and new energy. This change will come through the presence of these new people.

Gandini: *Looking toward the future, what are the focal points around which the thoughts and actions of this spirit of participation and shared experience will revolve?*

Spaggiari: There are several key concepts here. The first is *subjectivity*. There is no doubt that modern society is increasingly examining the growing demand for subjectivity that seems to be manifesting itself in people's attitudes. Whatever its origins, neo-individualism masks a strong desire to affirm one's identity and to have one's personal rights respected. The gamble that we must now face regards precisely this: the possibility of reconciling, and not placing at odds, the needs, the rights, and the desires of the individual with those of the group. In fact, we can see that the kinds of participation and cooperation that give the best results are those which accommodate and welcome many different personal contributions. This is precisely so because it is the individual who participates, and it is the individual who must find a reason for his or her participation. Moreover, today consideration of each individual identity is an essential condition for making participation worthwhile. Any activity that involves participation and cooperation, for it to attract others and be worthwhile, must be pleasurable, useful, and meaningful for the individual, rather than be based on the notion that one can cooperate only by sacrificing one's individuality.

How far the educational experience in the infant and early childhood centers will be a shared and coauthored experience with parents will depend on how well the opportunities created for socialization and exchange will be able to respond to personal expectations and to value individual contributions.

What's more, there are definite ways in which our institutions for young children become distinct and unique places. We have noticed that the process of "shared management" manifests itself in different ways in each school in terms of style and procedures, at times in extremely different ways. These differences that give each school its particular stamp, demonstrate that the reality of each separate governing process is the result of independent decisions and solutions.

Gandini: *And the second concept?*

Spaggiari: *Parenting.* There is no doubt that today the role of a parent has changed dramatically. In general, you do not become a parent accidentally, as used to happen. Instead, the birth of a child is usually thought over, desired, and planned. The decision to have a child is something that is carefully considered in the light of several important familiar variables: economic situation, living arrangements, stability of the couple, job security, guaranteed help, and so on. In general, therefore, a couple decides to have a child when they are sure of being able to offer that child the very best. All this places on the shoulders of the parents a high degree of responsibility and expectations. There is the awareness that the advent of a child will greatly modify the life of the couple, and that being the parent, especially the parent of a small child, will constitute a special experience, sometimes a unique experience that can be tiring, full of worries but above all full of educational responsibilities and duties toward the child.

Nowadays there is the widespread belief that a child's early years are particularly important in the future shaping of that person, that they are almost decisive in terms of his or her positive development. This conviction leads parents to invest much of their time and resources precisely in these early years. Today, however, parents are in the paradoxical situation of feeling and being highly responsible for an onerous educational burden for which they not only are unprepared but also have no points of reference or help. The educational know-how of the grandparents is no longer viable, and the general advice offered by manuals for parents is usually of little use because it does not take into account the uniqueness and the particular nature of individual circumstances. This growing preoccupation with the quality of the child's educational experience has undoubtedly induced many parents to become involved in the infant and early childhood centers in the belief that by doing so they can be closer to their children and better prepared to handle educational choices but also out of the conviction that they will enrich their own capabilities as parents. Against this background, the local school becomes the privileged seat of encounter and social exchange, the natural place where staff, parents, and children contribute on a daily basis to an educational community built on the premises of dialogue and cooperation.

Gandini: *And the third key concept?*

Spaggiari: *Communication.* In a community of people that is built on an ever-growing web of social interaction and a network of exchange, communication itself becomes the primary connector of the entire fabric of participation, the unifying agent that binds the most diverse and distant elements of this multiform and complex social system that we call a center or school for young children. Already, years ago when Loris Malaguzzi, with such thoughtful insight, developed a theory of the "pedagogy of communication," he endorsed the importance of the methods of communication and adopted them as the basis for the design and implementation of the early childhood educational program for our city.

Meaningful and effective communication is now consciously perceived as a way of determining and measuring the quality of social and educational experiences. Today, however, there is an urgent need to reach a deeper understanding and a clearer definition of the strategies for putting into practice this pedagogy of communication. We are well aware of the positive psychological implications of intense and sensitive communication that focuses on the personalizing of human relationships, the sense of belonging and of identity, the refinement of a common

BRINGING IN PARENTS AS EQUAL PARTNERS

As a pedagogista, Paola, what are your views on how parents are brought in as equals into the schools?

Cavazzoni: An infant-toddler center or a preschool which desires to practice participation must be able to mobilize itself and set in motion opportunities for individual and group exchanges even before the children and the parents come into the school. The teachers have to be able to plan and set up the tools (notebooks, diaries, etc.) for supporting the flow of the parents' ideas and their development over the course of time. The teachers have to know how to organize the infant-toddler center and preschool spaces as welcoming environments, space which is suitable for retaining the traces, testimonies, voices and the active presence of today's and yesterday's parents as part of the history of the school. Reggio Emilia has made the choice to believe in parents who are strong and powerful by virtue of their very parenthood, and this choice leads us to value family participation in the life of our schools. It also means that the teachers should not necessarily look for the kind of parents who come closest to the idealized model of the family, but instead recognize and value families or parents individually. This means listening to their questions, doubts, desires, and tailoring one's own approach accordingly while, at the same time, being able to build on these individual questions as opportunities for the school to discuss the values of education.

Are there ever times when the adults within the classroom, the parents or members of the larger supporting community at the school, truly disagree with some aspect of the philosophy, and do not want to engage in reflection or work to understand this way of supporting children's learning? What do you see as the role of the pedagogista in these situations?

Cavazzoni: Most adults who come into our centers are unprepared for this type of school, therefore, their belief in our overall educational project has to be developed. We feel that every adult who is exposed to our experience and whose child begins to attend our infant-toddler center or preschool is an important partner in the experience and has a right to be informed about the philosophy and the organization of our services. I think families have a right to communicate to the school the quality indicators they use to measure the degree to which the school provides a positive experience, and to request discussions about these or any other aspects of the educational process with which they may not agree or which they may not understand.

(continued)

Therefore, I think that debate and the possibility of exchanging opinions is important, and parents should be able to express their disagreement since this represents an important example of democratic participation. If parents feel they can do so, this generally means they have felt legitimated by the school to express their opinions and doubts. As to how to face the situation referred to in the question, I think this is the job of many people, including the teachers and the *pedagogisti*. The ways of arranging meetings with the parents are very important, though they may differ according to each situation. Sometimes individual interviews may be more useful for resolving problems in a more personal way. At other times, wider meetings which are more open to the other parents may be more effective and enriching. In both cases, the task of the school is to foster and increase the adults' awareness of and sense of belonging to the values of that particular school community.

—From an interview with Paola Cavazzoni in Gambetti, Sheldon-Harsch, & Kitchens, 2000, pp. 5–6.

dialogue, the feeling of attachment and reassurance. However, we have also realized that a program that seeks to create an integrated system of communication must directly involve all the aspects of the infant centers and early childhood schools. Among the factors that serve to determine the quality of the communication is the interaction between staff and parents, the collective decision making, the organization of the work and of the workplace, the planning of the calendar, the relationship between the administration and the children, the educational program and the use of materials, the interaction between the school and the community, and the timing and the organization of the meetings with families. At this level, we are still learning from our errors. In a world where communication has become the profession of many (newspapers, television, advertising, etc.), we are probably mere dilettantes. In our society that is bombarded with information, perhaps we, too, run the risk of abusing and misusing the techniques of communication.

Gandini: *Anything else?*

Spaggiari: I urge you to think of the value of *organization* as well. Few educational or pedagogical books discuss the value of organization. Many only think of organization as an administrative problem of the school, but we believe it is an integral part of the educational process. It is a decisive element of our project inside the school. Organization, in itself, is a pedagogical thought.

Gandini: *So, to conclude, could you summarize what you think are the key requirements for sustaining a successful program of participation?*

Spaggiari: One requirement is a diversity of activities meeting the various interests, needs, and aspirations of different families. Another is a focus on the classroom unit as the natural place of encounter for those who are interested in the educational experience of the school and as the starting point to becoming involved in the wider life of the community.

What we have seen in Reggio Emilia has been, and remains, an extraordinary educational experience. Yet what is most extraordinary is that this experience has been constructed for almost half a century—not by saints or heroes but by adults who are an everyday presence in our schools: teachers, cooks, auxiliary personnel, *atelieristi, pedagogisti,* and parents and families These participants have in their minds strong and well-rooted convictions; they respect and value all people without distinction and realize such respect is the keystone of the educational services.

James Heckman, Nobel Prize winner in economics, has spoken to us of three conditions that provide hope for change for disadvantaged children and young people. First, educational intervention has to start very early in children's lives. Second, it must be of high quality. Third, the schools must guarantee parents' participation. These conditions reinforce our deep investment in social participation and in making parents into full protagonists.

Participation is not an easy or comfortable choice. Certainly, it cannot be accomplished by delegating it to an "Office for Participation" that communicates with families by means of posters, pamphlets, phone calls, text messages, e-mail, or Facebook. Rather, participation depends on creating a culture of social concern. Such a culture nourishes our educational experience and puts all of us into the role of constructing human decency, spreading hope, and promoting emancipation. When we have the strength to bring a sense of civility to our work, then, as Paulo Freire would say, we join the army of liberation to free the destiny of people, and we offer children, families, and communities an opportunity to change and grow, thus transforming the infant-toddler centers and preschools into authentic laboratories of peace and humanity.

REFERENCES

Gambetti, A., Sheldon-Harsch, L., & Kitchens, H. (2000). The nature of professional development in the Reggio Emilia municipal infant-toddler centers and preschools: An interview with Paola Cavazzoni, part 2. *Innovations in Early Education: The International Reggio Exchange, 7*(4), 1–6.

Gandini, L. (2009). Renewal and regeneration of an educational community: An interview with Sergio Spaggiari. *Innovations in Early Education: The International Reggio Exchange, 16*(2), 1–6.

Gandini, L., & Kaminsky, J. A. (2007). Cooperative early childhood education services in Reggio Emilia: An innovative solution for a complex society. *Innovations in Early Education: The International Reggio Exchange, 14*(1), 1–5.

Scuole e Nidi d'Infanzia Istituzione del Comune di Reggio Emilia. (2009). *Bilancio sociale 2008.* Reggio Emilia, Italy.

Spaggiari, S. (2004). The path toward knowledge: The social, political and cultural context of the Reggio municipal infant-toddler center and preschool experience. *Innovations in Early Education: The International Reggio Exchange, 11*(2), 1–5.

Study Group on "Identities and Functions of the City and Childhood Councils." (2002). *Charter of the City and Childhood Councils.* Reggio Emilia, Italy: Documentation and Educational Research Center, Infant-Toddler Centers and Preschools, Municipality of Reggio Emilia.

Chapter 8

The Pedagogical Coordinating Team and Professional Development

Paola Cagliari, Tiziana Filippini, Elena Giacopini, Simona Bonilauri, and Deanna Margini

n Italy, the profession of *pedagogista,* or pedagogical coordinator, emerged during the 1970s, when a few municipalities (such as Bologna, Modena, Parma, and Pistoia, among others) began to open their own systems of first preschool and then infant-toddler education and care. This process spread throughout Italy, although slowly and unevenly; as a result, *pedagogisti* were found first and most commonly in northern Italy, with somewhat different definitions of their duties in the various locales.

This chapter was compiled by the editors based on an interview with Paola Cagliari and Simona Bonilauri in October 2010, conducted and translated by Lella Gandini; an interview with Tiziana Filippini in October 2009, conducted by Lella Gandini, Carolyn Edwards, and George Forman; a conversation with Angelica Liuzzi at Arcobaleno Infant-Toddler Center in May 2010 by Carolyn Edwards and Penny Fahlman; a visit to the Anna Frank Preschool by Carolyn Edwards as part of a study tour in May 2010; and on content adapted from all of the chapters and articles listed in the References.

The role of the *pedagogista* in Reggio Emilia is embedded in a system of relationships with teachers, other school staff, parents, citizens, administrators, public officials, and outside audiences. The *pedagogista* cannot interact with just one part of the system and leave the rest aside, because that would injure the whole. At this time, in 2011, there are 13 *pedagogisti* on the Pedagogical Coordinating Team who work collegially in their own working group but also interface with the "collectives," or working groups (composed of teachers, *atelieristi,* mentor teachers, cultural mediators, auxiliaries, cooks, and any other staff), within each school and with administrators, officials, and public bodies who are stakeholders in the Reggio Emilia "project" of early childhood education.

Currently there are 10 "direct" *pedagogisti* who coordinate the municipal infant-toddler centers and preschools. Each of us usually follows four centers/schools (except for a few individuals who follow a smaller number, because they have other special assignments). Additionally, there is another "direct" *pedagogista,* Ivana Soncini, who is responsible for the integration of children with special rights (see Chapter 11, this volume).

Overarching these 11 *pedagogisti* are two cross-cutting, or "transversal," *pedagogisti,* who coordinate the pedagogical system throughout its entire complexity. Tiziana Filippini and Elena Giacopini are responsible for the pedagogical coordination within the Istituzione of the Municipality of Reggio Emilia and for the professional development of the staff. Tiziana Filippini is also responsible for collaboration with a new city initiative, Officina Educativa, and Elena Giacopini attends to interfacing with the *pedagogisti* of the Emilia Romagna Region. The cross-cutting *pedagogisti* are new to the system and vital to continual professional development.

THE PEDAGOGICAL COORDINATING TEAM

We on the Pedagogical Coordinating Team are responsible for guaranteeing the quality of early childhood services in the municipal system and ensuring that they are consistent and unitary. The municipal infant-toddler centers and preschools of Reggio Emilia do not have on-site directors. Instead, administrative and supervisory functions are distributed across the system. Such administrative functions as hiring teachers and staff, admitting children, and collecting parent fees take place in the central office. Then, within each center and school, the educators and staff work as a collective to provide high-quality services. To accomplish this, they depend on their assigned *pedagogista* and the rest of the coordinating team for support in making choices and decisions and interacting with families and the public.

All of us on the Pedagogical Coordinating Team are often found in the centers and schools, but we meet together weekly to discuss policy and problems related to the whole network of our early childhood services. We engage in a continuous exchange of information regarding what is happening within the schools, new advances in theory and practice, and political developments. All of us seek to be flexible, sensitive, open, and able to anticipate change—in the same way as is expected of teachers and staff in the system.

We see ourselves as constantly transforming and growing professionally, through exchange with others. We are constantly striving for clarity and openness, one to another, and seeking to be forces for integration. In our work, we interact with city administrators and employees of many kinds (elected officials, civil service employees, and representatives of cultural and scientific groups) whose suggestions must be pulled together. Furthermore, our presence is active inside the infant-toddler centers and preschools because, together with the teachers, we support and integrate the various aspects of the experience of young children (for example, the learning experience that traditional thinking would divide into separate compartments).

Because all members of the pedagogical team are active at different levels of the system, our competence is multifaceted. We bring a high level of flexibility and a systemic point of view to our work. For example, we work with colleagues in the political and administrative branches of city government, contributing to executive and managerial functions. Another important part of our responsibilities is the in-service, ongoing professional development planned with teachers and staff.

These days, individual *pedagogisti* join others to support a certain number of infant-toddler centers and preschools, and each also bears other specific responsibilities within the system. For example, one of the *pedagogisti* serves as liaison to the state-run (national) preschools in our city, another has the charge of keeping abreast of new communication technologies, and so on.

Today, however, even more is called for regarding professional development because of the influx of new kinds of children and families, as well as the wave of newly hired teachers, *pedagogisti,* and other staff, who have entered the Reggio Emilia early childhood system. Paola Cagliari, the new director of the Municipal Infant-Toddler Centers and Preschools, and Claudia Giudici, president of the Istituzione, have worked closely together to conceive and lead a transformation of the professional development system that they call a *diffuse pedagogical system.* The diffuse system of professional development is not designed for linear and top-down transmission but instead creates many collegial zones of knowledge creation and exchange, where competences are deepened and enlarged in a forum that ideally promotes learning between older and younger generations, across job categories, around pedagogical issues of enduring concern. This new system amplifies tendencies of past years and sharpens earlier emphases, yet also reveals the capacity of the Reggio early childhood system to evolve and adapt to new conditions and challenges.

The diffuse system of professional development involves new arrangements of organization as well as of content focus. Organizationally, instead of a single *pedagogista* interfacing with each infant-toddler center and preschool, some professional development situations are created in which two (or more) *pedagogisti* interact with small groups of teachers and mentor teachers who may come from more than one school. In this way, new faces come into close contact with each other. The first focus on which they work is the feeling that they all belong; they are all entitled to express their own points of view and encouraged to offer their own experiences, while receiving ideas and learning from others. To reach this goal, they have to meet and encounter one another on repeated occasions to establish trust and rapport.

Regarding content, the intellectual content of professional development is currently focused on "conceptual knots" that can be explored in collaboration across educational roles. The "knots" are those everyday yet enduring thorny issues of teaching, such as how and what to observe; how children interact and learn; how and what to observe; ways to encounter the zone of proximal development of children, colleagues, and parents; and how one becomes part of and contributes to the educational action. These topics represent a departure, at least temporarily, from a focus on long-term projects, such as have been described extensively in the many publications and exhibit themes prepared by the Reggio educators (e.g., "City in the Rain," "Shadowiness," "The Long Jump," "The Importance of Looking at Ourselves," "The Amusement Park for Birds," "Reggio Tutta," "The Theater Curtain," to name a few that are well known to the outside world). Yet the patrimony of that kind of *progettazione* and documentation is not to be lost; instead, it will be kept alive through contemporary study and then revisiting with children some of those past themes, delving back for guidance into documentation preserved in the schools and the Documentation and Educational Research Center.

The ultimate intention is for the pedagogical team and teaching staffs to form, and inform, each other reciprocally. They will develop professionally together, supporting a mutual flow of exchange and learning. The heart of it is not in *when* or in *what size and composition* of groups the educators meet, but instead in *how* they meet, the form and spirit of the encounters. If the encounters take place in a genuine and open-minded way, then the meetings can achieve the intent to value—equally and maximally—all the thoughts that everyone can bring or contribute. It is the responsibility and special charge of *pedagogisti* to give value to all the contributions and then to integrate all the contributions of the protagonists in the conversation. They have to attune themselves and give value to everyone's thoughts and input, and they must integrate that input to give back to the group. This is parallel or similar to what they also do with children, as well as what they do with parents and families. If it is not done, the educators lose the opportunity to construct participation. Indeed, this is the very basis of participation.

WORKING WITH EVERYDAY "BACKBONE" SITUATIONS

In our work at the schools, we interact with all the adults (teachers, staff, parents) to help sustain and interpret the philosophy of the overall educational project.

We are deeply involved in the overall educational experience taking place within each infant-toddler center and preschool. We support the relationships there and promote the value of exchange and discussion as they go about helping the adults in the school confront everyday problems and issues. Many of these everyday issues involve basic operation and routine organization, the "backbone" of the system conceived as a living organism. To give just a few examples (Filippini, 1998), the *pedagogisti* might consider problems of scheduling, staff assignments and responsibilities, workloads, and shifts. We might consider issues about the physical environment, for example, reflecting on requests and goals of parents and teachers and then sharing these reflections with an architect who is designing building renovations or with parents and teachers who are building new furniture or equipment. We might learn of concerns from a parent about her child's adjustment to school or interaction with other children. In dealing with these situations, we support interpersonal relationships and help create effective alliances and solidarity through the everyday organization of work, time, and space.

WORKING WITH TEACHERS ON OBSERVATION AND DOCUMENTATION

We *pedagogisti* collaborate closely with the work groups at particular infant toddler centers and preschools regarding all sorts of educational issues and problems concerning children in which the ultimate goal is to promote teachers' autonomy rather than take over their problems and solve them for them. Observation, interpretation, and documentation are the processes that invite regular "reconnaissance" among these work groups, as Elena Giacopini (2007) and Paola Cavazzoni (Gambetti, Sheldon-Harsch, & Kitchens, 2000) describe. We act to sustain and nurture the collective, or working group, of all the adults (teachers, *atelietisti,* mentor teachers, cultural mediators, cooks, and auxiliaries) who promote children's learning at the infant-toddler center or preschool. Regarding children's ongoing experiences and inquiries, we reflect with the teachers on the relationships between theory and practice and how the investigation's initial thesis connects to the children's ongoing experience. These issues should be thought of in relation to the problem areas and skills that the children themselves may illuminate. The aim is to discover together the limitations and incongruities, as well as the aspects that may or may not emerge in the children's work and development of the educational experience.

In reflecting together on documentation, our role is centered not only on the final stage in which, for example, the documentation makes an experience visible via a poster, booklet, slideshow, or other product but spans across the entire process, through listening and contributing to the construction of the children's project and documentation of hypotheses as they unfold (Cagliari, 2004). Rather than acting as an expert, our role with the teachers is that of an active discussant,

Teachers working together preparing documentation.

in a position to sustain the teachers' critical interpretations, to suggest possible questions and queries that might bring out the teachers' narrative and interpretive abilities in relation to their ongoing projects. This means, for example, engaging in a dialogue with the teachers about the relationship between the thesis of a project and the way it is realized in experiences and articulated by the images (chosen and produced by the teachers), choosing together the most effective media for reflecting and demonstrating the complexity and value of the research being carried out by the children and adults. Our role also includes relaunching exchanges and discussions relating to the teachers' learning process to sustain the richness of the school's daily work with greater consciousness.

WORKING WITH TEACHERS TO PROMOTE PARTNERSHIP WITH FAMILIES

In Reggio, educators believe that an essential precondition for effective teaching is the creation of close teacher–parent relationships. Through in-service professional development that focuses on the processes and strategies of communication, we *pedagogisti* try to support in teachers and staff the competence to activate exchanges with parents, as well as among parents, and the willingness to listen to others' points of view.

We are also keenly concerned about whether the environment of the infant-toddler centers and preschools are welcoming and transparent to families (Giacopini, 2007). Keeping this up is an ongoing effort, and the pedagogical team is responsible for supporting work groups in the schools to find their own preferred ways to communicate. Documentation that is specific to each individual child as well as to the group as a whole must be kept up-to-date and cannot become a dry pile of papers or photographs that no one looks at; instead, it must remain a vital means of exchange. Some schools keep a daily diary that recounts the events taking place inside the classroom or the school. In others, there is a daily journal in which the focus is on what the children and teachers have found to be particularly important or interesting. The families contribute comments to these diaries and journals and sometimes take them home. The diaries and journals become useful instruments for reviewing a whole year of life inside the school and are extraordinarily useful for new staff members, who can find out about the experiences at the school. Developing such pathways of communication takes time and effort, and the pedagogical team supports the teachers in this work.

For instance, if we notice that some of our teachers think parents ask them mostly about routine matters, such as what children ate or how they slept at school, we help them consider how the parent is opening up conversation with the teacher and how the teacher might answer a question, then go on to offer an elaboration or discuss different considerations. This may lead to the sharing of interesting thoughts about the child and to raising new questions. In this way, we support teachers and parents in listening to and learning from one another.

WORKING TO PROMOTE MULTICULTURALISM IN THE SCHOOLS

In recent years, the increasing diversity of children and families in the schools has presented a focus of concern, and some members of our pedagogical team have demonstrated leadership in helping cultivate sensitivity toward other cultures among the teachers and increasing intercultural appreciation and respect in the schools (Margini, 2006, 2010). We have found that weekly meetings with the staff of the infant-toddler centers and preschools is important, as is encouraging the teachers to talk openly. We can ask the teachers how things are going with particular families and how they have been participating. We can support teachers in describing the experiences of the children and sharing how the relationships with the families are developing. Any teacher naturally feels deeply affected when a misunderstanding arises or when it seems that trust is not growing with a family, and we can encourage the teachers to talk about an episode that was not positive or was uncomfortable for a teacher, or in which she did not understand the intercultural nuances. At times, a teacher may misinterpret a family member's behavior because that person is from a different nationality or culture. In counteracting that, it can be helpful for educators to reflect together in staff meetings to better understand the experiences people are having and consider how to pay better attention to aspects of communication that the teaching staff might be underestimating or overlooking.

We can also help teachers work through their disappointment when families are not present for an experience. If a family is not present, we can discuss, for example, how the family was invited. The aim would be to focus with the teachers on the strategies that prime and enable participation for all families. It is important to inform families about the various possibilities for participation and to let them know about these invitations, so that families can choose to engage how and when they are ready to do so. We are reminded of one particular occasion during a meeting at a school when a teacher mentioned regretfully the lack of participation of immigrant parents. A parent from South America was present, and she said, "Don't worry. If we don't come, it means we need some time, but it's important that you never forget about us and continue to invite us!" These words were effective in reestablishing trust.

In recent years, a new role of *cultural mediator* has been created in the public services of Reggio Emilia. The six cultural mediators who work in the early childhood system are immigrant women of various nationalities (those most highly represented among the families) who have received training as cultural mediators. They interface on a close personal basis with children and families and educators, and they improve the educators' ability to mediate the inclusion of the various cultures.

Here is an example that illustrates how the cultural mediator work. At one preschool, the cultural mediator, who is Albanian, comes once a week. This mediator does not come to teach Albanian but rather to elicit and support the language and culture and to give the idea that there are many languages in the world; people can converse with one another even if they are not fluent in each another's languages. On one occasion, she observed a child telling his mother not to say he was Albanian; evidently he was ashamed. The mediator went into the classroom, which contained seven Albanian children, and said hello and some other words in Albanian. No one answered. The mediator was puzzled, wondering if the children knew their language. Yet the next time she came to the school, all the Albanian parents were there to greet her. Their children had come home happy, saying, "There is someone at our school who speaks Albanian!" From that incident grew many other favorable experiences in the preschool involving the exchange of language among children.

As a result of their intercultural experiences, we members of the pedagogical team, the cultural mediators, and the teachers and staff in Reggio Emilia have been able to gain a better sense of the points of view of the immigrant parents. The teachers, for instance, have come to realize how much insight they experience when the families begin to emerge in their individuality, to offer their

Two teachers and a *pedagogista* sharing the children's work and experiences with parents.

personal and cultural resources and speak about their lives: their particular path as an immigrant; the personal questions they have; worries about whether to create a family here; problems they may have in the relationship with families of their native country; or difficulties that the Italian laws and legal system continue to pose in the daily life of immigrants. Together, we play a facilitating role in creating an educational experience that is truly shared, in which choices and decisions can be made with the widest possible consensus and respect for the plurality of viewpoints.

WORKING TOGETHER TO PROMOTE PROFESSIONAL DEVELOPMENT

Professional development has always been a key part of the role of the *pedagogista*. We on the pedagogical team ensure that opportunities for in-service professional development are included in the teachers' work schedule in ways respectful of individual needs and preferences as to time and modality (Filippini, 1998). For example, given the complexity of their roles, we know that teachers benefit from a variety of meetings addressing educational theory, teaching techniques, and sound social relations and communication. Teachers appreciate ongoing support to improve their capacities for observing and listening to children, documenting projects, and conducting their own research. During the course of the year, we have some separate meetings for infant-toddler centers and preschool teachers—for instance, meetings connected to issues of child development and guidance at the various age levels—and then there are also joint meetings. We also have workshops devoted to the acquisition of technical proficiencies—for example, the design and preparation of documentation to make project work visible and to explain the school organization and functioning to parents and visitors. Another example is inviting an outside expert to give a lecture on a topic of interest. Also, the system makes it possible for teachers, staff members, parents, and citizens to participate in open discussions or forums, usually held in the spring, on contemporary scientific and cultural debates.

CONCLUSION

Pedagogisti are professionals who serve the early childhood system in Reggio Emilia by *not* separating theory and practice—that is, by *comprehensively* supporting the curricular and educational work in schools entrusted to them (Vecchi, 2010, pp. 54–55). Our role is complex, because we interface daily with all the levels and stakeholders in the system, and we must think about the implications

---

BECOMING A *PEDAGOGISTA*

Angelica Luizzi is one of the youngest and newest members of the Pedagogical Coordinating Team. Her story illustrates the diverse pathways through which individuals come to be pedagogisti and also the dedication and passion typical of all the ones who work in Reggio Emilia.

My educational path was not very linear.

My mother was an infant-toddler teacher at the Bellelli Center, and when I was young, I spent many happy days with her there, first as an infant in the center, and then as an older child visiting during school vacations. In secondary school, however, I found myself to be very good at mathematics, and I made plans and oriented my studies to go into engineering. Yet as time passed, I felt more and more that engineering was not what I really wanted. I felt compelled to turn to something that would be more meaningful for me.

(continued)

My family was worried about this change of heart and whether I would have a good future. It was a difficult decision for me, but I made up my mind and eventually graduated with a degree in pedagogy. I then secured a position as a *pedogogista* in the city of Bologna. There I learned many things, including the role of women in the Italian Resistance against Fascism and their important role in the founding of the Reggio Emilia preschools. I was working as an educator with children of many ages, also adults and young mothers, and I did some work with a publisher of children's books.

When I heard about openings for new *pedagogisti* in Reggio Emilia, I took the *concorso* (competitive examination). In preparing for the exam, I studied the publications of Reggio Children. Suddenly, I was able to put everything I was reading into relation, in line with my memories from long ago. All this was quite surprising to me. Because of my previous experiences, I found I had an open mind to the new concepts I was learning. Many people took the competitive examination with me, yet I passed it with positive scores.

Sergio Spaggiari, at that time director of the Istituzione Preschools and Infant-Toddler Centers of the Municipality of Reggio Emilia, called me to tell me how pleased he was with the results of my competitive examination. He said I was among the few people to become a *pedagogista* who was once a child in an infant-toddler center. The municipality was going to be able to hire six new *pedagogisti*, and I was among them. The other five were experienced teachers, who were already doing work as *pedagogisti*. For me, it was a new position.

I am very happy with my work now, and feel I have found everything I was looking for, and I continue to learn in my profession as a *pedagogista* inside the infant-toddler centers and preschools of the municipality of Reggio Emilia.

of issues from the most abstract to the most concrete aspects. When talking with teachers and parents, for instance, we need to keep the inspiring vision of the mayor as well as the financial constraints, explained by the financial office, in the back of their minds. It is a difficult job to balance the respective requests, requirements, dreams, and hopes of all the different segments of the community and to integrate theory with practice in an authentic way that is responsive to a changing society. Yet the welfare of the children and families demands that we not get either too mired in everyday concerns or too lost in theoretical arguments. We must balance a fresh and individualized empathy for people with frank and critical appraisal of the evolving philosophy of collaboration in which we believe.

REFERENCES

Cagliari, P. (2004). The role of observation, interpretation and documentation in understanding children's learning processes. *Innovations in Early Education: The International Reggio Exchange, 11*(4), 1–5.

Filippini, T. (1998). The role of the pedagogista: An interview with Lella Gandini. In C. Edwards, L. Gandini, & G. Forman (Eds.), *The hundred languages of children: The Reggio Emilia approach, advanced reflections* (2nd ed., pp. 127–147). Westport, CT: Ablex.

Filippini, T., & Castagnetti, M. (2006). The Documentation and Educational Research Center of the Istituzione Scuole e Nidi d'Infanzia, Municipality of Reggio Emilia. *Innovations in Early Education: The International Reggio Exchange, 13*(3), 1–11.

Gambetti, A., Sheldon-Harsch, L., & Kitchens, H. (2000). The nature of professional development in the Reggio Emilia municipal infant-toddler centers and preschools: An interview with Paola Cavazzoni. *Innovations in Early Education: The International Reggio Exchange,* Part 1, *7*(3), 1–3, Part 2, *7*(4), 1–6.

Giacopini, E. (2007). Observation, documentation, and interpretation as strategies for knowledge. *Innovations in Early Education: The International Reggio Exchange, 14*(3), 1–8.

Margini, D. (2006). A difference in ethics or an ethics of difference? Interview with Lella Gandini. *Innovations in Early Education: The International Reggio Exchange, 13*(2), 1–11.

Margini, D. (2010). Social justice and multicultural aspects in the Reggio Emilia experience. *Innovations in Early Education: The International Reggio Exchange, 17*(3), 1–7.

Scuole e Nidi d'Infanzia Istituzione del Comune di Reggio Emilia. (2009). *Bilancio sociale 2008.* Reggio Emilia, Italy.

Vecchi, V. (2010). *Art and creativity in Reggio Emilia: Exploring the role and potential of ateliers in early childhood education.* London: Routledge.

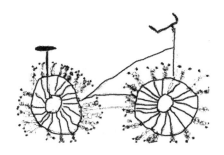

Chapter 9

Teacher and Learner, Partner and Guide: The Role of the Teacher

Carolyn Edwards

[O]ur image of children no longer considers them as isolated and egocentric, does not see them only engaged in action with objects, does not emphasize only the cognitive aspects, does not belittle feelings or what is not logical, and does not consider with ambivalence the role of the affective domain. Instead our image of the child is rich in potential, strong, powerful, competent, and most of all, connected to adults and other children. (Malaguzzi, 1993, p. 10)

[W]e need a teacher who is sometimes the director, sometimes the set designer, sometimes the curtain and the backdrop, and sometimes the prompter. A teacher who is both sweet and stern, who is the electrician, who dispenses the paints, and who is even the audience—the audience who watches, sometimes claps, sometimes remains silent, full of emotion, who sometimes judges with skepticism, and at other times applauds with enthusiasm. (Loris Malaguzzi, quoted in Rinaldi, 2006, p. 89)

I t is not easy to give a complete outline of the teacher's task," Loris Malaguzzi once said (1995, p. 18). In fact, the role of the teacher in Reggio Emilia is complex, multifaceted, and necessarily fluid, responsive to the changing times and needs of children, families, and society.

Yet teaching and learning are at the heart of it and therefore provide a good place to begin. In Reggio Emilia, the teacher's role in assisting learning is a subject of central and abiding interest and concern. Over the past 50 years, teachers and administrators have discussed and considered the responsibilities, goals, difficulties, and opportunities faced by the teachers in their public child-care system. They have evolved together a shared discourse, a coherent way of thinking and talking about the role of the teacher inside and outside the classroom, based—as are all aspects of their organization, environmental design, pedagogy, and curriculum—on an explicit philosophy about the nature of children as learners—young human beings who are learning and developing in reciprocity with peers, close adults, and their community—as well as about their educational values, focused on the search for truth and beauty in everyday life (see Part IV, this volume). This language of education serves to organize and bring together all of the participants in the Reggio system into one community. This chapter describes perspectives on the role of the teacher, drawing on recorded observations that illustrate teacher and child behavior, on examples from published sources, and "The Wonder of Learning: The Hundred Languages of Children" exhibit. The teachers' and children's words convey the distinctive meanings and ways of packaging ideas and communicating with others that are encountered in Reggio Emilia.

DEFINITIONS OF THE TEACHER'S ROLE IN REGGIO EMILIA

What is the role of the teacher in the early childhood classroom? When answering this question, a good place to begin is to analyze and list the various important dimensions as they are usually laid out in early childhood texts for North American classrooms. The roles typically include the following:

- Planning the curriculum to promote children's development in all domains
- Planning the overall program and preparing the environment
- Interacting with children to promote learning through play and appropriate instruction
- Providing nurturance and guidance to children
- Observing children and assessing their progress
- Educating parents and encouraging family involvement
- Engaging in advocacy to communicate the value of early education to outside audiences

These same aspects are seen in the work of teachers in Reggio Emilia, although they gain new nuances of meaning seen through their distinctive ways of talking about teaching. To quote Susan Fraser and Carol Gestwicki (2000, pp. 51–53), we can see that in the following:

- The role of teacher as curriculum planner changes to the role of the teacher as a *co-constructor of knowledge.*
- The role of the teacher as program planner emphasizes the role of *creator of the environment as a third teacher.*
- The role of the teacher in facilitating play changes to the role of the teacher as an *exchanger of understandings.*
- The role of providing guidance changes to the role of the teacher as a *supporter of the competent child.*
- The role of the teacher as an observer is extended to *documenter* and *researcher.*
- The role of the teacher as parent educator changes to the role of the teacher as a *partner with parents.*
- The role of communicator with outside audiences changes to the role of the teacher as *listener, provocateur,* and *negotiator of meaning.*

It seems clear that professional early childhood teachers, no matter their setting or society, agree on their basic range of responsibilities. Yet they do not think alike about these responsibilities: how they prioritize them, turn them into concrete tasks, and talk about the reasons for what they do. When asked to define the role of the teacher, for example, Reggio educators do not begin in the way typical to

The pair of teachers meeting with the *atelierista* at Diana Preschool.

North Americans, with a list of dimensions. Instead, they begin holistically and often speak of an idealized image—or rather, an idealized pair of images: teacher and child. The role of the adult as teacher complements the role of the child as learner; as Malaguzzi stated, "Your image of the child: Where teaching begins" (1994, p. 52). By creating shared meaning of the schoolchild's nature, rights, and capacities, members of a community also can come to agree on what kind of teacher is needed to educate and provide for this child.

Images of the Child and the Teacher

How to define this learning child? The educators in Reggio Emilia often say that young children are powerful, active, competent *protagonists* of their own growth. Children are protagonists in society, bearing the right to be listened to and to participate, to be part of the group and take action alongside others on the basis of their own particular experiences and level of consciousness. Children should never be thought about in an abstract, generalized way, disconnected from a concrete reality. Each unique child is tightly connected and linked to conditions in time and space. All children seek to realize their identity and make their voice heard within that specific context. Their particular context is the source of their individuality; through it, they express themselves using dialogue and interaction in the group and call on adults nearby to serve as partners, resources, and guides.

This intrinsically social view of children—as protagonists with unique personal, historical, and cultural identities—involves parallel expectations and possibilities for adults. Teachers are likewise protagonists—participants with children and parents in singular moments of time and history.

> The definition of the teacher's professional identity is thus not viewed in abstract terms, but in contexts, in relation to her colleagues, to the parents, and above all, to the children; but also in relation to her own identity and her personal and educational background and experience. (Rinaldi, 2006, p. 41)

Thus, any definitions of the teacher's role can never be accepted once and for all, but instead constantly undergoes revision—as circumstances, parents, and children change; the dynamics of their concerns and exchanges shift; and as more comes to be understood about the fundamental processes of teaching and learning. Questions about what teachers can and should do can never be finally answered but rather must keep returning to the starting problem: What kind of teachers are needed by *our* children—those real individuals in the classrooms of today?

Listening to Children

Carlina Rinaldi puts the act of "listening" at the heart of education (see Chapter 13, this volume). Thus, the teacher must not merely think about children as strong and competent but must act in such a way as to persuade children that they deeply share this image. "Listening" means being fully attentive to the children and, at the same time, taking responsibility for recording and documenting what is observed and then using it as a basis for decision making shared with children and parents. "Listening" means seeking to follow and enter into the active learning taking place. Tiziana Filippini, *pedagogista,* described this in one of her first U.S. lectures:

> Sometimes the adult works right inside a group of children and sometimes works just around the group, so he has many roles. The role of the adult is above all one of listening, observing, and understanding the strategy that children use in a learning situation. The teacher has, for us, a role as *dispenser of occasions*; and it is very important for us that the child should feel the teacher to be, not a judge, but a resource to whom he can go when he needs to borrow a gesture, a word. According to Vygotsky, if the child has gone from point **a** to point **b** and is getting very close to **c**, sometimes to reach **c**, he needs to borrow assistance from the adult at that very special moment. We feel that the teacher must be involved within the child's exploring procedure, if the teacher wants to understand how to be the organizer and provoker of occasions, on the one hand, and co-actor in discoveries, on the other. And our expectations of the child must be very flexible and varied. We must be able to be amazed and to enjoy, like the children often do. We must be able to catch the ball that the children throw us, and toss it back to them in a way that makes the children want to continue the game with us, developing, perhaps, other games as we go along. (Filippini, 1990)

Thus, the teacher needs to enter into a kind of intellectual dialogue with the group of children and join in their excitement and curiosity. Although learning is a serious matter, the teacher must approach it in a spirit of playfulness as well as respect. The metaphor of "catching the ball that the children throw us, and then tossing it back to continue the game" is a favorite one in Reggio Emilia. Thinking of teacher–child interaction as a badminton game was originally suggested to Malaguzzi by the Gestalt psychologist Max Wertheimer.[1] Malaguzzi talked about how, "for the game to continue, the skills of the adult and child need appropriate adjustments to allow the growth through learning of the skills of the child" (Chapter 2, this volume).

One example of this responsive teaching is documented in a little booklet from the Diana Preschool called "The Sun Is the Earth's Friend" (1998). Along with the 3-year-olds' drawings and quotations, the booklet includes the teachers' questions. From day to day, the teachers raised new questions for the children to wonder about, and these questions seemed to respond to the anthropomorphic thinking of very young age, and also to their interests about other beings. For instance, the children explored ideas about where is the sun, what it does, and how it stays up in the sky. They considered whether the sun has friends, and who are these friends. They compared the sun and the mooon, and they considered where the sun goes at night and when it rains, and whether children can touch it, or live on it. In talking about what happens to the sun when it's dark outside, children said:

A teacher stays near but just outside a group of children, to document without directly leading their work.

"It goes night-night."
"It disappears."
"It goes in its house, but it's yellow and far away."
"At night it goes on the earth, inside the earth, inside the sea, and the stars come out and then in the day the stars go in the sea."
"At night, there's the moon."

Yet another version of responsive teaching involves providing a next occasion for the children to follow their conjectures or probing children's drawing of how something works to help them clarify their theories. All of these supportive adult interventions are based on keying into the rhythm of the game and modeling an attitude of attention and care. The teacher seeks to extend the children's intellectual stamina and attention span; increase their range of investigation strategies; enhance their concentration and effort; and still allow them to fully experience pleasure and joy in the game.

SPIRALING LEARNING AND SHARED CONTROL

Thus, the teacher's role centers on provoking occasions of discovery through a kind of alert, inspired listening and stimulation of children's dialogue, co-action, and co-construction of knowledge. As in North America, such optimal teaching is understood to be a complex, delicate, multifaceted task, involving many levels and calling for much expertise and continuous self-examination.

Carlina Rinaldi has provided important insights on the educator's role. In many discussions, she has highlighted how a teacher's work should be grounded in political beliefs and advocacy. This perspective is rooted in Rinaldi's political philosophy, a leftist progressivism and idealism common among people in her city and region of Italy. Rinaldi is proud of the ancient heritage of her region—rooted in an agrarian culture and tradition of large cooperating farm households—of relying on communal rather than individualistic enterprise (e.g., see Hellman, 1987; Putnam, 1993). She believes that citizens have a moral obligation to invest public resources in children's welfare and to enter into continuous and permanent knowledge creation with children for her city, and society in general, to progress and improve human well-being. She also believes that the teacher's role must be imagined in terms that are holistic and circular, not segmented and linear. Such a circularity—or better, *spiraling*—is seen in the revisiting that is a frequent component of the learning process. Teachers' actions are not expected to take place in a set order, or one time only, but instead to repeat in cycles of revisiting and re-representation.

From this standpoint, the teacher appraises and assesses what is happening with children within a cycle of days taking place within larger cycles (weeks, months, or even years). Such a spiraling, rather than linear, way of thinking and proceeding is characteristic of Reggio educators—whether they are describing the course of child learning and development; narrating the story of a particular curriculum project; winding through theoretical points that illuminate an aspect of practice; or, as here, thinking about pedagogical roles.

Reggio educators believe in shared control between teachers and children. For example, the teacher leads the learning of a group of children by searching for individuals' ideas to use to frame group action. Sometimes this involves leading group meetings and seeking to strike a "spark" by writing down what the children say, then reading back their comments, searching with them for insights that will motivate further questions and group activity. At other times, it involves the teacher sitting and listening, noticing provocative or insightful comments, then repeating or clarifying them to help the children sustain their talk or activity. Malaguzzi often stressed the importance of tuning in to exactly what children say (verbally or nonverbally) so that the teacher can pick up an idea and return it to the group, and thereby make their discussion and action more significant. This is vital when children seem unable to proceed. Their work may have lost all momentum, or their interest to dissipate. The teacher can help the children uncover their own insights or questions, perhaps expressed by one child in a tentative or partial way—not fully clear to themselves or the group as a whole. The teacher, noticing and appreciating the idea's potential to restimulate the whole group, steps in to restate the idea in clearer and more emphatic language, and thus makes the insight operative for the children, a kind of intellectual spark for further talk and action:

> In this way the play of participation and the play of communication really take place. Of course, communication may take place without your assistance, but it would be important not to miss such a situation. (Vea Vecchi, group discussion, June 15, 1990, Diana Preschool)

At yet other times, especially at the end of a morning's activity, the teacher's intervention is needed to help the children search for an idea—especially one that emerges from an intellectual discussion or dispute between children—and shaping it into a hypothesis that should be tested, an empirical comparison that should be made, or a representation that should be attempted, as the basis for another day's activity by the group. Examining the question, hypothesis, or argument of one child thus becomes part of an ongoing process of raising and answering questions for all. With the help of the teacher, the question or observation of one child leads others to explore territory never encountered, perhaps never even suspected. This is genuine co-action of children.

As a project gets underway, teachers reflect, explore, study, research, and plan together possible ways to elaborate and extend the theme using materials, activities, visits, tools, and other resources. These ideas are then taken back to the classroom and investigated. The teachers work in co-teaching pairs in each classroom. The co-teaching organization is considered difficult, because the two adults must co-adapt and accommodate constantly, but nevertheless, it is powerful because it requires each adult to become used to peer collaboration, acquire a value for the social nature of intellectual growth, and become more able to help children (and parents) as they undertake joint learning and decision making.

Teachers communicate with parents about the current theme and encourage them to become involved in the activities of their child by finding necessary materials, working with teachers on the physical environment, offering supplementary books, and so on. In this way, parents are provoked to revise their image of their child and understand childhood in a richer and more complex way.

The teaching team works closely with other adults (at times the *atelierista*, at times the *pedagogista*) to plan and document what has transpired. This happens in different ways in different schools, but in general, documentation involves handwritten notes as well as backup audio-recordings and transcriptions of children's dialogue and group discussions; print and slide photographs or videotapes of key moments and activities; and collection of products and constructions made by children.

Throughout the project (as well as in other daily work), the teachers act as the group's "memory" and discuss with children the results of the documentation. This systematically allows children to revisit their own and others' feelings, perceptions, observations, and reflections, and then to reconstruct and reinterpret them in deeper ways. In reliving earlier moments via photography and tape recording, children are deeply reinforced and validated for their efforts and provided a boost to memory that is critical at their young age.

The teacher sometimes works inside the group of children and at other times outside, around the group. From either vantage point, the teacher observes and selectively documents the children's words, actions, interests, experiences, and activities. The teacher also observes and documents her own words and actions. Such observations are needed to interpret what is happening with the children and to make predictions and projections about how to go forward; on this basis, the teacher intervenes, joins with the children in their experiences and activity, and facilitates or provokes next occasions for learning—always in negotiation with the children and on the basis of agreement with them.

> What is involved is finding a special idea, all together, toward which the work will be directed, and the project can last for quite some time—even weeks or months—if the idea catches on and work turns out well. (Malaguzzi, 1995, p. 10)

The teachers constantly pay close attention to the children's activity. They believe that when children work on a problem of interest to them, they will naturally encounter questions they will want to investigate. The teachers' role is to help children discover their own problems and questions.

At that point, moreover, they will not offer ready solutions but instead help children to focus on a problem or difficulty and formulate hypotheses. Their goal is not so much to "facilitate" learning in the sense of "making smooth or easy" but rather to "stimulate" it by making problems more complex, involving, and arousing. They ask the children what they need to conduct experiments—even when they realize that a particular approach or hypothesis is not "correct." They serve as the children's partners, sustaining the children and offering assistance, resources, and strategies to get "relaunched" when they are stuck. Often teachers encourage children to continue with something or ask them to complete or add to something that they are doing. They prefer not to leave children to always work on their own but try instead to cooperate with the children's goals.

While working with a group of children, each teacher takes notes, including descriptions of her own words and actions. The notes should be taken in ways that are understandable to others and able to be communicated because they will always be discussed with others. Discussions takes place at different levels involving groups of different sizes, ranging from discussions with a few others (co-teacher, *atelierista, pedigogista*), to meetings of the entire school staff, to workshops designated for particular types of teachers, to large assemblies of educators from the whole municipality. Such discussions are integral not only to curriculum planning but also to teacher professional development. Analytic and critical activities are vital to the development of the individual teacher and, ultimately, the Reggio Emilia system as a whole. Systematic documentation allows each teacher to become a producer of research—that is, someone who generates new ideas about curriculum and learning, rather than being merely a consumer of certainty and tradition.

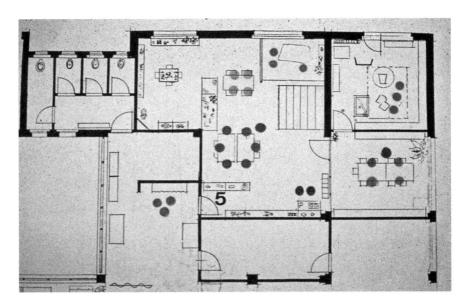

Map of the 5-year-olds room at Diana Preschool during the morning activities. The dots indicate where children and teachers might be positioned one day. One teacher works closely with a group of 4, and another floats among all the others (but is with a group of 6 at present).

THE SPECIAL DIFFICULTIES OF THE TEACHER'S ROLE

Educators in Reggio Emilia do not consider the teacher's role to be an easy one, with black and white answers guiding what teachers should do. They do possess, however, the confidence and sense of security that their approach to teaching, developed collectively over the past 50 years in Reggio Emilia, is the way they *should* be working. As teacher Laura Rubizzi put it, "It is a way of working not only valid but also right" (Interview, November 11, 1989). Her colleague at the Diana Preschool, Paola Strozzi, said: "We are part of a project that is based on the co-action of children, and on the sureness that this is a good way of learning" (Interview, June 14, 1990).

Finding Challenging, Satisfying Problems

The day-to-day work, nonetheless, involves constant challenge and decision making because of the use of emergent, or "projected," curriculum. One difficult task for the teachers is to help children find problems that are big enough and hard enough to engage their best energies and thinking over time. Many things happen every day; only some can be seized on. The teachers seek to discover what may be important and expected in the moments streaming by and then help the children breathe further life into them.

Identifying "Knots"

Not only must the larger project contain meaty problems, but even a daily work session should ideally contain sticking points, or "knots." Just as a knot (whorl) in wood grain impedes a saw cutting through it, and just as a knot (tangle) in thread stops the action of a sewing needle, any problem that stops the children and blocks their action is a kind of cognitive knot. It might be caused by a conflict of wills or lack of information or skills to proceed. Such knots should be thought of as more than negative moments of confusion and frustration, however. Rather, they are moments of cognitive disequilibrium, containing positive possibilities for regrouping, hypothesis testing, and intellectual comparison of ideas. They can produce interactions that are constructive not only for socializing but also for constructing new knowledge. The teachers' task is to notice those knots and help bring them to center stage for further attention—launching points for next activities.

Deciding When to Intervene

Teachers in Reggio have difficulty in knowing how and when to intervene because this depends on a moment-by-moment analysis of the children's thinking. As teachers Magda Bondavalli and Marina Mori stated:

> With regard to difficulties [in teaching], we see them continuously. The way we suggest to children things that they might do leaves things always open. This is a way to be with them through readjusting continuously. There is nothing that is definite or absolute. We try all the time to interpret, through their gestures, words, and actions, how they are living through an experience; and then we go on from there. It's really difficult! (Interview, June 14, 1990)

Also in the United States, teachers worry about how much and when to intervene, how to support problem solving without providing the solution. Children are "dangerously on the brink between presence that they want and repression that they don't want" (Malaguzzi, 1996, pp. 28–29). Thus, the teacher should not intervene too much and yet does not want to let a valuable teaching moment go by.

> But you are always afraid that you are going to miss that hot moment. It's really a balancing act. I believe in intervention, yet personally I tend to wait because I have noticed that children often resolve the problem on their own, and not always in the

way that I would have told them to! Children often find solutions that I would never have seen. But sometimes waiting means missing the moment. So it's a decision that you have to make very quickly. (Vea Vecchi, group discussion, October 18, 1990, Diana Preschool)

What they are describing here is a genuine commitment to emergent curriculum, not a subtle manipulation of the project theme so that it will end up in a certain place. The teachers honestly do not know where the group will end up. Although this openness adds a dimension of difficulty to their work, it also makes it more exciting:

I work in a state of uncertainty because I do not know where the children will arrive to, but it is a fabulous experience! (Interview, November 11, 1989)

[I]t is as if we are starting off together on a voyage. It could be short; it could be long. But there is an eagerness in doing it together. (Laura Rubizzi, group discussion, October 18, 1990, Diana Preschool)

Project work thus provides a supportive context for learning that takes off in unexpected directions, evoking

the idea of a dynamic process, a process that involves uncertainty and chance that always arises in relationships with others. Project work grows in many directions, with no predefined progression, no outcomes decided before the journey begins. (Rinaldi, 2006, p. 19)

Moreover, beyond being exciting, this way of working has the added advantage of the built-in support structures. The teacher is not expected to figure out what she should be doing all by herself. She always works in collaboration with other adults.

It's really the way to be in this school, where we compare notes continuously, and we talk to one another all the time. (Magda Bondavalli and Marina Mori, interview, June 14, 1990)

Such conferring takes place on an almost daily basis in short meetings between teacher and co-teacher, teacher and *atelierista,* and informal discussions between teachers of different classrooms at lunchtime (Strozzi, 2001). Teachers believe that by discussing openly, they offer models of cooperation and participation to the children and parents and promote an atmosphere of open and frank communication. More formal and extended analysis occurs during staff meetings of one's own school or some larger group meeting involving administrators, teachers from other schools, and perhaps even outside visitors or lecturers.

A METHOD OF EXTENDED MUTUAL CRITICISM AND SELF-EXAMINATION

It is important to note that analysis and feedback in Reggio Emilia involves both support and criticism. In contrast to a system in which concern for hurt feelings or ownership of ideas prevents extended examination and argumentation, in Reggio Emilia intellectual conflict is considered pleasurable for both adults and children. As Paola Strozzi said, "I am convinced that there is some kind of pleasure in trying to agree about how to do things" (Interview, June 14, 1990). The point of a discussion is not just to air diverse points of view, but instead to go on until it is clear that everyone has learned something and moved somewhere in his or her thinking. A discussion should go on until a solution or next step becomes apparent; then tension dissipates and a new, shared understanding provides the basis for future joint activity or effort.

Certainly, teachers and staff members offer each another emotional support and encouragement as well as concrete suggestions and advice. In addition, however, a method of extended mutual criticism and self-examination is very much accepted and an important part of teacher professional development in Reggio Emilia, where a small work group—composed perhaps of teacher(s), mentor teacher, *pedagogista,* and *atelierista*—observe and document a group of children together, then meet for lengthy discussion, analysis, and comparison of perspectives on what they were seeing (Rubizzi, 2001). This work illustrates a fourth important aspect of the teacher's role, *posing themselves important questions* (Malaguzzi, 1994).

Because it is difficult to describe to outsiders, this intensive process is sometimes simulated for study groups visiting Reggio Emilia. The simulation typically involves an introduction in which the small group who planned, conducted, and documented an experience with children will provide the audience or participants present with necessary context to enter the narration. They also will lay out the format and structure of the reflection phase to follow. Next, the documentation will be shown. Then, audience participants will engage in extended reflection on that documentation, listening respectfully to each speaker, following an implicit ethics giving everyone the right to participate (no one should dominate). Finally, each of the presenting educators will comment on and perhaps synthesize the reflections, offer final comments, and acknowledge the many insights offered and new questions raised.

As an example, Vea Vecchi (*atelierista*), Marina Mori (mentor teacher), and Loretta Bertani (teacher) led just such a simulation in October 2009 for an advanced study group, using as the documentation provocation a 27-minute videotape of a small group of children from the Robinson School working with clay. During the introductory phase, Marina provided necessary background and explained why the small group is the most favorable learning context for adults as well as children. This was followed by the viewing of the videotape, independent reflection by participants (broken into three smaller subgroups, each with a recorder), sharing of the groups' reflections, and, finally, response and summary comments by the Reggio educators.

Critical reflection of this kind on documentation of teaching and learning has been going on for many years in Reggio Emilia, although specifics of the small group format vary from year to year, and situation to situation, according to the annual plans for professional development formulated by the Pedagogical Coordinating Team. Small-group reflection is a method that teachers greatly appreciate, whether they are new to teaching or possess many years of experience. As one experienced teacher noted:

> Personally, I think we have debated very much [in our small groups], but I never felt that I was inadequate, or felt diminished when I was discussing. And I think that if you don't debate professionally, you won't grow. (Notes, "The Teachers Speak," feedback by teachers on working with a mentor teacher, Reggio Emilia, 2009)

Intellectual conflict is understood as the engine of all growth in Reggio. Therefore, teachers seek to bring out, rather than suppress, conflicts of viewpoints between children. Similarly, among themselves they readily accept disagreement

---

LORIS MALAGUZZI LEADS A WORK GROUP DISCUSSING THE TEACHERS' DOCUMENTATION

Our research team of Lella Gandini, John Nimmo, and Carolyn Edwards, studying the growth of cooperation among children, observed and videotaped the working group of adults at the Diana Preschool in October 1990. Each meeting, held over 3 days, lasted several hours and included teachers, *atelierista*, *pedagogista*, auxiliary staff, and Loris Malaguzzi.

Malaguzzi opened the first meeting by explaining the benefits of collectively looking at a videotape, obtaining a range of interpretations ("circle of ideas"), then working toward a common understanding or point of view. Laura Rubizzi, one of the teachers, then presented her edited videotape showing three 4-year-old boys working together to make a clay dinosaur and talked about what questions she asked herself after reviewing the session, suggesting which aspects of teaching were most on her mind and challenging for her. Did she miss an occasion when she should perhaps have gotten the boys to discuss together? Did she miss an important "knot" to the session by failing to notice how one child tried to make a neck for the animal but then dropped the task

(continued)

without having solved it? Finally, what should she have done to help the children gain more technical knowledge about how to stabilize three-dimensional clay structures?

At the second meeting, teacher Paola Strozzi presented an edited videotape of an activity in which four 3-year-olds had their second encounter with a new material. Paola explained to us how she presented the material (wire) to the children, what questions she asked them, and how she returned insights of individual children to the group. Her presentation was followed by a lengthy critique that addressed her pedagogical decisions. Had she overly "led" the children in creating verbal images about their constructions? Had she offered them an adequate range of materials so that they could compare and analyze the properties of wire? The next day, the wire activity was repeated with children, offering them a greater choice of wire thicknesses to study whether this change would lead to more experimentation and hypotheses.

At the third meeting, teacher Marina Castagnetti presented an edited videotape and behavioral analysis of a session involving two 5-year-old boys trying to draw a castle on a large piece of paper, using a Logo turtle activated by computer. She had created a behavior code and visually represented their whole interaction in a chart. Her presentation also led to lengthy discussion. Had the children been adequately prepared to solve the problem? Could they handle the computer commands? Did they need a set of rulers near at hand to stimulate ideas of measurement? Were they left too long to flounder on their own without the teacher's assistance? Did Marina let a "hot moment" go by, or "abandon" the children too long? Did the children's frequent language of joining ("Let's do this," "Let's try this," "Let's see," "We must," and so on) indicate productive collaboration or increasing desperation? Marina eventually asked, "As a teacher, what was I supposed to do that I didn't do?" but she was never offered a definitive right answer. The point of the discussion, evidently, was to think critically about difficult questions, not reach closure.

Our research team was impressed by the depth of discussion and lack of defensiveness by teachers. At the conclusion of the final meeting, we summarized our reactions to the working group and commented on their rigorous method of critical reflection. Loris Malaguzzi, with demonstrable affection for Marina, said, "Yes, we always have to have two pockets to reach into, one for satisfaction and one for dissatisfaction." (Group discussion, October 16, 1991) and expect extended discussion and constructive criticism; this is seen as the best way to advance. The teachers' pleasure in teamwork and acceptance of disagreement provides a model for children and parents.

EXAMPLES OF TEACHER BEHAVIOR

To give a fuller picture and provide concrete examples of the abstract principles just presented, we offer several short examples drawn from various sources. They illustrate different kinds of teacher behavior commonly seen in the Reggio Emilia infant-toddler centers and preschools.[2]

A Teacher Turns a Dispute Into a Shared Investigation

September 29: The Contested Doll
Laura and Silvia, both exactly 11.5 months old, sit next to each other on the carpet of the *Piccoli* ("Little ones") room of the Arcobaleno Infant-Toddler Center. They are playing with different objects. Laura holds a little soft doll that has a rattle inside.

When Silvia sees it, she wants it, and tries to take it from Laura. Laura resists briefly, then gives up the doll and bursts into desperate tears. Silvia witnesses this without reacting: she watches Laura cry but goes on holding on to the doll.

Only my intervention restores a little calmness between the little girls who, still next to each other, respond to my requests to point at the eyes, the nose, the hair of the doll.

This is the first time that Laura argues over a toy.

(Observation by teacher, Eluccia Forghieri, in Edwards & Rinaldi, 2008, pp. 39–40)[3]

A Teacher Observes a Child's Purposeful Play, and Curiosity (of Both) Is Aroused

October 12: Discovering the Drawer
The desk drawer is half open, and Laura becomes curious and goes closer. Laura has been walking for a few days, and she reaches the desk. After opening the drawer a little more, and exploring it, she tilts her heard and grabs a piece of paper. It's a very long paper with sticky labels, and Laura keeps pulling and pulling with large arm movements until all the paper is out. Laura's feet are completely covered by the paper, and the drawer is empty. Laura makes sure that there is no more paper in the drawer. She then looks at the long strip at her feet and picks it up, but she does not seem to think that this game is very exciting. What she finds interesting to repeat is the "emptying" game, and so she makes a connection (quite a brave one, we think) and she opens the other drawer, but then she looks

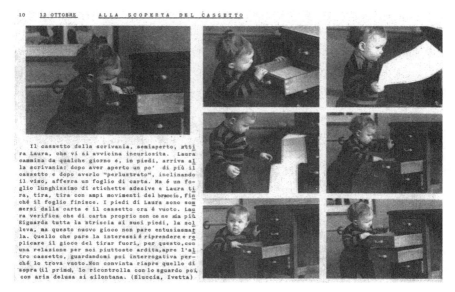

A page from the original Story of Laura, telling a story of infant exploration and surprise.

puzzled because she finds it empty. She is not convinced and she reopens the first drawer above, checks it again, and then she leaves, disappointed.

(Observation by teacher, Ivetta Fornaciari, in Edwards & Rinaldi, 2008, pp. 46–47)[4]

Teachers Follow the Children's Interests

On the day of this incident, the block area of the 3-year-olds in the Diana Preschool has been set up so the two classroom teachers could videotape a "cooperation episode." The teachers have prepared an inviting selection of blocks, tubes, and other lovely construction materials. Then something unexpected happens: the children discover a bug crawling through the blocks. Instead of interrupting, the teachers follow the children's interest, shaping it rather than canceling it, letting it grow into a problem-solving collaboration involving quite a group of the children. Many questions are posed implicitly by the children through their words and actions—questions that could possibly be followed up on another day—about what kind of bug have they found, is it dead or alive, is it dangerous or harmless, how best to pick it up, is it afraid of them, does it have a name, is it weak or strong, is it bad or good, is it disgusting or beautiful, is it a he or she? Even when new children join the group trying to save the bug, they immediately pick up on the original themes and elaborate them, in a circle of cooperation.

At the beginning of the observation, two girls are seen, whom we shall call Bianca and Rosa. To their surprise, they encounter a bug among their blocks. Their teachers are nearby (one videotaping the scene), watching quietly.

Bianca says, "Yucky! How disgusting. It's a real fly [a horsefly]," and Rosa responds, "It isn't a big fly, because flies fly."

Bianca observes, "Look, it's dead," but Rosa disagrees, saying, "No, it is moving its tail."

Rosa declares, "He has a stinger! Stay far away!" Bianca, also, is worried, as she says, "No, no, let's kill it!" Rosa repeats, "Look, he can sting you," and Bianca embellishes her earlier idea, "Yes, but I said that we kill it. I have a real gun at my house. Let's kill it! He moved! He isn't dead. Help! Help!" Rosa now murmurs, "Yes, he is dead. Try to . . . Hello, hello."

Bianca commands Rosa, "You kill it! You have pants on." Rosa says, "No, it will sting me." But Bianca counters, "No, not with your clothes he can't." Rosa isn't having it; she says, "It can sting me even through my pants," but Bianca says, "No, he can't sting you through the pants." Rosa insists, "He can sting me through the clothing."

Their nearest teacher intervenes. "In my opinion, he would prefer to be back on his feet. You children try to flip him because he can't flip himself, in my opinion. Why don't you try to take him outside on the lawn? So maybe you could try to save him."

The children accept this reframing. Rosa says, "Don't be afraid. He doesn't sting. Help me bring him outside. Grab the piece of paper [together] so we can carry him outside. We don't have to use our hands."

The commotion has attracted the other children. One child says, "We can carry him with the paper. Can you help me, Agnes?" Agnes says, "Yes, I can."

Rosa now has new thoughts about the bug. She comments loudly, "Oh, how beautiful he is." To the bug, she says comfortingly, "Don't be afraid. We are helping you." The children try to help lift the bug with a piece of paper. They utter various comments, "Not that way. Oh, poor thing. Grab this end of the paper. He even knows how to walk! You ought not to let him die! All right, what the heck, I will help you. Look, it walks! He is able to walk also. Did you see—Was I good? Where did he go? He is inside there [pointing], inside the paper. Here or here? Let's look. Let's open it [a roll of paper] . Where is it? Oh, it is there." Rosa looks and says, "Where? It is tiny. Oh, there it is!"

The children carry it, but then drop it. The teacher tells one child, "You aren't helping [with the carrying]," but that child protests, "I am helping." Another child cries out, "Help me, fence him in. Come on, help me. Yes, he is fenced in."

The second teacher now speaks up, "For sure, he is getting away. What would you like to do? Try to carry him outside."

The children try to carry the bug outside. Various children call out, "Oh, it fell. It hurt itself. It [the bug] is good. The bug is afraid. No, it is not afraid. Yes, it is afraid. It has fallen. No. He is afraid." Someone declares, "You killed him." This arouses many more comments from the group: "You have to believe, so you can save him. Look, look. You ought not to let him die. Yes, he is beautiful. He is very beautiful and good. I don't want to let him die. Let us put him in here. Put him in here. We must not let him die. Don't step on him."

One girl tries calling the bug, giving it a name, "Come here, beautiful. Beautiful, come here, *Topolone* ("Big Mousie"). Another child responds to her, "He doesn't want to come. Be careful or he will wind up squashed."

The children check on the bug's status. One boy declares, "He is still alive." The second teacher confirms, "He is still alive." She encourages the children, "Well, then, let's get him." A boy says, "He went under the table," and the second teacher guides, "Okay, grab him and take him outside."

The children are triumphant, "We captured him! We captured him. He doesn't want to get down [off the paper]. We got him! We are great!" Once outside, they let the bug go, saying, "He won't get down. Let's leave him, there, poor thing. Don't squash him. She's beautiful. Where is she?"

(Videotape from the cooperation study of Edwards, Gandini, & Nimmo, 1994)

A Teacher Provides Instruction in Tool Use and Technique

It is a morning in May 1988 in the *piazza* of Diana Preschool where teacher Paola Notari is working with eight 3-year-olds and large mounds of artists' modeling clay. She provides the children instruction in the correct use of the materials and tools as part of the process of facilitating, supporting, and encouraging. When asked about this, she says she tries to provide the help and advice that is needed for children to accomplish their own artistic and representational goals and not be defeated by the materials. For example, she knows that if children roll out the clay too thin, then it breaks during firing and children are upset.

The children are seated around a long rectangular table, while Paola stands and moves among them. In front of each is a large wooden tablet on which to work the clay. Paola is preparing each child a flat slab of clay: she tears off a hunk of clay, rolls it out thin with a rolling pin, cuts off the sides to make a neat square, then gives it out. She is using a knife to cut the clay and says, "This tool we can use to cut the clay when it is nice and thick."

The children have many cutting and rolling tools nearby. They are working on the problem of "representing movement, on a surface." With a knife, they can cut out a piece of the clay, then fold it up and over to give a sense of motion on the surface of the slab. (She explains later that some of the children don't actually succeed in getting any sense of movement into theirs. But Paola doesn't interfere and insist on her idea of movement. Because all are very involved in what they are doing, she does not impose her ideas on them. However, she does instruct them on matters of technique—showing them how to roll and cut the clay and use the tools.)

The teacher notices that children need help with something they are trying to do with the clay. First, she points and tells.

Then she decides they need her to actually show them what she means.

At the beginning of the episode, Paola is seen using a spatula to give a newly rolled slab of clay to a child. "Do you need this?" she asks. She tells another, "You are pressing too much. If you press too much, we will not be able to pick it up, and then we will not be able to fire it in the kiln. Don't press too hard." Then another child turns to her, "Is this all right?" "Yes, yes," Paola replies, "That's fine. If you want another slab of clay, I can prepare one for you."

She observes a little disagreement between two children. One wants the pastry cutter that the other has been using. That child protests, "This is mine. I had it before." "But they are all the same," says Paola, pointing out more cutters. "They really are all the same." She moves closer, and the first child shows here that in fact the desired cutter makes a different kind of track in the clay than the others. So she revises her opinion, "Oh, I see. Well, if you look in the tool box, there you will find another, precisely like this one." The child goes off happily to look.

She begins to prepare a slab of clay for one of the girls and, while doing so, looks up at the child opposite her. "What are you doing?" she asks. The boy shows, and Paola says, "That's nice."

Finishing the new slab, she takes it over to the girl needing it. Seeing her first piece, Paola comments, "Look at that marvel! Now you have to think about what else you want to do. You could put the same marks in it [the new slab] you did before. Of you could place these pieces folded, or standing up." She demonstrates, using little strips of clay. The little girl has in her hand a pastry cutter, which she moves over the slab without saying anything. Paola continues, "You only want to cut with this little wheel, don't you? It does make very beautiful marks."

Paola goes to the opposite side of the table where a very small child seems to be having difficulties. She asks him, "May I clean it up for you?" Her hand smoothes down his slab, using slip. She explains to him, "This is sort of like an eraser. And now I will show you how to use this tool [a cutter]. You can make a thin strip, like this, and fold it or pick it up." She shows him to lift one end of the strip. Then she puts the cutter into his hand and standing behind him, guides him in the use of both his hands. "With this hand, hold the clay. Now with this other hand, push very hard. More. This way. Okay? Now you can do it."

A little later, she asks all the children at large, "Do you want more clay? I can go get it." The children shout, "Also I!" "Also I!" "Okay," Paola says, "I'm going to get some more." She goes out of the room for a few minutes, leaving the children alone for a few moments. The observation continues in the same way when she returns.

(From a videotape in Carolyn Edwards's collection)

A Teacher Scaffolds Conceptual Understanding

In an episode recounted by Vea Vecchi (2010), the children in Marina Mori's classroom at the Diana Preschool are found drawing their classmate Sewaa. In a way that is customary in Reggio, children are divided into groups around the model, each with a different perspective.

One girl, Laura, wanders around and stops to speak to Martina, who is sitting at Sewaa's side. Laura tells Martina that what she has done isn't right. In a friendly way, she says, "You've drawn Sewaa as if she was like this, in front of you. . . . Instead you were supposed to draw her like this . . . from the side . . . in profile . . . with only one eye, only one leg, only one ear." She shows Martina her own side-view drawing, putting them side by side to compare. Martina, at first surprised, seems little by little to understand what Laura is trying to show her.

Marina, the teacher, comes close to Martina and says in a kindly way, "The drawing you have made is lovely." She pauses, then goes on to say, "But, to see it like this, where would you have to be sitting?" Martina points to the groups who can see Sewaa from the side, "There, at that table there."

Here is how Vea Vecchi analyzes Marina's method of intervention:

> The teacher does not say that the drawing is mistaken, rather she underlines that the drawing is a nice one, neither does she ask the child to redo it, but by her question she sanctions the difference between two points of view, front and side. Highly respectful of the child's sensibility, she does not immediately confront her with a further test in drawing because, by her reply, Martina shows that she has taken a first step toward understanding the problem, which is not simply a drawing problem but conceptual. There will be other times for advancing this awareness she has just acquired. (Vecchi, 2010, p. 52)
>
> (The full story, illustrated with photographs and the children's drawings, is described by Vecchi, 2010, pp. 51–53.)

A Teacher Relaunches a Project

In an investigation that involves mathematical thinking, the children at Diana Preschool are confronted with a real-life problem. How can they give all the necessary measurements to the carpenter so he can build them a new work table just like their old one? Five boys and one girl from the class of 5-year-olds have volunteered to work together on the problem.

In one of their initial encounters, Marina Castagnetti, teacher, invites the children to stand around their old table and offer their thoughts of how to measure it. Alan suggests, "You count and you measure with your fingers. You put one finger after the other, you count to 5 on your other hand and then up to 10." The children pursue this idea, then do some drawings, then continue measuring the table with their body parts. Eventually abandoning the idea of fingers, they next try measuring with their fists, their hand spans, and finally using their legs. One child even tries using his head. The children have moved from one unit of measurement to another without arriving at a definite choice. They are a bit stuck.

Marina and Vea Vecchi sit down together to study the observations that have been collected thus far and try to come up with an idea of how to support the

The children try using their body parts to measure the length of their table. They try with their fingers, hands, feet, even their hand. Eventually they become a bit stuck. What will the teacher do to help them out?

children. They reread the notes and hypothesize that the adults need to "push the children further into the disorder that they have created" as a way to accentuate the contradictions of their thinking. Perhaps this will help the children progress in their understanding.

In a next meeting, Marina suggests that the children try making long jumps and then measuring them. She asks them, "How can you measure your jumps?" The children reply, "You need two marks, one for the start and one for the finish, and you measure with your feet."

Tommaso makes a jump and then measures the distance, putting one foot in front of the other. His jump is four "feet" long. Now Marina measures the same distance with her feet, and it's three "feet" long.

Marco and Daniela jump next, and both times, the children's measurements are longer than Marina's. Finally, the children discover what is going on. They tell her, "Your foot is bigger, and it takes up more space. We have little feet."

This project continues on for many meetings, with the children using string, then their shoes, and eventually paper measuring sticks they have drawn themselves, as they construct knowledge for themselves and retrace the path of human history in understanding the need for a standard unit of measurement.

(The full episode, illustrated with photographs and the children's drawings, is described by Marina Castagnetti and Vea Vecchi, 1997, pp. 19–31.)

CONCLUSIONS

The role of the teacher in Reggio Emilia shows many similarities to the role as commonly conceived in the United States. In both settings, goals are set high—as ideals that are expected to be difficult to attain and sustain in practice. In both, early childhood education involves complex interaction with multiple constituencies (children, parents, colleagues, government, the public) and stimulating children's learning and development through the design of optimal school organization, physical environments, curriculum, and pedagogy. In Reggio Emilia, however, the infant-toddler or preschool teacher always works with a co-teacher. As a pair, these two relate to the other teachers, auxiliary staff, and the *atelierista* in their school and, moreover, receive support from *pedagogisti,* mentor teachers, cultural mediators, as well as staff assigned to the Documentation and Educational Research Center, REMIDA (the Recycling Center), and other laboratories and resource centers. They also interact and have a continuous dialogue with parents who support them and participate in the life of the school.

In their interaction with children, Reggio Emilia teachers seek to promote children's well-being and encourage learning in all domains (cognitive, physical-motor, social, and affective), at the same time taking advantage of key moments to instruct children in ever-more-sophisticated use of tools and materials needed to express themselves in the multiple symbolic and artistic media. From their own point of view, the teachers' classroom work centers on "provoking occasions" of genuine intellectual growth by one or more children—in particular, listening to the words and communications of children and then offering them back to the group to restimulate and extend their discussion and joint activity. Such a method of teaching they consider important, complex, and delicate, constantly evolving and changing, and a matter of collective effort and concern. Their tendency to engage with colleagues in extended mutual criticism and self-examination of their teaching behavior seems to distinguish the educators of Reggio Emilia. Just as they see children as learning best through communication, conflict, and co-action, so do they see themselves as learning in this way. They see the work and development of teachers as a public activity taking place within the shared life of the school, community, and culture; they place a strong value on themselves communicating and interacting within and outside the school. Striving to fulfill these ideals is demanding, they well know, but rewarding and sustaining as well, and vital to the progress of society and human well-being.

NOTES

1. Max Wertheimer (1982) famously described watching two boys playing badminton. One of the boys was much better than the other, and as the game went on, this older boy kept winning easily, and the younger boy's play became worse and worse. Then the boys decided to play a new game, where the objective was to see how many turns they could keep the birdie up in the air. Now both boys began to work in a complementary way, as the older boy had to adjust his play to assist the younger boy's efforts. The younger boy's playing improved, and both boys threw themselves into playing with effort and enjoyment.

2. Other vivid examples of teacher behavior were published in the second edition of this book. They can be found in "Partner, Teacher, and Guide: Examples of Teacher Behavior in Reggio Emilia." Available at http://digitalcommons.unl.edu/psychfacpub/503.

3. Quotations from Edwards & Rinaldi, 2008, edited by Carolyn Edwards and Carlina Rinaldi, copyright 2009 by Carolyn Edwards, the Municipality of Reggio Emilia–Istituzione Preschools and Infant-Toddler Centers, and Reggio Children S.r.l. Reprinted with permission of Redleaf Press, St. Paul, MN (www.redleafpress.org).

4. Quotations from Edwards & Rinaldi, 2008, edited by Carolyn Edwards and Carlina Rinaldi, copyright 2009 by Carolyn Edwards, the Municipality of Reggio Emilia–Istituzione Preschools and Infant-Toddler Centers, and Reggio Children S.r.l. Reprinted with permission of Redleaf Press, St. Paul, MN (www.redleafpress.org).

REFERENCES

Castagnetti, M., & Vecchi, V. (Eds.). (1997). *Shoe and meter: Children and measurement. First approaches to the discovery, function, and use of measurement.* Reggio Emilia, Italy: Reggio Children.

Edwards, C. P., Gandini, L., & Nimmo, J. (1994). Promoting collaborative learning in the early childhood classroom: Teachers' contrasting conceptualizations in two communities. In L. G. Katz & B. Cesarone (Eds.), *Reflections on the Reggio Emilia approach* (pp. 82–104). Urbana, IL: ERIC Clearinghouse on Elementary and Early Childhood Education.

Edwards, C. P., & Rinaldi, C. (2008). *The diary of Laura: Perspectives on a Reggio Emilia diary.* From a project originally by Arcobaleno Municipal Infant-Toddler Center, Reggio Emilia, Italy, in collaboration with Reggio Children. Minneapolis, MN: Redleaf Press.

Filippini, T. (1990, November). The Reggio Emilia approach. Paper presented at the annual meeting of the National Association for the Education of Young Children, Washington, DC.

Fraser, S., & Gestwicki, C. (2000). *Authentic childhood: Experiencing Reggio Emilia in the classroom.* Albany, NY: Delmar Publishing.

Hellman, J. A. (1987). *Journeys among women: Feminism in five Italian cities.* New York: Oxford.

Malaguzzi, L. (1993). For an education based on relationships. *Young Children, 49*(1), 9–12.

Malaguzzi, L. (1994). Your image of the child: Where teaching begins. *Child Care Information Exchange, 3,* 52–56.

Malaguzzi, L. (1995). Introductory remarks. In *The fountains* (pp. 6–23). Reggio Emilia, Italy: Reggio Children.

Malaguzzi, L. (1996). *The hundred languages of children: Narrative of the possible.* Catalog of the exhibit "The Hundred Languages of Children." Reggio Emilia, Italy: Reggio Children.

Malaguzzi, L. (1997). The invisibility of the essential. In M. Castagnetti & V. Vecchi (Eds.), *Shoe and meter* (pp. 10–13). Reggio Emilia, Italy: Reggio Children.

Putnam, R. D. (1993). *Making democracy work: Civic traditions in modern Italy.* Princeton, NJ: Princeton University Press.

Rinaldi, C. (2006). *In dialogue with Reggio Emilia: Listening, researching and learning.* New York: Routledge.

Rubizzi, L. (2001). Documenting the documenter. In Harvard Project Zero and Reggio Children, *Making learning visible: Children as individual and group learners* (pp. 94–115). Reggio Emilia, Italy: Reggio Children.

Strozzi, P. (2001). Daily life at school: Seeing the extraordinary in the ordinary. In *Making learning visible: Children as individual and group learners* (pp. 58–77). Reggio Emilia, Italy: Reggio Children.

Vecchi, V. (2010). *Art and creativity in Reggio Emilia: Exploring the role and potential of ateliers in early childhood education.* New York: Routledge.

Wertheimer, M. (1982). *Productive thinking.* Chicago: University of Chicago Press. (Originally published in 1945.)

Chapter 10

The Observant Teacher: Observation as a Reciprocal Tool of Professional Development: An Interview with Amelia Gambetti

Lella Gandini

Editors' Note: After 25 years of experience as a teacher in the preschools of Reggio Emilia, in 1992, Amelia Gambetti began to devote time to sustain the development of teachers in the United States, through conferences and educational meetings and also by supporting the evolution of schools for young children that have chosen to experience the innovative work inspired by the schools of Reggio Emilia. Her role at Reggio Children as Coordinator of International Exchanges provides her the opportunity to establish collaborations in northern Europe, Asia, South America, Africa, and the Middle East. The conversation that follows focuses first on her own experience as a teacher involved in her own development and second on how she has been transferring her learning in the U.S. context to help in specific situations with observing and sustaining teachers' learning with each another and along with the children.

Gandini: *I would like for you to begin by describing when you started to be in contact with visitors from the United States who had come to observe how teaching and learning happen in Reggio Emilia.*

Gambetti: There were some early visits to our schools, as you know because you came several times in the early 1980s. Later, groups started to come more regularly, from European countries as well as the United States, and I was observed very often. There were some particularly intense visits; for example, Baji Rankin came in 1989–1990 to spend a full school year of internship, and then Louise Cadwell came in 1991–1992. Let's also remember our collaboration with you and George Forman when you came together in 1992 to observe the project "Amusement Park for Birds." Remember how much we analyzed together the work done with children?

But to be clear, we had all along gotten a great deal of practice in learning to be observed and to reflect with Carla Rinaldi, who was then our *pedagogista*, and about what it means to be observed. At La Villetta Preschool, Carla observed us, and we teachers observed one another as well as the *atelierista*. It was a way to learn from others and with others how best to work with children. We would observe what each one of us did while at the same time being observed.

Gandini: *Carla's basic intention, I imagine, was to contribute to your professional development and show how reciprocally you could help each other to grow as teachers. What is notable is that her intention became a shared intention among all of you at La Villetta Preschool.*

Gambetti: Certainly, and this was taking place along with collective occasions of professional development that were held weekly at our school, and at times formally organized to include all the schools, with the goal of increasing our awareness toward the general objectives of our work.

When you accept being observed and understand the importance of it, you have to learn to separate your personal feelings from your professional role, of course not forgetting your identity and your personality. You have to assume a detached attitude from the person who is observing you while you are involved in actions with children. This is also true when you see yourself again in a video; you critique yourself, while being critiqued by your colleagues or the *pedagogista*. I think it is important that you learn to accept the comments in a constructive way because this improves the quality of your work. Others' points of view also increase your sense of responsibility for the actions you take. In fact, you have to learn to accept criticism and to do self-criticism. It is true that sometimes you see what you could have done better even before your colleagues mention it.

In fact, to observe better, we planned and adopted the use of videotaping. It was helpful for us to watch together, to see and criticize our work with children, together among colleagues. It was so important that in the discussion, all points of view emerged and were included in a shared assessment of various situations.

Gandini: *I find this reciprocal way of observing one another through the use of video and agreeing to use constructive criticism a powerful tool for growth. I* *am sure it requires a strong mutual respect and trust, and certainly, the support of the pedagogical coordinator as a coach and mediator was also essential to get started.*

Gambetti: The use of video was a way to help one also understand how one expresses one's thoughts in conversation among colleagues. How much space do you leave for others to express their thoughts or opinions and to speak up? It was also a way to understand, for example, how your way of thinking aloud in conversation works. How much room do you leave to the voice of others? How does one present her opinion without considering what the other is saying? If in all these exchanges you keep the intention of being a listener, it is easier to see the positive and less positive attitudes in the exchanges.

Gandini: *Was this a tendency that you had noticed among colleagues or also on your part, Amelia?*

Gambetti: I think we were all learning, and we were looking at collaboration as a deep resource.

Gandini: *It is a complex way of working that requires, it seems to me, a great deal of time and many meetings together.*

Gambetti: Yes, but it also happens with children; they also learn to do the same thing. I don't think it necessarily requires a great deal of time but rather an efficient use of time, so that instead of working more, you work better. When the children have established familiarity (this is a process), work in a group, and discuss something, their conversation is similar to a relay race. They refer to the words and thoughts of their peers to carry on the conversation. In fact, the more the group is capable of the strategies of communication, the more their conversation becomes articulate and full of meaningful details. This awareness about others' process of thought proceeds through the teacher to the children; parents also become involved and aware.

Gandini: *Could you tell us more about how this way of working by observing and being observed had developed? Was it a deliberate plan or strategy, and how gradual was the process?*

Gambetti: Carla Rinaldi has always urged us to include in our style of working—strongly based on theories and practice woven together—this attitude of observation. She used to suggest to us that we all had weaknesses and strengths, so that if we observed each other working in the school, we would learn from what others did differently and why. All of this facilitated the formation of an attitude of collaboration and collegiality rather than an attitude based on competition.

Gandini: *I am thinking about the time when George Forman and I asked Loris Malaguzzi if we could come to observe the teachers in action during a project. We were interested to learn how it is possible to describe and document the role of the teacher in the construction of learning with children. We were looking for an opportunity to observe very closely. I realize that the choice of La Villetta was not casual because there was a process of reciprocal observation that was already established there through great investment by Carla.*

Amelia Gambetti asks a child how she thinks water gets into a fountain. From "The Amusement Park for Birds."

Gambetti: The choice of La Villetta was not by chance. The process of observation was very much part of our daily work and, in particular, had already started in a more formal and intense way with the production of the video *To Make a Portrait of a Lion.* Giovanni Piazza, La Villetta's *atelierista,* and I had lived through that experience, observing each other while also being observed by Carla Rinaldi and Loris Malaguzzi. They were engaged in understanding in what way the development of a project could be documented. I really would like to underline that documentation as a process was and still continues to be part of our daily work.

That experience [with *To Make a Portrait of a Lion*] was a big step forward because there were many problems that emerged, and the strategies that we elaborated were a constructive learning and immensely useful. They were always generated by combining theory and practice. The goal was to succeed to show that a particular project could be documented in its integrity in its whole development and to make visible the very process of our work—that is, to show through the use of video the high points of communication within the various experiences that occurred and that we encountered. These experiences were very much connected to the theory of the hundred languages of children—the many ways that children express themselves, tell stories, and experiment in situations made visible in the video.

With regard to being observed, we should not forget to mention that after *Portrait of a Lion,* there was in Reggio a large project, "The City and the Rain," that involved various schools. As with *Portrait of the Lion*, this was documented in the exhibit "The Hundred Languages of Children."

Gandini: *I remember that Loris Malaguzzi was particularly invested in that project. He had given a great deal of thought to all the possible relationships and interpretations by children about natural changes and the changes of the city with the rain. When he came to the University of Massachusetts in 1988 to open "The Hundred Languages of Children" exhibit, "The City and the Rain" was included, and he gave for us a special narrative of that project. We three editors were very fortunate to hear his thoughtful and provocative analyses on that occasion.*

Gambetti: To be observed while you are involved in relationship with children is a situation that also helps you learn strategies of questioning and how to intervene and interact with them. It is difficult to find equilibrium within your different interventions with the children unless you know them very well, and even then, it is a complex situation that is always in front of you. If you know children well, you can use your intuition and enter the context as a listener. You can put yourself in a position to recognize the most appropriate moment to intervene. I would say that this intuition is based on knowing the children. What you learn is how to learn, even to make attempts to formulate questions that are very open. The formulation of questions itself could include an inquiry into how to modulate the tone of voice in particular way to keep the conversation or dialogue suspended, as it were. It is like "taking time" or giving value to a time that remains open to give the children the opportunity to formulate questions that might be generated by their train of thought. At times, the children accompany or guide you (maybe inadvertently) to understand which questions are best to ask; at times, just their attitude or tone of voice can suggest a question.

There are many ways to observe and be observed. You can observe and be observed through the strategy of taking photos and also using videos. For example, with "The City and the Rain," we observed one another using photographs when we were working together. It was not always possible to be observed by Carla or Loris Malaguzzi because they were responsible for following many other schools with the same project. When I was with the children, and Giovanni observed the situation by taking photos, we were documenting two levels of observation. We became aware of this by looking at the photographs together. We would see what Giovanni had photographed, and as a consequence what his choices were, and although I was observed from his point of view about how I was interacting with the children, the photographs were giving visibility to the choices I was making.

Gandini: *Comparing the various tools of observation—video, photos, audio recording, notes—do you think that they are all valuable for you, or do you have preferences?*

Gambetti: In my experience, they are all strong tools because they all contribute to learning both to observe and to be observed. They help one to understand how one is behaving within the particular context that is being observed. They can help to understand one's own motivations connected with the choices one makes.

Furthermore, these tools can help one to become aware and notice the evolution of one's way of working with children and also with colleagues and other adults.

It is important to build awareness about one's own personal way of working. I think that the more one becomes aware, the more critical one is with regard to one's own work. That critical attitude is necessary, in my view, because as educators, we have the responsibility to do the best work possible with children, families, and our colleagues. It has always helped me to start from the conviction that the person who observed me and eventually critiqued my work was neither angry at me nor disliked me. That was out of the question. The most important thing has always been to do the best one can do in working in contexts full of complexity. To be with the children always has to be at the highest level of one's own potential to create relationships of high quality. Therefore, to reach that level, one must succeed in becoming aware of each detail of one's own way of behaving. I believe strongly that this working with attention and listening is at the basis of the good work of all the educators.

This awareness did not come easily. At the beginning of my work, I invested a great deal of energy to understand the importance of observation. At times, it has not been a particularly pleasant process, but it has always been a study of attitudes that is useful in the construction of my role as a teacher. For example, if one does something that inhibits the children or says something that produces a disequilibrium in the understanding of a child who is next to you, if one has an attitude of listening, one might understand what did not work well; right away one can understand how to recuperate communication in a positive way. These attitudes, I think, can help a teacher to improve the quality of her relationships with children as well as adults.

In my professional life, I have been fortunate to be observed many times in many different ways. I started working very young, and to work while being observed has shaped me both at the personal and the professional levels. I was fortunate to receive my professional development mostly through Loris Malaguzzi and Carla Rinaldi. Both Carla and Loris knew well how to analyze the different personalities of teachers and had as an objective to work with us continually to enrich our knowledge—and theirs, too, I believe. With regard to my personality, I am stubborn, and my characteristics are to be tenacious and persistent; it is not like me to give up because of difficulties. However, I have to admit that professional growth has been complex and not always pleasant in its process. As a person, I am one who challenges herself all the time to do better and to do more. Both Loris Malaguzzi and Carla understood this trait of mine right away, and I think that this was why they invested so much in my professional development as a teacher.

Gandini: *It must have been an amazing experience to be accompanied in becoming a teacher by people of such caliber, dedication, and vision.*

Gambetti: During that period of time, when they saw that I reacted in a negative way, they would tell me, "Look more carefully. Listen but do not judge too

While explaining to Amelia how the waterwheel works, a child understands that he has to modify his construction. From "The Amusement Park for Birds."

quickly. Try to understand. Observe." This strategy helped me a little at a time to learn to evaluate myself, so I would be angry with myself because I had made those mistakes. Of course, I would get discouraged, but then I would use my frustration to work on improving my work as a teacher and as a person. I truly understood that children, and really everyone, deserve the best and sometimes even more than that.

I would share these thoughts with my colleagues, and I also do that now when I meet and collaborate with other educators. In the work as educator, one should not be content with approximations. One cannot think that children can do and understand only a little; we should not be satisfied with "just a little." If educators are content with a little, they might think that a child can reach only small objectives. By doing so, it is as if we diminished our vision of the child. If, instead, educators learn to invest more in children's potentials and capacities, not only will they offer more opportunities and possibilities, they will also offer more to themselves as educators. I have always pursued the objective that children can always do more; if one as teacher does not try to do more, I think that he or she will never learn enough about what children's potentials are.

Gandini: *I have noticed, Amelia, that when we are working together with teachers and the time comes to sum up our day of professional development with them (as happened recently), you find words of appreciation about their work;*

immediately, however, you express the point that what they do is not enough and that more could be done.

Gambetti: Yes. Because it is true, more can be done. I believe that there is a risk that, when people are pleased and satisfied with what they do, they start to be less curious about life and less interested in what more could be done. If I think about all the work we have done in Reggio Emilia, if I think of all the interest that we have constructed at the national and international levels, if we had started feeling satisfied and did not continue to invest in the evolution of our work, and on research in innovation, we would not have done our duty either to ourselves or toward all those educators who come to Reggio from many parts of Italy and the world. We have a responsibility to continue moving forward and to evolve by keeping in step with a changing society. We owe this to children, ourselves, our community, and society.

Now, when I happen to see a school, such as the one we recently saw together where the children's entire day is planned on a board with curriculum-imposed tasks rotating every 15 minutes and where the cluttered space is lined with desks, I feel that I am in a place where I do not see respect for the intelligence of children, teachers, and parents, and I know that we both feel sad and discouraged. But I remember right away what Malaguzzi used to say in similar cases, "I suffer when I see those schools. . . . We can no longer remain indifferent when we see that a child and human beings are not respected, and this is for me a kind of violence which is done especially to children."

I understand and share the determination that there is in Reggio, as well as the strong will to continue to do research for innovation. I can see how hard and exhausting it is, but it is truly more and more the right thing to do to continue in this direction. There are new people in our educational system; there are very young teachers who do not know our history, but being part of that history right now, they can see its quality. I consider myself a fortunate person as I have known, worked, and was taught by Loris Malaguzzi and Carla Rinaldi. With them, we participated in research—also with you—and we had the opportunity to do our work giving value to our actions, understanding the importance of the process, always with the objective of doing better.

Gandini: *In my own small way, I also feel fortunate for having worked with Loris Malaguzzi, in part as his interpreter when he was in the United States. Tell me about your experience in this country.*

Gambetti: I like to include the experiences in the United States in dialogue with Reggio Emilia because I keep fresh in my mind my development and history there and because I work for Reggio Children and am also a member of the Advisory Board of the Istituzione. The way I work with teachers is not decided by me alone, but together with the educators involved. When I work in a new context, I make a great effort to connect my own experiences as a teacher in Reggio with what I am living in the particular new context. The schools with which I collaborate might have followed different kinds of process of educational work. At times, the collaborations can be less difficult if there are organizational structures that support the context—in particular where an exchange among teachers, children, and parents is already in place. That type of situation can support and maintain the positive level of quality that can be reached in our collaboration. At times, schools in this process might try to widen their experiences by entering into dialogue and exchange with other experiences or other schools that are working to improve learning through relationship.

This is why I like to work on professional development together with Margie Cooper in Georgia and South Carolina. I appreciate this work because there has been a great effort to keep different types of schools in the network and to use their different identities to construct common and shared resources. Meetings organized to present innovation in education from Reggio Emilia or teacher's work process to educators or parents can be part of this process of giving quality to the work in which the group of schools is investing. I think it is a constructive choice and attitude that is generated in the process of improving the quality of a school. I am referring here to the good quality of an experience that respects the child and respects people as part of a community and society. It is a quality that is also obtained through continuous investment in professional development. All this work continues to give life to experiences that in turn, I hope, contribute to generate others of good quality.

In Atlanta, there are some schools involved in this type of experience. Margie Cooper continues to observe the depth of learning through the work of professional development based on projects of study and research and how each school could learn to have more autonomy and as a consequence take a leadership role. I am deeply convinced that in the work with teachers in schools, it is necessary to have high objectives to reach. I think that this way of working gives teachers the same opportunities to construct an attitude and a will to learn more to invest toward the objective of high quality in education.

I began my experiences in the United States at the University of Massachusetts, Amherst, followed by the Model Early Learning Center in Washington, D.C., and the Reggio–St. Louis Collaborative in St. Louis, Missouri. With time, my experiences continued with the First Presbyterian Nursery School in Santa Monica, California; with L'Atelier School in Miami, Florida; and with MacDonald Montessori School in St. Paul, Minnesota; these are definitely interesting examples of investing in quality in education. Our work together is based on continuity, on research and study, to give value to our different contexts in dialogue. I would also like to mention collaborations in Chicago, Illinois, with the Chicago Public Schools and Chicago Commons, as well as with Boulder Journey School in Boulder, Colorado, where among many shared experiences was also the one of hosting the grand opening of "The Wonder of Learning" exhibit. In San Francisco, California, I have collaborated with the Innovative Teacher Project, the director of which, Susan Lyon, initiated the Roundtable Discussions in the Bay Area early in the 1990s. These are still ongoing, based on professional development schools inspired by the Reggio approach. More recently I have entered into contact with the Riverfield School in Tulsa, Oklahoma; the Blue School and the Beginnings School in New York City; St. John's in Washington, D.C.; and Maplewood public school in St. Louis, Missouri, which also collaborates with Webster University.

It is rather complex to work with schools that have different identities. It is hard to support different processes of learning. I think that even when it is valuable to maintain the level of quality one has reached, to open up to new goals, it is necessary to have an administrative structure that is organized, strong, and open to support progressive change. Therefore, I think that a good opportunity for schools that are investing toward high quality is to widen the network of relations with other schools that have the intention to participate in growth based on innovation. These initiatives are not only instructive but sustain new interactions, build new connections, and give hope to the work of educators and children.

Gandini: *I understand that creating networks of schools so that the quality and quantity of professional development can be shared and increased at the same time can be an ideal strategy.*

Gambetti: When I become part of initiatives of professional development with a group of educators, I try not to guide their work. Even if it is difficult for me not to make an immediate connection with my work and my experience in Reggio, I understand and I strongly believe that it is necessary to respect the rhythm of work of the group of educators with whom I am working. This is why different schools with which I have interacted have developed their work in their own ways. Some schools have been capable of constructing collaboration with me by analyzing their experiences and giving visibility to those experiences through the process of documentation of the work we have discussed together. During encounters open to the public, all the educators have been able to answer questions posed to them, showing a high level of awareness, including the motivations behind their choices and experiences. By doing so, they realized what journey they had been through and how much they have grown by making visible and explaining their work. When these levels are reached, educators themselves feel motivated to continue to pursue higher levels. They also become more open to share and accept different points of view, and above all, they become capable and not shy to speak about their work and thoughts. In fact, teachers then tend to change their attitude and understand how important and necessary it is to teach and learn at the same time.

Gandini: *Could you explain more about the process and journey you and Margie Cooper undertook with these schools?*

Gambetti: All the same passages have taken place with some preschools and one infant-toddler center, respecting the diversity of each of these contexts. Then another school started to collaborate. Many of the educators have gone to Reggio Emilia. In my view, our professional work within each context arrives at a crucial point when a trip to Reggio Emilia is an important step in the teachers' professional development. It is important to go to the source of the experience that inspires them, and it is now in process.

Gandini: *I wonder if it is better to go to Reggio only after there have been a certain number of experiences of co-construction and learning through relationship? If it is too early in one's own learning, might the surprise and wonder be too much and impede careful observation of the deep layers of what is in the Reggio Emilia preschools?*

Gambetti: I have seen both experiences. In any case, there are always reactions that are emotionally strong. Sometimes coming to Reggio Emilia makes the visiting educators realize important values of life not as apparent in their own schools, perhaps because of the complexity of opportunities that may not be offered. Those elements are often connected to the identity of their own work context. Exactly because the schools of Reggio are so different from one another, even if they are inspired by the same philosophy, the interpretations of the philosophical principles are different, therefore the schools offer a different visibility of their identity. Even after these visits to Reggio, there are teachers who do not continue to go deeper with their work, and they ask me how "to do Reggio." I explain every time to them that they are the ones who have to explain to me if, when, and how much they want to enter into a dialogue with the experience of Reggio, by first focusing on understanding and giving identity to their own context.

As Howard Gardner says, one cannot transplant what is done in Reggio Emilia to another place as if it were a tulip bulb, but if people want to change their context, the observation has to start from what their context offers and the sense of belonging that is there.

Gandini: *Going back to the power of observation, does what you describe lead educators to observe themselves in their own context?*

Gambetti: I urge educators to observe themselves, to observe their context, and to take up an attitude of research. We could reflect long and hard on the change of attitude toward one's own work. At times, the staff of a school changes while the group of educators is reflecting together, thus adding more difficulties to their work. I am referring here specifically to the United States. In Miami, for example, in the many years of collaboration with the school L'Atelier that I lived through with the director Simonetta Cittadini, there has been a great deal of turnover of teachers, due to various factors. However, as Simonetta is a very determined person in her quest for high quality, she has invested in the role of some teachers who stayed in the school as pedagogical coordinators, and their presence has given constructive continuity within the school. Therefore, I also think that the changes of personnel in some cases can be counteracted if sufficient investment is made in the collaboration, collegiality, and, always, on the quality of the work.

Gandini: *I remember that you said it is important to observe a great deal before having a dialogue about what the teachers consider difficult and problematic.*

Gambetti: The observation of a classroom or a space with a group of children and their teachers in action is something I do after some time that I am in a school, and this is decided in collaboration with the educators in the school, because it is a delicate thing to do. It requires a great deal of respect for the situations that one observes. In particular, to report one's observations, one has to be attentive to avoid judgments, but rather encourage the teachers to interpret their own attitudes while they were observed. As a strategy, I always encourage teachers, directors, or pedagogical coordinators to observe one another.

In any case, when I observe, I take the role of a listener about all that happens. Sometimes I could predict why something does not work or how things could work better, but I try to accompany the teachers to think and reason in such a way that as they exchange their thoughts, they come to understand by themselves without my being the one who says what things work or do not work.

Gandini: *Considering your narrative, you have also gone through various phases in observing both your experience in Reggio Emilia and your work in the United States.*

Gambetti: For me, in almost 20 years of traveling and spending time abroad, I have always gone through a process of learning. I have learned also by making mistakes, by taking risks, by analyzing my own work. In the beginning, I felt hurried and I was too direct in sharing my reflections. Perhaps the fact that I had a limited knowledge of the English vocabulary and thus of appropriate terms made me use words that were too strong. Now I understand increasingly that in certain situations it might have seemed that I was giving a fast evaluation rather than helping people to understand. My transformation happened especially in examining and revisiting my own reactions and points of view; I have been practically learning to document myself while I work. This way, I read over the notes I have been taking at the end of the day at school, and I write pages of observations about my work and about the reactions of the people who were listening to me. I understood that at times my intervention was more than a contribution and instead an evaluation, even if, on the part of the teachers whom I was observing, I never encountered resistance and my points of view were always welcomed in a positive way.

But then I realized that this attitude on my part could give the impression that I was the only one who knew how to see or how to behave with the children and adults, and as a consequence, I was the one risking to teach them how to work. The more I tried to rethink and observe myself, the more I succeeded to change things, the more time I was giving to the process of understanding a situation that I was observing, the more this extended time gave the teachers an opportunity to understand more. We learned how to assess situations together.

Gandini: *I see that in a way you intend to relate to the teachers with whom you are working as you were when you were working with children.*

Gambetti: Now I truly try to proceed in this way, giving a contribution by starting from a contribution that the teachers give to me. I look and ask for the analyses of a situation and deep thinking by people who work with me. This "slowing down," as well as the continuity of our relationship, have contributed greater integrity and value to our roles and interactions. When I work in a school, I work in a context that belongs to others, and this context has a dignity that has to be respected. This is why I try to see and understand with care and to respect teachers' way of working.

Gandini: *If we think in terms of your history in the United States and the many years starting from your beginning in Amherst, people have understood your way of working with teachers (and therefore also with children and families), but not all of them have been able to transfer that knowledge to others. Yet I think about your way of forming and trying to help people to become deeply aware and able to help others to understand more deeply. I think, for example, about Mary Beth Radke, who first worked with you and is now a teacher specialized in the joy of reading and learning; I then think of Jennifer Azzariti and the way in which she helps teachers in their encounter with materials. She has a way that helps to bring out the best in teachers.*

There are many seeds that you have planted. You describe how teachers work with deeper awareness and find the way to work with and respect children, which tends to transform their school into higher-quality places of research in innovation.

Gambetti: There are various people with whom I collaborated in the United States who have roles of leadership in their work and have been able to create quality programs in their schools. In these schools, one can see an image of children, teachers, and also parents that are competent. All of this does not happen automatically. It requires an investment of time to give value to the needs or rights of all involved; it requires continuity, persistence, hard work with a sense of ethics, integrity, rigor, responsibility, and reciprocal respect.

FAi
IL BICICLETTIERE

Chapter 11

The Inclusive Community

Ivana Soncini

Editors' Note: Italy is a recognized leader in the general movement for integration and inclusion of persons with mental and physical disabilities. Since the mid-1970s, international organizations have pointed to Italian education for children with disabilities as the most inclusive of all the countries of Europe (Begeny & Martens, 2007; Gobbo, Ricucci, & Galloni, 2009; Philips, 2001; Vitello, 1991). This movement for integration and inclusion started in the 1960s when institutions for the disabled and the mentally ill were closed down, and health services were reorganized into decentralized units for each region. Reggio Emilia was never isolated from that movement but always stayed in touch and responded to the movement of those times. The deinstitutionalization movement in mental health created a parallel movement within education against segregation of students with disabilities and today is entering yet a new phase in shaping thinking about inclusive work with immigrant families and children.

In 1971, the Italian Parliament passed the first law concerning education for children with disabilities and established the right to a desegregated education of

This chapter, compiled by Carolyn Edwards, draws on interviews and material collected by Lella Gandini from Ivana Soncini in 2010 and 2009, as well as interviews with Ivana Soncini reported upon in Gandini and Kaminsky (2006), Kaminsky (1997), Palsha (2002), and Smith (1998). We acknowledge the contribution of Dr. Cathy Carotta of Omaha, Nebraska, for critical comments.

children in public schools. This law and a subsequent law in 1977 are directed to the entitlement of children aged 6 to 14 years to an inclusive education, unless a child's disabilities are so severe as to make it impossible to function in a regular class. However, health and education authorities recognize the need for early intervention, and many regions have long had programs serving children aged 6 months to 6 years (Cecchini & McCleary, 1985; McCleary, 1985). In the academic year 2004– 2005, 10,084 young children with disabilities were enrolled in the Italian state (federal) system of preschools—1.04% of the total number of students. They had various types of disabilities: mental and physical (9,270 children), sight (299 children), and hearing (515 children) (Organization for Economic Cooperation and Development, 2006, p. 363). Many other children with disabilities participated in municipal and private preschools.

According to the 1971 Italian law, a child with disabilities is defined as one with persistent difficulties in mastering skills and behaviors specific to the chronological age; the definition includes children diagnosed as having Down syndrome, cerebral palsy, mental retardation (IQ less than 60), aphasia, childhood psychosis, severe language disabilities, and severe learning problems. Deafness and blindness were included in following years. The local health service is the responsible agency for the diagnosis. The assessment is usually based on observations conducted in a variety of settings, neurological and psychological evaluations, and standardized testing where applicable. The local health service remains continually involved over the years, teaming with the child, family, and teachers. The same people usually remain on the team over long periods of time, providing continuity of service to the child, family, and school and aiding in transition across different levels of schooling. A holistic approach to the child is stressed, and for the most part, psychotropic drugs for behavior management and strict behaviorism are not well accepted (McCleary, 1985).

In 1977, another national law specified strategies for implementing integration in the public schools. A maximum of two children with disabilities may be integrated into any one class, and no more than 20 students are allowed in integrated classrooms. Extracurricular activities must include all students. Support teachers, who receive special training to work with children with disabilities, are paired with general education teachers in integrated classes, and both teachers interact with all students. Although no specific help is mandated for children with mild learning or behavior disorders, in practice, teachers and health service team members are aware of children below the norm and should provide them special attention without the disadvantages of labeling (McCleary, 1985). As a result of this legislation, Italy has made general education classrooms the primary educational setting for nearly all students of compulsory school age. Current research and anecdotal reports confirm that the large majority of parents and educators in Italy are supportive of inclusion (Vitello, 1991, 1994), although rigorous studies of student outcomes are by and large not available.

The Italian system of education for young children with disabilities is a downward extension of the integration model for the compulsory school years. At both levels, the philosophy of integration has progressed from physical integration ("mainstreaming" at least part of the school day) to full inclusion, with the child included in curricular activities and an accepted member of the classroom community. Italy has eliminated the deficit model and has placed the primary focus on changing the nature of the educational environment to serve all children (McGrath, 1999).

Several outside observers with special education expertise have commented on the atmosphere of welcoming and respect in the Reggio Emilia preschools and the way the learning environments stimulate senses and perception and support the developmental and social needs of children across the full range of abilities (e.g., Nurse, 2001; Palsha, 2002; Philips, 2001; Smith, 1998). These observers have also raised their own questions, for example, concerning the extent to which the regular documentation of children is used to monitor progress and set appropriate targets for individual children (Philips, 2001) and how teachers address learning and behavior issues of children not identified under the Italian system but who would be included as special needs under the broader definitions used in the United Kingdom (Nurse, 2001).

Children with disabilities or special needs are often referred to as "children with special rights" in Reggio Emilia; Ivana Soncini uses all these terms interchangeably.

I, Ivana Soncini, am a member of the Pedagogical Coordinating Team of the Istituzione Preschools and Infant-Toddler Centers of the Municipality of Reggio Emilia. I am responsible for the inclusion of children with special rights in the municipal infant-toddler centers and preschools of Reggio Emilia. I have a degree in psychology, but that was not a requirement, and I could have trained in another field, such as education or pedagogy. My specific role was created to facilitate the inclusion of children with disabilities in the municipal infant-toddler centers and preschools of Reggio Emilia. I work with all of the schools and all of the families of children with disabilities. Our founder, Loris Malaguzzi, thought it was important to include children with "special rights" in our schools. He felt that we could improve our pedagogical experience and understanding of all children as a result of this inclusion.

DIFFERENCES AMONG CHILDREN: CREATING A COMPLEX EDUCATIONAL CONTEXT

We wanted to embrace, not ignore, the concept of differences among children. We wanted to encounter these diverse children and try to understand what they could teach us. Loris Malaguzzi strongly believed that having the children with special rights in the schools could stimulate us, as teachers, to think in terms of a much broader pedagogical approach for all children, to broaden our horizons for all the children. Malaguzzi felt that differences could stimulate new thoughts and new ideas because when dealing with differences in all children, you cannot use homogeneous methods. The encounter with differences stimulates healthy uncertainty. It makes it necessary to interpret, understand, and observe more. Having these differences in the educational context trains the teacher to adopt an attitude of being able to use this new way of thinking for all the children.

In our view, a disability is just one of the possible differences a particular child could have. We are interested in looking at how this child has integrated a disability into her life and the strategies she has used. We want to get to know this child—to understand her subjectivity, the world she lives in, and the image her family has of her. We are interested in the same things in this child as we are in the other children. We want to have an encounter with these and all exceptions. Each child has his or her own exceptionality. Having a child with special rights in a class makes it necessary for the teachers to broaden the opportunities, possibilities, and communication codes for all the children. It forces the teachers to create a more complex educational context.

IDENTIFICATION AND REFERRAL: PROMOTING A THREAD OF RELATIONSHIPS BETWEEN SERVICES

We try to include children with special rights in our system as early as possible. We collaborate closely with the local health service where these disabilities have been certified so that we know who these children are even before the parents apply to our program. Nowadays there is a strong culture of inclusion in Reggio Emilia, and it has really changed our way of being and the way of being of these families. A generation ago, having a child with a disability meant a total breakdown of the equilibrium of the family. For example, many women quit their jobs to care for this child. However, when families have adequate educational and rehabilitative support, this equilibrium does not break down. We have seen some extraordinary situations of families of children with special rights helping and becoming resources to others. This can only happen when the parents feel supported.

The process of identification usually starts at birth in the hospital. When the babies are examined by the doctors at birth, they are referred to that family's pediatrician if there is any question that they may have a disability. The National Health Service certifies that the child has a disability that requires special services. Some disabilities, such as autism or other conditions, will not be identified at this early stage. The hospital acts as an agent of referral, and this works well in Italy. Resident immigrants, who are not Italian citizens, also have rights to free health services of this type for their children. The special services available to the children through the National Health Service include speech therapy, physiotherapy, psychomotor therapy, psychology, and social services. Here in Reggio, all of these health and support services are available to these families, and are all public.

The children with special rights have absolute precedence over all other children in admission to the municipal infant-toddler centers and preschools. Furthermore, we have chosen not to apply any specific criteria for accepting children or not accepting children with any kind of disability. Families do pay fees for enrollment in the infant-toddler centers and preschools, according to income like all others.

To promote inclusion in our infant-toddler centers and preschools, before the enrollment period begins each year, I visit the National Health Service doctors who do the examinations and screening of the infants. Because of the National Health Service network, the only cases we may miss are children who do not have status as residents. The pediatricians explain to the families that the children can attend the infant-toddler centers and preschools. Unless the child has a very serious condition, the physician encourages the families to apply to our system of infant-toddler centers and preschools. I get a list of certified children, and when the enrollments come in, I check to see who has not applied, so that I can contact the pediatricians of those children and see whether together we can encourage the parents to come in for a meeting to discuss our program. Thus, close relationship and coordination between systems is important.

In addition to receiving priority in enrollment, families of children with special needs have the right to select which preschool or infant-toddler center their child will attend. They sometimes base their choice on school location, presence of friends, or the physical structure of the school. For example, one family with a child who was blind chose La Villetta Preschool, which contains three stories and a narrow staircase. We were worried about this request and asked the parents about it, and they said, "We feel if our child learns to master La Villetta's environment under the careful guidance of the staff and children in the school, he will feel confident to tackle all other environments he encounters for the rest of his life."

"il sole . il fiume": Lorenzo

The sun and the river, by Lorenzo. From Looking at Lorenzo, Girotondo Infant-Toddler Center–Preschool, 2003–2004.

"io e Lorenzo stiamo giocando a palla di dietro nella scuola": Federico

Lorenzo and I are playing with the ball behind the school, by Federico. From Looking at Lorenzo, Girotondo Infant-Toddler Center–Preschool, 2003–2004.

In my role as pedagogical coordinator, I maintain the thread of relationships between the school, the family, the health services, and the therapeutic services. Because I am on the Pedagogical Coordinating Team, I coordinate with the other *pedagogisti* as well. We prefer the various specialists and therapists to work with the children in their center or school when it is appropriate so that this takes place in a normal context, not at a special office. When the various specialists or therapists come into the schools, we want this time to be in harmony with the child's normal experiences there. So even physiotherapists, for example, use the equipment and the furnishings that are already there in the school. I am in charge of maintaining the contacts, making decisions with these people about how much of this therapy is needed, and coordinating their work inside the schools with the children. It is also useful for them to have a point of reference within the school system, in that part of the child's life.

COMMON TYPES OF DISABILITIES IN OUR SYSTEM: EVERY CHILD HAS EXCEPTIONALITY

In past years, the most common types of disabilities we saw in young Reggio children were Down syndrome; motor disabilities, including paralysis; psychosis; schizophrenia; autism; blindness; deafness; developmental delays due to chromosomal abnormalities; and emotional and psychological problems (Smith, 1998). In contrast, today more than half of the Reggio young children identified with disabilities have a diagnosis of autism or autism spectrum disorder. Most of the others have intellectual/cognitive disabilities. These two categories are the most common. I want to make clear that the Italian health system does not formally identify as "childhood disabilities" all possible conditions, such as attention deficits and language delays. (This is different from some other countries.) Nevertheless, in the context of our infant-toddler centers and preschools, we do respond to those children's individual learning and emotional needs. Indeed, we seek to be responsive to every child's unique strengths and needs.

The number of children with Down syndrome has greatly diminished in our context. We have a few serious cases of children with cerebral palsy. We have few blind children currently, and no cases of diagnosed psychosis. Clearly, autism spectrum disorders and intellectual/cognitive disabilities are the most common kinds of problems we see in children today. For example, of 40 children identified with special needs who are currently in our system of municipal infant-toddler centers and preschools, there are 20 who have a diagnosis of autism spectrum disorder.

The increasing number of young children with autism spectrum disorders is startling, and mirrors a trend seen not only among elementary-aged children in Reggio but also in children throughout the region of Emilia Romagna, and in the world beyond.[1] It is an issue of concern that has been receiving great attention.

Of course, I am concerned by the numbers. How is it possible that in the past 10 years, we have gone from a few cases to these high numbers? The answer I often hear is that we are better prepared to notice and observe autistic-like behaviors, but truly this is not enough explanation for me. I have observed a great variety of differences among the children. It is only in a few cases that one can refer to the classical clinical description of autism. Often, children with diagnosed autism vary greatly one from another. I think that this should be a focus of further research.

THE TRANSITION PROCESS: A LONG AND GRADUAL ENTRY

All children in Reggio Emilia have a long and gradual entry into our infant-toddler centers and preschools. This period may be even longer for children with special rights to ease their separation process and closely attend to attachment. For example, in one case of a child with autism, the parent and child visited the center for an entire year before the child began to attend the program formally.

We do a number of things to orient the new child and family and pay particular attention to sleeping and eating patterns. In our meetings with the parents, we seek to alleviate any possible fears they may have about their child starting school. Our relationship with the parents has to be carefully planned and thought out. Building a positive relationship is the most important part of our preliminary work: all arrangements are made with the comfort of both the child and the family as top priorities. Parents report that when we ask them so many questions about their child, we give them confidence that we understand everything basic about their child's needs and requirements, their likes and dislikes. This is especially comforting to them when their child is an infant, and they may already be feeling guilty or reluctant to leave the child with anyone else. Also, the question-asking process provides a kind of modeling to the parents and encourages them to make their own inquiries about their child.

Work with a child who has special rights is considered to be a shared educational task involving the parents, the child's classroom teachers, the *pedagogista* of the infant-toddler center or preschool, and myself. This means that, like all our work with children, we begin with observation and documentation. Observation and documentation are always fundamental, but they are of particular benefit with regard to children with special rights.

What we do is this. When a child with special rights first comes into a class, we know the diagnosis that has been made of his disability and we know what we have learned in the direct interviews and observations with the parents. However, we do not know anything about the child's new situation and possible relationships in the environment of the center or the school. So, first of all, we need to get to know the child. At the beginning of the year, we offer the child the range of possibilities because we need to understand his choices, his desires. After a rather long period of

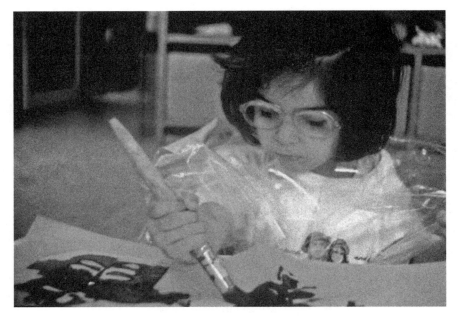

Sometimes a brush with a large handle and paint of a strong color help a child do satisfying work.

initial observation and documentation, we jointly compose what we call a "Declaration of Intent." This is a written agreement among the school, parents, and health service team to ensure collaboration. The declaration includes statements about the methods and materials we will probably use, as well as any ideas about how the work might be carried out. It puts a focus on relationships, with people, objects, and the environment. On the final pages of the Declaration, the projected plan of the year is outlined and includes goals for the child and family, classmates, teachers, and health service team who will support the education of the child.

The Declaration of Intent for the child with special rights is not a formalized, binding document that staff would have to follow without flexibility. In fact, as we get to know the child, the teachers are expected to revise, reinterpret, and refine the child's program continually, under the supervision of the school *pedagogista* and myself. The point of the plan is not to focus only on the child's disabilities but also on his or her tremendous capabilities. It is important for us to offer many rich possibilities and have high expectations. Our work is to help the child find the way, and we do this through motivation and interest.

You may wonder if there are expectations from the health or educational systems that are observable, replicable, and measurable. In our view, it is the role of the physicians and the health system following the children to collect data that can be evaluated for statistical purposes. Within the infant-toddler centers and preschools, we tend to avoid standardized assessments and instead use our pedagogical tools to follow the children. From the beginning, the children are assessed by the health system to evaluate their disability and their progress. That information is important, but then we go further. The collaboration we have built up with the health system is powerful, and we try to have constant and continuous relationships.

PARTNERSHIP WITH FAMILIES: EXCHANGING IMAGES OF THE CHILD

When the family is comfortable and feels it is possible to share this event of their lives with others, they have a much greater desire to be involved with the child and are more likely to be interested in the quality of their relationship with this child. For example, many years ago, the children with special rights stayed in school all day. Increasingly, we see that families are eager to take their children home early and spend time with them. I have also seen the families put amazing strategies into action and utilize the most unexpected resources to confront their situation. We need to change the attitude that we have to teach the families something new. We must not forget that they are the ones who have had the child at home, often for a year or two before the child comes to us, and they have a lot to teach us. Our attitude toward the families is to exchange together and offer our different points of view to build an overall educational project for the children. Perhaps our point of view, as teachers, is slightly more detached because we are not as emotionally involved as they are with their children.

Both perspectives are valuable. For example, many children with complex physical disabilities will learn to feed themselves at school. The mother teaches us a lot about the way the child holds her spoon, the way she sits. However, the mother may also say, "Don't give her any solid food. She might suffocate." Yet the health service may have told the school that it is all right to give solid food to this child. So, in trying to give this child solid food, we add something to what the mother has already begun. After seeing our experience, the mother may try to give the child solid food at home. It is this constant kind of exchange.

Very often, we see that some families have difficulty participating in the class meetings with other parents, and some decline to participate at all. This makes us ask, "Why is this happening?" and we work out other strategies. With such families, we schedule more frequent meetings with the family, teachers, and me. For example, we might show them a video or some other documentation that we have done with their child. Video is a powerful tool to use with children with special rights to know them better and to use in discussions with the families. With video, we can grasp the smallest details of the children's changes.

Besides the daily exchanges, we keep a very close watch on the overall home–school information exchange. It is extremely important that we document what happens at school for the children with special needs and share observations with their families. We need to produce photographs of the children in the educational context, images of how the other children relate with their child. Very often, there are certain things the parents are afraid to ask the teachers about their child—for example, how the other children view their child. Yet they are imagining what goes on and how the other children deal with their child. Very often they imagine a negative situation, and this is why they are afraid to ask.

Our goal is to give the families the possibility to construct a new image of their child. It often happens that the family goes home from the hospital not only with a child with a disability but with a whole list of what that child cannot do. What we want is to stimulate the families to imagine what can happen and what is possible, and this can only take place when children are included in the educational context. The children have the right to be respected in their growth and development; they do change and learn.

Let me relate a story about a girl who did not communicate verbally and would tap the lead end of her pencil on paper continuously, making dots on the page. It was irritating for the teachers. Once when we were filming this child, I asked the children, "What do you think she's doing?" There was no indication that the children saw this as bizarre in any way. They said, "She's leaving marks. She's leaving traces." The psychologist who had been working with this girl completely agreed with their point of view. It was the only way this girl could leave traces of herself, her identity, and it was the children who suggested this. As a result, we altered the direction of our educational project with her. We also shared the documentation with the family.

In all of the documentation of experiences in the classrooms, the children with special rights appear and therefore are visible to their own families, as well as all the other families. I do not think that the difficulty or reluctance of some of their families to participate in class meetings is due to the demands that the children make on the parents. I think it depends more on how much these parents can abandon the image they had of their child before the child was born, their idea of how their child would be. Some parents have talked to us about this, and they may have difficulty meeting with the other parents when they see these parents with the children they wanted to have. We cannot always help these families completely because this is a difficult situation and the problems are deep.

In the current era, our partnerships with families and the local health services have become supportive and sustained in important ways. The professionals at the health services in Reggio Emilia consider not only the medical but also the educational aspects of treatment to be very important to children's growth and development. Children with autism come to the clinic twice a week to receive speech therapy focused on the emergence of spontaneous language. They also receive behavioral intervention, what we call *structured pedagogy,* which involves a mild and flexible form of behavior modification.

Models for working with children with autism have proliferated, and the particular framework we favor in Reggio is based on an American approach known as the Denver Model[2] (Rogers & Dawson, 2009). By now, we have in our "collective DNA" a philosophy of relationship-based care and education for young children that has spread even within our health services. In our infant-toddler centers and preschools, great importance is given to relationships and their quality. Thus, also in the clinical setting, attention is paid to creating an emphatic child–adult relationship, a playful relationship, a relationship that takes into account who the child is. For instance, a young child with autism who does not want to participate in a structured interaction or to follow others is never forced to do so. The child is guided to do things that strengthen very precise cause-effect connections and support the therapeutic relationship of child to adult.

The health professionals are further convinced that this kind of formal adult–child intervention should never be all that is provided, because what the child learns in the clinical setting may not generalize to other settings. They recognize that the school also has a strong therapeutic influence and contribution to make. Therefore, the health services designate one of its clinic teachers to meet each child with autism once a week in the child's infant-toddler center or preschool. This professional, prepared in the field of autism, also works with the regular teachers in the center or school to show them how to talk to or behave with the child. Indeed, in our infant-toddler centers and schools in Reggio, we now use the principles of the Denver Model in our instructional interactions with children with special rights, and we find it useful as a way of listening to children and encouraging language. Of course, we contextualize the techniques to our situation. An example of this is provided in the observation of Matteo (see the following text box).

Finally, to complete the circle of partnership, the local health services employ sets of educators who make home visits to each family to see how the child lives in his or her own context and provide the parents helpful strategies with their child. All of this intervention involves an enormous financial commitment, and yet it is still not enough. Starting this year (2010), following our request, the health services have scheduled meetings devoted to parent education, or to put it better, group counseling and therapy, to support the parents with regard to their personal issues surrounding caring for their children with special rights. For example, there are parents who do not seem able to tell their own relatives or even their own parents about the diagnoses for their child. Others have difficulties getting together with their friends. These group sessions are an attempt to support the parents in dealing with their difficult emotions and concerns. It was high time for this to happen! Up until now, we in Reggio Emilia have not provided any formal group counseling or therapy services as they do in the United States for families of children with special conditions. We have not provided organized programs with psychologists or therapists, though we have had some families who have organized themselves into self-help groups.

MATTEO AND HIS SUPPORTING TEACHER

Matteo is a 5-year-old diagnosed with autism spectrum disorder.[1] He has been attending La Villetta Preschool for 3 years. In the beginning, he did not speak and tended to throw objects that were nearby, but he has improved greatly. Now it is snack time. The supporting teacher prepares three chairs and a stool in front of the bleachers where most of the children are sitting. Matteo is encouraged to sit next to the teacher, facing the bleachers. He touches her face. Rosi takes Matteo by the hand and guides him to the kitchen to prepare a fruit plate. She carries the plate, and Matteo follows her. He gets the fork from the plate and moves away from her. The teacher intervenes to stop him, while Rosi asks him, "Where are you going?" They return together to stand in front of the group sitting on the bleachers. Matteo sits on a chair between the teacher and Rosi.

The teacher says, "Call out the friends." She then gives Matteo, one at a time, the cards with the photo of each child. Matteo looks at each picture, then looks at the assembled children, and calls out the name of each child. The child who is called responds right away and comes to use the fork to spear a piece of fruit from the plate, which is sitting on the stool. When Matteo has called a name, he hands the photo card to Rosi, who holds a little box ready to collect them. The teacher smiles, and the children who are called look pleased as they come to get their piece of fruit. A couple of times, Matteo gets distracted, and Rosi pats his face. He smiles and goes on with the task, with the children responding nicely. Every time he says a name, the teacher or one of the children say, "*Bravo!*" or "*Bravissimo. Tommaso! Bravo!*" (confirming that it was Tommaso, in that case).

At a certain point, Rosi shows him, pointing with her finger, one of the pictures just handed to him by the teacher and tells him, "Look!" He says the name and adds, "At home." Several children say, "*Bravissimo!*" One says, "He did not even look for him!" When Matteo comes to his own photo card, he says, "This is me." Rosi caresses him and laughs and takes the photo card to place it in the little box she is holding. Matteo takes a piece of apple with the fork. When all is completed, Matteo and Rosi go off together to throw out the extra apple pieces.

1. Besides Soncini's examples and stories in this chapter, there are two additional published case studies from Reggio Emilia of children with special rights: Luca's story (see Gandini with Gambetti, 1997) and Stella's story (see Smith, 1998, pp. 209–213).

CLASSROOM ORGANIZATION AND COMMUNITY:
FRIENDS BEGINNING TO DREAM FOR THE FUTURE

When we include a child with special rights in a classroom, there is a third "supporting" teacher included in this classroom as well. She is not a special teacher, but a teacher like the others. In fact, part of my role is preparation of these support teachers because they have not received any specific training in special education. This is not a disadvantage; on the contrary, it is a positive choice because we consider the child with special rights as part of the group, as one child in the peer group. We continue to emphasize this exchange in observing the children from many points of view. The support teachers are chosen from the list of the teachers who participated in the competition for a regular teaching job. Currently, they are not required to have a special degree qualifying them for working with children with disabilities, although such a degree program now exists at the university level. Such a situation will not last much longer, however, as families are inquiring about the preparation of the support teachers.

Having a third (support) teacher permits the child with special rights to work in small groups. Working in small groups makes it possible for the adults to observe more closely and pay more attention to all of the children. It also enables the initiation and consolidation of friendships and relations in a kind of intimate context. It makes it possible for the adults and other children to create relationships with the child. We have found that routines, small everyday actions, are marvelous occasions for exchange, orientation, and giving value to emerging capabilities.

Generally, we include only one child with special rights per class in both the infant-toddler centers and preschools. There could be two but never with the same disability because we do not want comparisons made between the children. The teachers in the classroom are immediately stimulated to respond to and use the whole range of expressive strategies (vocalizations, signs, gestures, eye gaze, facial expressions, bodily postures, to name a few) in order for the child with special rights to be able to live and stay in this context.

Having a child with special rights in their class is highly educating for the other children because it forces them to adjust their behavior, language and communication, even their physical contact. This contributes to the children's acquisition of knowledge because it requires them to be more flexible. It stimulates the children to realize that the encounter with the child with special rights is possible. I have observed the most extraordinary encounters among the children in these classes, and I have never seen any of the other children hurt or harm a child with physical or motor challenges. I have seen many impressive examples of empathy and caring, as illustrated in the story of Marco in the accompanying text box. I have also seen children use some extraordinary body language in order to communicate with a child with limited verbal language. Children do not place a negative

MARCO AND HIS CLASSMATES

When Marco arrived at Anna Frank Preschool, he had already spent a year at the Salvador Allende Infant-Toddler Center. During that previous year, the shared objective had been to try to increase his social-relatedness and help him interact with the world and those around him. Born without eye lobes, he wore prostheses that needed to be periodically cleaned and reset, a process that may have been somewhat difficult for him. His family lived in an isolated way, and therefore, he was without contact with other children. His parents, above all his mother, were suffering feelings of grief and depression. His teachers wondered, what were Marco's perspectives? Who was and who is Marco? How could he be helped to find his way in the classroom space? How could we as adults make ourselves recognizable and known to him? Could Marco develop verbal language? What kind of exploration with his hands could we expect? What motivations could we develop in him to walk toward areas identified by their sound?

In the infant-toddler center, the decision had been to get to know Marco better by choosing spaces inside and outside the classroom that were distinctive for the sounds and resonance of their materials. For example, the teachers had made percussion musical instruments available in one area, bells attached to a climbing structure in another, construction materials involving metal and wood in a third, and a pillow made of furry material on which to sit at circle time. They also found a rug with a thick border that he could easily feel when he was crawling, and they placed it where he could play with other children.

The year at Salvador Allende was like a rebirth for Marco. He started to use verbal language, above all to construct utterances (phrases) that he used to ask for help. For example, he said, "Help me." "I want to get up." "I want to sit." "I want to stand." He also started to walk around accompanied by an adult and did not show difficulties of movement. He did not yet use language spontaneously to name objects, and his exploration of material with his hands was very limited.

When he entered Anna Frank Preschool, Marco showed great pleasure every day in meeting his classmates, who liked to greet him at the door when he arrived and help him take off his coat. His mother was also very pleased! He could easily find his cubby because it featured a three-dimensional shape of a little animal that was easy for him to recognize.

The teachers and children at Anna Frank discussed and shared the challenges of Marco to find solutions that might help him move from

(continued)

place to place independently. How could they help him know the path to the bathroom, directly connected to the classroom? How could they help him recognize the way to go from his classroom to the kitchen and to the *piazza*? Could the children find or place in the *piazza* something that he liked very much so that Marco would want to go there to play with them? All of these were relevant questions because Marco still made few attempts to move or walk around by himself and showed little spontaneous exploration with his hands of known objects even when they were made available to him.

To make a way for Marco to find his way toward the bathroom, the children thought of the idea to create a tactile path, using a strip made with a solid plastic rug with bumps in relief that he could feel with his feet as he walked. They experimented with different surfaces and types of carpets by walking with their eyes closed until they found the one they thought would be best. For the pathway to the kitchen, they thought about a rope with bells attached, and this was set along the wall, starting after the door of the classroom. Finally, thinking about going between the classroom and *piazza*, his schoolmates first chose elements in the *piazza* and the classroom with which they saw that Marco particularly liked to interact: a rocking horse near the door in his classroom and the piano in the *piazza*. Their ideas were many and demonstrated great variety; and they took into account Marco's needs, which were ever-changing, and the difficulties that they gradually encountered.

What was important to his teachers was that the children looked forward to playing with him and were trying to "think about Marco and think as Marco." They empathized with him and seriously pretended to have his limits and his possibilities. The children discussed the problems and possible solutions both in small groups and in the large group. Marco participated in the small group discussions, so that his opinion was involved. These discussions seemed to activate in Marco some spontaneous and independent movement. In particular—and we documented this on film—Marco used the piano keyboard and discovered the different tones from low to high. He began to play with the sounds in the company of one or two other children and to show great interest in moving around by himself at the piano, standing up easily to reach the keys of contrasting tonalities. He even created some games with a friend, consisting of a dialogue of sounds (stimulus and answer) and some patterns of rhythm. All of this was very encouraging in Marco's ongoing story.

connotation on these differences; rather, they recognize and, therefore, legitimate these differences. This is yet another example of how the teachers learn from the children. Whenever I go into the schools, it is always the children who suggest strategies and approaches for working with children with special rights that we can't always see. This is why Loris Malaguzzi always said, "Things about children and for children are only learned from the children."

An important question is how we promote small groups of children that form around their peers with special rights and offer a sense of belonging. Often the groups form by themselves during morning assembly in which the teachers share with the children the various possibilities for that morning. For example, "Teacher Luana is going to be doing a clay activity this morning. Who wants to work with her?" Very often, it is the children who choose to work in that group and also choose to include the child with special rights. When the teachers organize the groups, they tend to put the child with special rights into a group of skillful children who are good communicators. Very strong friendships have been built among the children, and we respect that in terms of their ability to organize themselves into groups.

Let me tell you about the development of a little boy named Umberto. When this child first came to our program 4 years ago, he could not sit up and spent his time lying down. We discovered that he had a very low tolerance for stimulation on his hands, but not on his face. The teachers worked with the other children in the classroom to encourage them to interact and form relationships with him. Once we observed a beautiful interaction between Umberto and two girls in his class. They were all listening to some soft, dreamy music, and the girls were pulling different colors of gauzy material over his face. They were also playing bells for him. Umberto was sitting on the floor and when he fell back, the girls would help him sit up. The teacher came in and out of the situation to interact when she felt it was important to encourage the children or make suggestions. She talked to Umberto about how to stay up and suggested ways the girls could help him. Once when Umberto started to fall back and caught himself, the teacher shouted from across the room, "*Bravo*, Umberto, *bravo!*" Umberto enjoyed this time with the girls very much. He smiled and clapped and made noises with his mouth. The girls were very happy to be with him as well. They would touch his face and sometimes he would pull the cloth off himself. The girls also helped to blow his nose and wanted to take care of him.

Very often the other children give us ideas and suggestions about how to work with children with special rights (just as they might do with other peers who are arousing reactions or protests for their behavior). For example, we might say to the children, "This is what we've got to do with Umberto. How can we do this?" Often they come up with ideas and suggestions that we have not considered, or pick up on the communicative signals, including gestures, and other nonverbal methods, used by the child with special rights.

The other children learn that the child with special rights can be wherever they are. Even if the child does not move on her own, she can still be kept close by. The important thing about offering all these possibilities to this child is that she becomes a part of our thinking and, consequently, becomes a part of the thinking of the other children. It is extraordinary how, over time, this child does become a part of their thoughts. They notice when that child is absent. They are working with certain materials and say, "Caterina has to come and do this with us." The spaces in the infant-toddler centers and preschools are not separating spaces but instead spaces that encourage meetings and encounters. There are always message boxes where the children can give and receive messages, and very often, the child with special rights is the one who receives the most messages in his or her box. These are all ways of keeping this child in the group and in the thoughts of the group.

Certainly, this spirit of belonging must start from the beginning. When a child with special rights enters a preschool classroom, we speak first with the other children and have an open discussion with them. (In fact, we do something like this when any new child is about to enter the classroom, to help the new friend be welcomed by the group.) We share information concerning the new child and engage the others. We might say, for example, "Your new classmate cannot talk just the way you do, so what can we do to communicate with him?"

Likewise, at the end of the school year, if the child is moving on to primary school, we try to speak with the other children about what advice we could give to his next teacher. In one case, we asked the classmates what could be transmitted about their special friend, Francesco, to the primary teachers. It was actually part of a project we called the "Bridge Project" to gather materials to accompany a whole group of children from preschool to primary school. The friends recognized the possibility of Francesco learning to read and write even if he needed a longer time to achieve this. They remembered all the small changes he had gone through during their 3 years together. We believe it is important that the classmates have dreams about their friends with special rights; they will continue to be peers and mediators in the future.

THE HUNDRED LANGUAGES OF CHILDREN: ENLARGING THE PALETTE OF LANGUAGES

When we are not able to use the accustomed codes of communication, predominately the verbal language, it forces us to remember that each of us is born with various sense organs that we use for encountering the world and communicating. When a child does not use verbal language, the teacher has an enormous responsibility in interpreting the alterative ways that child communicates. Being in this situation also reminds us that every child has his own individual timing and strategies for learning.

Inclusion of differences improves the general educational context in yet another way. By developing learning experiences with children, we cannot and do not want to look at final products or results. We try to keep our attention on the motivation and the strategies that a child puts into action to reach those results. The changes in the children with disabilities may be minimal, but these changes must be given value when they occur. Thus, their presence teaches us to be attentive observers. We are in debt to the children because their inclusion contributes so much to the quality of our educational approach and experience.

An extraordinary example is that of a 4-year-old I shall call Enrico, who was in his second year at Andersen School. He was diagnosed with a general psychomotor delay due to an undetermined genetic condition. His motor skills had improved, but he was much smaller than the other children. He had no oral communication, yet he understood a lot more than what the doctors had told us! He had developed his own complex sign language system, indicating he was making conceptual syntheses. For example, when he wanted to talk about other people, he indicated their characteristics that stood out to him. We used verbal language when we communicated with him, but our verbal language became enriched by his sign language.

That same year, across all of our centers and preschools, we were doing an investigation of how preschool children considered the identity of their city (Davoli & Ferri, 2000). The teachers asked the children questions and, from their answers, tried to understand the children's image of the city. At the Andersen School, we asked ourselves how we were going to learn about the way Enrico saw his city. How could we enable this child to communicate what he thought about the town? It was a big challenge. We had taken photographs of the children and the town during an outing around town, and when we went back to the classroom, we projected 10 images of this outing on a screen and asked Enrico to indicate what he liked about Reggio. We told him he could point, draw, or use sound materials to communicate his choices. Incredibly, Enrico indicated the sounds and noises in the town, with particular attention pointing to a saxophone player who had been playing on a street corner. It is important to understand the context of this situation. How can a child who does not communicate orally indicate his choices and "image of the city"? The palette of languages had to be very large for him to express his thoughts.

The outdoor garden invites children of different abilities to play together.

SOCIAL CONSTRUCTIVISM: CHILDREN SHOWING US THEIR APPROACH TO LIFE

I believe that children with disabilities have the right to live in a school that allows them to intersubjectively construct a positive representation of self—a representation that is in continuous evolution. When we refer to the philosophy of observation, to the process of documentation, we also refer to constructivism, in which knowledge is built through interaction with others. The object of knowledge, what is observed, is not considered separately from the subject who observes. To know children who have special rights is difficult. Therefore, in our work with children, to construct interaction and knowledge, we must reflect continuously and carefully on our own philosophical premises. We must always pay attention to the construction of semantic understanding on the part of the adults and their way of knowing. The children with special rights have compelled us to direct our attention to our own self-evaluation and to find instruments that would make it possible for us to self-evaluate in relationship to them. We agree with the ideas of Jerome Bruner and Franco Kayer, in that we believe we are responsible for building a structure, or scaffolding, to decode, deconstruct, and construct our communication with the children. It is essential for us to pay attention to our interpretive actions and to be aware of our limits and our creative potentials.

We have learned from the children with special rights, even more than with other children, that emotion and cognition are tightly connected. We have also learned, as I have described, to pay attention to other languages beyond the verbal. The children have motivated us to respect their time and rhythm but also to analyze our own interpretation of the idea of change. How do we interpret change? Traditionally, change has been perceived as a movement toward normality. Historically, the goal was to bring a child with special rights as close to a state of normality as possible. This idea of change focuses on the deficits of a child.

In Reggio, we are trying to see change in a realistic way by considering what is and is not possible in relationship to the child. This concept of change is especially relevant for children with the most complex conditions. This process is a long one, especially for the families who are anxious to see change in their children. Often, the families initially think about change in the traditional way, as a process of normalization. We are fortunate to be able to follow children over a long period of time, up to 6 years in the Reggio municipal infant-toddler centers and in the preschools. Therefore, we have the responsibility of helping the families to see the possibilities and the limits of their child realistically. The children often accept their limits more readily than their families. Our experience has taught us to be more attentive in listening to the families and trying to understand their expectations, rather than influence them with ours. The dialogue with the families regarding their expectations is delicate because if we do not understand what their expectations are, it becomes a dialogue between people who seem unable to hear one another. We, as educators, have had to learn to listen to the perspective of the families.

We have also learned that if we pay attention to the differences among children and, in particular, children with special rights, we can see that each child has a different way of being a child. It is important to let the children show us their approach to life. From their approach, we learn how to be with them. The children's approach to life is a kind of research to try to understand the world around them—a very human way to try to know. Our experiences with children with special rights have given quality to our work because we have become better observers. We are better able to discuss our own limits and expectations and to consider the children's interests in a deeper way. Because of their physical conditions, the evidence of the children's interests is often subtle and difficult to recognize.

Yet in Reggio, we have learned that each child has a different way of achieving intersubjectivity. We have combined our knowledge of pedagogy with the clinical suggestion to help children become more aware of others. We have found that in a situation rich in stimuli, the children with autistic tendencies tend to explore intersubjectivity through motion and movement. We have learned that children can become aware of others by, for example, taking turns throwing a ball into a basket. We have seen that when any three children sit at a little table with clay, they tend to glance at each other from time to time. In one case, there was a child who was overwhelmed by the circle of children, and it was suggested that the child be kept away from the others. However, this child found his own solution. While sitting in the circle, he put his hands over his eyes and gradually moved his fingers so that he could slowly see the group of children. He was accepting the group in his own time, which means that there was a possibility for exchange with the others.

PROFESSIONAL DEVELOPMENT: INCREASING THE CAPACITY OF TEACHERS TO SEE

Within Reggio Emilia

Professional development is critically important in a system like ours, if the progress that we have made is to be preserved and continued. My role is to serve as the psychologist and *pedagogista* responsible for the educational and rehabilitative project concerning children with special needs. However, I cannot be the only one who maintains the culture and history regarding the relationships with families, teachers, and the local health services. Therefore, the municipality has placed at my side a young *pedagogista* from the group on the Pedagogical Coordinating Team to start to give her professional development.

Considering that we live in a time of diminishing public financial resources, we are also seeking to organize more professional development for the support teachers (and others) who work with children in our preschools and infant-toddler centers. We are also bringing in the support teachers who work in elementary schools. All these educators work for the city, and we are trying to create a network of professional development among them because they all serve children with special needs who are aged from birth to 10 years. This exchange is absolutely fundamental because it is a way to connect past, present, and future in the children's lives; for instance, it allows teachers who support children in elementary school to know how the children were at younger ages.

We are becoming more intentional in providing professional development to the support teachers and in giving them observational tools more specific to their work. Keep in mind that we have an extraordinary context for the observation of children. For instance, a child who has delays in cognition can be studied as he constructs a tower with blocks or sets the table for lunch, both difficult tasks for such a child. The observations are always followed by planning discussions that include support teachers and classroom teachers about what intervention and support to give to the children. I have also obtained permission from the university for our support teachers (and other teachers) to audit or participate in the course on childhood disabilities.

In observing, we follow the same methods we use with all other children but take advantage of our long experience in the schools as well as our constructivist approach. For example, a support teacher might approach a 4-year-old child who is well adjusted in many ways but who has no idea about how to start building with blocks or making a drawing. The child might first be perplexed by questions that seek to elicit higher-order reasoning, such as "What do you think we can do with these blocks?" or "You just did that, how do you think we should proceed next?" or "How could you draw that idea?"

With all children, we look for the ways in which they recognize choices and possibilities and represent their experience. Mental representation is learning; it is a way of knowing. Children who appear to lack the ability to plan or represent may find help through a teacher intervention that encourages them to start to plan or begin a drawing concerning the part that is of most interest to them. If we gently suggest and gradually help children focus by asking questions, then we are working in a way that is in line with our philosophy, as inspired by Loris Malaguzzi and the psychological theories of Lev Vygotsky and Jerome Bruner. We must learn to help each child exactly where the child finds difficulties; it is as if we are making a choice to proceed with greater attention, although at a pace that is slower than the way we usually do.

Relevant to this discussion is the fact that we have also had an influx of new teachers entering our system. With this influx comes a need to return to studying how children learn. When an educational system such as ours has consolidated good practices that were originally based on close knowledge of a particular set of children, and then time passes, a risk arises that the set of practices becomes separated from a deep knowledge of contemporary children and families—that is, from the particular ones who are with us today. Rather than jumping quickly into decisions about techniques, I feel that we should go back to studying the processes of learning by different children. We must always remember that we have a new generation of teachers and greater diversity of children than 20 years ago. The educational style of parents is changing; children come to us from different countries and economic backgrounds. Therefore, it is important to return to the fundamentals of observing individual children and recognizing that each one has unique ways of learning and developing.

Through our research, we also want to add to the literature on longitudinal development of children with disabilities. In starting this initiative, we have gained the assistance of Tiziana Filippini, who now will dedicate a number of work hours to support us in this collaboration. The documentation effort, called Officina Educativa (Educational Forum), will be a system of collaboration among educators who work on issues related to children with disabilities from birth to 10 years of age. We are also trying to involve the support teachers in Reggio who work for the state (national) preschools.

Long ago, Lorenzo Milani wrote in *Lettera a una Professoressa* (*Letter to a Teacher,* Scuola di Barbiara, 1967) that a secular and truly democratic school should provide opportunities to everyone, considering all the differences (and societal inequalities) to allow each person the possibility of offering the best of himself or herself. Schools should not advantage the rich over the poor; all children have the right to equal possibilities no matter their background. Milani's message has been influential in Reggio Emilia, but the young generation of teachers does not know this heritage, and therefore, we have to recapture and present it to them. I realize that we who are older have this history inside of us, and we can help younger educators encounter it. For example, reflections about differences are more than appropriate because of the differences found in our schools today. Because we live in a small city, it is possible to do it. We can widen the circle of learning and the exchange of knowledge acquired in the field through professional development.

Reaching Out Beyond Reggio Emilia

Besides the professional development that we conduct inside our city, we often conduct professional development sessions in Italian schools outside Reggio. While viewing videotapes of experiences from one of these schools during a professional development session, we observed that the children with special rights were well cared for by the teachers. However, we also observed that these children sometimes did not interact with the other children at all. While viewing the videos from the Reggio schools, teachers from elsewhere have been surprised to see so many children interacting with children with special rights. They told us that their children do not approach children who cannot speak because children with disabilities might be afraid of the others; this of course makes interaction difficult. However, it seemed as if the teachers were imposing their own interpretations on the children—it was the teachers' belief that children with disabilities would be afraid if other children approached them and would not be able to communicate with them.

How can children with special rights construct their own subjectivity, their own sense of self, when they only see other children at a distance? We realized that in many of these situations, the teachers or therapists were acting almost like bodyguards who stayed close to the child, trying to anticipate all his or her needs. The adults seemed to be helping out of a sense of pity rather than a belief in the potential of the children. In other situations, there were adults who were so clinically specialized, who knew so much about the diagnoses of the children, that they tended to approach them from too narrow a framework that placed constraints on what they thought would be relevant or possible.

In both situations, artificial barriers or limits influenced children with special rights in their efforts to develop a sense of self. Instead, we, as adults, have to become aware that we might be the obstacle to children's development of subjectivity. The most important thing that teachers, other adults, and other children can do to support the development of a positive representation of self is to recognize those efforts and attempts that the children with special rights are making on their own behalf in interacting and learning in the classroom and at home.

The competence of children with special needs is sometimes missed because teachers fail to see it, as if they are blind to it. If we are aware of this tendency, then we can do something about it. Observation and documentation are essential. The more situations we create when we can observe and document the children, the more we will be able to see. For example, one child might shut down in a situation that has to do with exploration of materials but open up for a game at a table. Therefore, we must prepare many situations, then document and interpret them. In fact, I am encouraged when teachers share inconsistencies in a child's behavior because it shows that they realize there are different ways for a child to reveal what is going on in her mind. Videos, in particular, record minute changes and painstaking efforts that teachers do not easily perceive in the moment; they allow us to study and review moments that are difficult to notice without this visual tool. We can also use video to reveal long-term changes in children. We have found that during professional development sessions for teachers who are going to be placed in supporting classroom roles, it is crucial to show videos of experiences with the children with special rights during the course of the previous year. Such sessions allow us to hear the interpretation of the new teachers and integrate them with the interpretations of the teachers who worked with the children the year before.

On the basis of all we have learned about working with the children with special rights and competencies, we need to start thinking about passing on our experiences to the city at large to have other places and other spaces that are welcoming for young children with special rights, to make the whole community more open and accessible to them. I would hate to think that the children are included only in our preschools and infant-toddler centers and are not visible outside those walls. Those of us who were pioneers have a huge responsibility. We need to talk more directly with city planners, architects, and designers and move these ideas out into the community at large.

NOTES

1. Autism, first described in 1943, is no longer considered a rare, stigmatized disorder. In fact, the range of developmental disabilities now known as "autism spectrum disorders" affect an increasing number of individuals worldwide. Some have pointed to environmental toxins or other factors that may be behind the "explosion" of cases, whereas others believe that the increased incidence reflects improved awareness by the public, evolving diagnostic criteria, and better reporting. For further discussion of the historical and cultural elements of the condition, including description of the experiences of families of autistic children in several countries, the editors recommend the recent book by Roy Richard Grinker (2007).

2. The Denver Model, or Early Start Denver Model, is a developmental approach to treating autism originally developed by Dr. Sally Rogers, who was then at the University of Colorado. She provided preschool intervention for young children with autism that was first called the "play school model" because intervention was developed in the course of children's play activities. The theoretical foundation for this approach was Piaget's theory of cognitive development. Over the years, the Denver Model has incorporated some behavioral procedures, or Applied Behavior Analysis, but has retained its focus on engaging the autistic child's social initiative. The Denver Model, like other relationship therapies, focuses on the child's unique concerns and on establishing relationships with other people.

REFERENCES

Begeny, J. C., & Martens, B. K. (2007). Inclusionary education in Italy: A literature review and call for more empirical research. *Remedial and Special Education, 28,* 80–94.

Cecchini, M., & McCleary, I. D. (1985). Preschool handicapped in Italy: A research-based developmental model. *Journal of Early Intervention, 9*(3) 254–265.

Davoli, M., & Ferri, G. (Eds.). (2000). *Reggio tutta: A guide to the city by the children.* Reggio Emilia, Italy: Reggio Children.

Gandini, L., with Gambetti, A. (1997). An inclusive system based on cooperation: The schools for young children in Reggio Emilia, Italy. *New Directions for School Leadership, 3,* 63–76. Also published in *Innovations in Early Education: The International Reggio Exchange,* 1997, *5*(3), 7.

Gandini, L., & Kaminsky, J. (2006). To know a child with special rights: An interview with Ivana Soncini. *Innovations in Early Education: The International Reggio Exchange, 12*(1), 1–11.

Gobbo, F., Ricucci, R., & Galloni, F. (2009). *Inclusion and education in European countries. Final report 7: Italy.* INTMEAS Report for Contract. Lepelstraat, Netherlands: DOCA Bureaus for the European Commission's Directorate General for Culture and Education.

Grinker, R. R. (2007). *Unstrange minds: Remapping the world of autism.* New York: Basic Books.

Kaminsky, J. A. (1997). An interview with Ivana Soncini. *Innovations in Early Education: The International Reggio Exchange, 5*(3), 1–6.

McCleary, I. D. (1985). Overview, Italy. *Journal of the Division for Early Childhood, 203.*

McGrath, B. (1999). National policy on inclusion of students with special educational needs in Italy, Ireland, and the United States (unpublished paper). Available at http://www.eric.ed.gov/PDFS/ED436875.pdf.

Nurse, A. (2001). A question of inclusion. In L. Abbott & C. Nutbrown (Eds.), *Experiencing Reggio Emilia: Implications for pre-school provision* (pp. 62–71). Philadelphia: Open University Press.

Organization for Economic Cooperation and Development. (2006). *Starting strong II.* Paris: OECD Publishing.

Palsha, S. (2002). An outstanding education for ALL children: Learning from Reggio Emilia's approach to inclusion. In V. R. Fu, A. J. Stremmel, & L. T. Hill (Eds.), *Teaching and learning: Collaborative exploration of the Reggio Emilia approach* (pp. 109–130). Upper Saddle River, NJ: Merrill Prentice Hall.

Philips, S. (2001). Special needs or special rights? In L. Abbott & C. Nutbrown (Eds.), *Experiencing Reggio Emilia: Implications for pre-school provision* (pp. 48–61). Philadelphia: Open University Press.

Rogers, S. J., & Dawson, G. (2009). *Early Start Denver Model for young children with autism: Promoting language, learning, and engagement.* New York: Guilford Press.

Scuola di Barbiana. (1967). *Lettera a una professoressa* [Letter to a teacher]. Florence, Italy: Libreria Editrice Fiorentina.

Smith, C. (1998). Children with "special rights" in the preprimary schools and infant-toddler centers of Reggio Emilia. In C. Edwards, L. Gandini, & G. Forman (Eds.), *The hundred languages of children. The Reggio Emilia approach: Advanced reflections* (2nd ed., pp. 199–214). Greenwich, CT: Ablex.

Vitello, S. J. (1991). Integration of handicapped students in the United States and Italy: A comparison. *International Journal of Special Education, 6,* 213–222.

Vitello, S. J. (1994). Special education integration: The Arezzo approach. *International Journal of Disability Development and Education, 41,* 61–70.

Interlude

From Messages to Writing: Experiences in Literacy

Laura Rubizzi and Simona Bonilauri
Describe Their Research

Laura Rubizzi is one of the most experienced teachers in Reggio Emilia. She teaches at Diana Preschool. Simona Bonilauri is the pedagogista *for Diana and has been supporting Laura in this research on children's emerging literacy. For a long time, teachers in Reggio have supported children in sending messages. Visitors always notice the message boxes in all the preschools that are used by children to communicate with one another. In this way, children gradually become aware of the importance of writing, and their teachers appreciate that sharing a message with an audience represents a necessary mind-set for children to maintain as they continue to learn how symbols work. To introduce the conversation, we hear about the project background from Claudia Giudici, Pedagogista and President of the Preschools and Infant-Toddler Centers, Istituzione of the Municipality of Reggio Emilia.*

Claudia Giudici:[1] The approach to "codes" and, in particular, the alphabetic code is not a new idea in our experience because for quite some time, we have intentionally prepared contexts and strategies that give attention to symbolic

213

learning. The research projects on this topic took place in all infant-toddler centers and preschools some years ago. The shared notion from the beginning was the development of the capacity to use symbols, which is present in children from birth.

We encounter that capacity when very young children—even before the emergence of language—begin to use their body and objects symbolically. Next children develop the ability to use symbols separate from the objects to which the symbols refer, and subsequently, they develop the capacity to use the alphabetic and numerical code.

What were the assumptions and aims of this inquiry? We began with the idea that written language is a cultural invention. It must be an object of knowledge before it can convey knowledge. While the children try to understand this "object" in reality, they also reinvent it. That is, they personally and subjectively reconstruct it by creating original linguistic theories that are individual or group driven.

I would like to clarify what we mean when we say that a child reinvents writing. First of all, we do not mean that children reinvent letters but, rather, that they reconstruct the rules of the code. To use the system of writing productively, a child must understand the process of its construction and the rules of its production. In other words, the child destructures and restructures writing.

We have noticed that even very young children in the infant-toddler centers, without specific invitations or requests, try to explore the alphabetic code and begin to differentiate writing from drawing. These attempts are spontaneous as children are immersed today more than ever in a society in which "visual" communication predominates. We have valued and documented these first initiatives by children.

The theoretical references that we used to begin the inquiry are connected to research by Emilia Ferreiro and Ana Teberosky, part of a group of researchers who have elaborated on this research, including Cristina Zucchermaglio. Their research is longitudinal and transcultural. They highlight a process that is at the basis of the construction of the written language and focus on children through four years of age.

We have given a great deal of attention to these studies because they are based on a socioconstructivist approach:

- They recognize an active and constructive role in the process of knowledge building in the children. Children do not simply receive information from their context, they transform it in order to understand it.
- They recognize that to read and write is much more than "learning the alphabet" and that it is not only limited to the learning of "instrumental" techniques.
- They maintain that literacy is not only the acquisition of a technique of transcription of the code but the discovery of the rules by which the code functions.

Therefore, these research studies move the concept of writing from an instrumental view, which is based mainly on motor-perceptive skills and abilities, to a

From Messages to Writing

Teachers in Reggio always have done much work with *messaggerie*, the process of using mail boxes and message exchange, as part of the general exploration of communication and emerging writing and reading.

Teachers of the Diana Preschool 4-year-olds classroom decide to try something different, by starting this year without the message boxes. They meet with the parents to explain their intentions and ask them to join in looking closely at the emergence of writing and reading among the children.

Teacher Laura Rubizzi observes the 4-year-olds writing. "Do you want to write your name? How are you going to do it? What do you need?"

"We need letters," they say. The children now want to talk about and write the letters in their names. They try to write certain letters using different pens and papers. One child practices the letter A over and over.

Another child carefully writes O, a letter that has been of special interest to the children. "Is this the true O?" the children wonder.

The child shares his O with his friend. Children discuss what they are doing and compare their various viewpoints.

One girl stands to read some of the posted letters, pointing as she identifies them, reading (in this case) from left to right. Note that this is the same girl seen previously, writing with her left hand.

Regular meetings are held by the teaching team to discuss what they are observing and what they might do next with the children.

The children take serious pleasure in writing and reading words in small groups. In this way, they are able to consult and help one another.

Children write letters or words on Post-it notes that they like because they can be placed on a surface and moved around easily. One day, many notes involve three words, MAMMA E PAPA ("Mom and Dad"), arranged in various orders. Two children (LUCA ZINI and ANGELICA) have printed their names.

Throughout the weeks, documentation is collected and studied by the Pedagogical Coordinating Team. Tiziana Filippini and Simona Bonilauri meet with teachers at Diana Preschool.

As time goes by, all over the preschool, the older children's letters are turning more and more into words and phrases. In the 5-year-olds classroom, a girl places on a large board her strip of paper saying, GRASIE SEI UN VERO . . . ("Thanks, you are a true . . .").

Among other legible words on the board are BUON COMPLEANNO ("Happy Birthday"), CUORE ("Heart"), and a clearly printed, but slightly misspelled, COME SEI BELA ("How beautiful you are"), where the large C wraps expressively around the message.

Emerging literacy involves all the ages. The entire preschool gathers for the grand opening of the store of the 5-year-olds class.

The store contains many signs. One in the window says, COMPRATE TUTTE LE COSE ("Buy all the things"). Three sets of signs declare the store's name, PUNTO IMPRONTA.

conceptual view of writing that focuses on the existence of progressive conceptualization. These studies are useful on a didactic level as well. Our investigations confirm that if we know how to observe children, we will be able to understand the processes that children activate and participate in their learning paths in a way and time that best supports their growth and evolution.

It is important to eliminate right away the perplexity that could result from this statement at the infant-toddler centers and preschools. We are not trying to refer to an anticipation of the formal teaching of reading and writing that takes place in the primary schools in Italy. Rather, we are trying to think toward a different quality of literacy.

The objectives of our work were as follows:

- to investigate how children explore in original ways the written code when they have not yet received any formal instruction and
- to make it possible for the children to be accompanied in transforming their theories as they come closer to the conventionalization of the alphabetic code.

Laura Rubizzi: We have done so much work with the *messaggerie* (the process of using messages, as part of general exploration of communication and writing). Yet, I thought that it was time to explore other ways for children to encounter the written word. So I thought of the many aspects that are part of communication and also what happens when children show their interest in communicating and when they have a teacher next to them.

Last year (in fall of 2009), I was ready to begin to change my approach to introducing the written word to children. I had a new group of 3-year-olds, as well as the support of Simona Bonilauri and other *pedagogisti*. With that support, I deliberately did *not* set up message boxes in the usual way or speak about "messages" with the children. Instead, we decided to take more time to document through video how children who are 3 years old communicate with one another and with their group. We started to observe first with the still camera how children communicated their emotions with their faces and bodies.

We took pictures and then showed the photos to the children involved and asked them, "What were you communicating?" We showed the photos right away and then again after some time and found that the children were interpreting the same photos differently. Then we started to play some games in which the children were trying to make their friends guess what they were trying to communicate with each other. We took more photos and tried to create an "alphabet of emotions" in which the children were trying to communicate different things, such as "I like that" or "That's funny," with their eyes, mouth, or body. The intention was to see whether children could communicate in a different way from just using words.

Usually, when children turn 4 years old in our preschools, they are invited to write their names, and they become very passionate about it because it is almost as if they are representing themselves—in fact, creating a symbol of themselves.

That is true of children from any national origin; they are pleased with themselves when they can write their own name. We see that children who are quicker at that want to help their friends learn to write their names.

Now it is October 2010, and my 3-year-olds from last year have become a group of 4-year-olds. I moved up with them to the 4-year-olds' classroom, as we always do in Reggio.

In line with our research, what I did at the beginning of this school year was to ask the parents to wait on teaching their children to write their own names or any other words because I wanted to study this transition. I also explained to the parents that we hoped to study and document this transition when the children discover the world of signs in our classroom and learn about letters and writing their names.

So we tried not to put any signs or symbols in the classroom that would indicate individual children, and we have noticed that the children, when the parents came to pick them up, would pick up their own work and show it to the parents. We have seen that the children were eager to document and make known what they were doing. The children were showing us they needed a way to identify their individual work and space, and the ones of their friends as well. So that was when we started to help the children to write their names, and we noticed that some children were already able to recognize certain letters.

The Italian language has the advantage of being highly phonetic in its orthography. The children start to recognize the first and last letters of their name and their friends' names. On the wall of the 4-year-olds' classroom, there are the traces of the communication center from last year's group, the marks where the mailboxes had been. Because we were not going to use the mailboxes this year, on each box space, we wrote "*Ciao*" ("Hello"), and so this became a greeting, "*Ciao, Ciao, Ciao.*"

When the children saw the writing, they said, "Oh how nice! You have written our names."

"Are you sure?" I asked. "Do they look the same?"

"Yes," they answered.

"Do you all have the same name?" I asked. "Are you all the same?"

"No," they said.

"How could we write your names?" I asked.

Simona: It is important to provoke curiosity, thinking, in the children.

Laura: At this point, the children became curious and motivated about writing their names. We think that by proceeding this way, we help the children think about the way names are written and consider that different-sounding words go with different letters or sequences of letters. In general, we ask children who are 4 years old, "Do you want to write your name? How are you going to do it? What do you need?"

Usually the children will answer, "We need letters." (They say it as if this were easy.) So I say, "Would you like to do it?" And they will try and make marks, and then they encounter their first difficulties and conflicts. If they succeed in writing a letter, or a mark that is almost a letter, such as the letter "O," then the children typically begin to be surprised that the same mark or letter can be in two names. One thing we have noticed is that children have such a strong sense of possession about their name that it is difficult for them to accept that a certain letter can be found in more than one name. Or perhaps for some children, it just doesn't make sense that two people (who look so different) could have names that look the same.

Then when the children try to write a letter, they are also concerned that they write it correctly, or as they say, make "a *true* letter."

Simona: We discussed this with Jerome Bruner and told him that the children had used the word *vero* ("true"). Bruner said they didn't really mean true in the sense of "truthful," but instead they meant true in the sense of "right" (that is, correct). They wanted to find an agreement about what was the right "O" (the true "O"). This behavior on their part made us understand that they were ready for conventionality—that is, they wanted to find a "convention," a shared formula for the letter "O."

Laura: Such a moment of discovery is also a time in the life of the class when the children, who have been together for a year, or more than a year, are beginning to search for ways to establish shared rules. Thus, this moment also involves the construction of group rules.

Simona: They are in transition from an individual way of being together to a shared way.

Laura: They feel the need to find rules. Not a rule that is imposed on them, such as *in school you do it this way,* but rather in *finding the right way,* so that everyone will be able to understand each other and do things correctly. How could we agree on how to do this? Let us try this rule in our community. We might change it, but we will see that all respect it.

It is a very particular moment in the growth of children. It is a very particular moment in their development in which they discover the need and the pleasure to decide and choose, and agree about, something together. We have seen this happen with regard to writing, in particular, and it is especially significant because it is a wish shared by all of the children.

And yes, they also like invention. What has particularly surprised me during the past 2 years that I have been working on this research with this particular group of children is their strong attitude of autonomy. They have never asked me to write something for them. They have never asked, "You, who know how to read, how do we write this?" Instead they say, "Wait a minute. We are going to try."

But every year, so consistent is the effort of 4-year-olds to find the right way to write that as the year progresses and many of them turn 5, they try to write a word that has an "h" in it, or a word with major orthographic problems, and they might spend even half an hour on it. In my view, they are making valuable attempts, as a group. They say, "Let us try. No . . . It is not right yet." The children's goals become larger, and they write stories, they create newspapers. They have never changed this sort of attitude, and they always work in this way. It seems very beautiful to me because later when they are about to go off to elementary school, they continue to write. Then what they say is, "According to you . . . In your view . . ." Or they ask the girl in the group who seems most competent, because there is this attention and awareness that you need the others to proceed.

Now, with this particular group of children, at 4 years of age, they have had long and difficult discussions, and we see that they do not yet distinguish what is arbitrary from what is convention. For example, they were writing indifferently from right to left or left to right. They were trying and did not have an order to proceed in reading.

And in this discussion, they could not reach certainty. However, we understood that this transition was valuable. What could be the "right" (*vera*) letter? So we opened the discussion to all the children in the class. If it is truly such a big problem, each one of you should write his or her own "right" letter. Therefore, we divided them into groups, and we asked each child to write his or her "right" letter. We decided to divide them into groups in such a way as to help them make progress. It was important for them to realize that their problem was understood and that they were supported.

The children were more or less at the same level of research, and it was important for the teachers to show them that with all of us in this together, they could succeed. As we went forward, it appeared as if the children, working together with the teachers, were going to write a set of rules—what I called, the "tables of the law," our own law. The children got the idea of this new way of supporting each other (with the teachers), and they realized that they could work this way, arranging themselves in different places around their classroom environment, and they started to write their "right" letters.

After that, the children became more relaxed. They had written all the letters, one after the other, and now they could write words.

Then there arose from the group the children's first theories about writing words—a collection of very different theories. For example, someone suggested making a series of letters and photocopying them, but the question arose, were the letters then too much the same?

Each child wanted to contribute ideas. Then there was a new process, with all the children trying to write words, but now in groups of four or five children; inside some of those groups, even smaller subgroups formed or groups reformed in other ways. For example, there might be two children working together who would look for the help of a friend whom they thought was more competent than they were or who had discovered something special.

The documentations we have are mostly about six children working together. At the beginning, each child seems to feel certain and self-assured. As they work in their group, they nevertheless look at each other's work, and also consult each other. Sometimes, one child says, "We need this letter!" or "We have placed this letter, and now we need . . ." and they try to read and sound out the letters. They try to read, even if they do not know the sound of all the letters.

Simona: But they do call the letters by name. At least the children who know them do.

Laura: Yes, some children know, and there are some children who absolutely want to write. For example, we had two children who had established together that they wanted to write, so they spent an immense quantity of time writing the letters, also drawing on some knowledge they had acquired from an aunt or their mother. The other children treated these two as consultants, even though they usually had doubts, even with regard to the teacher's knowledge!

In one of the first videos that we took, I proposed to the children that we would all write the same word, and that word would be the name of an animal. I suggested this idea because the children were wanting to transform the *atelier* and fill it up with the names of animals. It was an incredible goal of theirs, considering that they did not have the competency. But I said, "Fine. With which animal's name are we going to start?"

I suggested the symbol of our Diana Preschool, "Zebra," and they said, "No, that is a small name!"

"So which one is a big name?" I asked. "Is it squirrel?"

"Yes, yes, but . . ." and there began a long discussion about the size of a name and the size of an animal. (Young writers often think long objects should have long names, and short objects should have short names; they still blend drawing and writing in their minds.) It is a delicate matter for the teacher to be present but also to be ready to step a bit back and not push too much. Instead, I want to help them to be aware of the knots that are present in what they are constructing.

For example, I wrote, and they copied, "ZEBRA."

"Are you really sure you have written ZEBRA?" I asked them. "Try to convince me."

One child said, reading the word, "AR-BEZ."

"No," I said, "ZEBRA is written there."

"No, no," said the child, pointing to the end of the word. "You have to start to read from here!"

"But one cannot read as one likes, one time from right to left, and one time from left to right," another child declared.

This is the usual tone of our encounters.

In another group in which there were two children who were quite competent, I said, "Let us try. I will write, and you dictate the letters to me." So in that case, I made mistakes on purpose, and they corrected me. That became very interesting!

In one of the families, there was an older brother who was in second grade and very competent. He entered into our research and was very much loved by all the children as a consultant. For me, it was also interesting to observe this child who had experienced a traditional type of teaching. He knew all the rules, but he learned through the exchange with the younger children *why* the rules were that way. He had learned rules as procedures without understanding the reasons they exist. Therefore, it seems to me that older children who have learned to write in the traditional way may still have a lot to learn from younger children who construct their own learning.

What was interesting for me was to explore the children learning to write in this autonomous way, something that had not been previously explored through our use of the *messaggerie*. In the past, when children wanted to write important messages, they would say to us, "Will you write it for me? Then *I can copy it.*" In that situation, the children learn less about the construction of words, because they are seeing the message as a whole and not attending to the parts—the words and letters. This time, I wanted to understand more about the processes of learning when children use a different strategy and become more fully the authors of their own writing and reading.

Furthermore, this research involved starting with the 3-year-old children. In contrast, the system I had used previously, in which children copied messages, could only really start at age 4; the younger 3-year-olds simply shared objects in their message boxes. That prior system provided a good beginning and an interesting way of working. It depended on the teacher establishing a rule for the 3-year-olds about what was allowed to be placed in the message boxes—for example, objects and toys, materials nicely wrapped in a package, messages cut out from newspapers, or an audio cassette on which the child had recorded a message. That prior way of using the message boxes was above all connected with the idea of presenting a *gift.* It was satisfying to the children and communicated friendship and love, and sometimes it involved children using their personal symbol to indicate the sender of their message, but it did not specifically involve *words.* It was more a way for the 3-year-old children to cut and glue, thereby creating something special for another person. At times, teachers or parents might add a message in words to the child's production, but the main focus remained the gift.

In this research, I instead wanted to focus less on *giving* and more on *communication* with the 3-year-old children.

Simona: With this new focus, the teacher can initiate very different experiences with the children. The situation changes significantly. Our task previously with the youngest children had been to create a richness of material and objects. But in this research, there is a completely different register. The focus begun last year with the 3-year-old children discovering that they could "read" others' facial expressions and physical movements.

Let me remind you that in 2004, we conducted another study of children's knowledge of writing in which we were looking not only at 3-year-olds in their first year of preschool but also at 2-year-olds in their last year of the infant-toddler center. Any research study begins with a definition of the situation, and when we did that earlier study, we were focused on children's earliest graphic expressions. (Part of this research is included in the exhibit "The Wonder of Learning: The Hundred Languages of Children," in the theme "The Enchantment of Writing.") In fact, I now understand that we were creating a different context in which to look at the development of writing. We became open to seeing different things than we had in the past, so we actually began to see them. Now, in this current project, we are trying to synthesize this new research with what started about 5 years ago. We have documentation from that earlier phase, but we only began to collect good video documentation in 2008–2009.

Laura: The way we started this new research was with an initial period of professional development for all the staff of the Diana Preschool, guided by Professor Catellani of the University of Modena and Reggio Emilia and Professor Giacomo Stella. As part of that process, we teachers at Diana took videos covering specific moments, and then, with Simona's support, we studied and reflected on them. We would discuss and make decisions on how to move on with the children, thus adjusting and relaunching our work with them on writing. We edited the videos, and they were used for professional development at other schools in Reggio, along with those same professors. In that way, other schools became engaged with us in the discussion of how children learn.

Simona: During that time, Laura was a mentor teacher, but she did her mentoring here at the Diana Preschool. The videos include important passages showing diverse parts of the process, as Laura changed the groups of children who worked together and also altered details of strategy. However, for one little boy and one little girl, we can observe the entire journey over a year and a half period of time. The collection of videos is difficult to share for professional development with outside teachers because they are so extensive, but I have selected some stories out of them to use. Those of us involved in the research have all made comments, and we are trying to put together the notes and the video excerpts.

We should add that many things took place at Diana this year that are part of the context of the inquiry and the schoolwide focus on the emergence of writing. The classroom of 5-year-olds, for example, decided to open a store. They conducted research by visiting their favorite shops in town, and then they gathered items to sell and organized prices and publicity. They named their store *Punto Impronta,* which means "place of impressions," "tracks," "traces," such as fingerprints, footprints, or other marks left behind. An interesting metaphor, don't you think? The signs they made called on many of their new writing skills, and also showed how much children this age infuse their emotions and concepts into the figurative way they draw letters. The whole preschool attended the grand opening of *Punto Impronta.*

As a last word, let me say that this experience, which we call "La Vera O" ("The Right O"), is useful to describe, because it involves an important principle: *Learning does not begin when we feel the need to teach the children.* Rather, when the children feel the need to render their communications conventional (shareable), they become ready to learn to write in a very short time. They are ready to construct by themselves (with our support) all the rules of the written code. We have discussed this with the teachers at the elementary school because it is important that we reciprocally understand each other. We know that there are different functions at the two levels, but when the children go on to first grade after the kind of experience we are describing, they really are ready to start writing. We also had an advocacy goal in mind. Through this research, we could fight the idea that reemerges periodically in Italy of starting formal schooling at age 5 years instead of 6.

NOTE

1. Claudia Giudici, "The enchantment of writing: Between signs and writing. How children approach the written codes," paper, 2005. Published in *Innovations in Early Education: The International Reggio Exchange,* 2011, Spring Vol. *18*(2), 1–4. Reprinted with permission.

Part III

Documentation as an Integrated Process of Observing, Reflecting, and Communicating

Chapter 12

Pedagogical Documentation: A Practice for Negotiation and Democracy

Gunilla Dahlberg

THE POWER OF PEDAGOGICAL DOCUMENTATION

Running through the work of Reggio Emilia, as it does through the chapters that follow, is the practice of pedagogical documentation. Most simply expressed, pedagogical documentation is a process for making pedagogical (or other) work visible and subject to dialogue, interpretation, contestation, and transformation. It embodies the value of subjectivity—that there is no objective point of view that makes observation neutral. It is rather a base for nurturing negotiation by making perspectives explicit and contestable through documentation with others, be they

Earlier versions of some portions of this chapter appeared in Rinaldi, Carlina. *In Dialogue with Reggio Emilia: Listening, Researching and Learning* (New York: Routledge, 2006); and in *Beyond Quality in Early Childhood Education: Postmodern Perspectives* edited by Gunilla Dahlberg, Peter Moss, and Alan Pence (Philadelphia: Falmer Press, 1999). Reproduced by permission of Taylor & Francis Books, UK.)

children, parents, educators, politicians, or other citizens. The value of subjectivity also means that the subject must take responsibility for her or his point of view; there can be no hiding behind an assumed scientific objectivity or criteria offered by experts.

Pedagogical documentation promotes the idea of the school as a place of democratic political practice, by enabling citizens, young and old, to engage with important issues, such as childhood, child care, education, and knowledge. It is a practice that opens up a *public space,* a forum in civic society, where dominant discourses can be visualized and negotiated.

One could say that pedagogical documentation, as used in Reggio, is a *specific attitude about life.* It starts with active listening, a form of listening that builds on a serious engagement and inquisitiveness in the here-and-now event. While documenting, we must try, as the French philosopher Maurice Blanchot has said, to hear that which tries to make itself heard. This implies a listening that takes us beyond a tendency to think in either-or terms. It is a trusting and affirmative listening that welcomes an infinity of possible responses and that has been described so sensitively and thoughtfully by Carlina Rinaldi (2001, 2006; Chapter 13, this volume).

With inspiration from the early childhood services in Reggio Emilia, many teachers around the world have begun to use pedagogical documentation as an important device for the construction of an ethical relationship with the "Other" and the world—what could be termed an *ethics of encounter* (Dahlberg & Moss, 2005). Whether a school becomes a place for an ethics of encounter, and for democracy, depends on teachers being open to experimenting with the children. Do the teachers have the courage to be open to the unexpected and unpredictable? Such an openness requires attitudes that do not rely on a scheming or transactional mentality—the kind of thinking that characterizes the marketplace and purely contractual relationships.

By making pedagogical work both visible and subject to a democratic and open debate, pedagogical documentation provides the possibility for early childhood education to gain new prestige and legitimacy in society. Yet we cannot increase that legitimacy under contemporary conditions unless the costs of early childhood education are more closely linked in the minds of the public with the values it provides. A prerequisite for this is that educational practices and purposes must be made visible outside the domain of preschools and child-care centers; they must become part of public awareness and discourse. This requires the participation of a variety of concerned groups and an educational practice based on participation and negotiation among parents, staff, administrators, and politicians (Dahlberg & Åsén, 1994).

Pedagogical documentation is important for other reasons, too. It has a central role in the discourse of meaning making. Rather than relying on some standardized yardstick of "quality," pedagogical documentation enables us to take responsibility for our actions and for our way of making meaning. As a tool for

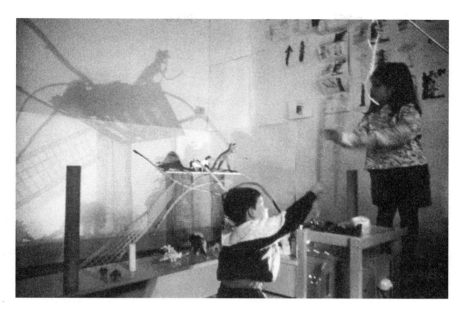

The language of shadows is a powerful one for young children, and many experiences can be created for them.

assessment and evaluation, pedagogical documentation represents an extremely strong antidote to the proliferation of assessment and evaluation tools that have become ever more anonymous and decontextualized—objective and democratic in appearance only. Rating scales and similar normative tools that evaluate against a set of criteria (assumed to be stable, uniform, and objective) represent one "language of evaluation"—namely, the *language of standards and accountability*. That kind of language builds on a highly administrative rationality, a rationality seeking the best methods and procedures for delivering a predefined body of knowledge and predetermined outcomes. The measurement techniques most often used are supposed to ensure control, prediction, and performance by offering objective and universal knowledge.

Instead, pedagogical documentation represents an alternative language of evaluation—the *language of "meaning making"* (Dahlberg, Moss, & Pence, 2007). This kind of language assumes that we must take responsibility for our actions and practice—always in relationship with others—as part of an act of a *democracy in a process of becoming*. This alternative language of evaluation opens to examination, or "problematizes," the complex process of early childhood education, with its contestable images of the child, knowledge and learning, and the environment. Instead of reducing complexity, which is the goal of using standardized tools to measure quality, it opens up the complexity, so that we can work and learn from it.

PEDAGOGICAL DOCUMENTATION AS A WAY
OF CHALLENGING DOMINANT DISCOURSES

Teachers in Reggio Emilia bring to their work a special intellectual awareness, serenity, and way to follow, through documentation, children's and teachers' strategies of experimenting and learning. These habits of mind allow them to follow individual and cooperative learning processes and thus open a space for them to examine and "border-cross" the usual frameworks embedded in our traditional constructions of childhood, knowledge, learning, and the environment. One could even say that pedagogical documentation opens a totally new landscape of childhood. When teachers cross into this new territory, they take part in the kind of professional development on which Reggio places such great importance, not least through the idea of the teacher and the child being understood as both a learner and a researcher.

Through documentation, we can more easily study and ask questions about our practice. What image of the child do we hold? Which discourses of teaching and learning have we bought into? What voice, rights, and respect do children receive in our early childhood programs? Do we merely *talk* about the "competent child," "creativity," "participation," and "reflective practice," or do these ideas actually permeate what we *practice?*

The point of departure here is that the greater our awareness of our teaching practices, the greater the possibility we can promote change by constructing a new space, where an alternative discourse can be established. In this process, pedagogical documentation will encourage us—as it has the teachers in Reggio— to make the familiar seem unfamiliar, to make invisible assumptions and values more visible, and to make explicit the thoughts that are largely tacit in the way in which we govern and are governed (Dean, 1999, p. 36). We will gain insight into the possibility of seeing, talking, and acting in a different way and hence being able to cross boundaries, in particular to transgress the whole grandiose project of modernity and its determination to map all human life in relation to a supposed "Truth." This is a question of taking control over one's own thinking and practice, whether as a teacher or a child.

Because documentation can be kept and revisited and must be seen all the time as a living record of educational practice, the process of pedagogical documentation can also function as a way to revisit and review earlier experiences and events. By doing so, it creates not only memories but also new interpretations and reconstructions of what happened in the past. In this way, teachers will be able to build on and utilize well-established experiences and simultaneously take part in constructing new theories concerning children's learning and knowledge construction, with documentation as a base. In other words, the teachers can participate in the production of new knowledge. This presupposes, however, that teachers engage in continuous scrutiny of the use of expert knowledge as a form of power over others. This requires a high degree of professionalism but can also serve as challenge and inspiration for a deeper engagement. When educators in Reggio Emilia embark on projects with children, an enormous creativity is released, and children's explorations and learning are transformed. The documentation process helps teachers follow children's transformations and trajectories, and it forges relations and connections through which new "becomings" are produced. Of course, the teachers must first be capable of the art of becoming surprised and amazed by children and their potentialities, as Loris Malaguzzi always urged us.

PEDAGOGICAL DOCUMENTATION AS A DANGEROUS ENTERPRISE

Pedagogical documentation can never be an innocent activity; it always has social and political implications and consequences. It can be dangerous, and we do not have any guarantees, as Michel Foucault (1970) argued. Foucault drew our attention to the fact that an educational system built on a discourse of formal neutrality and equality, despite its best intentions, may still be viewed as a potential act of power and control. What we make evident through our practices of representation, perception, and recognition, as well as through our technologies and apparatus of documenting and experimenting, does not exist outside of our theoretical and conceptual frameworks. Such frameworks inform and play a constitutive role for our practices. Thus, if we are not alert and observant, pedagogical documentation may get swept up into strategies to "predict and control" children more effectively through processes of normalization and surveillance. In this case, our observational tools may function as tools for deciding whom to include and whom to exclude. Through abstract categories and labeling, children can all too easily be made into mere "objects" for our understanding. Hence, singularity and the new disappear.

Considering these risks, we must always pose questions concerning what right we have to interpret and document children's doings and what is ethically legitimate. We cannot assume that documentation automatically is a way to resist the power/knowledge nexus. Whether the documentation process becomes democratic must be related to whether it realizes its potential for active listening and for taking in multiple perspectives. If it invites other constructions and perspectives, then documentation has the potential to reveal the concrete ways in which knowledge is constructed in our schools and then lay the basis for the ethical responsibility that each human being gets when she or he acts.

OPENING UP A FORUM

By constructing services for children as forums for engagement and dialogue, for an ethics of an encounter, educators have an important role to play in opening up new potentialities, in which a reconstructed welfare state and democracy are based on the visibility and inclusion of children and families. We can view services for children as forums in civil society and thereby provide opportunities for children and adults to come together and engage in projects of social, cultural, political, and economic significance. This will give these services a specific meaning, as a *community*, in which the life and work of the children can be seen as contributions not only to that particular place but also to the wider global context. In this respect, children and teachers can take part as citizens of the world by engaging with the most vital questions of our present and future (Kemp, 2010). The role of pedagogical documentation in the construction of such early childhood services is critically important. It offers an important starting point not only for dialogue but also for trust and legitimacy in relation to the wider community, by opening up and making visible what goes on in early childhood services.

Thanks to pedagogical documentation, each child, teacher, and school can gain a public voice and a visible identity. That which is documented can be seen as a narrative of children's, teachers', and parents' lives—a narrative that can show the school's contributions to our society and to the development of our democracy. In the words of Carlina Rinaldi (1995):

> Documentation can offer children and adults alike real moments of democracy—democracy which has its origin in the recognition and the visualization of difference brought about by dialogue. This is a matter of *values* and *ethics*.

Combined with the idea of the hundred languages of children, pedagogical documentation may, through having a trust in life, contribute to *vitalization of life*. It enables us to build our lives into a plateau of intensity—of an *aesthetic vibration*, as Loris Malaguzzi used to say.

REFERENCES

Dahlberg, G., & Åsén, G. (1994). Evaluation and regulation: A question of empowerment. In P. Moss & A. Pence (Eds.), *Valuing quality in early childhood services: New approaches to valuing quality* (pp. 157–171). London: Paul Chapman.

Dahlberg, G., & Moss, P. (2005). *Ethics and politics in early childhood education.* London: Routledge.

Dahlberg, G., Moss, P., & Pence, A. (2007). *Beyond quality: Languages of evaluation.* London: Routledge.

Dean, M. (1999). *Governmentality: Power and rule in modern society*. London: Sage.

Foucault, M. (1970). *The order of things: An archeology of the human sciences*. New York: Random House.

Kemp, P. (2010). *Citizens of the world: Cosmopolitan ideals for the 21st century*. Amherst, NY: Prometheus Books.

Rinaldi, C. (1995, June). Observation and documentation. Paper presented at the Research Conference, Reggio Emilia, Italy.

Rinaldi, C. (2001). Documentation and assessment: What is the relationship? In C. Giudici, C. Rinaldi, & M. Krechevsky (Eds.), *Making learning visible: Children as individual and group learners* (pp. 78–89). Reggio Emilia, Italy: Project Zero and Reggio Children.

Rinaldi, C. (2006). *In dialogue with Reggio Emilia: Listening, researching and learning.* New York: Routledge.

Chapter 13

The Pedagogy of Listening: The Listening Perspective from Reggio Emilia

Carlina Rinaldi

LISTENING AND THE SEARCH FOR MEANING

Listening plays an important part in achieving an objective that has always characterized our experience in Reggio Emilia: the search for meaning. One of the first

Earlier versions of portions of this chapter were presented by Carlina Rinaldi in *Innovations in Early Education: The International Reggio Exchange,* and published by Wayne State College of Education in Detroit, Michigan, as follows: "The pedagogy of listening: The listening perspective from Reggio Emilia," 2001, *8*(4), 1–4; "The teacher as researcher," 2003, *10*(2), 1–4; and "The relationship between documentation and assessment," 2004, *11*(1), 1–4.

Excerpts also come from *The Diary of Laura: Perspectives on a Reggio Emilia Diary,* edited by Carolyn Edwards and Carlina Rinaldi. Copyright © 2009 by Carolyn Edwards, the Municipality of Reggio Emilia-Istituzione Preschools and Infant-Toddler Centers, and Reggio Children S.r.l. Reprinted with permission of Redleaf Press, St. Paul, MN; www.redleafpress.org.

The photographs come from an experience, "Laura and the Watch," that appeared in "The Hundred Languages of Children" exhibit and catalog. The original story took place in Arcobaleno Infant-Toddler Center in 1983, when Rinaldi was *pedagogista.*

questions we ask ourselves as educators is: "How can we help children find meaning in what they do, what they encounter, and what they experience? And how can we do this for ourselves?" In the search for meaning, we must ask: "Why?" "How?" and "What?" These are the key questions that children constantly ask, both in and out of school.

It is a difficult search, especially for children who have so many reference points in their daily lives: family, television, school, and the social places they frequent. Yet we cannot live without meaning, because that would leave our lives empty of identity, hope, or sense of the future. Children know this; they have the desire and the ability to search for the meaning of life and their own sense of self as soon as they are born. This is why we, in Reggio, view children as active, competent, and strong, exploring and finding meaning, not as predetermined, fragile, needy, and incapable.

For both adults and children, understanding means being able to develop an interpretive theory, a narrative that gives meaning to the world around them. For us, in Reggio, these theories are extremely important in revealing how children think, question, and interpret reality, and their own relationships with reality and with us. Expressing our theories to others transforms a world not intrinsically ours into something shared. Sharing theories is a response to uncertainty. This is the reason why any theory, to exist at all, needs to be expressed, communicated, and listened to. Herein lies the basis for the "pedagogy of relationships and listening" that distinguishes the work in Reggio Emilia. The capacity for reciprocal listening and expectation, which enables communication and dialogue, is a quality of the human mind and intelligence that is clearly present in young children. From the moment they are born, children develop this attitude of being part of the identity of others. The educators in Reggio have had the opportunity to reflect on the relationship between individual and group learning. We have learned the value of learning that is collective, collaborative, and democratic.

WHAT IS LISTENING?

- Listening should be sensitive to the patterns that connect us to others. Our understanding and our own being are a small part of a broader, integrated knowledge that holds the universe together.
- Listening should be open and sensitive to the need to listen and be listened to and the need to listen with all our senses, not just with our ears.
- Listening should recognize the many languages, symbols, and codes that people use to express themselves and communicate.
- Listening to ourselves—"internal listening"—encourages us to listen to others but, in turn, is generated when others listen to us.
- Listening takes time. When you really listen, you get into the time of dialogue and interior reflection, an interior time that is made up of the present but also

past and future time and is therefore outside chronological time. It is a time full of silences.

- Listening is generated by curiosity, desire, doubt, and uncertainty. This is not insecurity but the reassurance that every "truth" is so only if we are aware of its limits and its possible falsification.
- Listening produces questions, not answers.
- Listening is emotion. It is generated by emotions; it is influenced by the emotions of others; and it stimulates emotions.
- Listening should welcome and be open to differences, recognizing the value of others' interpretations and points of view.
- Listening is an active verb, which involves giving an interpretation, giving meaning to the message, and valuing those who are listened to by others.
- Listening is not easy. It requires a deep awareness and a suspension of our judgments and prejudices. It requires openness to change. It demands that we value the unknown and overcome the feelings of emptiness and precariousness that we experience when our certainties are questioned.
- Listening removes the individual from anonymity (and children cannot bear to be anonymous). It legitimizes us and gives us visibility. It enriches both those who listen and those who produce the message.
- Listening is the basis for any learning relationship. Through action and reflection, learning takes shape in the mind of the subject and, through representation and exchange, becomes knowledge and skill.
- Listening takes place within a "listening context," where one learns to listen and narrate, and each individual feels legitimized to represent and offer interpretations of her or his theories through action, emotion, expression, and representation, using symbols and images (the "hundred languages"). Understanding and awareness are generated through sharing and dialogue.

Thus, the pedagogy of listening is not only a pedagogy for school but also an attitude for life. It can be a tool, but it can also be something more. It means taking responsibility for what we are sharing. If we need to be listened to, then listening is one of the most important attitudes for the identity of the human being, starting from the moment of birth. Before we are born, we live for 9 months in the body of our mothers. Therefore, we grow up as a listener surrounded by dialogue, and listening becomes a natural attitude that involves sensitivity to everything that connects us to others——not only to what we need to learn in school but also to what we need to live our lives. In fact, the most important gift that we can give to the children in the school and in the family is time, because time makes it possible to listen and be listened to by others.

It is also essential that we listen carefully to ourselves, to who we are and what we want. Sometimes we move so quickly through our lives, and we lose the courage of meeting ourselves. What are you doing? Where are you going? This courage to listen, this attention to what is inside ourselves, is a sort of interior listening and reflection. Listening means being open to differences and recognizing the value of another's point of view and interpretation. Thus, listening becomes not only a pedagogical strategy but also a way of thinking and looking at others. Listening is an active verb that involves giving meaning and value to the perspectives of others, a form of assessment. This kind of listening is a way of welcoming others and their differences, and a way of welcoming different theories and perspectives.

Our way of listening means to be open to doubts and uncertainty. This listening means to be open to being in crisis, to accepting frustration. When I was in the United States, many, many teachers were worried because a child was in crisis, or they themselves were in crisis. It is not always bad to be in crisis, because it means that you are changing. The problem is, if you are not in crisis, it might be because you are not really listening to people around you. To be open to others means to have the courage to come into this room and say, "I hope to be different when I leave, not necessarily because I agree with you but because your thoughts have made me think differently." That is why documentation is so fascinating and so difficult to share. Documentation as visible listening can help you to understand and change your identity; it can invite you to reflect on your values. Listening also means welcoming uncertainty and living in the zone of proximal development. Only when I have doubts can I welcome others and have the courage to think that what I believe is not the truth but instead only my own point of view. I need the point of view of others to confirm or change my own point of view.

Real listening requires the suspension of judgments and prejudices. The relationship between peace and prejudice concerns the ability or disability to be good listeners. This is where education for peace begins. There is a connection with the pedagogy of listening. Peace is a way of thinking, learning, and listening to others, a way of looking at differences as an element of connection, not separation. Peace is a way of remembering that my point of view is not the best, and I need to hear and understand others' points of view. Here we find the roots of participation in the school as a place to encounter differences. We must have the courage to share and to agree or disagree. Listening provides the opportunity for professional and human development.

A "listening context" is created when individuals feel legitimized to represent their theories and offer their own interpretation of a particular question. We enrich our knowledge and our subjectivity by listening to others and being open to them when we learn as a group. When children are working together, each is developing his or her own process by learning from the processes of others. If you believe that others are a source of your learning, identity, and knowledge, you have opened an important door to the joy of being together. We are not separated by our differences but connected by them. It is because of my difference that I am useful to you because I offer another perspective. To learn as a group means to learn from the learning of others. This learning from others is visible not only because of documentation but also because there is a context of listening in which my theories are shared with others.

CHILDREN AS LISTENERS

The capacity for listening and reciprocal expectation is an important quality, enabling communication and dialogue, and demands to be understood and supported. In fact, it abounds in young children, who are the greatest listeners to the world that surrounds them. They listen to life in all its shapes and colors. They listen to others—adults and peers. They quickly perceive how listening is essential for communication.

From the beginning, children demonstrate that they have a voice, that they know how to listen, and that they want others to listen to them. Sociability is not taught to children; they are naturally social beings. Young children are strongly attracted by the ways, the languages (and thus the codes) that our culture has produced as well as by other people. Listening, therefore, seems to be an innate predisposition, present from birth, that supports children's process of socialization and acculturation. This is where the school comes in; it should first and foremost be a "context of multiple listening," involving the teachers and children, individually and as a group, who should listen to each other and themselves. This concept of a context of multiple listening overturns the traditional teaching–learning relationship. The focus shifts to learning—children's self-learning and the learning achieved by the group of children and adults together.

TEACHERS AS LISTENERS:
THE PROCESS OF DOCUMENTATION

As children communicate their mental images or theories to others, they also represent them to themselves, developing a more conscious vision. This is what "internal listening" means. By moving from one language to another, and one field of experience to another, and by reflecting on these shifts, children modify and enrich their theories. Yet this is true only if children have the opportunity to make these shifts in a group context—with others—and if they have the chance to listen and be listened to, to express their differences and be receptive to the differences of others. The task of those who educate is not only to allow the differences to be expressed but to make it possible for them to be negotiated and nurtured through exchanging and comparing ideas. In this way, not only does the individual child learn how to learn, but also the group becomes conscious of itself as a "teaching place," where the languages are enriched, multiplied, refined, and generated, so that they collide and hybridize with one another and are renewed.

In addition to offering support and mediation to the children, the teacher who knows how to observe, document, and interpret these processes will realize his or her own full potential as a learner—in this case, learning how to teach. Documentation can be seen as visible listening: it ensures listening and being listened to by others. This means producing traces—such as notes, slides, and videos—to make visible the ways the individuals and the group are learning. This ensures that the group and each child can observe themselves from an external viewpoint while they are learning (both during and after the process).

A broad range of documentation (videos, tape recordings, written notes, and so on) makes visible the learning processes and strategies used by each child, though always in a partial and subjective way. It also enables reading, revisiting, and assessing these actions to become integral to the knowledge-building process. Finally, it seems to be essential for meta-cognitive processes and for the understanding of both children and adults.

Observation, documentation, and interpretation are woven together into what I would define as a *spiral movement* in which none of these actions can be separated out from the others. It is impossible, in fact, to document without observing and interpreting. By means of documenting, the thinking or the interpretation of the documenter becomes tangible and capable of being interpreted. The notes, recordings, slides, and photographs represent fragments of a memory. Each fragment is imbued with the subjectivity of the documenter, but it is also subject to the interpretation of others, as part of a collective process of knowledge building. In these fragments lie the past and also the future (i.e., "What else could happen if . . ."). The result is knowledge that is bounteous, co-constructed, and enriched by the contributions of many.

Documentation, as we have developed in Reggio, does not mean to collect documents after the conclusion of experiences with children but during the course of these experiences. Traditionally, the recording and reading of memories take place at the end of an experience and may become part of a collection of archives. For us, documentation is part of the daily life in the schools. It is one of the ways in which we create and maintain the relationships and the experiences among our colleagues and the children. We think of documentation as an act of caring, an act of love and interaction. We believe that both the teachers and the children are learners. For us within the Reggio experience, documentation is an integral part of the learning and teaching process of the children and teachers. In the process of learning through documentation, we become aware of learning and its value; we assess it. Therefore, we believe that assessment is also an integral part of the learning and teaching process. We believe that the relationship between documentation and assessment is fundamental to our experience. This belief has not only completely changed our approach to documentation but has also helped us to understand the relationship between documentation and testing. We see more and more often the risk of considering testing as a tool of assessment. In reality, testing assesses only children's knowledge of the test's content, not the true learning of children.

Our interpretation of documentation has evolved from a fundamental question that we ask ourselves as teachers and educators. We don't have to teach them to ask "why" because inside each human being is the need to understand the reasons, the meaning of the world around us, and the meaning of our life. We believe that it is important to try to reflect on the children's questions and understand *why* they are asking why. What are their connections? What are their reflections? *Why* do they ask this why? Children ask "why" not only when they speak directly but also through the hundred languages. There is a mix of practical and philosophical concerns in their questioning attitude, in their effort to understand the meaning of things and the meaning of life.

But children not only ask "why?" They are also able to find the answers to their whys and to create their own theories. One could ask why we, in Reggio, talk about *theory* and about *constructing theory*. Why, among many words, did we choose the word *theory?* Many people refer to theories only in the scientific realm of men like Galileo and Einstein. Can children build theory? If we accept the idea that our search, as human beings, to find the meaning of the world around us is essential to life, then we can accept that we can build the answers to our questions. We tend to build theory as a satisfactory explanation that can help us to understand the whys that are inside of us. We are inviting you, the reader, to think about this essential element that is expressed in the children, because the children them-selves are one of the best expressions of our being human, when they create their own theories as satisfactory explanations. Observe and listen to children because when they ask "why?" they are not simply asking for the answers from you. They are requesting the courage to find a collection of possible answers.

Children also are better able to develop theories as satisfactory explanations that can be shared with the others as a point of view. A theory is much more than an idea. Theories must be pleasing and convincing. They must be useful and able to satisfy our intellectual and aesthetic needs. Theory is an expression of our point of view about things and about life. Because of this, theories need to be shared with the others not only to gain an ethical perspective but also to encounter an indispensable element for learning and understanding. The theories that the chil-dren can elaborate have to be shared with the others and communicated using all the languages that we know in order for them to exist. This is one of the roots of the pedagogy of listening and one of the roots of documentation as visible listening, beginning from the idea that the children are able to elaborate theories as explanations about life. This attitude must be preserved as essential for our development as human beings.

This attitude of the child means that the child is a real researcher. As human beings, we are all researchers of the meaning of life. Yet it is possible to destroy this attitude with our quick answers and our sense of certainty. How can we sup-port and sustain this attitude of children toward constructing explanations? If a child says, "It's raining because God is crying," we could easily destroy his theory by telling him that it's actually because of the clouds. How can we cultivate this child's intentions to research? How can we cultivate the courage to create theo-ries as explanations? In his childhood attitude, we can find the roots of creativity, the roots of philosophy, the roots of science, the roots of curiosity, and the roots

of ethics. In this childhood capacity to construct theories, we can observe the freedom to collect elements of ideas to put together in an original way. In this childhood search for answers, we see the roots of a philosophical attitude. This childhood habit of asking "why" is the only way to maintain what is essential in our life: curiosity. Humanity exists and endures because we have developed our capacity for curiosity. In the search for reasons and information lies the roots of doing what is right and good—that is, it is the foundation of ethics.

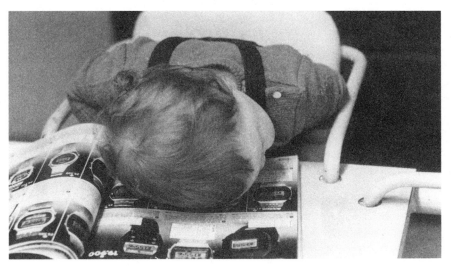

TEACHERS AS EVALUATORS:
THE PROCESS OF ASSESSMENT

For us in Reggio, *making listening visible* means to be open to the theories of children. The elements of observation, interpretation, and documentation are strongly connected. It is impossible to observe without interpreting because observation is subjective. It is impossible to document without interpreting, and it is impossible to interpret without reflecting and observing. When you choose something to document, when you take a photograph or videotape an experience, you are making a choice. That means that you are giving value or evaluating this experience as meaningful for the children's learning processes and for your own learning processes as well. When you document, you are sharing the children's learning and your own learning—what you understand, your perspective, and also what you value as meaningful. Within the word *evaluation,* there is the word *value.* Valuing means giving value to this learning context, and to certain experiences and interactions within that context. This is what we offer to the learning processes of the children and to those of our colleagues.

Here, in my opinion, is the genesis of *assessment* because, in producing the documentation, you make the element of value, as well as the indicators you have applied, visible and sharable. From your documentation, the children can understand not only their processes but what you value as meaningful for their learning processes. In this way, assessment becomes more democratic. Thus, the children can see the meaning that the teacher has drawn from their work. When you share your documentation with the children, you demonstrate that what they do has value and meaning. The children discover that they exist and can emerge from anonymity and invisibility, seeing that what they say and do is important, that it can be heard, valued, shared, appreciated, and understood.

Therefore, you cannot document without assessing. Assessment becomes part of the learning processes as you become aware of your choices and your values, as you come to understand your ethics. When you enter our schools and your own schools, perhaps what you see documented are not only experiences but values—in other words, things that the members of the learning community have assessed and valued as important. For instance, if we want to create a school for education, and not a school for instruction and information, then we can hope that education for peace also begins from the moment of birth. Education for peace is a way of thinking about the others and the world, a way of looking at the reality as the children do, without prejudice. Children can teach us because they welcome everything. They can teach us how to be open to others and to their differences. They can teach us to be open to understanding that we are extraordinary because we are unique, because we are different. Listening is a metaphor of encounter and dialogue. Because we believe in the pedagogy of listening, the experience in Reggio tries to honor the children by listening to that expression of the human being. Perhaps the pedagogy of listening may be a pedagogy for supporting a way of living with the hope that it is possible for human beings to change.

Children feel that we value what they say, and therefore what they think, because we record it, transcribe it, and reflect on what it might mean. The children know that we seek for indications connected with the processes of research and learning that they are experiencing. Above all, they feel that by giving value to their thoughts, we give value to them as unique individuals who are saying something important; they feel how important they are to us. From very early on, children understand that drawing is not merely a way to kill time but gives witness to a thought, an emotion, a way of knowing that might indicate the direction of their processes of knowing and therefore of expressing. This happens because teachers place much value on the children's drawings. The children also recognize themselves in photographs and videos and realize what was happening to them or their group of friends with regard to both actions and emotions. They recognize the efforts they make in discussing their respective points of view and understand the value that cooperation has within the group. They become aware that they are contributing different opinions, sustaining their own ideas, but at the same time participating in constructing a joint result. Children thus feel that each one of them is valuable and competent. At the same time, they appreciate that the knowledge they have constructed together acquires an added value because it is a shared result and has deep meaning related to how education builds community.

Beyond what they come to feel about themselves, through the listening process, children also recognize that each trace of their processes of learning and development is welcomed. This happens across the different fields of knowledge, for example, with respect to their first letters that appear mixed in their drawings, their first written numbers that indicate measurements of the table they want their parents to build for them, or their beginning attempts at music produced with the instruments they have available, which is then recorded and listened to as a musical exploration or as background to their daily activity. Each of these signs of learning is welcome as precious and is supported with new materials and activities that provide possibilities for further meaning, either replicating the experiences or expanding them into new contexts. What they are learning becomes evident to them because teachers give value to their processes of learning about letters, numbers, music, and other subjects of knowledge and make them visible in their daily teaching.

Children feel emotion and participate with passion and barely concealed pride when they see images of these learning processes displayed in their classroom, collected in a publication, or organized in a video or digital presentation. Those products will be shown and shared with other teachers or with parents at the regular class meeting. Self-esteem and appreciation from others, along with the perception of being an essential part of the community, become things of value not only declared as abstract objectives but also as experiences rendered palpable and manifest in the concrete actions, lived in everyday space and time.

A learning community thus takes shape. It involves the teachers who learn that their way of looking bestows value and who therefore develop a deep sense of responsibility and reciprocity. Beyond the teachers, however, it also involves the parents. To parents, their own son or daughter is important not only as a child but also as an individual with a certain kind of personality or a specific way of learning. That child needs and has a right to times and spaces, friends, and materials and strategies that are personalized as much as possible. Yet the parents also discover that although their son or daughter is unique, that child has within himself or herself the rights of all the children in that community. They learn that to do something for their own son or daughter means to do something for all the children. From the concept of "my son" or "my daughter," the parents easily develop a concept of the children of "our school" and "their rights."

Through meeting other parents and reflecting on ways of knowing, playing, and being together with other children, the parents open up to dialogue about the diverse ways to deal with common problems and about styles of informal education that individuals adopt in relation to each of their sons and daughters. The educating community is a community that gives value to the rights of everyone.

This learning community is therefore an ethical and democratic community. It possesses the democracy of the communal construction of knowledge and of values that inspire and motivate that knowledge and that can strongly, through documentation, communicate with the wider community in which the school is placed.

On the basis of such a foundation, documentation that begins in schools for young children evolves into something that moves beyond them, in the form of an exhibit perhaps or books, opening up debates that speak not only a verbal language but also the language of images and more. We speak of the "hundred languages" through which the children communicate and discover pathways to the new and unexpected, to the courage that education asks for and then proposes—the courage of values that we want to construct together with our children, values that accept the challenge of contemporary life and the richness of change.

TEACHERS AS RESEARCHERS: EDUCATION AS LIFE

When teachers make listening and documentation central to their practice, they transform themselves into *researchers*. Why is the concept of "teacher as researcher" so important? Why, among the many possibilities, do we emphasize the qualification of "researcher"? Research is a word with many meanings that can evoke laboratories, chemical formulas, and science. It generally represents a clear and recognized methodology and implies objectivity. The word research has a serious tone and tends to be reserved for the few people who work in relationship with certain established and conventional procedures. It is a concept that inhabits universities or specialized centers for research. It is a word that does not circulate in the streets and squares of the city. Research is not a word with common usage, and above all, it is not a concept that we normally think about putting into practice in our daily lives.

In schools, the word research usually means to gather a collection of information and compile what is already known about a certain topic. Emotions and experiences that characterize so-called scientific research, such as curiosity, doubt, the unknown, error, crisis, theory, and confusion, are not usually part of school work or daily life. If they do enter into the context of life in the school, they are viewed as weak moments, moments of fragility, of uncertainty, that must be quickly overcome.

In my opinion, this is why true innovations are so difficult to accept and appreciate. They shake up our frames of reference because they force us to look at the world through new eyes. They open us up to what is different and unexpected. All too often, we human beings tend to accept things as they are, the status quo, what we know and have already tried out, even when we are not satisfied, even when that makes us feel stressed, confused, and hopeless. So, in this way, we try to defend our normality, the norms and rules we already know, to the detriment of the new. Yet only searching and researching are guaranteed to lead us to that which is new, that which moves us forward. In contrast, the status quo of normality excludes research as the approach to be used everyday and therefore excludes doubt, error, uncertainty, curiosity, marvel, and amazement as important values in our daily lives. The preference for the status quo places normality in opposition to research. Instead, I would like to propose the concept of the "normality of research," which defines research as an attitude and an approach in everyday living—not only in schools but also outside of them—as a way of thinking for ourselves and thinking jointly with others, a way of relating with other people, with the world around us, and with life.

Where and how can we find the strength and courage for this radical change? Once again, we must start with the children. The young child is the first great researcher. Children are born searching for and therefore researching the meaning of life, the meaning of the self in relation to others and to the world. Children are born searching for the meaning of their existence; the meaning of the conventions, customs, and habits we have; and of the rules and the answers we provide.

Children's questions (such as, "Why are we born?" and "Why do we die?") are precious, as are their answers, because they are generative. Children's theories (such as, "The sea is born from the mother wave" and "When you die, you go into the belly of death and then get born again") highlight the strongest characteristic of the identity of children and of humankind: searching for and researching meaning, sharing and constructing together the meaning of the world and the events of life. All children are intelligent, different from each other, and unpredictable. If we know how to listen to them, children can give back to us the pleasure of amazement, marvel, doubt, and the "why." Children can give us the *strength of doubt* and the *courage of error,* of the unknown. They can transmit to us the joy of searching and researching, the value of research, as well the openness toward others and toward everything new that is produced by the encounter with others.

These concepts give strength to the notion of education and personal formation as an ongoing process of research. They are also at the root of the value of documentation and of making listening visible, which is not simply a technique that can be transported but a way of guaranteeing that our thinking always involves reflection, exchange, different points of view, and differences in assessment or evaluation. They are seen not only as didactic strategies but also as values that inspire our view of the world. The documentation materials we use attest not only to our path of knowledge regarding children but also to our path of knowledge about the child and humanity, and about ourselves. They also attest to our idea of the teacher as researcher, of school as a place of research and cultural elaboration, a place of participation, in a process of shared construction of values and meanings. The school of research is a school of participation.

Moreover, this concept of the normality of research is the best way to express what I believe is one of the particular aspects of our experience, one of the most topical "cultural knots" in these complex times: the relationship between theory and practice. Theory and practice, considered as a dichotomy that has weighed heavily on the world of school and on our culture, could find a true dialectic and synthesis in this concept of research in which theory generates practice that, in turn, generates new theories and new perspectives on the world. The theories come from the practice but also orient and guide it. The theories are practical thoughts. My theories produce my interpretations of reality. This is why theories should be continuously questioned and verified in an exchange with others.

When we say that school is not a preparation for life but *is* life, this means assuming the responsibility to create a context in which words such as *creativity, change, innovation, error, doubt,* and *uncertainty,* when used on a daily basis, can truly be developed and become real. This means creating a context in which the teaching–learning relationship is highly evolved—that is, where the solution to certain problems leads to the emergence of new questions, new expectations, and new changes. This also means creating a context in which children, from a very young age, discover that there are problems that are not easily resolved, that perhaps cannot have an answer, and for this reason, they are the most wonderful ones because therein lies the "spirit of research." Even though the children are very young, we should not convey to them the conviction that for every question, there is a right answer. If we did so, perhaps we would appear to be more important in their eyes and they might feel more secure, but they would pay for this security by losing the "pleasure of research," the pleasure of searching for answers and constructing the answers with the help of others. Children are capable of loving and appreciating us even when we appear to be doubtful or we do not know how to answer, because they appreciate the fact that we are right there by their side in their search for answers: the child-researcher and the teacher-researcher. Only in this way will children return with full rights among the builders of human culture and the culture of humanity. Only in this way will they sense that their wonder and their discoveries are truly appreciated because they are useful. Only in this way can children and childhood hope to reacquire their human dignity and no longer be considered "objects of care" or "objects of cruelty and abuse," both physical and moral. Life is research.

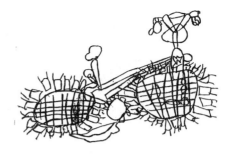

Chapter 14

Negotiated Learning through Design, Documentation, and Discourse

George Forman and Brenda Fyfe

Reflective practice of teaching must stand on a well-defined theory of knowledge. Otherwise, we know not where to go. One needs a definition of knowledge to serve as a standard for effective teaching. The theory of knowledge to which we subscribe is constructivist—more precisely, social constructivism as found in Doise, Mugny, and Perret-Clemont (1975) and co-constructivist as found in Berger and Luckmann (1966), Tudge and Winterhoff (1993), Vygotsky (1986), and Wertsch (1985). We hold that knowledge is gradually constructed by people becoming each other's student, by taking an inquiring stance toward each other's constructs, and by sincere attempts to assimilate or reconcile each other's initial perspective (see Jankowicz, 1995; Palincsar & Brown, 1984). We further hold that knowledge is never verifiable through listening or by observation alone, but rather it gains clarity through a negotiated analysis of the communication process itself,

for example, "Was that a question or a statement of fact?" This analysis necessarily contains tacit knowledge that is inferential and not literally "in the data"
(Bruner, 1957; Polanyi, 1958/1998; von Glaserfeld, 1995).

Once this premise is accepted, our educational practice changes radically from
a study of facts to a study of how we study and how we move from facts to
meaning. The education of children now lies in helping them study their ways of
making meaning, their negotiations with each other in a context of symbolization
(Gardner, 1983), communication, (Tharp & Gallimore, 1988), narrative (Engel,
1995/1999; Taylor, 1993), and metaphor (Bruner, 1990).

The principles of this epistemology lead to practice similar to what we have
observed in Reggio Emilia, a practice that we prefer to call *negotiated learning*. This term captures the centrality of the social, co-constructivist principles
just mentioned. In negotiated learning, the teachers seek to uncover the children's
beliefs, assumptions, or theories about the way the physical or social world works.
Their study goes beyond simply identifying the children's interest. Their analysis
reveals the reasons behind the children's interest—not strictly what is familiar,
but what paradox or curiosity drives their interest qua topic. Children are encouraged to talk about what they know before they begin their projects. In a similar
way, preverbal children are allowed to explore new objects or materials so that a
teacher (observing the children's strategies) can infer what might be the children's
theories, given those strategies (Forman & Hall, 2005). In this co-constructivist
curriculum, the teachers form a community of learners with the children and with
the parents and other teachers (see Rinaldi, 1996).

They discuss the social and symbolic processes through which meanings
are negotiated toward some level of shared understanding. The curriculum is
not child-centered or teacher-directed. The curriculum is child-originated and
teacher-framed. The children discuss many interests—for example, making an
amusement park for the birds that come to the school playground. The teachers
reframe the goals into slightly more general concepts—say, how to make the birds
feel less anxious about being away from home (see Forman & Gandini, 1994).
Then specific follow-up activities are proposed and negotiated with the children
and, at the more general level, with the parents (see Fyfe & Forman, 1996).

On the other hand, the curriculum could be teacher-provoked and then child-
engaged. What is important here is that the teacher engages children's minds and
interests in the topic proposed. For example, a teacher might invite a small group
of children to join her in observing the squirrels that play outside their classroom
window (something they had previously not noticed). As children and teacher
comment on what they notice and converse about what the squirrels seem to enjoy
doing, the teacher is engaging the children's interests. The teacher may ask probing questions (e.g., "What do you think the squirrels like about this tree?" "Are the
squirrels playing or working?" "Why are they gathering nuts?") to engage children's minds. Once children are engaged and interested, the teacher can help children ask questions that give meaning to continued observations, investigations, or

experiments. All the while, the teacher is guiding and supporting children toward intended learning outcomes (e.g., develop inquiry skills and knowledge about the natural world).

We will specify three components that define negotiated learning as a dynamic system of causes, effects, and counter-effects. These components are *design, documentation*, and *discourse*. In general, these three components create a system such that academic skills are engaged within the context of meaningful problem solving, reflective practice, and communication among constituents. For example, when teachers document children's work and review these documents with the children, the net result is a change in the image of their role as teacher, a change from teaching subject matter to studying and learning with children (see Rinaldi, 1996). Furthermore, asking children to design their future work changes the way children talk about their work. Their talk becomes the discourse of prediction and explanation.

THREE COMPONENTS OF NEGOTIATED LEARNING

Design refers to any activity in which the designer (child or adult) makes a record of a plan or intended solution. A drawing is a design if it is drawn with the intent to guide a future reader in the construction of the items drawn or to specify for the reader a sequence of actions. For example, children at the Eighth of March School in Reggio Emilia drew the traditional sequence of acts in a "Drop the Handkerchief" game so that children unfamiliar with the game could learn the rules by reading the drawings. Children at La Villetta Preschool in Reggio Emilia drew fountains and amusement rides knowing that these drawings would be used to guide the actual construction and layout of these amusements in their outdoor playground. Designs can be in many media: a clay fountain to guide the construction of one made from pipe and hose, a wire figure to portray the movements of a dance for others to learn. Because the design will be revisited later to guide another person's actions, it must be crafted to be read. Thus, the designer should consider the readability of the representation as opposed to how precise or realistic it is. Indeed, it is often the more schematic representations that communicate the best. The educational value of design flows from the special attitude of the designer, an attitude of building a relationship with the reader, even with oneself as a revisiting reader of the design (Dunn & Larsen, 1990; Kafai & Harel, 1991).

Discourse connotes a deep desire to understand each other's words. Discourse is more than talking. Discourse connotes a more reflective study of what is being said, a struggle to understand, in which speakers constructively confront each other, experience conflict, and seek footing in a constant shift of perspectives. In effect, discourse is an analysis of communication, a meta-linguistic process in which meaning is questioned in the name of growth and understanding (Gee, 1990; Stubbs, 1983). Discourse is the voice we use for schooling and learning

(Goodman, 1992). Design and documentation serve to focus, maintain, and improve the discourse during the negotiated process of learning.

Documentation refers to any record of performance that contains sufficient detail to help others understand the behavior recorded. Whereas design represents a prediction or plan, documentation records the performance during a learning encounter as well as the documenter's interpretation of that performance. Thus, a single drawing by a child would not be considered documentation because it is not a record of the performance. However, a video clip of the child creating that drawing or a set of redrawn portions to plot the process that lead to the final drawing would be considered documentation. (A single photograph with text that describes and then interprets the unrecorded behavior, could be treated as documentation but is a less-than-ideal method for deep understanding.) The intent of documentation is to explain not merely to describe. Documentation is more than "work samples." Documentation may be publicly displayed, such as panels of photographs with explanatory text placed on the classroom walls, or may be filed in a portfolio and later studied as a collection. Strictly speaking, documentation is not a form of assessment of individual progress but is a form of explaining to the constituents of the school the depth of the children's learning and the educational rationale of curriculum activities. Documentation is central to negotiated learning, and much of what this chapter discusses deals with the relation between documentation and the two other components: design and discourse.

These comments contain a distinction between design and documentation. Design seeks to instruct; documentation seeks to explain. Design is prospective; documentation is retrospective. Both are more than the physical records. Thus, we use the word *documentation* instead of *document,* and *design* instead of *designs* to put the pedagogical function of these records in relief.

A Diagram for All Relations

To ease our discussion of this pedagogical system, we have provided the following diagram. This diagram contains all three action components and four constituents (children, teachers, parents, community). We have deliberately made the connection between the four constituents and the three action components rather loose. Otherwise the diagram would look like a tangle and cease to be useful. We describe specific relations in the text of the chapter.

These three components, design, documentation, and discourse, form a system of relations that is everywhere reciprocal. Design can be used to improve documentation. For example, the children's drawn designs can be placed within the wall panels to help explain the learning encounter. Documentation can be revisited to improve discourse by serving as a database for reflective teaching. Discourse can be documented and then used to improve a second design session. We use the flow among these components as a scheme to organize the segments of this chapter. (Please note that as we describe the interrelation among these three components, we will venture into some suggestions for practice that have not necessarily been seen in Reggio or anywhere else.)

These components serve a variety of constituents—children, teachers, parents, and the general public. Consider how design helps children. Selected records of the children's assumptions or plans certainly serve the children as they revisit their own ideas to deepen and broaden the application of their concepts. Design helps teachers plan follow-up activities. Design helps parents who want to extend the child's study into the home, and it helps the general public understand the vision and objectives of the school.

These relations to constituents are neither simple nor one way. Constituents often work together around one component to improve another component. Teachers and children together engage in a design activity, and this improves their level of discourse when they study their designs. The design sessions are also documented. Teachers and children revisit these documents, and this in turn improves discourse further.

Traffic Within the Diagram

A useful theory not only specifies the components of a system but also makes propositions about traffic among those components. A theory tells us what to expect when one path is taken rather than another. In reference to the flow chart in Figure 14.1, here are some paths that exemplify the use of documentation to enhance discourse:

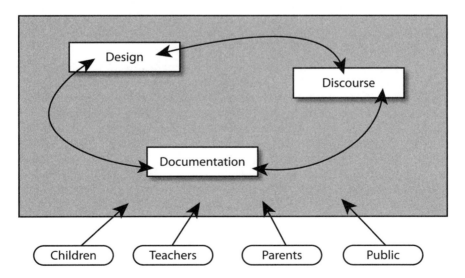

Figure 14.1 Components of negotiated learning.

Four children draw their plans for a village on the Moon, including vehicles with sticky wheels (*design*). Then they use their drawings to explain the buildings and vehicles to peers who ask them to clarify (*design affects discourse*). The teachers use an audiotape of these explanations to study the assumptions children have about how things work on the Moon (*discourse of children is documented*). By working in a small group, the teachers, using this shared referent of the audiotape of the children's conversation, discuss which comments to transcribe and how to explain this activity in a wall panel they make (*discourse of teachers affects documentation*).

PASSAGES TOWARD GREATER UNDERSTANDING

This diagram can illustrate principles of negotiated learning. We present these principles as a set of passages, from an initial understanding of a teaching practice to a more comprehensive understanding. We begin with the passage from description to design, which is a passage from a narrow view of representation as record to a broader view of representation as a recommendation for action.

From Description to Design

As we mentioned briefly, design has an instructive intent that is beyond mere description. This difference applies to many media not just drawing. However, for illustration's sake, lets consider the passage from drawing an object to using a drawing as a design. A drawing may be judged good if its referent can be recognized by another person. Granted, a realistic drawing can improve discourse, because it serves as a common referent, but such a drawing remains no more than a picture of something else.

A design, in contrast, is made to build something or instruct someone on how to do something. The designer needs to capture action in the marks and needs to help a new reader discern these implied actions. Somehow the "reader" must translate the marks on the paper into a set of acts to accomplish some desired result. For example, a drawing used to build a toy wooden boat might be drawn with less detail regarding the textures of the woods and more detail for the manner in which the parts are articulated. The interface between two parts carries more information for building the boat than does the texture detail. The design also includes marks that carry a message of action and sequence that is more than a static record of the features of a stationary object. Arrows, numbers, and a row of progressive drawings are some common techniques of representing actions. This shift from visual analysis of detail to the representation of a set of procedures is a fundamental shift in science and education (Piaget, 1970, 1978). This same shift underlies the high level use of representations in negotiated learning. Furthermore, the child's desire to explain how something should be done implies an audience, an audience that vicariously participates in the co-construction of knowledge (Vygotsky, 1986;

Wertsch, 1985). The dual emphasis on procedural knowledge and communication interfaces Piaget and Vygotsky in negotiated learning.

Here is an example of the description to design passage:

> A group of children were interested in the huge sunflowers outside their window. They were absolutely amazed that the blossom head contained so many seeds. The teacher thought that this prolific blossom should be preserved in the children's memory somehow, so she suggested that the children make their own rendering of this blossom using paper and colored pencils. The drawings were beautifully done, with great attention to the individual seeds in the center of the huge flower. The teacher and children agreed that the drawing activity had sensitized them to details that they would not have noticed had they not taken pains to draw these details on paper.

On a second thought, we decided that this flower drawing activity was too limited. We asked the children why they were amazed about the seeds in the flower head. They told us that they remembered the seed that they had placed in the ground 6 weeks earlier, and now the flower has seeds in the blossom that look just like the one they planted. So we asked them to draw pictures that showed how these seeds were produced—that is, draw what they could not see, draw what they thought were the steps that took place inside the sunflower to produce the seeds. In essence, we were asking them to design a seed factory.

The drawings were diverse, clever, and revealing. The children did not give as much attention to the graphic realism of their drawing but rather became more interested in communicating their ideas about the procedures that yielded seeds in the flower's head. One child drew a set of drawings that portrayed the original seed advancing from the ground, inside the straw-like stalk of the sunflower, the same seed popping out of the blossom in the last picture! Through these designs of seed growth, the teacher found many more opportunities to engage the children's minds about their theories than were possible with the descriptive drawings of the sunflower per se.

From Display to Documentation

The passage from display to documentation travels the path from informing to educating and thereby changes the teacher's perspective from observing children to studying children. Museums, particularly science museums, are places to find examples of both displays that inform and documentation that educates. Take this frequently found exhibit, a row of silhouettes that show the changing profile of the human skull over the past 100,000 years. The display of these silhouettes is not itself documentation of an evolutionary process. The panel merely displays the evolution, informs us of its occurrence. Documentation, on the other hand, would make an explicit attempt to walk us through an explanation.

For example, we could add a caption to this row of skull silhouettes. "As humans evolved, the thickness of the brow ridge decreased, and the cranial capacity increased, indicating a decrease in a defensive structure and an increase in brain size." Now the row of silhouettes exemplifies an interesting principle and can be studied for other features that exemplify similar principles. What might the reduction of jaw length mean? Good documentation provokes a study of the graphics because the text helps frame the graphics as examples of something more general than the features themselves.

When applied to negotiated learning, displays should be converted to documentation by adding interpretation and explanation to the graphics. A set of photographs pasted to poster board showing a trip to the farm is a display. A set of photographs captioned with the children's words would still be a display. The panels need commentary to qualify as documentation.

Imagine this set of photographs with a display of the children's words. One child, looking at 12 piglets suckling on the same sow, says, "Do all the piglets get enough to eat?" Elsewhere on the panel, an account is printed about how the children continued to talk about this relation between the supply of one mother and the demands of 12 children. The one child added, "If she [the sow] eats a lot, she can feed them all." The documentation printed more than the children's words; it also speculated on the general issues that were implicit, such as the fear that a mother might not be able to nurture her young. Documentation invites inquiry about the children's thinking and invites predictions about effective teaching. A panel with only pictures and the children's words could describe but not explain. The teacher's commentary is necessary to frame the data as examples of something more general, some principle that can be applied in new contexts. Display invites pleasure and satisfaction but is not deliberately designed to provoke hypotheses. Documentation is a research report used to enhance discourse rather than a mere record of a past event.

This brings us to a difference between documentation in negotiated learning and the portfolios that are popular in American schools (Glazer & Brown, 1993; Tierney, 1991). Portfolios are touted as a more authentic form of assessment, primarily because portfolios include the actual artifacts that children produce as they work, which can include drawings, diagrams, math sheets, photographs, and even videotapes that when studied chronologically in all their qualitative detail, present a unique path of progress for each child.

Documentation, as we mean it here, is more focused on children than on a child. Even when a child is featured in documentation, the intent is to have the viewer treat this child as a representative child. The documentation presents the spirit of the school, the pedagogical principles at work, which may include Shawn as the protagonist here and Rane as the protagonist there. Be aware that the interest of a featured child's parent could be inversely related to the interest of the other parents. The other parents need a message to which everyone can relate.

Documentation tries to raise questions about children's thinking and teaching strategies rather than to mark the progress of each individual child. The viewer is asked to assume that what one sees in the documentation of four children has happened at other times with all the children. Documentation presents the wisdom of the teachers who write the explanations and provocations, but documentation, by itself, is not a systematic evaluation of instruction. These two objectives, evaluation and documentation, should be kept separate, at least when evaluation means applying some standard of achievement or skill. Documentation should not be constrained from presenting unique stories that reveal forms of thinking no book of standards contains.

From Talking to Discourse

We talk almost all the time. Sometimes we listen to our own words and to the words of others to understand more deeply. It is this meta-linguistic attitude toward talking—that is, talking itself as the object of study—that defines the discourse of schooling (E. A. Forman & McPhail, 1993; Palincsar & Brown, 1984; and especially Isaacs, 1930).

Take for example the following conversation among several children:

Erica: Look, my legs are long, but I am not split all the way up.

John: Yeah, but your hand is split into five fingers.

Tim: Well, your legs aren't split, they are just two.

Erica: What?

Tim: There are just two. They have always been two. You could say, "My legs are apart."

Erica: Oh.

Tim thought about Erica's choice of adverbs. Split means "once together, then separated." Although he was certainly thinking about the process of a continued split of one's legs, he was also thinking about how to word the more accurate facts. We call this form of negotiating the meaning of words *discourse*. Tim wanted to present an alternative word as a strategy to make explicit his alternative understanding of the future of Erica's legs. Is this a real example? It seems far-fetched from the conversations that happen in early childhood (preK–third grade).

As a team of teachers, we could read this transcribed conversation. Indeed, the way this conversation was analyzed in the previous paragraph exemplifies discourse. Teachers talk among themselves as they study a transcript to discover the children's theories, assumptions, false premises, misapplications, and clever analogies—all ambiguities that are pieces to be negotiated into shared meaning by the group of teachers. Teachers continually say such things as, "Would you then say that the children knew that would happen?" or "I am not sure I would call it collaboration; maybe parallel play." The teachers work to understand the meaning of the words they use to interpret their observations. This discourse mind-set carries over into teachers talking to parents, to the public, and all possible relations portrayed at the bottom of Figure 14.1.

Discourse also changes as it is affected by design and documentation, and of course, discourse changes design and documentation. As we study the children's designs, hear them explain their plans, and revisit our documentation of these projects, we begin to speak differently about our subject matter, the children. We speak of them as exemplifications of growth, development, and power. Furthermore, as we take explicit note of how we speak differently, we become conscious of our own professional development. Instead of saying, "The children seem to enjoy the activity," we say, "The children enjoy watching the birds without being noticed." We observe that we now use more "verb talk" than "noun talk," such as, "You made that mark by pressing down very hard on the pencil," as opposed to, "I see that you made a dark line with your pencil." We think about how our patterns of speaking to children are changing. These are not trivial or jargon differences in discourse. They bespeak fundamental shifts in one's level of analysis and one's theory of learning (see Solisken, Wilson, & Willette, 1993).

From Remembering to Revisiting

Teachers of young children can serve as a memory, a record of an experience that can be revisited. This function can be served by writing down what the children say and then reading these words back to them on a later day when the children are trying to extend their understanding of something. Or the teacher can show a photograph or replay a video recording of an experience and ask the children to reflect on their intentions, purpose, expectations, and assumptions regarding the actions they see in the photograph or video. Note that compared with a static photograph, a video recording "uploads" the memory of the actual action into the recorder, thereby allowing children to use their mental space to think about things not seen, such as purpose and intention, the "why" of behavior rather than the "what."

There is a difference between remembering what one did and revisiting the experience. For remembering, the children are content with a simple listing of what they did, "We saw a pig. We rode the tractor. We looked down into the deep silo." But revisiting is more than remembering. Revisiting is just that, a return to a place to reestablish or to discover the significance of that place, like going to one's hometown after a long absence. As a visitor, you now look on the experience as an outsider. You no longer reside in the experience, but you seek to establish a new meaning and new feelings from that experience. You are a bit more detached as a nonresident but no less eager to be there. The past is reconstructed from the new perspectives of the present. You look for patterns to create meaning; you look for causes and relations that were not obvious while you were resident in the experience.

A teacher, reading from a transcript, says, "Yesterday you said that the man on the tractor made it turn by stopping one of the big wheels. How can stopping make something move in a new direction? Lets remember what you were thinking and try to figure out what you meant." The teacher has invited the children to revisit their assumptions or explanations about how things work on the farm. In regard to an experiment with shadows, a teacher might say, "Here is a photograph of you jumping as you look at your shadow on the ground. Tell me what you were thinking just as you were in midair over your shadow." The teacher has invited the two girls to confront an earlier curiosity they had about whether one's shadow is always attached to one's feet. Note that the teacher does not ask, "Look at the photograph and tell me if your feet are attached to your shadow." The focus is on memories about the children's thinking, not photographic evidence of an answer.

While the initial question might be to recall a thought or an observation, the teacher carefully chooses memories that will draw the children into conversations about something that was unresolved or an action that is incomplete. It is the intent of revisiting to take children further and not simply list the places they have been. Photographs should be treated as a door to enter a world of possible events, not as a window that pictures a single time and place (G. Forman, 1995). Video should be treated as an opportunity for the children to abstract the theory, assumption, belief, or expectation that makes a strategy reasonable to them using that particular strategy and possibly create sufficient dissonance to motivate a reconstruction of those theories, assumptions, beliefs, and expectations.

From Symbol to Language to Languages

As we ask children to represent their thoughts, it is important to understand the concepts of a symbol and a language. We have often heard the phrase from Reggio Emilia, "the hundred languages of children." What does this mean? It could refer to the 100 ways children can use their native language to express their general attitude toward something, as in the phrases *multiple realities* or *multiple perspectives.* More literally, it could mean that there are 100 symbol systems that have enough systematicity and syntax to be called languages, languages that children could use if the classroom culture would allow it (see Gardner, 1983). For example, several children choose to use readable gesture to retell the story of a lion capturing a gazelle. Others use musical symbols that capture the action in tone, timber, and rhythm, and still others draw stick figures to show the crouch, pounce, and capture across three sequenced frames. Although children may not have 100 languages available to them, they certainly have more than the spoken words of their native tongue.

Perhaps the first idea of multiple perspectives can best be translated as differences in *voice,* as in, "He speaks with the voice of authority," or "She speaks with the voice of experience." Children have a hundred such voices. We also know that voice is central to revelations about gender differences in communication styles (Tannen, 1982, 1989). Although the concept of voice is important, it is probably not the meaning implied in the phrase *a hundred languages of children*. Let's look more closely at the second meaning, different symbol systems.

A language is more than a set of symbols. A language contains rules of combining these symbols to convey meaning. Thus, a panel where each child's photograph contains a little animal stamp to stand for that child's identity is not a language. But a child's stamp followed by an arrow and another child's stamp could mean, "Amy likes Zoie." A simple syntax is born, and with it a new language for children to invent and explore relations. Likewise, a clay figure of a runner is a symbol but is not of itself a language. However, when 12 children make different clay figures to tell the other children how to play "Drop the Handkerchief," these clay figures become the elements in a proto-language. Tree leaves can be arranged on poster board in rows, but this is not a language of leaves because it tells us nothing. However, if the children tried to arrange the leaves to show the presence of a strong wind or a weak wind, then the relation among the leaves would constitute a proto-syntax, and the whole enterprise would engage the children to think about the language of leaves and what the leaves can tell us. These various media, when their elements are combined to tell a story, form the 100 languages.

In summary, we need to move children beyond the level of making symbols on to the level of inventing language and from the stance of using only the native spoken language to the use of many symbol systems: leaves, gestures, rubber stamps, clay, and so on. It is the nature of the relation among the symbols that converts the medium into a message, and it is the presence of an intended message that motivates children to negotiate shared meanings and to co-construct knowledge.

Hattie says to Tom, "You can't do that, that's Lisa's name."

From Listening to Hearing

We can give ourselves time to listen to children. We can say that our classroom is child-centered. We can transcribe the children's conversations and affirm the importance of their words. We may listen, but what do we hear?

In negotiated learning, it is essential for teachers to listen with the third ear, to hear the implied meanings of children's words. Take the case of Hattie, who was upset with a teacher, Tom, who was wearing a life-size photographic mask of Lisa, another teacher. Hattie says to Tom, "You can't do that, that's Lisa's name" (G. Forman & Kuschner, 1986, p. 216). We can listen to Hattie's exact words, we can print them on a panel that documents the encounter, but what is the deeper structure of Hattie's complaint. What have we heard her say?

Hattie, like other four-year-olds, probably has some difficulty distinguishing between words that refer to objects and words that refer to words. The word *Lisa* refers to, at a minimum, the unique face, an object; but the word *name* refers to the spoken word we use to identify that unique face. Hattie more likely treats words as symbols that refer to objects. So it makes sense to her to say *name* when *face* would be better, albeit the removable face (the photo mask) is psychologically somewhere between the concepts of name and face. Nevertheless, the idea that the word *name* refers to another word (*Lisa*) is a bit beyond the ken of the average four-year-old. So we listen to Hattie's exact words, but our third ear hears the struggle she is having with the more difficult forms of reference. We also hear the objection to Tom pretending to be Lisa. Why wasn't Tom wearing his own photographed face? Was Hattie upset or amused at the joke of Tom wearing the "wrong" mask? There are many meanings to her words, and we try to hear them all. From this attempt to understand, we discover better follow-up questions to scaffold her reflections on her assumptions.

From Understanding to Provocations

Continuing the example of Hattie, what might we do with this understanding? Granted, teachers using a negotiated curriculum become researchers, but they must translate their study of children into a design for education. Do we simply ask Hattie, "What do you mean?" Do we ask Hattie, "Why did you say *name* instead of *face?*" Asking such direct questions would be like asking an infant why she repeatedly throws her cup from the high chair. We have to design encounters that cause children to engage the differences between these concepts—symbols for objects versus symbols for words.

The photographic mask was one such encounter, albeit an unplanned one. We construct negotiated learning by extending these fortuitous discoveries into a variety of contexts. Ideally, teachers will meet as a team and discuss Hattie's comments, look in their documentation for other episodes in which children are dealing with this transition to word–word relations, and plan ways to provoke the children to reflect on these different types of symbols. It could be that the teachers and children will revisit the photographic mask game in which Lisa wore Tom's photograph and Tom wore Lisa's photograph mask. Together with the children, a new game could be planned. Perhaps the children want to place their own photograph mask over their best friend's face or place a printed sign saying *chair* on the table and a sign with the word *table* on the chair. If the children invent this game of inverting the markers for identity, they may be provoked to think, for the first time, about the range of referents that words can have, and eventually that the word *name* refers to a word (*Lisa*), not an object (Lisa's face).

From Encounters to Investigations

Interesting learning encounters can occur during ordinary moments in the classroom. Much can be learned about the children's thinking, interests, dispositions, and emotional engagement during these ordinary moments. When possible, our understanding of a momentary learning encounter can guide us toward some planned possibilities that expand the spontaneous encounter into a longer-term investigation. Here is an example.

> A group of four-year-olds in Honolulu were outside playing when a gust of wind blew across the yard. "That's the windy wind," one child said. The teacher asked, "The windy wind. Are there different kinds of wind?" Soon a gentle breeze wafted across their faces and another child said, "There, that was a gentle wind." From this brief encounter with two different winds, the teacher arranged trips to other parts of the island. Eventually the children discovered and named 19 different winds from the monster wind to the mountain wind, invented marks that distinguished them, and even, with the help of high school students, animated their drawings of their winds.

This investigation of the winds involved a number of educational objectives: creating symbols that were schematic yet readable characteristics of their winds, creating a homespun mythology of the wind population, thinking about what happens when two winds of different types cross paths, the shape of wind currents as they are influenced by terrain, learning how to identify one wind from the other in the field, and so forth. An investigation uses the original encounter to give continuity to the various encounters and to maintain a high level of emotional engagement. The children continually revisit new encounters to relate them to both the original encounter and planned possibilities.

It is important for teachers to find the concepts within the children's interest and scaffold the children's thinking about that concept. An interest is not sufficient. One does not simply bring in more dinosaur pictures and plastic models if the children have an interest in dinosaurs. In the educational setting of a school, it behooves the teachers to speculate on what drives the interest and scaffold the concepts, not necessarily the interest. The progression of the investigation should be considered on track not when children learn more about dinosaurs but when children learn more about the concepts that drive their interest in dinosaurs. For example: What would it mean to my feeling of safety if huge lizards walked in the forest today? Could I have a pet raptor? If there are no more dinosaurs, will there be no more of us after a while? When the teachers focus on the concepts and not the surface interest, the investigation can take branches that do not include dinosaurs at all, such as watching a mahout guide an elephant in a logging operation or an investigation of the relation between climate and current animal population. The teacher tries to identify the fear, the paradox, the curiosity, the anomaly that drives the interest, and then embeds the energy from this more emotional engagement into the investigations—not just to motivate the children but also to address their personal questions.

When possible, learning encounters should be expanded to investigations, but not necessarily long-term projects. *Investigations* have a somewhat longer duration than learning encounters, have more contexts that provoke a given set of concepts, have a community atmosphere to them, involve more children as they progress, and progress to more complex concepts as they run their course. *Projects* have all the same things as investigations, and in addition some central themes to which children have an emotional investment. This is one of the most important differences between learning encounters and projects.

In a negotiated curriculum, teachers and children get excited about what they are doing. They do things that are big and wonderful and often rather ambitious, like building an amusement park for the birds that visit their playground or holding an Olympic-style long-jump contest for the entire school. These projects, however, can emerge from an episode such as the learning encounter between Hattie and the photographic mask.

In a class meeting, the children and teachers decide that pictures placed in the wrong place, like Lisa's photograph on Tom's head, can be confusing, but pictures placed in the correct place can be helpful. By degrees and in the course of several meetings, the teachers and children decide to study pictures they see outside. One child mentions the pictures he sees on the road, such as the picture of children playing that is a warning for cars to be alert. The children decide to add pictures all over their classroom and playground that will inform people about what to do, what to watch out for, ground rules, and so forth.

A variation of this project was actually done at the Eighth of March Preschool in Reggio Emilia. Eventually the children invented an entire fantasy about a dragon, snakes in a pit, and a princess held captive in a tower that required road signs for all rescuing knights. The medieval adventure of this project motivated the children to invent these symbols, while not in the least diminishing their high-level thinking about how symbols convey meaning. In fact, these children invented the convention that any pictures drawn inside a triangle meant "danger," and any picture drawn inside a circle was a directional pointer.

From Assessment to Study

Assessment, as we view it in negotiated learning, involves the ongoing study of children. This study enables teachers to plan responsive curriculum that supports individual and group development. It is not done to compare children, to determine placement or inclusion into programs, to label, or to grade. It is done to understand children—their schema, feelings, interests, dispositions, and capabilities. This knowledge makes it possible for teachers to plan learning experiences that are meaningful and yet challenging to children.

Assessment of this nature is not focused on what children cannot do but on what they can do, independently, with assistance, and in different kinds of social contexts. It is a dynamic and flexible process. It does not aim to freeze the child in time to quantify achievement or development through a score, rating, or grade. It is an alive, contextualized process that aims to understand children within ever-changing life experiences and situations. Documentation, as we have described it, is at the heart of this kind of assessment.

Much attention has been given in recent years to promoting democracy in the classroom, to developing a sense of community in schools, to cooperative learning, but we seem to assess the effects of these kinds of strategies on only the individual. Our work with parents, in like manner, is solely focused on their own child, not the group. Sometimes we present what the child can do in group situations, but generally these are cases in which the child's behavior within a group is extracted to characterize the individual child, not the group.

The educators in Reggio Emilia study and assess the development of the individual, but also the development of the group, the development of a community of learners, a community of caring people. They celebrate how children learn from and with each other. By presenting documentation on the work of the group, and relating particular children's progress to the development to the group, teachers, parents, and children focus on the social dynamics of learning. Through negotiated learning, educators collaborate to develop a social consciousness about the rights of all young children.

From Parent Involvement to Intellectual Partnership

Many teachers view parent involvement as parent education. This could mean that the teacher's job is to share her expert knowledge with parents. From this standpoint, teachers might consider organizing documentation panels to give information to parents about their children's learning. If teachers operate on this assumption about the teacher's role in relationship to parents, documentation is likely to be used as a one-way communication. Parents are not seen as designers, nor are they invited to engage in discourse with teachers. Parents may be encouraged to ask questions about documentation but not to debate or supplement. Parents are expected to look to the teacher as a source of information.

On the other hand, if we apply the principles of negotiated learning to our work with parents, documentation of children's experiences can be used by teachers to support interactive communication and provide a focus for discourse between teachers and parents. The observations teachers have documented through photography, audiotaping, anecdotal records, note taking, video, or collections of children's work can be shared and explained and then serve as a base for further inquiry, discussion, and analysis. Just as teachers share such documentation with each other to gain multiple perspectives that lead to new insights into children's thinking, they can do so with parents. Parents offer different kinds of insights. They have knowledge of children outside the classroom. Their observations, combined with the teachers' observations, can lead to an even deeper understanding of children's thoughts, feelings and dispositions. By engaging in such discourse, parents and teacher may be able to negotiate an understanding of the learning documented. They become study partners. Designs for future learning experiences naturally flow from this kind of study.

In negotiated learning, teachers invite parents, whenever possible, to think with them not only about how to support children's learning (Fyfe, Strange, & Hovey, 2004) but also about how to best communicate with other parents. If panels or other forms of documentation are to be read by parents, what better way to test the readability than to invite a representative parent to consult in the process?

Another example that illustrates the shift from family involvement to intellectual partnership could focus on family participation in field trips. This is a perfect opportunity to invite parents or other adults to observe and document children's learning processes through photography, taking notes, or videotaping. In preparation for a trip to a farm, for example, the teacher could have a meeting or phone conversation with the family member(s) who will participate in the field trip. She could share what she and the children anticipate they will be exploring during the trip and then probe what parents or other volunteer adults think the children will be most interested in learning and experiencing. This conversation could reveal what prior experiences, if any, the children have had with farms; it could focus on the kinds of questions adults might pose to engage children in thinking about the animals they encounter, the smells they notice, the work of the farmer, and so on. This reflective talk before the visit can help family members develop plans (design) for their observations and conversations with children during the field trip.

A critical part of the negotiated learning process would involve the reflection and analysis of documentation after the field trip. Again, a teacher could meet with the parents or other family members, have telephone conversations, or engage in e-mail exchanges to probe reflections and analyze documentation, always being open to looking at unanticipated learning as well as the anticipated, examining learning processes as well as outcomes (e.g., vocabulary developed or used during the field trip, questions asked by children, interactions among children and farmer, etc.). As noted, the documentation collected during the experience should be used as a platform for supporting these conversations, analyses, and reflections (discourse). Finally, family members could then be engaged in thinking with the teacher about what could happen next; what experiences or conversations could be designed for school or home to extend the learning? Thus the full cycle of discourse, documentation, and design is used to negotiate learning and build intellectual partnerships with families of young children.

Records of parent involvement can promote partnership with families. It is important to keep records of any form of parent involvement (e.g., parent–teacher committee meetings, parent–teacher conferences, parent participation in contributing and organizing materials for the classroom). Records might take the form of photographs, written descriptions of events, minutes of meetings, videotapes of family celebrations or field trips, written records of parent questions or comments. These records are then converted to documentation by revisiting them with parents to understand the roles of family members in negotiated learning. Such records can provide a common reference for discourse, a common memory of experiences or accomplishments that otherwise may have been forgotten or remembered differently. This conversion of records to documentation paradoxically can generate richer experiences in the future, much as reading last year's journal about a trip will enrich this year's trip. If the journal is not revisited, the current trip stands to yield only the same discoveries forgotten from the first—or even worse, the failure to generalize our subtle insights to new experiences. Our subtle insights are most easily forgotten and require the support of documentation to yield growth from experience.

Documentation of parent involvement can be displayed as panels on school walls or notebooks in family lounges, or used in slide presentations for school events. This kind of documentation should invite the viewer to recognize the many and diverse opportunities for parents to become intellectual partners in curriculum support. The display, again, becomes more than an accounting of parent involvement if it includes notes about the process, purpose, and value of the involvement. Quotes or questions from parents can be added to panels to communicate parent perspectives on the experiences. Teachers can even display photographs of parents looking at classroom panels with their children. Such moments, captured and displayed, give a visible presence to parental involvement in the study of their children's work and a clear message of the partnership among teacher, child, and parent, as well as the essential and tangible form of this trilogy. Photographs of parents looking at panels about projects express the "study of study" that defines discourse and negotiated learning.

Parent involvement documentation can be organized and disseminated in many other forms, such as newsletters, phone messages, binders of information, videotapes, or content on school or classroom websites or Facebook pages. The form of documentation should suit the population for whom it is targeted. Take the example of a class in which parents bring their children to school or frequent the classroom regularly. In this case, printed wall panels or video panels may be an efficient means of communication. On the other hand, for a program in which parents seldom visit the school or frequent it only occasionally, other vehicles for documentation may be more effective in communicating and affirming parent involvement. A newsletter or minutes of parent meetings could be sent home or posted to a website. A lending library of video clips or multimedia of family involvement inside or outside the classroom might be made available on a website or on CDs. Making documentation accessible to family members is critical, but the full cycle of negotiated learning will only happen if the documentation is designed and used in ways that invite response and dialogue about learning.

From Cooperation to Co-construction

The components of design, documentation, and discourse have the power to transform teacher–teacher relations, to move the teaching team from routine cooperation to truly generative co-construction of new knowledge. In the first case, team members can cooperate by staying within a defined role, acknowledging each member's area of expertise, and providing material and psychological support for each other. However, these features of cooperation may not lead to growth through co-construction in which each team member is seen both as a learner and a teacher and each team member feels comfortable about making suggestions regarding another member's work. The dynamics of negotiation involve the creative use of confrontation and conflict.

Collective reflection and analysis of documentation at planning meetings leads to more coordinated planning in which teaching teams make better decisions about how to organize themselves and their time, to share their work yet differentiate it to best support the diverse needs of children within small-group projects, individualized activity, or larger group learning experiences.

Another aspect of organization that supports collaboration among teachers is the documentation of team discussions and planning. In negotiated learning, teacher planning is complex and time-consuming. It involves the collective study of the words and work of children and then planning for possible experiences that connect with or challenge children's current schema. When such study and planning for possibilities has been done, the team must then agree to strategies for presenting the plans to children so that they will want to participate. Teachers must determine the roles that one or more team members will play with regard to facilitating small group activities, and another monitors the activity of the rest of the children. They must plan strategies and allot time for documenting ongoing observations of learning; they must determine who will have responsibility for organizing appropriate documentation tools (e.g., camera, camcorder, tape recorder, paper and pen) and who will use them; they must schedule time to analyze the ongoing documentation that is collected and to involve parents through documentation and discourse. As the project evolves, they need to examine ways to use documentation (e.g., photographs, slides, videotape, transcripts of children's dialogues, and children's drawings, writing, paintings, constructions) to sustain children's interests and involvement in the project.

Minutes preserve the collective memory of the group about these teacher agreements and remind the team members how they will coordinate their work. Without documentation of this sort, complete team efforts can easily fall apart. It is relatively easy simply to divide work among teachers in a preset and fixed curriculum, but to coordinate the flow of work within a negotiated learning system requires ongoing communication and collaborative planning. Such planning, organization, and co-construction of purposes and possibilities enables teachers to function efficiently and flexibly in ways that are responsive to children.

From Co-construction to Advocacy and Community Support

Just as it does with other stakeholders, documentation can give educators and the public a common platform for discourse about what goes on in schools. It gives to the public something tangible, visible, and accessible. If done well, it invites dialogue among educators, parents, and public. It can provide better facts to address long-held beliefs. Take the case of four-foot rope lengths, placed as loose strands on the classroom floor. These rope strands are used in many preprimary schools in Reggio as a play material. The legal-minded public often has the initial reaction that ropes are too dangerous as a free play material for young children. However, actual photographs and videos of how children use the four-foot spans of rope, as pretend fire hoses, as a two-way telephone line, as a line to guide block building on the floor, as a pulley rope when looped around a table leg, and even as a game in a supervised tug of war, would dispel the fear that braided cotton rope is a dangerous material.

Too often we use sweeping generalizations when we attempt to change public opinion about our schools. We loudly make claims such as the following:

- Children learn best in small groups!
- Children need hands-on materials to help them learn!
- Teachers need more time for planning and reflection!
- The environment is the third teacher!
- Children need meaningful projects, not drill on skills!

We may even back up these positions with evidence from research. We may be articulate in communicating these positions and needs for resources and occasionally succeed in swaying votes on a particular school referendum. Nonetheless, such accomplishments are often short-lived. Public opinion can easily change when someone or some group speaks louder and stronger.

If we apply the principles of negotiated learning to our efforts in gaining community support, we are less inclined to proclaim to the community and more inclined to engage community members in discourse about educational issues. We often feel that the community is not interested in the details of our work, so we present the sweeping "should" and "ought" to gain their support. However, our assumption that community members feel too distant from our class projects ensures that they will remain so. We have learned from Reggio Emilia that documentation can be a powerful tool for engaging the public in reflective discourse (Rinaldi, 1996). Documentation can make visible the work of the schools and the capacities of children. Real examples of documented learning offer the public a more particular kind of knowledge that empowers and provokes them to reflect, question, and rethink or reconstruct the image of the child and the rights of children to quality education.

When the children of Reggio Emilia interview the farmer about the process of harvesting grapes or ask the street worker about the city's underground drainage system, they and their teachers are giving community members firsthand experience with the kinds of active learning processes that are characteristic of good schools. The documentation of these community-based activities can be returned to the community members as small booklets. These booklets can be sent to the Audubon Society volunteers who helped hang the birdhouses or to the public works people who helped add a new water supply. They can be posted on city websites or developed as articles for local newspapers. These documents build personal bonds and meaningful connections between children and adults in the community. Such documents often increase attendance to open-house events at the schools, which in turn provide opportunities for discourse among educators, parents, and community members.

Educators begin to ask community members for intellectual contributions, not just manual or monetary ones. They treat the community as a "fund of knowledge" for children (Moll, 1992). This kind of treatment is an expression of respect, a way to build connections through shared experience leading to shared conceptions of being and a sense of belonging. It strengthens the "we" identity of a community that cares about each other and helps all members learn and live more productive lives. These are the ingredients of effective advocacy.

We have to be careful not to assume that any contact with the community will engender support for the schools or that such contact is an inherent good. The community members involved—let's say in a class project—need to hear good questions from the children, to sense that the teaching staff has prepared the children for the field trip, and to learn how the experience will be used in the classroom in the future weeks. No one likes to feel that they have provided only a diversion for children, an outing to the fire station, an emotional high that is isolated from true educational objectives, a trip to a celebrated place leaving with only a plastic fire hat as a memory.

Once again, this is where the combined components of design, documentation, and discourse can assure more generative encounters with community members. Children, before meeting the community members, will discuss their expectations in group meetings. With support from a teacher, they will design a purpose, a set of questions, a reason for making the trip. They may even draw what they expect to see and then take these drawings with them as hypotheses to check out. They will bring a camera and an audio recorder to document the experience, which in turn will indicate to the community members the seriousness of the trip for the children. They may bring their sketchpads in some cases. As was mentioned, the children will also share these records with the community members later when they create a documentation for public viewing. This cycle—from designing the purpose of the experience to documenting the experience to engaging the community in discourse during and after the experience—is essential to create an informed advocacy and community support.

SUMMARY OF THE DESIGN, DOCUMENTATION, AND DISCOURSE SYSTEM

To summarize how these three components affect each other, we will follow the traffic of a classroom activity using Figure 14.1. Lets say that a group of children want to enter a checker tournament with another school in the town. Two children know how to play checkers fairly well, but they do not know how to explain their skill to others. The class decides to take notes on how these two children play. These notes are written in a notation system that the children invented (*documentation*). These notes are then summarized and organized into a guide for more novice children (*design from documentation*). The expert players use the guide to walk the more novice players through a variety of board setups. The novice and expert discuss the rationale contained in the notes (*discourse from design*). The teacher videotapes the lessons (*documentation from design*) so that the students can revisit these lessons. The children discuss how effective the lessons were and how well the checkers strategies worked (*discourse from documentation*).

The parents study the documentation and marvel not only at how well the children play checkers but also at how well they can explain their expertise to others and how well the novice players explain what they need in order to understand. The parents listen to each other as they study the documentary video (*discourse from documentation*) and make plans for how they will help the children learn other board strategies (*design from discourse*). These plans are brought before the children for discussion (*discourse from design*).

Documents of the design meetings by the parents and the lessons from the more expert children are revisited by the teachers (*discourse from documentation and from design*). The teachers create panels using video prints and printed words from the documented activities. The teachers add their own commentary to these panels that explain what the children, teachers, and parents learned from these experiences (*documentation from discourse*). Then new parents and the general public come to the school to read these panels. The panels become the focus of a discussion for continuing the co-constructive thrust of the school (*discourse from documentation, then design from discourse*).

In these various ways, the community of the school produces the following results:

- Drawings function as design.
- Descriptions transform into documentation.
- Talking elevates to discourse.
- Remembering supports revisiting.
- Symbols combine into languages.
- Listening includes hearing.
- Understanding leads to provocations.
- Encounters expand to projects.
- Assessment is replaced by study.
- Parent involvement develops into intellectual partnership, and what could be dismissed as only a beautiful example of cooperation becomes a generative case of co-construction, with the special consequence of creating an informed public that will advocate for the continued success of the school program.

REFERENCES

Berger, P., & Luckmann, T. (1966). *The social construction of reality*. New York: Irvington.

Bruner, J. S. (1957). Going beyond the information given. In J. S. Bruner, E. Brunswik, L. Festinger, F. Heider, K. F. Muenzinger, C. E. Osgood, & D. Rapaport (Eds.), *Contemporary approaches to cognition* (pp. 41–69). Cambridge, MA: Harvard University Press.

Bruner, J. (1990). *Acts of meaning*. Cambridge, MA: Harvard University Press.

Doise, W., Mugny, G., & Perret-Clemont, A. N. (1975). Social interaction and the development of cognitive operations. *European Journal of Social Psychology, 5*, 367–383.

Dunn, S., & Larsen, R. (1990). *Design technology*. New York: Falmer Press.

Engel, S. (1995/1999). *The stories children tell: Making sense of the narratives of childhood*. New York: W. H. Freeman.

Forman, E. A., & McPhail, J. (1993). Vygotskian perspective on children's collaborative problem solving activities. In E. A. Forman, N. Minick, & C. A. Stone (Eds.), *Contexts for learning* (pp. 213–229). New York: Oxford University Press.

Forman, G. (1995). Constructivism and the project approach. In C. Fosnot (Ed.), *Constructivism: Theory, perspectives, and practice* (pp. 172–181). New York: Teachers College Press.

Forman, G., & Gandini, L. (1994). *An amusement park for birds* (90-minute VHS video). Amherst, MA: Performanetics.

Forman, G., & Hall, E. (2005). Wondering with children: The importance of observation in early education. *Early Childhood Education and Practice, 7*(2). Available at http://ecrp.uiuc.edu/v7n2/forman.html.

Forman, G., & Kushner, D. (1986). *The child's construction of knowledge*. Washington, DC: NAEYC Publications.

Fyfe, B., & Forman, G. (1996). Negotiated curriculum. *Innovations in Early Education: The International Reggio Exchange, 3*(4), 4–7.

Fyfe, B., Strange, J., & Hovey, S. (2004). Thinking with parents about learning. In J. Hendricks (Ed.), *Next steps in teaching the Reggio way: Accepting the challenge to change* (pp. 96–105). Upper Saddle River, NJ: Merrill Palmer.

Gardner, H. (1983). *Frames of mind: The theory of multiple intelligences.* New York: Basic Books.

Gee, J. (1990). *Social linguistics and literacies: Ideology in discourses.* New York: Falmer Press.

Glazer, S. M., & Brown, C. S. (1993). *Portfolios and beyond.* Norwood, MA: Christopher Gordon.

Goodman, K. (1992). Why whole language is today's agenda in education. *Language Arts, 69,* 354–363.

Isaacs, S. (1930). *Intellectual growth in young children* (with an appendix on children's "why" questions by Nathan Isaacs). London: Routledge & Kegan Paul.

Jankowicz, A. D. (1995). Negotiating shared meanings: A discourse in two voices. *The Journal of Constructivist Psychology, 8,* 341–348.

Kafai, Y., & Harel, I. (1991). Learning through design and teaching. In I. Harel & S. Papert (Eds.), *Constructionism* (pp. 85–110). Norwood, NJ: Ablex.

Moll, L. (1992). Creating zones of possibilities: Combining social contexts for instruction. In L. Moll (Ed.), *Vygotsky and education: Instructional implications and applications of sociohistorical psychology* (pp. 319–348). New York: Cambridge University Press.

Palincsar, A. S., & Brown, A. L. (1984). Reciprocal teaching. *Cognition and Instruction, 1,* 117–175.

Piaget, J. (1970). *Science of education and the psychology of the child.* New York: Grossman.

Piaget, J. (1978). *The development of thought: Equilibration of cognitive structures.* London: Blackwell.

Polanyi, M. (1998). *Personal knowledge. Towards a post critical philosophy.* London: Routledge. (Original work published 1958.)

Rinaldi, C. (1996). Malaguzzi and the teachers. *Innovations in Early Education: The International Reggio Exchange, 3*(4), 1–3.

Solisken, J., Wilson, J., & Willette, J. (1993). Interweaving stories: Creating a multicultural classroom through school/home/university collaboration. *Democracy and Education, 2,* 16–21.

Stubbs, M. (1983). *Discourse analysis: The sociolinguistic analysis of natural language.* Chicago: University of Chicago Press.

Tannen, D. (1982). Ethnic style in male–female conversation. In J. J. Gumperz (Ed.), *Language and social identity* (pp. 217–231). New York: Cambridge University Press.

Tannen, D. (1989). *Talking voices: Repetition, dialogue, and imagery in conversational discourse.* New York: Cambridge University Press.

Taylor, P. (1993). Pluralism, and decolonization: Recent Caribbean literature. *College Literature, 20*(1), 78–89.

Tharp, R. G., & Gallimore, R. (1988). *Rousing minds to life: Teaching, learning, and schooling in social context.* Cambridge, MA: Harvard University Press.

Tierney, R. (1991). *Portfolio assessment in the reading-writing classroom.* Norwood, MA: Christopher Gordon.

Tudge, J., & Winterhoff, P. A. (1993). Vygotsky, Piaget, and Bandura: Perspectives on the relations between the social world and cognitive development. *Human Development, 36,* 61–81.

von Glaserfeld, E. (1995). *Radical constructivism: A way of knowing and learning.* London: Falmer.

Vygotsky, L. S. (1986). *Thought and language* (A. Kozulin, Trans.). Cambridge, MA: MIT Press. (Original work published 1934.)

Wertsch, J. V. (Ed.). (1985). *Culture, communication, and cognition.* New York: Cambridge University Press.

Chapter 15

The Relationship between Documentation and Assessment

Brenda Fyfe

What is the relationship between the Reggio concept of documentation and conventional understandings of assessment? What does the term *assessment* mean in the United States, Italy, and other parts of the world? What does the concept of documentation mean in the preschools and infant-toddler centers of Reggio Emilia?

Dominic Gullo, an American professor and author of a widely referenced book on assessment in early education (2004), defines the concept of assessment as "a procedure used to determine the degree to which an individual child possesses a certain attribute. The term assessment can be used interchangeably with measurement" (p. 6). He goes on to state that assessment is a decision-making tool. It can be formal or informal in nature. Formal assessments can include readiness tests, developmental screening tests, and diagnostic tests. Informal assessments,

The photos in this chapter were taken by Jennifer Strange. The author acknowledges the collaboration of Jennifer Strange and Joanne Ford in the work described here.

in contrast, can include direct observation, use of interviews, anecdotal records, checklists, and collecting samples of children's work.

The concept of documentation, as it is used in the preschools and infant-toddler centers of Reggio Emilia, is a procedure used to make learning visible, so that it can be recalled, revisited, reconstructed, interpreted, and reinterpreted as a basis for decision making. Documentation may reveal a child's skills and knowledge (or attributes), but more important from the Reggio perspective, in-depth documentation can reveal the learning paths that children are taking and processes they are using in their search for meaning. As Rinaldi (2001) stated, "We place the emphasis on documentation as an integral part of the procedures aimed at fostering learning and for modifying the learning-teaching relationship" (p. 79). Documentation is a tool for helping teachers and children reflect on prior experience; listen to each other's ideas, theories, insights, and understandings; and then make decisions together about future learning paths. Thus, documentation, from a Reggio perspective, cannot be used interchangeably with the term *measurement*. Measurement is generally considered an exact science looking at a magnitude of quantity that is established through a standardized unit of measurement. Documentation may consist of "traces of learning" but no trace of learning is limited in its interpretation to a standardized unit of measurement.

Formal assessments, as described by Gullo (2004), are not part of the Reggio concept of documentation. However, some of the informal assessments he describes (e.g., direct observation, anecdotal records, and collecting samples of children's work) could be viewed as documentation practices if done for the purpose of gathering "traces of learning" that make reflection and interpretation possible.

This is not to say that formal assessments are not administered and used to inform educational programming for children in Reggio Emilia. It is most likely that such assessments are used for determining and analyzing the status and progress of children with disabilities (see Chapter 11 by Ivana Soncini, this volume).

FORMATIVE ASSESSMENT AND DOCUMENTATION

The literature on assessment often refers to two basic types: (1) *formative,* which is usually carried out throughout an educational experience, and (2) *summative,* which is conducted at the end of an educational experience. If we reflect on the ideas of Carla Rinaldi, expressed in her chapter "The Pedagogy of Listening" (this volume), it might be reasonable for us to surmise that formative assessment is more closely related to the Reggio concept of documentation, which is used throughout the educational experience to inform teaching and learning.

When thinking about the relationship between formative assessment and the Reggio Emilia concept of documentation, it is important to reflect on how different theories and philosophies of learning can differentiate social constructivist practices of formative assessment from those practices that are informed by a behaviorist or empiricist philosophical orientation. For example, when formative assessment is understood from a behaviorist or empiricist philosophical orientation, it can be viewed as evaluative, judgmental, corrective, or take the form of reinforcement feedback from teacher to child during the process of learning. The practice of documentation, which comes from a social constructivist philosophical orientation, is conducted, in contrast, in a way that supports the learner to participate in looking at his or her own learning to construct or reconstruct new and deeper understandings. As Rinaldi explains, it is done to make learning visible so that the learners can "observe themselves from an external viewpoint while they are learning" (Chapter 13, this volume). Traces of learning such as notes, transcripts, slides, photos, and videos are examined by teaching teams and with parents, but they are also shared with children so that they can examine their own work, experience, actions, and comments. Teachers scaffold children's reflections on these documents with probing questions, encouragement to take the idea further, or challenges to look again at their ideas or actions and clarify them for others. Children in Reggio schools are enabled to use documentation to revisit and rethink their work and expressed ideas. Ultimately, the goal is to help children self-assess.

The message center of the Maplewood–Richmond Heights Early Childhood Center in St. Louis, Missouri.

The theoretical framework of social constructivism guides teachers to presume the learner to be an active participant in the assessment process, just as it presumes the learner to be an active participant in the learning process; in contrast, when learners are given evaluative, corrective, or reinforcement feedback during the learning process, the learners are more likely presumed to be (or at least treated as) passive recipients of knowledge—recipients whose behavior is shaped by external reinforcement rather than informed by external feedback.

Although making learning visible through documentation can be reinforcing to a child who sees his or her words and work valued through this process, the use of documentation is aimed at helping the child to reflect, revisit experiences, or self-assess, not to shape his or her inclination to repeat such behavior or work. Revisiting can support children's attempts to make sense of their theories and to deal with assumptions that with extra inspection do not make sense.

Here is an example that might illustrate feedback of various kinds. In response to a child who announces that he has completed a message for his friend, a teacher might say something like, "I see that you wrote a message, but you need to sign it" (*evaluative/corrective feedback*). Another teacher might say "Your message is almost finished, but you need to put your name on the bottom so the person to

Teacher and child look into a mirror, in preparation for the child drawing her self-portrait.

whom you are sending it will know it's from you" (*This might be considered a loan of knowledge, from a Vygotskian perspective*). Or she might say to the child, "When you started this message, you told me you were writing it for your friend, Sam, but after you put it in his mailbox, I wonder how he will know it's from you" (*using the child's expressed comments to help the child reflect on whether the message is, indeed, finished*). The teacher might also show the child a documentation panel of messages exhibited above the message center and suggest the child look at them to see what he notices, asking the child, "What are some features of these messages that seem important for helping the receiver of the message know who sent it?" (*using visual documentation of other children's work to provoke this child's thinking*). Any of these responses may be helpful in providing constructive feedback that comes from formative assessment, but which teacher responses will encourage the child to think and rethink his concept of message making? Which enable the child to distance himself from his work, to question and reflect on it, and to self-assess?

CAN ASSESSMENT PRACTICES LIMIT THE CHILD'S SEARCH FOR MEANING?

Those of us who aspire to the pedagogy of listening agree with Carla Rinaldi that it supports the search for meaning, and this meaning is made visible and possible through the processes of observation, interpretation, and documentation. As Rinaldi says, "Documentation can be seen as visible listening: it ensures listening and being listened to by others. . . . This ensures that the group and each child can observe themselves from an external viewpoint while they are learning (both during and after the process)" (Chapter 13, this volume).

Yet how does or can the process of assessment support the search for meaning? More specifically, we must ask how our own particular processes of assessment support the search for meaning. Do they support or do they sometimes inhibit or limit the search for meaning? The examples previously given about various kinds of teacher responses (coming from different philosophical perspectives) may help us to reflect on this question. However, another direction we might take in answering this question is to look at how our conventional understandings of curriculum and developmental expectations may inhibit or limit the search for meaning.

A commonly shared principle of good assessment is that it should be aligned with the goals or standards for learning. However, Reggio educators caution us to refrain from imposing a preestablished frame of analysis that will limit, in advance, how we will interpret and use documentation with children. They encourage us to keep an open mind to look beyond the learning that may have been anticipated or planned, to look beyond the goals of the curriculum.

Dahlberg, Moss, and Pence (1999) expressed concern that too often educators try to categorize and classify according to predetermined schemas:

As a consequence, all we know is how far this or that child conforms to certain norms inscribed on the maps we use. Instead of concrete descriptions and reflections on children's doings and thinking, on their hypotheses and theories of the world, we easily end up with simple mappings of children's lives, general classifications of the child of the kind that say "children of such and such an age are like that." The maps, the classifications and the ready-made categories end up replacing the richness of children's lived lives and the inescapable complexity of concrete experience. (p. 36)

In a later book, Dahlberg and Moss (2005) questioned whether this emphasis on standardization could be considered ethical practice. They explained that in society today,

the concept of quality is about establishing conformity to predetermined standards. It seeks closure, in the sense that it wants certain answers about conformity, often reduced to numbers. The discourse of meaning making, in contrast, is first and foremost about constructing and deepening understanding. . . . It assumes that the meaning of pedagogical work is always open to different interpretations. (p. 88)

In *Schools that Learn,* Peter Senge and colleagues (2000) wrote,

states become preoccupied with establishing standards and measuring student outcomes through tests. Educators focus their attention on techniques and strategies to respond to the policymakers' mandates, often narrowing the curriculum and increasing the emphasis on rote learning. (p. 281)

As a result, a de-emphasis or no emphasis is placed on the thinking or meaning making of the child in relation to the curriculum, much less the thinking of the child that may appear unrelated to the curriculum goals driving instruction.

The concepts of a responsive curriculum and negotiated learning (Chapter 14, this volume) that put *documentation, discourse,* and *design* at the heart of the teaching–learning process are certainly not supported in many school systems today. Even when pre-kindergarten teachers do not have to abide by the direct mandates of meeting predefined standards and measurements of outcomes, they often experience tremendous pressure that comes indirectly from parents, colleagues in the elementary grades, and the community at large to rush children through a curriculum of procedural knowledge and skills that are perceived to prepare children for the screening and testing that is to come. Teachers who are feeling this pressure often become more teacher- and curriculum-centered. They feel they have no time or encouragement to support a negotiated learning process, where children's ideas (especially those that appear disconnected from curriculum goals) are given serious consideration. There is no place for questions and uncertainty, especially when learning must be measured for assessment purposes.

Assessment in U.S. schools most often focuses on determining children's levels of competency, not on uncovering children's theories or revealing the child's processes of meaning making or ways adults can support that search for meaning. It is used to give parents an understanding of how their child is performing according to standards and in comparison with other children, not to help parents gain insights into the thinking of the child.

I am concerned that some of our early childhood documents on best practice in the United States still have the tendency to narrow and limit our image of the child, boxing them into predetermined expectations about learning. The heavy emphasis on goal-driven instruction and assessment is not balanced with an openness to going into uncharted territory with children. In the latest edition of *Preparing Early Childhood Professionals* (Hyson, 2003), Standard #3 addresses the importance of observing, documenting, and assessing to support young children and families. At first reading, it appears that this standard is very much aligned with Reggio's emphasis on the ongoing and integral nature of documentation and assessment in the learning process. This document from the National Association for the Education of Young Children (NAEYC) indicates that teachers demonstrate their understanding of this standard "by embedding assessment-related activities in curriculum and in daily routines, so that assessment becomes a habitual part of professional life" (p. 33).

The document goes on to emphasize *alignment:* "good assessment is a positive tool that supports children's development and learning, and that improves outcomes for young children and families" (p. 33). The basic concepts described in this document are sound, but I am concerned about what is not stated. For example, there is little or no discussion of the importance of using documentation to help children self-assess. There is no mention of using documentation with children to reflect on their own learning or to think about their thinking. There is no mention of interpreting and reinterpreting to develop (with the children) theories that give meaning to events and objects in their world. Rather, this NAEYC document places emphasis on using observation and documentation "to capture each child's unique qualities, strengths and needs" (p. 33). There is no mention of using documentation to study and develop children's ideas, current schemas, or theories; no talk of using documentation with children to help them to ask good questions (Forman, 1989), to support them in the search for meaning.

The social constructivist approach that Carla Rinaldi describes encourages us to go beyond identification of qualities, strengths, needs, and interest. The teachers in Reggio Emilia "seek to uncover the children's beliefs about the topics to be investigated. . . . Their analysis reveals the reasons behind the children's interest, the source of their current knowledge and their level of articulation about its detail" (Forman & Fyfe, 1998, p. 240; see also Chapter 14, this volume).

I go back to the plea from Dahlberg, Moss, and Pence (1999; see also Chapter 12, this volume) to suggest that in the United States and other nations where standards and goals are highly valued, where evaluation is considered essential, we must seek balance when it comes to combining frameworks of normalization (standards or developmental scales) and openness to meaning making that goes beyond or outside the boundaries of standards and scales. This involves the use of multiple frames (curriculum goals, developmental progressions, and open-ended questions about learning and thinking) for examining children's learning and meaning making.

COLLECTING, ORGANIZING, AND INTERPRETING DOCUMENTATION AT THE END VERSUS DURING AN EDUCATIONAL EXPERIENCE

Frequently, teachers who are new to the study of the Reggio Emilia approach collect, organize, and interpret documentation only at the end of an experience or project, rather than during the process of the experience or project. In *Making Learning Visible,* Steven Seidel (2001), the director of Harvard's Project Zero, commented that in the United States, "the practice of assessment is most often thought of as synonymous with evaluation and, in an American context, evaluation is a process of judgment, measuring and placing one work in relation to the others' works" (pp. 304–305). I think Seidel's observation could explain why many U.S. educators who document observations or collect samples of children's work wait to interpret and use it (as if it were evaluation data) to judge or describe the final learning outcome at the end of a series of experiences, rather than as part of the everyday teaching–learning process.

Evaluation is generally focused on the summative rather than the formative character of assessment. Assessment, when viewed as evaluation, is seen as a tool for grading and comparing students, for rating them on a scale to determine a level of competence or development, for classifying them for special services, or for deciding whether to retain or pass them on from one grade to the next. The concept of documentation as described and practiced by Reggio educators is a tool for teachers, children, and parents to reflect on learning processes and learning outcomes, not only of individuals but also of groups.

Today, a growing number of teachers who have studied the Reggio approach in-depth are interpreting documentation as part of their daily work, rather than only at the end of an educational experience. Moreover, even when documentation is analyzed only at the end of a unit, project, or extended period of time, there is value. Anytime learning is made visible through real examples of children's work, words, or actions, there is opportunity to gain insight into the thinking and potential of children. There is opportunity to offer parents an inside view of the mind of a child, an opportunity to think together with teachers about learning. Although much is lost that could have come from the use of documentation in the formative sense (with children, parents, and teachers) during the set of experiences, documentation of the sort Rinaldi describes can provide a rich base for interpretation and study at any moment in time. This interpretation at the end of a project or long-term study can be considered "formative" in the sense that it can be used by teachers to inform future teaching and learning. When such documentation is reflected on with children and parents, it can support their understandings of themselves as learners and provoke new directions and ideas for further research or application in other settings.

The culminating documentation of a project from one school year can become a provocation for a new set of learners in following years. It could also be used as a bridge between preschool and kindergarten or kindergarten and first grade to reconnect children and teachers to prior learning and experience, creating a spiral curriculum and cultural situatedness of meanings (Bruner, 1977) that helps to bring continuity to the history of children's experiences and studies from one year to the next. Documentation of this sort can help teachers circle back to earlier experience and intuitive knowledge that can serve as a foundation for deeper learning. Too often, teachers in kindergarten or first grade know nothing about the in-depth learning experiences and research that they should be building on. End-of-year documentation can become that link or bridge for such teachers.

In Reggio Emilia, it is a common practice for each school or, at times, single classrooms to produce a booklet presenting a long-term investigation, research, or community project. The children and teachers from Martiri di Sesso Preschool, for example, have produced such documents (e.g., *Ippolito, Ascoltare con le mani . . . , Come in un Giardino, Gli Uccellini del Parco*) the contents of which would have been used in various ways during the project to inform learning but when organized and presented at the end of the year have another value. They tell the entire story and study of the project. They illustrate the learning of individuals but, more important, the learning of the group. This documentation that is organized and presented at the end of an educational experience has tremendous value in celebrating the accomplishments of the community of learners. It gives value to the collective intelligence and accomplishments of the children, parents, teachers, and community who collaborated in the experiences.

INCORPORATE DOCUMENTATION
AS PART OF DAILY PRACTICE

Teachers typically experience several changes in mind-set as they begin to view documentation as critical to teaching and learning (Chapter 14, this volume; Fyfe, 1998; Fyfe, Geismar-Ryan, & Strange, 2000). One of these is a shift toward thinking about teaching and learning as a process of collaborative inquiry, a process of ongoing collaborative action research. It requires a search for new patterns of organization and communication with children, parents, and fellow teachers. Collaborative action research involves an understanding of the interdependence between organization and collaboration, one of the fundamentals of the Reggio approach (Gandini, 1993). It is a collaborative style of work that asks teachers to think, plan, work, and interpret together (Rinaldi, 1994).

This practice of collaborative inquiry, when applied to the concept of assessment, insists that teachers look at evidence of learning and documented observations of learning processes together. Documentation offers a kind of raw data that has not yet been interpreted. It gives the teaching team a common platform for thinking together about learning, for drawing on multiple perspectives to enrich the possible interpretations.

This paradigm of teaching as a collegial and research-based activity requires the following: "(1) that we make our observations visible so that we can share them with colleagues; (2) that we consider each others' perspectives as we dialogue, debate, and negotiate shared interpretations; (3) that together we formulate hypotheses, predictions, and projections about future learning experiences that we might propose to the children; and (4) that we organize diversify, and coordinate our work in light of these agreements" (Fyfe, 1998, p. 21). Loris Malaguzzi (Chapter 2, this volume) states that this shift "represents a deliberate break from the traditional professional and cultural solitude and isolation of teachers." Malaguzzi was speaking of a shift that had happened long ago in his Reggio Emilia schools. This shift has yet to happen on any scale in the United States. Mike Schmoker (2006) cited numerous studies that testify to the fact that teaching in the United States is still, for the most part, an isolated practice, and he made the case that isolation is the enemy of improvement. He stated:

> Unlike other professionals, and despite near-universal agreement on the importance of teaming, teachers do not work in teams. They do not prepare lessons and assessments together, and they do not test and refine their lessons regularly on the basis of assessment results. (p. 18)

It may be easier for pre-K teachers to team within a classroom (in preparing learning experiences, carrying them out, and reflecting on their effectiveness), because it is common to have two teachers per pre-K classroom. However, the norm in the United States is to have a lead teacher and teacher assistant, rather than two teachers with equal authority and credentials, as is the norm in the Reggio Emilia preschools. Unfortunately, lead teachers do not always cultivate egalitarian relationships with their teacher assistants, inviting and supporting them to participate in the collection and analysis of documentation or assessment data. Some school district structures (e.g., in regard to union rules, time and compensation, and so on) may even directly or indirectly prohibit teacher assistants from participating in such activities.

Educators who have made the shift toward this collaborative style of continuous action research can use pedagogical documentation to rethink the meaning of "assessment," to question their certainties about what is significant learning and what is not. Collaborative action research, by its very nature, uncovers new questions and suggests new paths of learning, rather than just evaluation of pre-determined goals.

FINDING AND ORGANIZING TIME FOR COLLECTIVE REFLECTION AND ANALYSIS OF LEARNING

Finding and organizing time on a weekly or biweekly basis for interpretation of documentation or assessment data is most often identified as a major barrier for teamwork and collaborative action research. However, I have observed that even when time is available during the workday, it is often used inefficiently.

Because time of this nature is so precious, it needs to be organized for optimal productivity. Efficient use of such time requires preplanned agendas for meetings with agreements among team members about what documentation will be presented and who is responsible for bringing the documentation in a form that will make it easy for the team to examine (e.g., multiple copies of transcripts and appropriate technology when needed, such as a smart board or computer screen for viewing such documentation). The meeting space should support focused and serious discourse, a space that is free of distractions. At the meeting, multiple perspectives and interpretations should be encouraged and debated. Teams should give a significant amount of time to reflect collectively on what the documentation reveals about children's ideas, interests, feelings, opinions, assumptions, or working theories. I have observed that many teachers want to move too quickly through this part of the process, jumping ahead to implications for teaching. Only after considerable analysis of what the documentation reveals (in terms of children's theories, understandings, and misunderstandings) will teachers be in a position to formulate hypotheses, predictions, and projections about future learning experiences that have continuity with children's current thinking—experiences that will challenge and engage a particular group of learners at a particular time and place (Dewey, 1998). Finally, teachers must plan how they will organize, diversify, and coordinate their work in light of their interpretations and projections (Fyfe, 1998).

Another less obvious barrier that can prevent teachers from committing to the regular practice of placing documentation and assessment at the heart of the learning process is a concern that it takes time away from the teaching of children. Amelia Gambetti once commented in a consultation visit with St. Louis teachers that we must think of this as "time for children." The time adults spend observing and documenting and then interpreting and reinterpreting documentation will make our time with children all the more meaningful and responsive. In addition, teachers learned the value of interpreting and reinterpreting documentation with children. As Carla explains, this is done to develop with the children theories that give meaning to events and objects in their world (Rinaldi, 2006).

In Reggio Emilia and all great school systems that support collaborative inquiry and formative assessment, teachers and administrators devise school structures

Teaching team studying documentation together.

that deal with the resource of time. The viability and sustainability of learning organizations that give value to collaborative inquiry are dependent on such structures. The widely acclaimed work on "understanding by design" by Wiggins and McTigue (2007) is grounded in collaborative inquiry. They stated that "Finding new chunks of time to permit work groups to meet is, of course, a challenge. It requires creative thinking and political skill (because finding 'new' time means stealing 'old' time, in most cases" (p. 189). They offered many suggestions based on their work with schools. A few of these practices (Wiggins & McTigue, 2007) are similar to what I have observed in U.S. schools that are committed to the process of collaborative inquiry and collective reflection on formative assessment data:

- Each grade-level or departmental team is allocated 2 hours per week, with coverage provided by other teams, administrators, resource specialists, student teachers, or substitutes.
- Teachers meet for an extended lunch and during resource periods or scheduled assemblies.
- Roving substitutes, hired for a day, provide release time for grade-level or departmental teams.

RECIPROCAL EXPECTATIONS AND DIALOGUE WITH CHILDREN: A FOUNDATION FOR SELF- AND GROUP ASSESSMENT

Teachers who have begun to understand the pedagogy of listening often express a significant insight. Back in 1992 when a number of us in St. Louis began a university–schools collaboration to study the Reggio approach, the phrase *slowing down to listen* could be heard in conversation after conversation with teachers who were beginning their study of the Reggio approach. Teachers were continually amazed at what they learned from young children when they slowed down to ask the children's opinions, to listen to their ideas, to wonder about the meaning of a child's comments, or to ask for clarification from the child, to check on their understanding of the child's understanding. Teachers reflected that this kind of interaction with children was not possible when they were focused solely on guiding, directing, and assessing children every moment through a preestablished and narrowly designed curriculum.

Teachers who are new to the Reggio concept of documentation and the pedagogy of listening often need to be helped to deconstruct what they have learned about the process of learning, the role of the teacher, and the role of the student (Dahlberg et al., 1999; MacNaughton, 2005). I would add that teachers also must deconstruct their concepts of the purposes and processes of assessment. With the support of an ongoing professional development system, teachers in our St. Louis group were able to deconstruct prior assumptions that guided interactions with children. Teachers were encouraged to take the risk of changing their normal patterns of behavior (e.g., from guiding, directing, and facilitating to slowing down to listen and having genuine conversations with children), and they were given the time and opportunity to reflect on these new experiences with colleagues (Fyfe, 1998). As a result, expectations changed.

Teachers reported that through listening, they could truly be "in the moment" with children. Through listening, they were better able to support and challenge a child spontaneously to extend his or her thinking. However, they also learned that reciprocal expectations of dialogue must be developed over time with some children. Many children are not used to teachers who want to understand their opinions and emerging theories. Children may not trust the teacher's motives, assuming that the interest in their ideas is really a test rather than genuine curiosity and interest in the child's thinking (Kaminsky & Gandini, 2002). Teachers who have embraced the pedagogy of listening may have to persist through a period of disbelief and mistrust from children. My observation is that when children build relationships of mutual trust and respect with adults, and those adults engage them regularly in meaningful dialogue, the children, as well as the teachers, develop reciprocal expectations in regard to dialogue.

I have observed that teachers who embrace the pedagogy of listening have an image of the child as someone whose ideas are worth listening to, whose comments and opinions are not just frivolous and cute but instead intelligent efforts to make sense of the world. They learn that staying in the frame of mind of the child is critical to helping children to ask good questions (Forman, 1989). I have observed that the more teachers develop the reciprocal expectations of the pedagogy of listening, the stronger the image of the child grows—in the minds of teachers, children, and parents.

Reciprocal expectations in the schools of Reggio Emilia go beyond child–teacher relationships. The intersubjectivity of children within groups and the group's ability to function as an effective learning community is also cultivated through reciprocal expectations. Peers are expected to support each other's learning. Through group learning experiences, children learn not only how to support but go further to become responsible for each other's learning.

In Reggio preschools and infant-toddler centers, great attention is given to the form, function, and understanding in learning groups. Mara Kreschevsky (2001) of Project Zero presented a set of seven propositions about learning groups in early childhood that were identified by Reggio educators. The last of these propositions focuses on indicators that learning groups are supporting and demonstrate understanding. One indicator related to this proposition is "assessment and self-assessment have a strong presence inside the learning group and serve to guide and orient the learning process" (p. 247).

It has been my observation in the United States that, although we give a lot of lip service to the importance of children learning how to function within a group, we seldom give value (through assessment or research) to the understanding of learning groups and the learning outcomes of the group as well as the individual. We may examine and assess how an individual child contributes to a group discussion or cooperates with his or her peers to accomplish a task, but we seldom think about or give value to the learning dynamics, accomplishments, and context of the learning group. In Reggio Emilia schools, children are viewed as individual and group learners (Giudici, Rinaldi, & Krechevsky, 2001). Teachers and children reflect on and assess not only their individual performances or contributions in a group, but also the collective efforts, cooperation, and interactions that enabled a group to achieve or not achieve its goals. Much of the documentation we see in Reggio Emilia intentionally focuses on the relationships, subjectivity, and interdependence of the learners (children and adults) within the school. It often reveals what some would call distributed or situated cognition (Kirshner & Whitson, 1997; Ross, 2007; Salomon, 1997; Woodhead & Light, 1991) of a group of learners. It reveals young children's ability to engage in mutual learning and to build a learning community where each child is responsible for the others' learning. It illustrates how the culture of participation and "the value of democracy . . . is embedded in the concept of participation" (Giudici et al., 2001, p. 42).

Assessment processes in the United States seldom focus on this social and collective aspect of learning. Teachers, children, and parents could benefit from expanding our concepts of assessment, moving beyond a focus on the individual learner (as described by Gullo at the beginning of this chapter) to a focus on individual as well as group learning.

IN CONCLUSION

The images used to illustrate some of the practices of documentation and assessment that I have discussed in this chapter were taken at the Maplewood–Richmond Heights (MRH) Early Childhood Center. This school serves children from age 3 years through first grade in a racially and economically diverse, urban public school district adjacent to the city of St. Louis, Missouri, in the United States. My Webster University early childhood faculty colleagues and I have partnered with this district for the past few years through an embedded professional development model. Jennifer Strange, an adjunct faculty member from Webster University works side by side with teachers and the principal of this school for 2 to 3 days per week, mentoring them, modeling Reggio-informed practices, and assisting them in the process of observation and documentation. Jennifer is able to draw from her experience over 20 years as a master teacher and now national consultant as she works directly with MRH educators while also bridging a professional development school connection with Webster's School of Education students and faculty. As a way to conclude this chapter, I would like to share a reflection written by Jennifer Strange and Joanne Ford, one of the MRH teachers, as they looked back at a turning point for teachers in their first year of working together to understand the pedagogy of listening and the power of documentation.

> Educators at the Maplewood–Richmond Heights Early Childhood Center, preschool through 1st grade, in St. Louis had been reading and thinking about Reggio-inspired learning for some time. A *pedagogista* was hired to work with teachers and children in the fall of 2006. Reggio-inspired work began in earnest.
>
> The image of the child began to be seen in the hallways of the school through photographs on identity boards outside of each preschool classroom. Accompanying self-portraits were initiated by the *pedagogista*. The classroom teachers became intrigued and quickly assumed support of this ongoing work with the children. As the identity boards of photographs and self-portraits began to be posted in the hallways, teachers, children, and family members from throughout the school began to stop and admire the results of each child's image.
>
> The preschool educators soon recognized the importance of these self-portraits in relation to the children's and their own learning. One teacher said, "At first, scaffolding the skills for drawing a self-portrait seemed odd to me. However, when I thought about how we might support the writing of letters to improve the effort, it seemed fine to use similar language and techniques for drawing." Children voiced their pleasure regarding the results of their work. A child said, "I drew my teeth and they look like my Dad's teeth . . . wow!" While educators were documenting these responses, they did not fully anticipate how the portraits would become a tool for communicating the depth of this new way of thinking and doing to others.

A father stops to admire and take a photo of the children's self-portraits.

Early one morning as the *pedagogista* came out into the hallway, she saw a parent taking a photograph of his child's self-portrait panel. While pleased at this father's interest, she was also curious and asked why he was taking a picture. He replied, "These drawings of the children are so great. I want a picture of them to hang in our living room." The *pedagogista* was profoundly moved. All of the educators became increasingly aware of family members' interest that the self-portraits were generating.

In collaborative meetings preparing for fall conferences, the teachers decided to use the self-portraits as a focus for dialogue. Describing the process of the self-portraits provided an insight for parents regarding the relationships being built between children and teachers as they collaborated on this meaningful work. The developing observational, expressive, and reflective skills of the children especially came to light in these conference dialogues. This particular conference was so different in comparison to previous conferences that dealt more with checklists and standardized assessments. Both parents and teachers came away from these meetings filled with appreciation for the children's work and with excitement for what might be possible in the coming months.

I believe this story illustrates teachers' efforts to put documentation into relationship with concepts of assessment. These educators have deconstructed former concepts of assessment as strictly focused on evaluative data. They have found that parents learn from each other and the teachers through an exchange of what they see in the documentation, what they question, and what they interpret. It was clear to me from this reflection that Jennifer and Joanne viewed assessment as a social construction of knowledge through the study of children's learning made visible. This does not mean that they no longer utilize checklists or standardized assessments, but instead they believe and have experienced that parents as well as children need to engage in the process of meaning making, rather than being treated simply as the recipients of evaluative information. They view assessment as meaning making, and they know that good documentation can support that process of learning. They use documentation with children and parents to build reciprocal expectations about learning. They help children to reflect on their own and each other's ideas and to assess each other's ideas and contributions to the group.

Today, first-grade teachers at MRH like Heather Bailey, who loops for 2 years (K–1) with her children, are putting documentation into relation with assessment as they work with children and communicate with parents. Heather recently reported that as a result of sharing documentation of children's story generation, writing, and editing processes at parent–teacher conferences, a new level of parent participation has emerged. One parent, for example, drew insights for his own teaching of older students and has initiated an ongoing exchange between his older students and the first graders. Other parents have expressed appreciation for having this window into their children's thinking and experience, saying it gives new and enhanced meaning to progress reports. The children of this first-grade teacher have developed dispositions to raise the bar of expectations for themselves and each other as they collectively critique documentation of their work and learning experiences.

For these teachers, children, and parents, documentation has become a necessary and driving force for creating responsive curriculum and for promoting and assessing individual and group learning. They have found meaningful ways to use documentation as a complement to more formal assessment data, all of which inform better teaching and learning.

REFERENCES

Bruner, J. (1977). *The process of education*. Cambridge, MA: Harvard University Press.

Dahlberg, G., & Moss, P. (2005). *Ethics and politics in early childhood education*. London: Falmer Press.

Dahlberg, G., Moss, P., & Pence, A. (1999). *Beyond quality in early childhood education and care: Postmodern perspectives*. London: Routledge-Falmer.

Dewey, J. (1998). *Experience and education: The 60th anniversary edition*. West Lafayette, IN: Kappa Delta Pi.

Forman, G. (1989). Helping children ask good questions. In B. Neugebauer (Ed.), *The wonder of it: Exploring how the world works* (pp. 21–24) Redmond, WA: Exchange Press.

Forman, G., & Fyfe, B. (1998). Negotiated learning through documentation, discourse and design. In C. Edwards, L. Gandini, & G. Forman (Eds.), *The hundred languages of children: The Reggio Emilia approach to early childhood education* (2nd ed., pp. 239–260). Norwood, NJ: Ablex.

Fyfe, B. (1998). Questions for collaboration: Lessons from Reggio Emilia. *Canadian Children, 23*(1), 20–24

Fyfe, B., Geismar-Ryan, L., & Strange, J. (2000). The potential of collaborative inquiry. *Innovations in Early Education: The International Reggio Exchange, 7*(4), 7–19.

Gandini, L. (1993). Fundamentals of the Reggio approach to early childhood education. *Young Children, 49*, 4–8.

Giudici, C., Rinaldi, C., & Krechevsky, M. (Eds.). (2001). *Making learning visible: Children as individual and group learners*. Reggio Emilia, Italy: Project Zero and Reggio Children.

Gullo, D. F. (2004). *Understanding assessment and evaluation in early childhood education*. New York: Teachers College Press.

Hyson, M. (Ed.). (2003). *Preparing early childhood professionals: NAEYC's standards for programs*. Washington, DC: National Association for the Education of Young Children.

Kaminsky, J. A., & Gandini, L. (2002). The role of culture and community in children's learning and development: An interview with Barbara Bowman. *Innovations in Early Education: The International Reggio Exchange, 9*(3), 4–12.

Kirshner, D., & Whitson, J. A. (Eds.). (1997). *Situated cognition: Social, semiotic, and psychological perspectives*. London: Psychology Press.

Krechevsky, M. (2001). Form, function, and understanding in learning groups: Propositions from the Reggio classrooms. In C. Giudici, C. Rinaldi, & M. Krechevsky (Eds.), *Making learning visible: Children as individual and group learners* (pp. 246–269). Reggio Emilia, Italy: Project Zero and Reggio Children.

MacNaughton, G. (2005). *Doing Foucault in early childhood studies: Applying poststructural ideas*. London: Routledge.

Rinaldi, C. (1994). Staff development in Reggio Emilia. In L. Katz & B. Cesarone (Eds.), *Reflections on the Reggio Emilia approach* (pp. 55–60). Urbana, IL: ERIC Clearinghouse on Elementary and Early Childhood Education.

Rinaldi, C. (2001). Documentation and assessment: What is the relationship? In C. Giudici, C. Rinaldi, & M. Krechevsky (Eds.), *Making learning visible: Children as individual and group learners* (pp. 78–89). Reggio Emilia, Italy: Project Zero and Reggio Children.

Rinaldi, C. (2006). *In dialogue with Reggio Emilia: Listening, researching and learning*. London: Routledge.

Ross, D. (2007). *Distributed cognition and the will: Individual volition and social context*. Cambridge, MA: MIT Press.

Salomon, G. (1997). *Distributed cognitions: Psychological and educational considerations*. New York: Cambridge University Press.

Schmoker, M. (2006). *Results now: How we can achieve unprecedented improvements in teaching and learning*. Alexandria, VA: Association for Supervision and Curriculum Development.

Seidel, S. (2001). Understanding documentation starts at home. In C. Giudici, C. Rinaldi, & M. Krechevsky (Eds.), *Making learning visible: Children as individual and group learners* (pp. 304–311) . Reggio Emilia, Italy: Project Zero and Reggio Children.

Senge, P., Cambron-McCabe, N., Lucas, L., Smith, B., Dutton, J., & Kleiner, A. (2000). *Schools that learn: A fifth discipline fieldbook for educators, parents, and everyone who cares about education.* New York: Doubleday.

Wiggins, G., & McTigue, J. (2007). *Schooling by design.* Alexandria, VA: Association for Supervision and Curriculum Development.

Woodhead, M., & Light, P. (1991). *Learning to think.* New York: Routledge.

Part IV

The Idea of the Hundred Languages of Children and Its Evolution

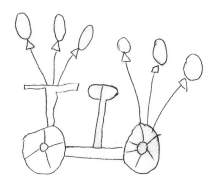

Chapter 16

Is Beauty a Way of Knowing?

Margie Cooper

What if we were living in a time of shifting paradigms in our understanding of the relationship between learning and teaching? Would we be aware of it? Would we welcome it? Would we take it up as our charge to gain more insight and perspective in our roles as educators?

It could be argued that the last *major* shift in our field was brought about by the contributions of social constructivist theorists who advanced our perceptions of the important and essential influences of *others,* whether peers or adults, in terms of the ways we humans build up learning and meaning. Because ours is a field responsible for constructing the most positive conditions for human learning, what if we have been missing or misunderstanding other important and essential contributors to or conditions for learning?

The theory of the hundred languages, as proposed by Reggio Emilia educators, offers a new vantage point for seeing children in their brilliance and competence in constructing and advancing their own understanding. Nearly 5 decades of close observation of children and adults in the real life of schools, critical and social

An earlier version of this chapter was published in Cooper, M. (2009). "Is beauty a way of knowing?" *Innovations in Early Education: The International Reggio Exchange, 16*(3), 1–9 (Michigan: Wayne State College of Education).

interpretation of those observations and experiences, and detailed documentation of learning processes enacted by children and adults is pointing to a crucial human endowment that both urges and satisfies humans along their particular, unique course of development.

This endowment or sensibility might be called an aesthetic dimension and, when given the space and time to develop in relation to all other human facilities, becomes a powerful tool for driving and connecting learning along the course of the human experience. Up to now, "aesthetics" is a field that has been claimed by philosophy and art, as evidenced by the extensive literature on the subject in those disciplines. It is interesting to note that a major publication from those disciplines states, "aesthetics is thriving as a field of scholarly inquiry, and demand for courses in aesthetics equals or surpasses demand for any course in philosophy at many universities" (Gaut & Lopes, 2005, p. xviii).

Concomitantly, from 5 decades of experience, educators from Reggio Emilia are now more clearly aware and better able to articulate, with a humble sense of confidence, their observations and theories of human development in relation to the presence and contribution of an aesthetic dimension. What follows is a discussion of these ideas, taken from a weeklong study experience in Reggio Emilia in April 2009. The week was full of sunshine, long days, and challenging thinking. I was especially captivated by the contributions of Vea Vecchi, *atelierista* of Diana Preschool for 30 years. Having retired in 2000, Vea continues to collaborate with Reggio Children, particularly in the areas of publishing, exhibitions, research projects, and concepts of the *atelier* and the theory of the hundred languages. Her contributions across the week were not only through her words but also through her passion, spirit, pleasure, and positive energy. Her first sentences of the week gave a glimpse of the complexity we would encounter:

> We cannot have a discussion of the *atelier* if we do not have a background discussion of the culture of education. And I think also that we cannot have a discussion without poetics, aesthetics, epistemology and ethics. These are difficult concepts but are a framework for the idea of the *atelier* without which the *atelier* becomes impoverished. The risk is that the *atelier* simply becomes a place for activities. We use a lot of techniques and materials quite well. The risk is that our gestures are rushed and hurried, not only children's but the adults' as well. We lose the relationship to what we are doing. Only if we are able to give meaning to our actions from the *atelier* can we get the vital lift in our work. Giving meaning is central. . . .
>
> The question that should be accompanying us this week is how and in what way would processes of learning and teaching be modified and enriched if school culture welcomed the poetic languages and an aesthetic dimension as important elements for building knowledge? This is not an abstract concept—it has been made real inside the infant-toddler centers and preschools here.

Never more powerfully have I noticed the underlying commitment to "research for innovation" as the concept of the *atelier* was discussed throughout the week.

Entrance to the park near the Diana Preschool.

Claudia Giudici, longtime *pedagogista* who attended the Diana Preschool as a child, retraced the early thinking behind introducing both the physical space of the *atelier* and the profile of *atelierista:* "our theoretical intuition suggested a new element was needed in schools to make work more complex and to encounter children's complex ways of knowing the world around them."

Although it certainly must be true that expressive languages were felt by Malaguzzi and colleagues as readily available cultural resources to bring into the schools in the beginning of their experience, it is interesting that the key energy for the innovation of a new educational paradigm was, as Giudici offered, the urge to understand deeply "children's complex ways of knowing the world around them" to better craft an educational approach worthy of children. This would contrast with the way we sometimes misinterpret the role of the *atelier* as simply a place of making art or duplicating crafts, and the role of the *atelierista* as simply an art teacher who supplies expressive materials and teaches techniques from an external vantage point. A stronger interpretation of the role of the *atelier* is to interpret it as a rich and well-appointed research environment, and the *atelierista* as a thoughtful, skillful researcher of children's and adults' ways of knowing who, at the same time, remains a playful, nurturing companion in ongoing experiences with children, families, and colleagues. From this, we must also extrapolate these concepts to include the whole school environment, thinking metaphorically of the entire school as an *atelier.*

Malaguzzi referred to the *atelier* as "a retort to the marginal and subsidiary role commonly assigned to expressive education . . . [and] a reaction against the concept of the education of young children based mainly on words and simple-minded rituals" (Gandini, Hill, Cadwell, & Schwall, 2005, p. 7). The choice of the *atelier* was a strong declaration of the importance given to expression, creativity, and aesthetics as natural fibers within education, and the broad human search for understanding and meaning.

Because schools are cultural places for supporting, expanding, and creating learning of children *and* adults, the presence of the *atelier* from the beginning inside the infant-toddler centers and preschools of Reggio Emilia has advantaged their collective understanding of the nature of learning and contributed significantly to our field's ongoing curiosities of epistemology. In a strongly firsthand way, deeply rooted in ongoing cycles of observation, interpretation, and documentation, Reggio educators have borne witness to child learning from its earliest genesis and in its *least restrictive environment,* to borrow a concept from the field of special education in the United States. Least restrictive environment, in this case, refers not to an "anything goes" chaos but an environment liberated from false boundaries and external caveats that inadvertently impede or unnecessarily parse the complex development of children. Instead, the whole school environment of Reggio infant-toddler centers and preschools is positively influenced by the presence of the *atelier.* Teachers endeavor to continually provoke children's natural propensities to search for meaning, to pose questions of themselves and others, and to interpret the phenomena of their own lives.

In the early 1930s, John Dewey contributed significantly to key foundational underpinnings interpreted by Malaguzzi and colleagues. Although prolific on many aspects of education and society, it was his seminal *Art as Experience* that offered Malaguzzi and his colleagues another vantage point to weave within their retort to traditional education approaches. In discussing the importance of the space in which the human experience communes with the everyday, ordinary experience, Dewey's originality marries the concept of aesthetic to experience:

> In order to **understand** [emphasis in original] the esthetic in its ultimate and approved forms, one must begin with it in the raw; in the events and scenes that hold the attentive eye and ear of man, arousing his interest and affording him enjoyment as he looks and listens. . . . The man who poked the sticks of burning wood would say he did it to make the fire burn better; but he is none the less fascinated by the colorful drama of change enacted before his eyes and imaginatively partakes in it. (Dewey, 1934, p. 3)

Often, Reggio educators use the phrase *rich normality* to describe the physical, social, emotional, and cognitive environments to which they continually aspire, calling important attention to the promise of ordinary moments. For it is the stringing together of ordinary moments that ultimately gives shape and quality to human life over time, just as it is the stringing together of ordinary moments that ultimately gives shape and quality to infant-toddler centers and preschools. Educators everywhere are deeply cognizant of the professional demands, moment by moment, in building a day together with children and families and the exponential demands of stringing together a sequence of days and a sequence of years that eventually constitutes a well-lived childhood. Although compelling and seductive, the long-term project work of educators and children in Reggio Emilia that has captured our attention will never be fully understood until we more carefully attend to and examine deeply the style of the daily life that surrounds, lives within, and gives birth to the longer research journeys that have captured our imaginations and emotions.

How much positive attention do we give ordinary moments in our programs for young children in North America? For example, the physicality children naturally express in their everyday encounters—running fingertips along a fence line, spinning and darting in open spaces, breathing deeply the fragrances of the natural world, handling objects to view every angle—are wide ways children build understanding through natural dispositions for researching worlds *polysensorially*—that is, through all their senses. Within these natural ways of children, there lives an aesthetic dimension, described by Giudici as the "pursuit of loveliness, of harmony, of balance, poise, equilibrium and sensibility to relations" that exists epistemologically. It could be argued, as Dewey and Malaguzzi have concluded, that aesthetics is not a separate dimension from experience but rather an element of it.

Dewey (1934) used the metaphor of a mountain to convey this conceptual wholeness:

> Mountain peaks do not float unsupported; they do not even just rest upon the earth. They are the earth in one of its manifest operations. It is the business of those who are concerned with the theory of the earth, geographers and geologists, to make this fact evident in its various implications. (p. 2)

Likewise, it has been taken up as the business of educators in Reggio Emilia, geographers and geologists of epistemology, to make evident epistemology's "manifest operations." The original contributions of children and adults in Reggio Emilia, in terms of research for innovation, have birthed the new theory of the hundred languages of children, within which the importance of aesthetics, plurality, and complexity is underscored in connection to learning processes and knowledge building.

Stephen Hawking, the renowned contemporary physicist, states, "we live in a strange and wonderful universe. Its age, size, violence and beauty require extraordinary imagination to appreciate" (2005, p. 3). His view further supports Dewey's and Malaguzzi's positions that scientific thought and imagination are not separate mental operations but are different points within the complexity of human intelligence that work to build our knowing of the universe, as well as the identity and meaning of our lives. Dewey (1934) suggested that the artist and scientist differed

Study tour outside the Bruno Munari Preschool.

only in the style in which they approached the world: "The difference between the esthetic and the intellectual is thus one of the places where emphasis falls in the constant rhythm that marks the interaction of the live creature with his surroundings" (p. 14).

Here are some of the quotes from Vea Vecchi that most stirred me and that I still continue to ponder. Many of them echo the writing in her new book (Vecchi, 2010).

> [I]t is quite difficult to say simply what we mean by the aesthetic dimension. An attitude of empathy toward things around us, perhaps comes first, an aspiration for quality that makes you choose one work over another or one piece of music over another or the taste of one food over another. This, with other more complicated things, is an attitude of care and attention toward things. So perhaps the aesthetic dimension could be defined as the opposite of indifference or conformism and it could be defined as the opposite of the lack of participation and involvement. Thus, a conscious awareness together with the presence of the aesthetic dimension would raise the quality of learning processes. . . .
>
> Because we human beings are part of a whole cosmos and if we lose this sense of being a part and in relationship with everything else, we lose something very critical to our experience. Each language is made of rationality and imagination—*all* languages, not just art. An educational culture that separates disciplines loses a lot of the meaning of holding things together.

A biological part of our makeup is to think in a complex way. If part of that complexity is not recognized, then our ways of thinking and our learning processes will be impoverished. Imagination has cognition and rationality. In all learning processes, these elements are kept connected. It is not an easy task, and we cannot always do it but that is what our objective should be.

Beautiful products are a testament to beautiful processes. The pursuit of beauty and loveliness is a part of all of us. If you think back to past eras, not just works of art but objects of everyday life—vases, jewels, clothes—the simplest, most everyday things through all eras and all cultures, you will find this search for loveliness and attention for the shape of things, the form of things. . . . I continue to believe beauty constitutes salvation for men and women. I believe they must be considered rights of humans rather than needs.

In aesthetics as we mean it—the promoter of relations, connections, sensibilities, freedom and expression—vicinity to ethics appears natural. As far as education is concerned, we cannot renounce bringing aesthetics and ethics together. . . . When placed together, they are one of the greatest barriers to violence and oppression. The aesthetic experience is the freedom of thought. It is no coincidence that avant garde research is always oppressed in dictatorships. The aesthetic sense goes beyond the border of visual languages into every other discipline. Once, a mathematician said, "When God sang, he sang in algebra." This notion communicates numbers as beautiful. Beauty in no way diminishes the rigor and cognition of studying numbers.

From the doorway of these key but not exhaustive orientations to the theory of the hundred languages, it is possible to realize the original contributions of this theory to the body of epistemological insight continuously being built. We can observe that their disposition for relations, connections, plurality, differences, and expression has given rise to new perspectives regarding what Carlina Rinaldi calls "the art of knowledge." We can view "art" not as a discipline but as a "fusional [integrative] part of the learning experience," as Rinaldi said in her lecture. In this way, educators everywhere are offered new potentials for strengthening experiences within programs for young children.

In mentally revisiting and remembering the experience of the April study week, I realize anew that it is not a minor detail, the way in which our colleagues from Reggio Emilia laughed together, teased each other, and levied serious criticism and suggestions to each other during the course of conversation. These are expressions of educators who have devoted themselves and their careers to the defense and promotion of children's rights. Along this path, they have also researched, defended, protected, and promoted the right of education to embrace forms of knowledge that have beauty as the center of the human experience. To visit their infant-toddler centers and preschools is to witness the bounty of such an approach.

As it always does, thinking about the educational project in Reggio Emilia causes us to think about and wonder about our own educational projects here in North America. I am always deeply struck by the devotion, determination, seriousness, playfulness, and willingness to remain present for long discussions about the meaning of experiences underway in the municipal infant-toddler centers and preschools of Reggio; the capacity for thinking, creating, and projecting; and the sheer depth of familiarity with historical and contemporary literature from the arts and sciences displayed by the Reggio Emilia team.

I have come to believe that we child advocates of North America are better supported in our vision for children, families, and educators the more we borrow *dispositions and attitudes* from Reggio Emilia, rather than techniques and examples. The deep message I witnessed during this particular week of study was the promise that beauty affords us as learners. Inside difficult thinking is pleasure, harmony, and poise that rewards and sustains the human experience. I wish for all of us, in our ongoing quest to give more excellence and quality to education, to question ourselves as Vea questioned us, asking us whether we can't have teaching and learning that include wonder, ethics, beauty, pleasure, and rigor—all of them, not just some preferred subset of them.

REFERENCES

Dewey, J. (1934). *Art as experience.* New York: Berkley Publishing Group.

Gandini, L., Hill, L., Cadwell, L., & Schwall, C. (Eds.). (2005). *In the spirit of the studio: Learning from the atelier of Reggio Emilia.* New York: Teachers College Press.

Gaut, B., & Lopes, D. (Eds.). (2005). *The Routledge companion to aesthetics* (2nd ed.). New York: Routledge.

Hawking, S. (2005). *A brief history of time.* New York Bantam Dell.

Vecchi, V. (2010). *Art and creativity in Reggio Emilia: Exploring the role and potential of ateliers in early childhood education.* New York: Routledge.

Chapter 17

The *Atelier*: A Conversation with Vea Vecchi

Lella Gandini

Gandini: *Please tell us how the* atelier *began.*

Vecchi: In the 1960s, Loris Malaguzzi introduced an *atelier* into every preschool in Reggio Emilia, along with a teacher with an art background. This was an unusual choice but a brave one, for then, as now, it represented a strong and tangible statement of the importance attributed to imagination, creativity, expressiveness, and aesthetics in the educational processes of development and knowledge building. As Malaguzzi said:

> For us, the *atelier* had to become part of a complex design and, at the same time, an added space for searching, or better, for digging with one's own hands and one's

This chapter is based on interviews conducted with Vea Vecchi by Lella Gandini and published in the English (1993, 1998) and Italian (1995) editions of *The Hundred Languages of Children* (C. Edwards, L. Gandini, & G. Forman, Eds.); on Vecchi's essay, "Poetic Language as a Means to Counter Violence," in *Children, art, artists: The expressive languages of children, the artistic language of Alberto Burri* (pp. 137–143), edited by Claudia Giudici and Vea Vecchi, published by Reggio Children, Reggio Emilia, Italy, 2004; and on two interviews conducted with Vea Vecchi by Lella Gandini in October 2009 and 2010.

Vea Vecchi and Carlina Rinaldi talking together in the *atelier* of the Diana Preschool.

own mind, and for refining one's own eyes, through the practice of the visual arts. It had to be a place for sensitizing one's taste and aesthetic sense, a place for the individual exploration of projects connected with experiences planned in the different classrooms of the school. The *atelier* had to be a place for researching motivations and theories of children from scribbles on up, a place for exploring variations in tools, techniques, and materials with which to work. It had to be a place favoring children's logical and creative itineraries, a place for being familiar with similarities and differences of verbal and nonverbal languages. (Gandini, 2005, p. 7)

Gandini: *What is the purpose of the* atelier*, and how does the* atelierista *work in the school?*

Vecchi: The *atelier* serves two functions. First, it is a space that makes it possible for children to encounter interesting and attractive contexts, where they can explore many and diverse materials as well as techniques that have expressive and combinatorial possibilities. Second, it assists the adults in understanding processes of how children learn. It helps teachers understand how children invent autonomous vehicles of expressive freedom, cognitive freedom, symbolic freedom, and paths to communication. The *atelier* serves to shake up old-fashioned teaching ideas. Loris Malaguzzi (Chapter 2, this volume) talked about this and expressed our views.

Let me tell you how an *atelierista,* such as I, works on a daily basis with the teachers in his or her preschool. The teachers and I meet several times a day. Every morning, I do a tour of each classroom. I am particularly interested in what is happening at the beginning of the day, both with regard to the larger ongoing projects and the smaller, independent activities. Teachers and I briefly talk about how to introduce certain things to the children and what to anticipate and then what to do about it. Sometimes, I also suggest the use of particular materials. Often, in the middle of the morning, I do another circuit, being sure to go where something of particular interest might be happening. Or sometimes, a teacher comes to ask advice or to get me to come and see. Then, at the end of every morning, I find at least 15 minutes to consult with each teacher. Often, we gather as a group to discuss something.

An important part of my role is to ensure the circulation of ideas among teachers. I am really their constant consultant. Because of my schooling and background, I can help them see the visual possibilities of themes and projects that are not apparent to them. I may even intervene directly with the children to create possibilities that have not occurred to others.

Let me offer an illustration. The school has a great deal of precious material that makes it possible to reveal and interpret our ways of observing, taking initiatives, and documenting the children's sequences of responses. Here are two small stories of the adults' provocation and the children's responses.

The adults taped a little paper bird onto the glass of a large window in the preschool, where we know the sun shines through brightly in the morning. After 2 days, a few children, aged 3, discovered the shadow of the bird on the floor. A teacher suggested that they trace it using a piece of chalk. The children then went out to play. When they came back, the shadow of the little bird had moved beyond the boundaries of the chalk outline they had drawn. Their hypothesis: the teacher made a mistake, or else the little bird wants to move.

The children now wanted to stop the bird and keep it with them. Therefore, they started a passionate study, rich in attempts to solve problems. The children first tried to build a cage on the floor out of tape, but the little shadow bird continued to move and escape their cage even while they were still constructing it. The children next tried to seduce the bird to stay, by offering it bread crumbs, but the bird didn't give up and continued to move along the floor. The children constructed a house out of bricks and blocks. They even tried putting some desirable toys into the house, but the shadow bird, instead of entering their house, climbed over the wall.

The 3-year-olds didn't know what else to do, so they went to the class of the 4-year-olds, who offered various hypotheses but no definite solution, and the problem remained suspended. The next day, as the 3-year-olds noticed that the shadow of the little bird was moving, following the same trajectory as the day before, they again discussed the problem with the 4-year-olds:

Alan (4:1):	"I know why it always goes the same way."
Veronica (3:6):	"Because he likes to."
Daniela (3:8):	"The sun helps him to mirror himself there."

Alan: "The sun points his reflection onto the bird because the shadow of the
bird knows this road, just as we know the road to go to our house. Early
in the morning, the shadow is still sleeping. Then the shadow goes into
the sun, and the sun points his ray, so that we can see the shadow of the
bird. The next day, when the sun comes up, the ray understands that it
has to go along the same road that it went before."

Daniela: "Ah, it is the sun that is driving [with] the steering wheel."

Another time, I noticed that the sun, shining behind one of the trees outside the
window, cast a shadow of the leaves onto the glass. I taped a sheet of translucent
white paper onto the glass. As children came in that morning, they exclaimed
with surprise and pleasure at the sight of the shadows on the paper. On a later day,
it happened that two girls, aged about 6 years old, stopped and looked at the glass window
and said to each other:

Agnese: "It is a drawing made by little bits of sun."
Cecilia: "They seem to be tiny leaves of sun."
Agnese: "It is the shadow of the leaves that is reflected."
Cecilia: "But is it a drawing by the sun or by the shadow?"
Agnese: "It is like a clock. I saw it also yesterday, and the other day; when that
drawing comes up [pointing to the signs on the translucent paper], it is
time to go to lunch."

Is this art? Is this science? The children with great wisdom do not separate the
exploration of reality into separate compartments. Observation and documentation
become cultural animators, or steps toward further interpretation and deepening.
This attitude of research continues to help to construct through time new types of
teachers and *atelieristi*.

Certainly, I follow very closely all of our major and longer-term projects. Always
I find most interesting and wonderful the project on which we are currently working,
because it seems to me that with each project, we advance and learn a little more,
and so we can do better work with the children. For example, we have found that
shadows offer extraordinary educational possibilities. The project about the shadows was described in our book, *Everything Has a Shadow, Except Ants* (Sturloni
& Vecchi, 1999), and it involves an integration of acts of visual representation with
scientific hypothesis testing. It goes far beyond the emphasis on aesthetic expression
and perceptual exploration with which I began my work many years ago.

Gandini: *What is the influence of the* atelier *on the functioning of the school?*

Vecchi: I am convinced that including an *atelier* within a school can render
the educational process and the learning experience for children more whole and
complete. The expressive languages are just as essential as the academic disciplines and should not be considered optional or marginal. I am further convinced
that the specific structure of the expressive languages used in the *atelier* (visual,
musical, and others) weaves together emotions and empathy with rationality and
cognition in a natural and inseparable way. This weaving together, in turn, favors

What does a paper bird stuck onto the window have to do with a shadow bird on the floor?

the construction of the imagination and a richer approach to reality, and it can contribute to the formation of a wider and more articulate perspective on learning. I think these concepts are an essential part of the foundation for further reflection.

The connections and interweavings among different disciplines with the languages of the *atelier* often produce, in our projects, a shift in established points of view and favor a more complex approach to problems, revealing the expressive, empathic, and aesthetic elements that are inherent in any discipline or specific problem. Therefore, it is not surprising that the integration of digital technologies has had a different impact in the preschools of Reggio Emilia than in most other schools: this experience has been rich in imagination, a stimulus to socialization, and full of merriment.

I am fully aware that it seems ingenuous to suppose that it would be sufficient to introduce an *atelier* and an *atelierista* into a school and expect that everything would automatically be transformed and enriched. Such a transformation can take place, in my view, only if the entire educational program is based on rich and vital bases of learning and teaching. Furthermore, I believe that for the *atelier* to fulfill its role efficaciously today, work needs to be done deliberately in four areas.

First, we have to consider that the art world often has the function of stimulus; it suggests new concepts to explore and to elaborate, offering us poetic, nonconformist views and unconventional interpretations of reality. Therefore, I believe that it should continue to be one of the primary sources of inquiry and inspiration in schools, as long as we ensure that the children and young people remain the protagonists of their personal itineraries. We do not want to place them in a culturally marginal position with regard to complex artistic events, emerging from sophisticated cultures and often from distant contexts. It is important not to absorb only the formal part of works of art, as often happens, but instead to work on ideas and concentrate attention on the concepts that generated the work of art.

Second, we have to render evident and visible, through observation and documentation, the vital interweaving of cognitive and imaginative ways of knowing. We must also reveal the personal as well as the social elements that are a part of every representation that is supported by vital teaching and learning. At the same time, it is necessary to render more visible the contribution the *atelier* gives through documentation to the development of projects carried out in other fields of knowledge, such as literacy, mathematics, science, and so on. Third, we have to give closer attention to the processes of learning through the digital media, a subject still little explored with children. The digital experience is much too often exhausted simply in its functional and technical form. However, in addition to its technical aspect, if it is also used in creative and imaginative ways, it reveals a high level of expressive, cognitive, and social potentials as well as great possibilities for evolution. It is necessary to reflect on and better comprehend the changes that the digital language introduces in the processes of understanding. We have to be aware of what this adds, takes away, or modifies in today's learning. The presence and the contribution of the *atelier* can be surprisingly innovative in the approach and exploration of the digital material, as some experiences that have taken place over the past several years in our schools demonstrate.

The fourth and last aspect to consider is the relationship of the schools with the city. It is a relationship that the communicative structure of the *atelier* can greatly support by constructing contexts for dialogue, visibility, and knowledge about the culture of young children and school children. It is a culture that, if correctly received and recognized, can contribute more than commonly thought to a radical reconsideration of the city and to an improvement in the quality of life. Documentation has also been a democratic way to make known, to share and discuss, what happens in the schools, and it serves as a reminder of the value and importance of education.

Gandini: *And all together, do you see transformations in the climate of the life and space?*

Vecchi: Above all, the *atelier* brings the strength and joy of the unexpected and the uncommon to the process of learning. It supports a conceptual change that comes from looking through a poetic lens at everyday reality. This kind of looking is what some define as an "aesthetic project," but in fact, it is a biological process that evidently belongs to our species. This process, in its apparent levity, is capable of unhinging many commonplace events and banalities and of giving back relevance and centrality to aspects of life and thought that are often not given enough importance by the greater part of school and social culture. This is because they pertain to unpredictable processes that are not easily measurable or controllable.

However, they reveal themselves to be indispensable for the birth of cultural events that make us grow and move forward and without which our life would be less full and less interesting.

Although I am not sure that we *atelieristi* have always lived up to the expectations held for us, I am at least convinced that having the *atelier* in every preschool has made a deep impact on the emerging educational identity of our system. Certainly, the *atelier* itself has changed with the passing of time, although the basic philosophy has remained the same. And of course, the personality and style of each *atelierista* make each *atelier* a different place. Working together, accompanying the children in their projects, teachers and I have repeatedly found ourselves face to face—as if in looking in a mirror—learning one from another, and together learning from the children. This way we were trying to create paths to a new educational approach, one certainly not tried before, in which the visual language was interpreted and connected to other languages, all thereby gaining in meaning.

Children painting in the *atelier* of the Diana Preschool.

Gandini: *Are there changes that the work of the* atelier *has brought to your thinking and work?*

Vecchi: Our interests have gradually shifted over time toward analysis of the processes of learning and the interconnections between children's different ideas, experiences, and representations. All of this documentation—the written descriptions, transcriptions of children's words, photographs, and videotapes—becomes an indispensable source of materials that we use everyday to be able to "read" and reflect critically—individually and collectively—on the experience we are living, the project we are exploring. This allows us to construct theories and hypotheses that are not arbitrary and artificially imposed on the children. Yet this process of work takes much time and is never easy.

Gandini: *Children, art, and artists—I know you have reflected a great deal on their interrelationships.*

Vecchi: Yes, people often ask about the relationship between child and adult artwork. The way one should examine what children do is very different from evaluating adult artwork. It often happens that some of the children's products are so original that one wants to compare them to the work of famous artists. But that kind of comparison becomes dangerous and fraught with ambiguity, especially if one tries insistently to make comparisons. It leads to false conclusions, such as that the behavior of children unfolds innately or that the product is more important than the process. To make comparisons that go beyond a simple and playful resemblance shows how little one has understood of either children or artists.

On the other hand, I think that artistic discoveries—conceptual breakthroughs made by artists—should circulate among the adults in our schools, because we can learn from them. For a sense of volume, all are very interesting and help us explore new paths with children.

Gandini: *What is the role of the* atelier *in a socioconstructivist choice in education?*

Vecchi: All this material is indispensible to make possible children's reading and rereading of individual and group exploration as they are discovering various fields of knowledge. This also allows the construction of theory and hypotheses of work that are interesting and that try to take into account the points of view and times of children without distorting them.

The presence of the *atelier* in the schools is seen as a means to safeguard the complexity of the knowledge-building processes with the aim of using the imagination as a unifying element for the different activities and of viewing the "aesthetic knowledge" (Lori Malaguzzi spoke about *aesthetic vibration*) as a drive that is rooted within us and leads us to choose among patterns of thinking and among visual images. Gregory Bateson, a great influence on my thought and work, examined closely the complexity of relationships between the things that surround us. He was reflecting on the importance of the aesthetic approach as a major and significant connector of elements of reality, and he provided a definition of *aesthetic* that is so close to my way of thinking and so beautiful that I would like to quote it verbatim. "By *aesthetic,* I mean responsive to *the pattern which connects*" (Bateson, 1979, p. 8). This lucid statement and this approach help us investigate and highlight the hidden patterns of reality, create new maps that can combine logical and emotional processes, and connect technique with expressiveness—an excellent background for learning as well as a goal to keep constantly alive in schools and in education.

The *ateliers* in the municipal infant-toddler centers and preschools of Reggio Emilia have chosen the visual language not as a separate discipline, devoted to traditional activities; rather, they have focused on the visual language as a mean of inquiry and investigation of the world, to build bridges and relationships between different experiences and languages, and to keep cognitive and expressive processes in close relationship with one another, in constant dialogue with a pedagogical approach that seeks to work on the connection rather than the separation of various fields of knowledge.

My focus is always on the children. To make my reflections most clear, if space allowed, I would describe the processes adopted by the children as they produce their work, on their own or in groups, which the teachers and *atelierista* so keenly observe and so carefully document. Indeed, I always illustrate and discuss these processes in my conference presentations, as a necessary prelude of any kind of discussion topic. These documentary materials never fail to surprise the audience for the acuteness the children show in dealing with the most diverse situations, and also because of equally diverse and unforeseen—and at times unimaginable—solutions that children find to overcome hurdles. It also needs to be emphasized that the cultural and social situation around us is constantly changing; furthermore, we should realize that children and their mental images—their perceptions, theories, and products—never remain frozen and unaltered in time, but live and evolve within different contexts. The visual language is conceptual and cultural before being formal.

This work of investigation and documentation makes us realize how little we know about the strategies that children use, and our knowledge of children must be constantly expanded, revised, and updated. The crucial starting point of any of our proposals should always come from the children.

We are conscious of the value of the processes that the visual language can sustain and the contribution it can make to other languages, but also of the fact that the visual language itself can be modified and enriched through a dialogue with the others. These are the links we particularly and consistently focus on in our work, and we feel this approach sets us apart from that which the school environment traditionally calls "art education."

Our main task as teachers is to create situations within which creative processes can be experimented with, grow, and evolve. This means devising and implementing generative contexts, paying attention to procedures, and creating the right conditions to make possible the fruition of the creative process that we aim to sustain and stimulate.

Gandini: *And the children?*

Vecchi: The starting point for all these will always be the child and the group of children, with their mental images and exploratory strategies. This is what we are attempting to do as we observe and document the strategies through which they explore in an effort to improve our understanding of their knowledge-building and expressive processes, promote the creation of educational situations, and propose encounters with materials that are in tune, as much as possible, with children's way of being and, consequently, more capable of generating a high level of participation, interest, and quality. Some tell us about the impossibility of seeing these processes, but for many years, we have been aware of the precious nature of the fragments we are able to capture and document and of the extent of how these fragments bring us closer to the children, increasing our respect for their intelligences and sensibilities. This can render our proposals more well thought out, discussed, and perhaps less certain, but we hope less liable to betray the children. Joseph Brodsky (1995) wrote, "Seen from the outside, creativity is the object of fascination or envy; seen from within, it is an unending exercise in uncertainty and a tremendous school for insecurity" (p. 300).

A moment of encounter with materials.

We hope that on the teachers' part, there will be an underlying emphasis on doing a great deal of listening to the children's strategies. Without listening, without being responsive to the ideas of others, there can be neither learning nor teaching.

Gandini: *Recently, we had a conversation about the new exhibit, "The Wonder of Learning: The Hundred Languages of Children," on tour in North America. One aspect to underscore, because it doesn't always emerge with clarity, is the contribution made by the* atelier *to the development of pedagogical documentation in Reggio Emilia—documentation that uses dual languages, the written language and the language of images.*

Vecchi: Documentation, such as we see in "The Wonder of Learning," is part of a particular communicative structure that is not so common in education. Carla Rinaldi and I have defined it as *visual listening.* The *atelier* generates a visual culture in schools. The process of documentation by teachers corresponds to the attention given to the aesthetic dimension in the pedagogy of Reggio, or, as Jerome Bruner likes to define it, a *poetic dimension,* which is as important in the learning of children as in the learning of adults. For infant-toddler centers and preschools, teacher documentation has always simultaneously contributed to give us a deeper look at meanings in children's work, to give us a gratifying testimonial to the work of children and adults. It has also been a democratic way to make known, to share and discuss, what happens in the schools, and it serves as a reminder of the value and importance of education.

Documentation, like any topic, can be examined in different ways. We are convinced that teachers' growth and development are only possible through discussion and sharing, and documentation provides the most fertile terrain for such reflection. Certainly, so that we may reflect together, it is necessary that the documents (for example, the observational notes, images, and samples of children's work) arising from a documentary journey must also be consultable and comprehensible to those who were not present during the observations. No matter what working tools the teachers use (there is no single preestablished model), and no matter what kinds of documents they collect and prepare, the intention that underlies the structure must always allow for the work to be verified; it must allow for exchange or comparison of ideas between and among different points of view. If this intention is made clear from the beginning, then documentation will allow for important and precious re-elaboration over time.

One of most innovative parts of the exhibition "The Wonder of Learning" is the new work we have done to deepen its communicative structure. To work on the communicative structure means to recognize and deepen the meanings of the work that was originally carried out. What we have wanted to communicate convincingly in this new exhibit is a *contemporary* image of the child. By contemporary, I intend to convey an image that is projected toward the future. I do not want to say that it is only a "modern" image or an image that is "actual." If one considers communication today, it does not correspond only to something that is happening now but has a complexity that is projected toward the future. For example, "The Wonder of Learning" is flexible and can be adjusted according to the different places or contexts where it will be shown. It contains certain concepts that are not simple to communicate and that may be understood or interpreted differently depending on the context. For instance, there are diverse views on pedagogy in different places, and other kinds of social, political, or economic conditions that might create a need to modify how the exhibit is set up and shown. It is important for us in Reggio Emilia to allow for this flexibility; it is what we want. We wish for the exhibit to be a *piazza* in which ideas can be discussed in different realities far away from Reggio Emilia, maybe China, India, or Japan. We want a complex image of the child to be communicated in different realities, and then, in response, those faraway places and realities will communicate to us things that we do not know.

Lella: *You and I have also wandered together through the exhibit "Ariadne's Thread," a revisitation of the documentation of the Reggio infant-toddler centers and preschools from the 1981 to 2008, on display in the Malaguzzi International Center. The exhibit's name comes from the Greek myth in which the hero Theseus slays the Minotaur with the help of the princess Ariadne, who has given him a sword and a ball of red yarn so that he can find his way out of the Minotaur's labyrinth.*

Vecchi: I would like to speak about that exhibit and how it can show the development of our thoughts and experiences. It contains segments on "The Crowd" and "The City and the Rain," which were projects with children that came one after the other in the 1980s. At that time, we were already entering a way of thinking that even a small thing contains great complexity, as if it were a large thing. One thing can have as much complexity as a city. The categories *small* and *large* do not pertain to two ends of the continuum of complication; instead, they are both complex. I remember vividly that this thought came to us as we were discussing one day in the school.

Another segment of "Ariadne's Thread" concerns the children's study of the leaf of the plane tree ("In Pursuit of a Plane Tree Leaf," Municipality of Reggio Emilia Infant-Toddler Centers and Preschools, Reggio Children, 1996, pp. 94–97). In fact, already back then, in considering the idea of exploring the plane tree leaf, it was my thinking that a leaf has inside itself a great deal of complexity (like a city), and it includes great possibilities for exploration and use of materials. Starting from that outline, and refusing to take on an academic way of thinking about drawing, I wondered how that complexity could be brought out and reinterpreted with the children. As shape, as background, as system—all of these could be explored by looking at details.

I made the deliberate choice, with awareness and intentionality, to see whether my theoretical research and reflections would support me in constructing a meaningful experience for children. We had already been exploring with children parts of the body—hands, eyes, ears, and mouths as elements that could be examined in their details and complexity, using photos and drawings. Thus, we began to explore the leaf of the plane tree. Nowadays, there is more awareness of ecology, and therefore, in looking at the leaf, it would probably also be considered in its relationship to the tree. Yet our intention in exhibiting these early documentations is not to suggest that we would do everything the same way today. Rather, the intention is to pose these traces of our history to teachers of the present time, so that we can examine them on the basis of all our layers of experiences and levels of awareness. We can pose questions: How would you explore a tree now? What would you do that is the same or different from what we did? Such discussions can include both preschool and elementary teachers.

In those days, back in the 1980s, in creating documentation,

Children using their bodies to assume the shape of the plane tree leaf.

we did not yet use quotations of the children's words. Thus, we were missing something important that we discovered later. But one very important aspect was that children made observations about the *life* of the leaf. (They entered imaginatively into the leaf as another living being.) Also, our explorations included the metaphorical basis of children's perceptions and conceptions of the leaf. We would choose the materials and set up the exploration, and then the children moved freely within our organized choices. The children reflected about the life of a leaf in ways that were nonfigurative and abstract: the life of a living entity. Similarly, they created interpretive metaphors for the leaf. We adults chose the tools, materials, and techniques children would use, and they explored through experiments with light or on the windowpane against the light, and in different contexts, such as leaves in the rain or in the sun, wet or dried out.

Today, what we do instead is provide the children more time to process these variations and more choice in which expressive media they use. We have a different trust about the choices that children are able to make about tools and techniques. This change has happened slowly, a bit at a time, and in my view, it may have been observation and documentation that brought us to this greater awareness of children's capacities. We now have much more faith and trust in the children.

What we say today about children and what we do with them has come about gradually. In my early days, I did not always know how to widen the possibilities for teachers to enter more deeply into children's processes. It was professional development that brought us forward. Malaguzzi set us down this path, but I needed his support and encouragement to go forward. Both of us were struck by how children could play and represent through metaphors. One event that occurred completely spontaneously was that six children arranged themselves on the floor of the *piazza* to create with their legs and torsos the outline of the shape of the leaf, with its five sharp points and long stem. They shouted, "We have made the leaf!" Afterward, we designed ways for them to explore more with their bodies the shape of the leaf.

The project "The City and the Rain" was explored first by the Diana Preschool ("Rain in the City," Municipality of Reggio Emilia Infant-Toddler Centers and Preschools, Reggio Children, 1996, pp. 78–87). Malaguzzi realized that this subject, like the study of the leaf, had great possibilities for sensory and perceptual exploration, including through sound, and so he suggested the same topic to the La Villetta, Neruda, and Anna Frank preschools. Some of us went to photograph at the other schools, and we tried to capture the joy of the children playing with the rain and the water in puddles. We should always include a playful exploration. Perhaps the puddle could have become an important subject of a project if we had better supported the children's expressivity!

Some things emerged in a similar or parallel way in the different schools, and this was the first time we began to examine and compare children's theories. It was very beautiful and significant to have many schools come together as if in chorus, as also happened recently in the citywide project "Reggio Tutta" (Bonilauri &

Filippini, 2000). There was at this point a strong relationship among the schools and a desire to communicate to others.

In many ways, even in those days, we were very aware of the children, but what we did not know was when and how to leave the room. We did not know how to leave enough space for the subjectivity of children, and we did not know how to document the children's subjective thinking. We prepared documentation, but we did not document the processes of learning sufficiently. However, the goal that we set for ourselves with our recent research experiences is, to paraphrase James Hillman (1999), to return color and taste, sound and structure, to the things of the world. Without an exercised imagination or a tension that allows us to "see" the things we encounter, to renew them (and renew ourselves) through a sense of wonder and the establishment of empathic relationships with the things around us, there is a risk that we may respond to the sensitive world with our senses and mind anesthetized by everyday life. To benefit fully from opportunities, we need to ensure that our senses, and our curiosity, expectations, and interests, are kept constantly alive.

REFERENCES

Bateson, G. (1979). *Mind and nature: A necessary unity*. New York: E. P. Dutton.

Bonilauri, S., & Filippini, T. (Eds.). (2000). *Reggio Tutta: A guide to the city by the children*. Reggio Emilia, Italy: Reggio Children.

Brodsky, J. (1995). *On grief and reason: Essays*. New York: Farrar, Straus & Giroux.

Gandini, L. (2005). From the beginning of the *atelier* to materials as languages: Conversations from Reggio Emilia. In L. Gandini, L. Hill, L. Cadwell, & C. Schwall (Eds.), *In the spirit of the studio: Learning from the atelier of Reggio Emilia* (pp. 6–15). New York: Teachers College Press.

Hillman, J. (1999). *Politica della bellezza* [The politics of beauty]. Bergamo, Italy: Morettie Vitali.

Municipality of Reggio Emilia Infant-Toddler Centers and Preschools. (1996). *The hundred languages of children: Narrative of the possible*. Catalog of "The Hundred Languages of Children" exhibit. Reggio Emilia, Italy: Reggio Children.

Sturloni, S., & Vecchi, V. (Eds.). (1999). *Everything has a shadow, except ants*. Reggio Emilia, Italy: Reggio Children.

Chapter 18

Connecting through Caring and Learning Spaces

Lella Gandini

Following are children's ideas about a sense of place:

- A place is here. (Benedetta, aged 2 years, 3 months)
- You recognize a place by the air. (Matteo, aged 5 years)
- A place is a city where I scared some birds, where there are those fake lion statues. (Sara, aged 3 years, 9 months)
- You go inside the place . . . and after that your body decides whether to receive it or not. (Pietro, aged 4 years)
- You walk around a little to discover what's there. (Gabriele, aged 5 years)
- A place is my mommy. (Pietro, aged 2 years, 7 months)
- You can listen to the noise of a place; a tree, for example, tells us about the wind. (Pietro, aged 4 years)
- To listen [to a place] you have to call your brain. (Lucia, aged 4 years)
- When I make a really big silence, I can hear the silence. (Omar, aged 4 years)

—Quotations from Vecchi, Filippini, & Giudici, 2008, pp. 14–15

PEDAGOGY AND ARCHITECTURE

Place and Space as Essential Elements of the Educational Approach

A visitor to any institution for young children tends to size up the messages that the space gives about the quality of care and about the educational choices that form the basis of the program. We all tend to notice the environment and "read" its messages or meanings on the basis of personal experience and the knowledge we have acquired about child development; all this also shapes our own ideas about childhood.

We can, however, improve our ability to analyze deeper layers of meaning if we observe the extent to which everyone involved is at ease and how everyone uses the space itself. We can then learn more about the value and meaning of the relationship among the children and adults who spend time there.

In the entryway of a school in Reggio Emilia, we are already aware of the value given to communication and openness of information. There is an intention to make the identity of the school visible. Sometimes the history of the school itself is presented first, accompanied by photographs of each team of two teachers (those who teach the 3-, 4-, and 5-year-old children) then photos of the *atelierista*, the cook, and the auxiliary staff members, along with their names and welcoming smiles. On the same wall are posted schedules of events: professional development sessions, meetings with parents of each age group, meetings of the whole school, meetings with other schools, field trips, and celebrations.

On another wall, there might be words of the children about their rights: "We've got to have rights, or else we'll be sad." Or there might be observations that become poetic metaphors: "The leaves fall because they hold on with only one hand." We learn that, in addition to the children's words and expression through other symbolic languages, their photographs are important for the children's own identity, and their sense of belonging depends on how they are displayed.

We also realize these messages that the school space offers are addressed especially to the parents, who enter the school mornings and afternoons. Moving from the entryway, we find the spacious central area bathed in light, inviting us to explore and become involved.

Through the years, educators in Reggio Emilia have evolved a philosophy based on partnership among children, teachers, parents, educational coordinators, and the community. They have succeeded in developing their programs for children from birth to age 6, during a time period when other cities in Italy have had to relinquish their municipal programs to the national state system. For lack of funds and energy, some cities have lost the city schools they created through years of effort and political action to obtain public funding and local support.

Early in the development of their educational program, the participants in this collaboration appreciated the educational significance of space and invested a great deal of their energy into thinking and planning about it. More and more, the educators in Reggio Emilia have given attention to the connection between pedagogy and architecture and to the power of aesthetics as a connecting principle. They have continued to develop the organization of space in their schools by considering these theoretical perspectives in continually renewed ways.

The structures, choice of materials, and attractive ways in which educators set them up for the children become an open invitation to explore. Everything is thoughtfully chosen and placed with the intention to create communication, as well as exchanges among people and interactions between people and things in a network of possible connections and constructions. This process engages everyone in dialogue and offers tools, materials, and strategies connected with the organization of space to extend or relaunch those ideas, to combine them, or to transform them.

The children also see the adults as a support through the way the adults organize and use the space to discover and learn with the children. At the same time, the wider system of organization (i.e., the cooperating system of the whole school staff, the *pedagogisti,* parents, and community) sustains teachers, directly and indirectly, in and around the environment of the school, and makes it possible for them to work at this high level of engagement.

Educators in the United States are well aware of the importance of the environment. This is evident, for example, in their imaginative use of outdoor spaces, a marvelous American resource not so readily available to, or so easily tapped by, Italian teachers, who often work in a highly urbanized environment. However, American teachers have often faced funding limitations and thus have been forced to make compromises with regard to indoor space. The unfortunate result, as seen in many child-care centers and schools for young children, has been a set of discouraging physical conditions, especially the lack of natural light and uncluttered space.

> Research in neuroscience and social science confirms that our identity develops from our experiences of the environment as well as our genetic history. We develop our senses and cognitive abilities through interaction with our environment. Children are a laboratory for the senses with each sense activating other senses. . . . As a result, the child's environment cannot be seen just as a context for learning or a passive setting for activities; it is an integral part of learning and helps define their identity. (Zini, 2005, p. 22)

The Architecturally Planned Space and the Extended Space Around the School, the City, and Beyond

In the process of formulating and rendering more explicit the dynamic aspect of their philosophy and choices in their educational program, Reggio Emilia educators planned and worked out the structure and arrangement of space. Following the idea that the education of young children is a community-based concern and responsibility, children's centers ideally had to be integral parts of the urban plan. Moreover, there is now a variety of schools in the city, from some newly designed and built, to some carved out from an apartment building, a restored old school, or even a villa. They have been placed in full view of neighborhoods, where the life of children and teachers would be a visible point of reference for the community. The presence of the school in the neighborhood is a pronouncement about respect for the rights of all children and families. This is a pointed statement made visible by the choice to construct places in a peripheral area of the city where there is low-income housing and workers and immigrants live. Among those are Nilde Iotti (a combined infant-toddler center and preschool) and the restoration of the Locatelli cheese factory and warehouse, which houses the Malaguzzi International Center and includes preschool and the first few primary-grade classrooms.

For each building, whether built completely anew or modified from an existing one, pedagogical coordinators, teachers, and parents met to plan with the architects. These people who were going to work and live there for so many hours had to be participants in every choice: a wall that was too high or the lack of a partition could modify the possibility or the quality of interaction in an educational approach where partnership and interaction are paramount.

In fact, as Tiziana Filippini pointed out, educators in Reggio Emilia speak of space as a "container" that favors social interaction, exploration, and learning, but they also see space as having educational "content"—that is, as containing educational messages and being charged with stimuli toward interactive experience and constructive learning (Filippini, 1990). Therefore, the structure of interior spaces tends to evolve along with everything else about the educational program in Reggio Emilia.

Loris Malaguzzi, in an interview together with Vea Vecchi in 1992 about the space in the Diana Preschool, said:

> In 1970 we were processing many things that we had not yet fully worked out. To be sure, some were in place already: the transparency of the walls, the flood of light, the continuity between inside and outside. We already had the *piazza,* but it was not until we lived in it that it acquired its full significance. The *piazza* does more than extend the classrooms, for it encourages many different encounters and activities, and we assign still other purposes to it. For us it represents the main square of the Italian city, a space where people meet, speak to one another, discuss and engage in politics, conduct business, do street theater, and stage protests. The *piazza* is a place of continuous passage, where the quality of the exchange becomes more intense, whether among children or adults. The more they meet, the more ideas circulate among adults and children. We might say that the *piazza* is a place where ideas arrive and depart.

At this point in the interview, Vea Vecchi remarked that traditional schools also have large central spaces, and the issue is not simply having space but how it is used.

Malaguzzi: That's right. These large spaces are used for recess, for "recreation," because between 10:00 and 10:30 there is supposed to be a break, yet in truth there are neither objects nor structures, not even any purpose, except for the hypocritical and ignorant one of handing the children a space so that they can do what they want for half an hour!

Vecchi: It was precisely this that I wanted to point out. If we call that central space a *piazza,* it means that we have a theory about its use. Spaces could look more or less alike, but if they are part of a culture and subject to some pedagogical reflection about their use, their significance changes completely. The objects and structures found here, in the space of the Diana School, allow purposefully for a variety of encounters.

Malaguzzi: The *piazza* is also a passage. In part it is structured by the objects in it, but there are also the children, and it allows them to flow through, to walk, or to linger as they wish. It is necessary to keep in mind how influential the environment is with regard to the affective, cognitive, and linguistic acquisitions. The environment becomes part of the individual so that any response to a request we make of the children or to a request children make of adults is facilitated or obstructed by the environment and its characteristics. In general, what architects ask is: "How many children do you have? Twenty, thirty? The place for the desks?" Already we know that they are thinking of a school where learning takes place sitting down. For a school where children stand up and where they learn moving around, their way of measuring is useless. We have to consider that each child is an organic unit who needs personal space for action and movement in his or her own personal way, and we have to reflect on that; we cannot use the tape measure.

Vecchi: An architect and a *pedagogista* could also build a beautiful school, but then if the teachers who go to work there neither reflect on nor prepare to deepen their understanding about what is the meaning of living in a space, nothing happens. One has to return to the initial ideas that determined choices about the space. For example, to inhabit the space according to philosophical choices that respect children transforms mere hygiene into genuine care and transforms interaction with objects into communication. Without a philosophical basis that gives meaning to the educational experience to be lived in a space, the identity of the space will not emerge; in fact, the risk is to try to live an experience disconnected from the space. Often one walks into a well-built building that is used for a school for young children, and one sees many things done to that space that run against its own important positive features creating a dissonance and fragmentation. (Malaguzzi and Vecchi, interview, 1992)

The teachers also value what is special about the spaces that surround their schools, considering them extended classroom space. Part of their work with children involves taking children to explore neighborhoods and landmarks in the city. One example of the extension of the school is a project undertaken for many months by several schools and also La Villetta Preschool, during which children went out to explore how the city is transformed during rainstorms. This project brought the children and teachers to explore first the reality of the city without rain, taking photographs in both familiar and less familiar places, and then making

Piazza of Diana Preschool.

hypotheses about how the rain would change them. Because that year the seasonal rains were so late to arrive, the children had weeks to prepare the tools and equipment they thought would help them observe, collect, measure, photograph, and record everything about the rain. In the meantime, the children's expectations grew tremendously. Every day, the teachers and children went up to the school's roof terrace to gaze hopefully at the sky, gaining much knowledge about cloud formations and wind direction.

When a good rainstorm finally arrived, the experience was feverish and exhilarating. The children noticed how people changed their speed and posture in walking, how the shining reflections and the splash from the puddles changed the streets, how the sound of the raindrops differed depending on whether it was falling on the pavement, the hoods of cars, or the leaves of trees. Then, after experiencing the rainstorm, and following the customary procedure in Reggio Emilia, the children became engaged in representing many of its aspects. This, in turn, led to more questions, hypotheses, and explorations that the teacher and the *atelierista* thoroughly documented. The whole exploration was eventually recorded in "The City and the Rain" segment of "The Hundred Languages of Children" exhibit and serves to tell us of the many ways in which the familiar space of the city can become the stage for and subject of activities and constructive explorations (Municipality of Reggio Emilia Infant-Toddler Centers and Preschools, 1996).

In recent years, there has been an intensive dialogue between pedagogy and architecture, which has oriented the thinking and design of space for young children in the educational landscape of the Reggio Emilia municipal infant-toddler centers and preschools. This dialogue has involved teachers, *pedagogisti,* designers, and architects and has contributed to a culture respectful of the rights of children by enriching the identity of their spaces. This has taken place through the consideration of learning through relationship and participation as a central aspect of education. Paola Cavazzoni (2007), *pedagogista,* stated, "An environment of daily life continually activated and modified by explorations and research by all the protagonists—children, teachers and parents—marked by traces of events, social and personal stories, becomes an empathic place, a place of learning and suggestive of actions and change."

A key aspect in the development of the dialogue between pedagogy and architecture is the relationship between the Reggio municipal government and the community of architects through their active participation and work throughout the city. This relationship is a strong factor in the development of construction and design for sites devoted to the education of young children from birth to 6 years of age in Reggio Emilia. In particular, the municipal administration has chosen to address the dilemma created by families' increasing requests for places for their children in infant-toddler centers and preschools, the number of places available, and the long waiting lists for these places in a city with an increasing birth rate (which is unusual for Italy) and also a large influx of immigrant families (which is now common throughout Italy).

The architectural design of the Reggio municipal infant-toddler centers shows the deliberate effort to create places that guarantee the well-being of children and teachers as they construct learning together and welcome family members who are considered active participants. Loris Malaguzzi characterized these places as *amiable spaces,* and in the 1970s and 1980s, new buildings began to grace various neighborhoods of Reggio Emilia. These became reference points for the community as the site of various meetings of families and citizens.

The premises for the architectural characteristics and descriptive qualities for these buildings were elaborated collectively through time by the pedagogical team, teachers, and *atelieristi* and were published by Reggio Children and Domus Academy in the book *Children, Spaces, Relations: Metaproject for an Environment for Young Children* (Ceppi & Zini, 1998). The book analyzes a series of descriptions and terms (key words and metaphors) that are all connected and have been developed by architects and teachers working together. This critical examination of the experience in the schools of Reggio Emilia helped to formulate some general criteria and situations that indicate the desirable characteristics and qualities of an environment for young children. These ideas, described in the subsequent paragraphs, are based on the fundamental principles of pursuing relationship and constructing educational experiences by observing and listening.

Overall softness. Softness, as a metaphor, refers here to the psychological quality of the space and the creation of an amiable place, livable and serene. Traditionally, spaces for young children have tended to be organized in a rather rigid fashion that separates the different parts for different activities throughout the school. This deliberate separation is intended to protect the autonomy of the classrooms and of the teachers, but the risk is that it can limit communication. The choice, therefore, is to consider an environment that is functional while remaining aware that different dimensions and relationships can coexist and that the people involved can communicate and work together (for example, infant-toddlers and preschoolers sharing common spaces). How is that possible? It can be realized through cooperation, organization, and a strategy of listening and welcoming. It is by being open and giving attention to others that one invites dialogue and exchange. (This is one of the values in the Reggio Emilia philosophy.) The objective is to create a context of empathy in which listening is a way of respecting children in their many different expressions (even in their silence) and of respecting the ideas and intentions of adults involved.

A relational space. The network of relationships and communication makes possible, through sharing creative ideas and strategies, the creation of many specialized explorations, inquiries, and constructions among adults and with the children. The different identities of adults and children can find harmony through relationship and the interpretation of what happens in the school. By learning together and exchanging points of view and ideas about new paths to explore together, these connections contribute to creating an awareness of the value of relationships and a pleasant aesthetic sense.

Continuity with surroundings environments and social connections. The relationship among people can be extended as a dialogue with the world of objects. (Objects "speak" with their shape or through where they are placed, for example.) Furthermore, relationship creates continuity with all that is within the space of the school and with what is outside. (Think about the impact of your outside space.) What is socially connected to the school permeates it and is filtered by the values and the educational philosophy of the school itself (a philosophy that has been shared in advance with the parents). It is important to cultivate the enriching relationship with the community, other institutions and organizations for children, libraries, parks, landmarks in the city, and so on.

Multiple sensorial experiences. Infants and young children discover reality through sensorial explorations and construct their knowledge and memory through them. This personal way of experiencing the world can be extended to group exploration.

How can this be supported? An environment that invites sensory experience by creating a variety of features, stimulating perceptions, and helping children become aware of them can support meaningful sensorial experiences. This attention can help children to make connections that lead to cognitive discoveries. It is here that exchanges or conversations with children are crucial. It is important to note that the quality of a space (or environment) results from many factors: size and shape, functional organization, and sensory experience, color, light, and materials, as Michele Zini (2005) suggests:

> Design processes that have been found are those which make use of color, light, sound and smell. This is because these correspond to young children's cognitive processes. The image of the center is therefore derived not only from the layout and furnishing of the space, but also from the sensory richness of its material.
>
> **Color.** For color, this means it is necessary to use a chromatic range with many shades. This is far removed from the banal and simplified red, yellow, and blue color system that adults often associate with the child. Instead the aim should be to offer children a more subtle color scheme with many colors.
>
> **Light.** Lighting should offer an environment illuminated from a variety of sources: incandescent, fluorescent, vapor, halogen, etc., in order to make optimal use of the full range of possibilities. Light should be able to create shadows. This is possible when using incandescent lighting but not with fluorescent lights. Lighting should provide concentrated as well as diffuse light and different color "temperatures": warm white, cool white, rose white.
>
> **Materials.** The materials used should be rich and varied. They should create a multisensory setting with surfaces which are smooth and rough, wet and dry, opaque, bright, translucent, and transparent. They should have different features

The space outdoors can become an *atelier*.

which change over a period of time (wood, stone, flowers, fabrics) or remain un-
changed (glass, steel). (p. 24)

There is not a single, optimal solution in combining these factors, however,
because we all have individual differences in sensorial threshold. It is better to
avoid overstimulation and instead choose a moderate tone and variety of sensorial
possibilities so that one can find an agreeable niche.

Flexibility and adaptation.   A space for learning has to be adaptable in a
flexible way so that the children who live in it day by day can either signal to
adults the need to modify it, or they can directly proceed to modify the space as
they use it. This flexibility contributes to group learning as the children together
often construct changes through action within an existing educational environment. How can respect for all the children and for the intentions of the teachers
be maintained? The adults in the school have a shared responsibility to sustain
an active dialogue with the children and the teachers to understand together the
motivations and needs of the school community: questions, responses, and negotiations are important strategies for the children to learn.

Community and participation.   Community in a school, inspired by relationships, respect, and participation, has the children, teachers, and parents at
its center. All participate in generating the educational design and the life of the
school. Often the quality of space favors dialogue, reciprocity, and exchanges
by providing a sense of belonging and enjoyment in being part of a learning
experience.

Social constructivism.   The school is a workshop or laboratory where
knowledge is constructed continually—not in a linear or progressive way but in a
dynamic, active, and often social context. Personal knowledge is co-constructed
in the exchanges with others, be it among adults, with children, or among children. Through shared experiences and exchanges, aspects of knowledge, skills,
and strategies are modified, negated, affirmed, consolidated, connected, intercon-
nected, refined, and revised. Teachers have the creative responsibility—on the
basis of their observations of children—to identify or create experiences, as well
as to provide a variety of materials and tools to serve as sources of exploration and
discoveries. These experiences, with teachers scaffolding, then become sources of
shared learning.

Narration.   Jerome Bruner (1991, 2004) wrote that if we do not tell about
our experiences, we do not exist. In the philosophical context we are discussing,
there is a tendency to consider two layers of narration that a school should pursue.
Communication is essential, and space offers a strong possibility to let people
who enter the school know about the care teachers have for the well-being and
learning of young children, for the teachers' own professionalism, and for the
participation of parents. This is one layer of narrative to be found in a school. Visibility and transparency in the classroom reflect what is happening in that space.
However, it is through documentation that the processes of the children's and

teachers' research and action can be seen. A variety of documentation can be prepared. Words, drawings, materials, colors, and objects can carry the voices and thoughts of children and tell about them also during their absence. This is the second layer of narrative in the classroom and school.

Intense richness everyday.   Every day, as we observe and listen to children, we can note the wonderful inventions and discoveries they make in and around our small world of the school. There are so many opportunities for learning in an organized and well-thought-out environment. The sense of well-being comes from harmony, equilibrium, and positive interactions of different elements; in a way, it is a symphony. Rich, intense, generous, interesting normality can result from a balanced combination of many different elements, "Just as the white light of the sun is the sum of all the colors of the spectrum" (Cappi & Zini, 1998, p. 27).

The publication of *Children, Spaces, Relations: Metaproject for an Environment for Young Children* was an accomplishment that formalized a long-standing connection between the thoughtful pedagogical and aesthetic choices developed through many years in the experience of municipal preschools and infant-toddler centers in Reggio Emilia. This newly formulated and now public perspective, along with the increasing participation of others in the private and public sector in the city of Reggio Emilia (including efforts to create new enterprises), has determined the development of various projects and activities in the city that are visible in public spaces.

The relationship of the city with the schools for young children has been enriched by several gifts, and others invited and received, for architectural projects, including the restoration and refurbishing of the Loris Malaguzzi International Center, an admirable architectural feat. One example is the Villa Sessa Preschool gift of Anna and Gianni Iotti. Another case in point is the gift from the Maramotti Foundation in 2005 for the construction of an infant-toddler center through an agreement with the Municipality of Reggio Emilia and the Istituzione Preschools and Infant-Toddler Centers, with the organization and support of Reggio Children. This synergy between the public and private sectors seemed to have answered the various needs of a city with an increasing population due to birthrate and immigration.

One New Infant-Toddler Center Is Born

The gift from the Maramotti Foundation was made in honor of Giulia Maramotti, an exemplary figure in the history of the art and craft of designing and making women's clothes. Her work in developing and teaching dressmaking methods was the origin of the design brand Max Mara.

In 2004, the Maramotti Foundation, in collaboration with Reggio Children and with the patronage of the Order of the Architects of Reggio Emilia, announced a contest for the realization of a new infant-toddler center named after Giulia Maramotti. The competition was open to architects and engineers under age 35. Its

Young children gazing at their new infant-toddler center, Giulia Maramotti.

main objective was to offer young professionals in the Emilia Romagna region the opportunity to design an educational space for children inspired by high-quality pedagogical and architectural criteria and values.

Paola Cavazzoni, the *pedagogista* who followed and supported the architectural activities related to the Maramotti Infant-Toddler Center, was interviewed with Carlo Margini in September 2009 after we visited the school together. This is what they described:

Cavazzoni: In the end, the project selected was the one prepared by the architects Francesca Fava and Carlo Margini. Their project demonstrated great attention to the experience of very young children. They designed a space open to the outdoors that included movable *ateliers* and could be placed close to the building in the winter and further out toward the grounds in the summer. The selection was based on the coherence of ideas about space that are part of the values of Reggio Emilia. Their proposal was for a building that contained key concepts consistent with the "Metaproject for the Environment"—mobility, transparency, and transformation—along with giving attention to the context and the physical and cultural space. We selected the project by Carlo Margini and Francesca Fava because it included careful attention to relationship, which is one of our basic values. We also found their care about including and considering the continuity between interior and exterior space to be a positive aspect of their proposal. In their plan, there was a flower garden where colors and aromas were specified and made visible, so that they could be offered to the children and adults within the educational community. A vegetable garden to be planted with parents was also included in their design.

Gandini: *When listening and observing the teachers for a short time today, it was interesting for me to see how they live this space as something new and special that has to be handled with special care in a very delicate way.*

Cavazzoni: The teachers are all very young and find that it is an extraordinary adventure to be in this infant-toddler center.

Gandini: *I heard the teachers ask themselves, "If we add this or that to the space, how would the space change?" It is clear that this is a very fresh experience for them.*

Margini: In effect, the basic premise is the idea of continuous change. It was one of the cardinal points of our project: to create a space that is in continuous transformation with parts that are movable. Our thought was and still is that transformation should be possible through the daily use and life in the space. As you observed, we are still experimenting. We are aware that there has to be a delicate balance between a space that is reassuring and familiar and a space that can be changed by the action and interest of children and teachers.

Gandini: *Did you have a chance to observe the children's many types of constructions and how the teachers are documenting their processes? They are beautiful and complex, and the children seem to work together on them intensely.*

Margini: The children seem to be influenced by the structure of the building. It is so interesting to see how the children use the space. For example, to see what can happen in relation to the large glass windows, playing with light and shadows, or trying to capture the rain drops when the weather changes is very affirming. The way in which the children use the space is important to us. It is true that we had thought about the many possibilities, but to see them in action is so beautiful.

Gandini: *The materials that the teachers offer establish a relationship with the space that surrounds the children. Paola, how did the development of the various constructions begin? Was this a result of conversations among teachers? Or did they evolve spontaneously from the children within a newly constructed place?*

Cavazzoni: The teachers imagined the choice of materials that were appropriate for construction, and a request was made to the parents to bring a variety of construction materials to the *nido*. Children perceive the importance adults give to materials, and it is evident that the children use the language of these materials. It is an explicit invitation to them.

Gandini: *Certainly the children's interest in construction is not a coincidence. They know how new and amazing the building is. There are photographs in the center's documentation that show children pointing from a field in the distance to the building and its structure, which may seem to them to be a construction with blocks or a toy.*

Margini: The structure of the building *is* like a toy . . .

Cavazzoni: What has been done there serves as a reference with regard to our values. It is not that we intend to transfer an architectural project from one place to another. It is a question of values that become part of every project.

And in a later interview (December 2009) with both Carlo Margini and Francesca Fava, these concepts were elaborated.

Gandini: *Carlo, you said that this project is so much a part of the two of you that you feel the need to return often to see the* nido. *Which uses of space or transformations that children and teachers together do or have done surprised the two of you most?*

Margini: The space interpreted by the children with their color and warmth renders the place changeable and in continuous transformation. For us to always find new interpretations during our numerous visits is truly satisfying, and I think this is one of the most important reasons why Francesca and I are architects. Each detail of our project is lived in the *nido* in several modalities. We think that this is the result of architecture that is centered on listening . . . listening to the place, and to the ones who have lived in children's places currently and in the past. Listening that way sustains our relationship with the *pedagogisti,* the teachers, and the children. In preparing the project and building the *nido,* perhaps Francesca and I played as children, becoming little ones once again.

Fava: During a recent visit and because of the transparencies of the place, Carlo was exchanging smiles with a little girl. At first, she hid out of shyness, and then they began to play a game of hide and seek, feeling the emotion to be there and not to be there anymore, ending up with beautiful shared laughter. Space is an element that generates contact, along with evolution and transformation (Gandini, 2010).

EDUCATIONAL AND CARING SPACES

The Welcoming Space as a Reflection of Layers of Culture

When one enters the schools for young children in Reggio Emilia, as in the example we saw at the outset, one immediately senses a welcoming feeling, an atmosphere of discovery and serenity. Moreover, one gains an overall impression of richness in the quality and types of the activities of children, as well as of high professional standards and care on the part of adults. These impressions come from the way the environment is thoughtfully organized, and especially from seeing how children, teachers, and families move about in the schools. Yet how does all of this come about? Loris Malaguzzi (interview, June 1990) said:

> To be sure, our schools are the most visible object of our work. I believe they give multiple perceptions and messages. They have decades of experience behind them, and have known three generations of teachers. Each infant-toddler center and each preschool has its own past and evolution, its own layers of experience, and its own

peculiar mix of styles and cultural levels. There has never been, on our part, any desire to make them all alike.

The space in many ways reflects the culture of the people who create it and, on careful examination, reveals even distinct layers of this cultural influence. First of all, there is in these schools a great attention to the beauty and harmony of design. This is evident in the functional and pleasing furnishings, often invented and built by teachers and parents together. It is also evident in the colors of the walls, the sunlight streaming through large windows, the healthy green plants, and many other details, such as careful upkeep of the space. This special care for the aesthetic appearance of the environment and the methodical care for the living space of the home, along with the design of spaces that favor social interaction, are essential elements of Italian culture.

Built into the organization of the environment for activities and routines are features, such as spaces organized for small groups, that favor cooperation, a concept with strong social and political value in the Emilia Romagna Region, where a century-old organization of producers' and consumers' cooperatives is still thriving. Further regional touches can be heard in the language, seen in some of the materials and implements available, and in the typical food that the cooks prepare

Teacher and children in the 4-year-olds classroom in the Bruno Munari Preschool.

fresh each day, much to the children's delight. The culture of the city can also be detected in the documentation on the walls about outings and activities that involve city landmarks and people. One example is the famous visit to the stone lion, who sits forever waiting for the children in the market square of the city.

The next layer is the culture of the school, of each particular school. The school itself, through each and every person that directly and indirectly participates in its life, constructs a culture, starting from the particular story of how the building was chosen, designed, and built, moving on to the experience that each child and each family brings from home and the way the participation of parents is manifested in the life of the school. All this contributes to the construction of a distinct culture along with the sharing of the special events and daily rituals. In Reggio Emilia, it is considered particularly meaningful that the environment of the school, besides being welcoming, shows the traces of those children who spend so many hours in those rooms for a cycle of 3 years. There are individual and group histories carefully documented, and there is a daily weaving of routines that are meaningful stepping stones in the life of all involved. All these contribute to the creation of symbols and metaphors that are elaborated and constructed together and become part of the common discourse.

Materials that children and families bring into the school contribute to creating a particular culture. Some are natural materials, such as displays of pine cones, shells, or pebbles arranged by size, shape, or color. There are transparent boxes that contain treasures collected during a special excursion or simply exploring the garden surrounding the school. There are implements and objects brought from home, from the kitchen or the sewing box, or even the toolbox. The children bring these objects and materials to the school, but the parents help place them inside the transparent bags that go back and forth, creating a connection between school and home lives.

Furthermore, the action of the children contributes to mold the space in a specific way. The history of the children who were there before creates special characteristics, but the adults have great flexibility and interest in continuous renewal. The environment mirrors the new relationships that bring new ideas and continue to nourish the life of the school.

All this contributes to render each school different and to create a specific culture. The creative solutions, the care of the environment, the attention to details, and the reflection of the reality brought in by children and families are common elements in this system, and they leave distinct traces in each school.

Space and Time

An environment is a living, changing system. More than the physical space, it includes the way time is structured and the roles we are expected to play. It conditions how we feel, think, and behave, and it dramatically affects the quality of our lives. The environment either works for us or against us as we conduct our lives (Greenman, 1988, p. 5).

When one observes children and adults in the schools of Reggio Emilia, one perceives that there is a particular connection between time and space and that the environment truly works. The consideration of the children's own needs and rhythms shapes the arrangement of space and the physical environment, and in turn, the time at their disposal allows for the use and enjoyment, at a child's pace, of such carefully thought-out space. In fact, the way time is thought of in the Reggio Emilia approach is influenced by at least three factors. First of all, their experience has extended since 1963 when the first municipal school was established, and that in turn was based on the parent-run schools established immediately after World War II. Therefore, what we see in the arrangement of spaces is based on many changes and much learning through long experience. As a consequence, educators do not push to obtain immediate results.

Second, parents and their children establish a long-standing rapport with the program, because many start sending their sons and daughters to the infant-toddler center before age 1. When they are 3 years old, the children transfer to the municipal preschools, which take them between the ages of 3 and 6 years. The system allows teachers to be with the same children for 3 years as they move from beginning to end through the preschool. The relationships that are established during this long stay of the same groups of children, parents, and teachers shape the space, which, in turn, becomes a familiar niche for them. Because there is no separation at the end of the year, and thus no period of adjustment to new relationships, there is less pressure to reach certain goals, to finish the year's work with a clean break or start each year with a clean slate.

Third, the public programs for young children in Italy are not divided between education and day care. These programs do differ but only because they cater to children of different ages; they are all supposed to provide both care and education. The programs are considered social services, with flexible schedules. Although most of the children stay in the municipal centers between 8:30 a.m. and 4:00 p.m., there are parents who need to leave their children as early as 7:30 a.m. to as late as 6:20 p.m., and still others prefer to pick up the children right after lunch, at 12:30 or 1:00 p.m. Most of the children, in fact, spend many hours in group living. Accordingly, the educators provide a leisurely social setting for their meals; a quiet, protected environment for their naps; and several areas with a great deal of interesting and engaging proposals for their activities, which are carried out at a generally unhurried pace. Together they create a sense of security, self-esteem, and the opportunity to work through problems. Loris Malaguzzi commented, "One has to respect the time of maturation, of development, of the tools of doing and understanding, of the full, slow, extravagant, lucid and ever-changing emergence of children's capacities; it is a measure of cultural and biological wisdom" (Chapter 2, this volume).

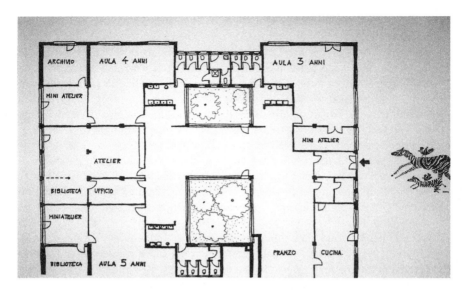

The floor plan of the Diana Preschool.

Social Space, Active Space, and a Space for Hands and Mind

For the educators in Reggio Emilia, social exchange is seen as essential in learning. Through shared activity, communication, cooperation, and even conflict, children co-construct their knowledge of the world, using one child's idea to develop another's or to explore a path yet unexplored. Because social development is seen as an intrinsic part of cognitive development, the space is planned and set up to facilitate encounters, interactions, and exchanges among children. The space has to guarantee the well-being of each child and of the group as a whole. At the same time, the space is set up to favor relationships and interactions of teachers, staff, and parents among themselves and with children. For example, adults can meet, work in small or large groups, discuss problems, and eat together inside the school. The well-being of the adults who work in the schools and the trust of parents, who entrust their children to the school before going about their activities, are essential for the educational project to work. As stated by Loris Malaguzzi (interview, June 1990):

> We have tried always to help and maintain strong ties between work and research, a healthy cooperation with the school staff and with the families, an unfailing faith in the potential and capacities of children, and, lastly, a ready willingness to think about and discuss what we do.

In the Diana Preschool (see photo above), the classrooms for the children aged 3, 4, and 5 years are open toward the large common space designated by the same term used for a city square (*piazza*). The other interior spaces are open toward this *piazza* or common space. The classrooms are subdivided in two or three spaces because the teachers are convinced that smaller spaces can offer opportunities for children to work well in small groups, to listen and be listened to, and therefore to communicate. This arrangement also gives the teachers the opportunity to set up situations that invite constructive exploration and action.

Among the other interior spaces that open toward the *piazza* of the Diana School, there is the large *atelier,* a library with space for computers, an archive, and a storage room. All the children and adults in the school use the *atelier* (a workshop or studio). The teacher in charge of the *atelier,* the *atelierista,* has preparation in art education or, more and more frequently, in various aspects of expressive arts, such as dance, music, and design. The *atelierista* is co-organizer of children's and teachers' experience and serves as editor and designer of the documentation of the work done in the school. Each age group has a classroom (a large room) and next to it a mini-*atelier,* which distributes the tools and activities of the *atelier* throughout the school.

Continuing our visit to a school, we see the kitchen, which is always an important space where the cook and her helpers include a few children every day in the food preparation. Recently there has been great attention to the "languages" of taste and food and to the children taking turns with the responsibility of setting

The mini-*atelier* of La Villetta Preschool.

tables, which helps develop their mathematical and aesthetic understanding (Cavallini & Tedeschi, 2007). The dining room is an important relational space, as is the washroom with sinks for washing or water play, and the bathrooms, which are all laid out in efficient and pleasant ways. Nothing is considered a marginal space; for example, the mirrors in the washrooms and bathrooms are cut in different shapes to inspire the children to look at their image in a playful way. The ceilings are used as host to many types of aerial sculptures or beautiful mobiles, all made with transparent, colored, and unusual material, built by children and set up by teachers. There are glass walls to create a continuity between interior gardens and outside gardens; they contribute much natural light and give occasion for playing with transparencies and reflections. Glass walls also separate working spaces to create a communal feeling. However, if one desires to be or work alone or chat with one friend, there are various options, such as the space of a mini-*atelier* or other comfortable small enclosures to which one can retire and spend time.

The organization of the day and of the active space shows the attention to individual children as well as to the group of children. Every morning around 9:00, when all the children have arrived at school, each classroom has a meeting. In some schools, the meeting space is on something similar to bleachers. Then, once the children have chosen from among the activities available or to continue with one of the projects in progress, they will find the necessary materials and tools set up on tables, light tables, and easels, or placed in convenient spaces. They will be able to find everything else they need on well-organized open shelves, stocked with recycled and other materials. Those materials have been previously selected and neatly placed in transparent containers with the help of teachers.

The arrangement and use of space for activities, for constructive exploration of materials, or for work on projects and themes is critical. Loris Malaguzzi said:

> What actually goes on in the schools is a basic test for all of us. The continuous activity is the most important thing for us and represents that which can contribute the most to keeping fresh (a term dear to Dewey) our interest and the continuous mobility of our thought and action. I believe that our schools show the attempt that has been made to integrate the educational project with the plan for the organization of work and architectural and functional setting, so as to allow for maximum movement, interdependence, and interaction. (Malaguzzi, interview, June 1990)

One of the images that Malaguzzi used to make a point about setting up the space for stimulating and meaningful centers of activity is that of "market stalls" where customers look for the wares that interest them, make selections, and engage in lively interactions.

Space Appropriate for Different Ages and Levels of Development

In the infant-toddler centers, the attention given to the physical environment has a particular quality that reminds one of the need that the youngest children

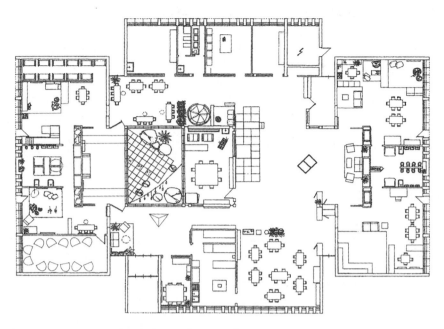

The floor plan of the Arcobaleno Infant-Toddler Center.

have for closeness and nurturing exchanges. Right at the entrance, comfortable wicker chairs invite parents to take time to pause with their infants, meet with one another, or converse with the teachers. There are rooms covered with carpets and pillows where children can crawl safely or snuggle up with a teacher to look at a picture book or listen to a story. There is a large space with equipment appropriate for movement with ramps and rolling carts, built by a parent, that children can enter or push. There is a space for toileting, washing, and changing between the two rooms of the youngest children. One detail, included to invite the child's participation during change, is a mirror hanging over the changing table. But there is also an *atelier* where the children explore with paint, markers, flour, clay, and much more. The glass partitions are used especially in the infant-toddler centers, where children tend to feel a greater sense of separation. There, glass walls are used to allow one to see into the kitchen and into the room where the children's clothes are changed, or to look back and forth between the rooms where children of different age groups play. The ways that very young children come to feel a sense of belonging about their entire infant-toddler center is described in a book, which also provides a floor plan of Nido Arcobaleno and the context of the well-known story of "Laura and the Watch" (Edwards & Rinaldi, 2009).

Similarly, in the preschools, in the classroom of the youngest group, more space is left for play with unstructured materials such as blocks, Legos, toy animals, and recycled materials. The area covered with rugs is larger to allow the children to play on the floor. Furthermore, the housekeeping space is wide and rich with small replicas of pottery and glassware commonly found at home, jars of pasta of different sizes, and beans of different colors.

Entering the mini-*atelier* in the late autumn, one might notice that the children are exploring the properties of three materials: clay, paper, and wire. They spend several weeks on each of these materials. In later months, teachers and children will return to these materials to use their higher level of skills and understanding. Through the year, as they acquire more self-assurance, these children carry out many explorations and projects in the main *atelier* as well.

Space That Documents

According to Loris Malaguzzi, "The walls of our preschools speak and document. The walls are used as spaces for temporary and permanent exhibits of what the children and the adults make come to life" (Chapter 2, this volume).

One of the aspects of space that strikes visitors is indeed the quantity and quality of the children's own work exhibited all around the schools. In fact, this is one of the ways in which children and teachers contribute to shaping the space of their school and to constructing the culture of a particular school. They do it through the mediation of the *atelierista,* who with the teachers selects and prepares the displays with great care. Most of the time, these displays include the teachers' reflections and, next to the children's work, photographs that tell about the process, plus a description of the various steps and evolution of the activity or project. These descriptions are meaningfully completed with the transcription of the children's own remarks and conversation (often tape recorded) that went along with this particular experience. Therefore, the displays, besides being well designed and contributing to the general pleasantness of the space, provide documentation about specific activities, the educational approach, and the steps of its process.

The process of documentation itself, which is done collaboratively through observation, collecting a variety of documents, and interpreting them, gives teachers the opportunity to make informed curricular choices to assess the process and the results of the children's activities. In fact, documentation contributes notably to their professional growth. Of course, it also makes the children aware of the regard adults have for their work. Finally, to document the educational process is a way to make parents, colleagues, and visitors aware of the children's potential, their developing capacities, and what goes on in the school. Malaguzzi commented on documentation:

> Today, we would need other kinds of space. It is clear that where there is an image of the child as being active and productive, the form, distribution, size, and organization of space has to be taken into account. One thing is a school that speaks; another a school that is silent. If it is a school that speaks, we have to consider and help it to

speak. We should create a space that includes documentation where parents can tarry or take time. I would like to set up a specific space, with comfortable armchairs, where parents can pause and receive a flow of messages that will be continuously transformed. We should organize a place where parents, visitors, and teachers have dialogues and exchange thoughts and ideas. It is not casual that an archive has become a notable element of our work. The archive has resulted from our own need to document. But if one documents, for whom does one document? I document only if I have an organization that includes the family; otherwise the messages bounce away. What I want to say is that the archive and the documentation change completely the professional stature of each person who is within the school. This complete change comes about because if one must document, one must not only record, but also make predictions—that is, think carefully about what to document and why that particular thing and not another. Our school, of course, has to be physically attached to the earth, but, as an image, it has to be a ship in movement. This means that parents will always be on board with us to see different landscapes, transformations, phenomena, and so on; that is what one sees when one follows the children's interest. Parents have to have an idea of a school in motion, because the children move around all the time and not only physically; for their minds and social exchanges are in continuous motion, just as their language is. We need to become able to have this open vision of the school. (Malaguzzi and Vecchi, interview, 1992)

Space That Teaches

The environment is seen here as educating the child; in fact, it is considered "the third educator" along with the team of two teachers.

To act as an educator for the child, the environment has to be flexible: it must undergo frequent modification by the children and the teachers to remain up-to-date and responsive to their needs to be protagonists in constructing their knowledge. All the things that surround and are used by the people in the school—the objects, the materials, and the structures—are seen not as passive elements but, on the contrary, as elements that condition and are conditioned by the actions of children and adults who are active in it. In the words of Loris Malaguzzi (personal communication, 1984):

> We value space because of its power to organize and promote pleasant relationships among people of different ages, create a handsome environment, provide changes, promote choices and activity, and its potential for sparking all kinds of social, affective, and cognitive learning. All of this contributes to a sense of well-being and security in children. We also think as it has been said that the space has to be a sort of aquarium that mirrors the ideas, values, attitudes, and cultures of the people who live within it.

The schools in Reggio Emilia thus could not be just anywhere, and no one of them could serve as an exact model to be copied literally elsewhere. Yet they have common features that merit consideration in schools everywhere. Each school's

View from the *piazza* into the *atelier*, in the new school, Martiri di Sesso, gift of Gianni and Anna Iotti.

particular configuration of the garden, walls, tall windows, and handsome furniture declares: "This is a place where adults have thought about the quality of environment." Each school is full of light, variety, and a certain kind of joy. In addition, each school shows how teachers, parents, and children, working and playing together, have created a unique space—a space that reflects their personal lives, the history of their school, the many layers of culture, and a nexus of well-thought-out choices.

> Our hope is that a sensitive approach to our surroundings can constitute a positive element for participation and conscious solidarity with others and with that which surrounds us, an indispensable attitude for the future of democracy and humanity. (Vecchi, Filippini, & Giudici, 2008, p. 11)

REFERENCES

Bruner, J. (1991). The narrative construction of reality. *Critical Inquiry, 18*(1), 1–21.

Bruner, J. (2004). Life as narrative. *Social Research, 71*, 691–710.

Cavallini, I., & Tedeschi, M. (Eds.). (2007). *The languages of food: Recipes, experiences and thoughts.* Reggio Emilia, Italy: Reggio Children.

Cavazzoni, P. (2007, April). Pedagogy and architecture encounters. Lecture at the University of Modena and Reggio Emilia.

Ceppi, G., & Zini, M. (Eds.). (1998). *Children, spaces, relations: Metaproject for an environment for young children.* Reggio Emilia, Italy: Reggio Children and Domus Academy Research Center.

Edwards, C. P., & Rinaldi, C. (2009). *The diary of Laura: Perspectives on a Reggio Emilia diary.* From a project originally by Arcobaleno Municipal Infant-Toddler Center, Reggio Emilia, Italy, in collaboration with Reggio Children. St. Paul, MN: Redleaf Press.

Filipini, T. (1990, November). Introduction to the Reggio approach. Paper presented at the annual conference of the National Association for the Education of Young Children, Washington, DC.

Gandini, L. (2010). The relationship between architecture and pedagogy in the experience of the Reggio municipal infant-toddler centers and preschools. *Innovations in Early Education: The International Reggio Exchange, 17*(1), 1–11.

Greenman, J. (1988). *Caring spaces, learning spaces: Children's environments that work.* Redmond, WA: Exchange Press.

Municipality of Reggio Emilia Infant-Toddler Centers and Preschools. (1996). *The hundred languages of children: Narrative of the possible* (catalog of "The Hundred Languages of Children" exhibit). Reggio Emilia, Italy: Reggio Children.

Vecchi, V., Filippini, T., & Giudici, C. (Eds.). (2008). *Dialogues with places* (catalog of the exhibit). Reggio Emilia, Italy: Reggio Children.

Zini, M. (2005, April). See, hear, touch, taste, smell and love. *Children in Europe, 8,* 22–24.

Chapter 19

The Use of Digital Media
in Reggio Emilia

George Forman

We can find current uses of digital media in the Reggio Emilia preschools that delight, surprise, and inform our understanding of early education and the competence of young children. I will discuss these innovations here, but first cover their use of digital media in ways that are currently familiar. At times, I will compare what is now done with digital media that was previously done without it, such as using acetate sheets rather than Photoshop overlays. In this way, we can discuss the rationale for the change and consider the gains or losses in shifting to digital media.

By digital media, I mean any type of files that reside on a computer, even if later printed to paper or recorded to videotape. The digital format provides great flexibility in how the asset is distributed, stored, edited, retrieved, composited, and layered with other symbols, such as text with video or photographs with animated graphics.

Regarding a move toward conventional uses of digital media, we have seen in the traveling exhibits from Reggio a shift from large hanging panels that could not be reproduced easily to the lightweight freestanding columns with graphics stored digitally ready to produce a copy. "The Wonder of Learning: The Hundred

343

Languages of Children" (Reggio Children, 2011), the most recent traveling exhibit, includes the addition of seven or eight monitors with DVDs that loop or can be controlled by the visitor. We have seen increasing use of computers to print images and documentations to grace the walls of the schools and more use of CDs sent home as a graduation gift to the family.

The CDs sent home to families contain text files, audio files of the child's voice, video files, and a way to navigate the assets that cover a 3-year period. These CDs capture the actual process of an experience at school in ways not possible with the older practice of giving the children a portfolio filled with notes, photographs, and drawings from the previous year. These digital photographs come from a large archive that can be used and reused to make documentation panels for the wall. The fact that the photographs are now digital allows children, parents, and visitors easy access to a much larger database, and one that is much less cumbersome than in the past, when the large wall panels were stored in stacks on shelves.

There are printers, scanners, video monitors, and video projectors in many of the *ateliers.* The children are taught how to use this equipment to produce images on paper and images, animations, and video clips on the computer screen. A few groups have used the Lego Mindstorm blocks (computerized modules) that can be programmed to respond to light, sound, or physical barriers.

I have also seen increased use of digital video both with the children to revisit an experience and for the adults to study a project or investigation. For example, at an advanced study week on documentation and assessment (October 2009), a working group of *atelierista,* teacher, and mentor teacher showed the international participants a 20-minute video of three boys collaborating to build miniature clay chairs to the same scale as a clay table they had made earlier. Obviously, there were many hours of video footage taken beyond the samples placed in "The Wonder of Learning" exhibit. No doubt this footage did not fall on the cutting room floor but exists as a digital database for reviewing, evaluating, planning, and disseminating their work with children.

DIGITAL MEDIA AND CHILDREN

The Signature of the Reggio Emilia Teachers

These uses of digital media sound modern, but not extraordinary. Let's drop in and listen carefully to how they use these media, however. I think you will see a convergence between the conventional use of digital media and the pedagogical principles that have defined this work in Reggio for the past 30 years. For example, the teachers often list "relationships" as a primary and core objective. One might wonder how a project at La Villetta using computerized blocks could support this principle. Giovanni Piazza and Elena Giacopini reported on how this was done. A tree in the yard had lost a large branch during a storm the previous night. The children brought the branch into the patio of the school but then wondered if the branch (the "child") was lonely for its tree (the "mother"). The children, using the Mindstorm blocks from Lego, created a way for the tree to say hello to the branch. These blocks have sensors that respond to light by turning on other switches. As the sun rose in the morning, its light reflected from a mirror placed on the tree and hit a light sensor the children placed on the branch. At this point, the light sensor triggered a soundtrack that said, "Good morning Mommy."

The point for me was, how wonderfully typical of the educators in Reggio. Most teachers would have worked with the children to have one motorized block stop to a clap of the hands or back up if it hit the leg of a chair. What for me was typically Reggio was finding a way to integrate the robotic world to the social world—to use the intelligence of the computerized blocks to reestablish the loving relationship between a tree and its broken branch. This empathic reframing of the computerized blocks made me smile.

Chestnuts Go Digital

During the production of *The Amusement Park for Birds* video (Reggio Children, 1992), I saw how the teachers would help children think about the inside of something or the growth of something by layering acetate sheets over a drawing. In one case, the children showed the morphological changes of a sunflower by drawing the stages of the sunflower's growth on overlapping acetate sheets. In another case, the children drew the path of the water through a fountain by placing an acetate sheet over their prior drawing of the fountain as seen by the naked eye. With new technology, this method of drawing on different layers that reveal the layers below can be done on a computer using Photoshop or other graphic applications. But why would one want to do this?

No doubt the reasons were discussed in staff meetings. There was no assumption that new media was inherently better than old media. In Reggio, there has to be a reason that derives from their understanding of how children learn or what the media affords. Here are a few examples of how some older techniques have been modified via digital technology.

In the new exhibit, "The Wonder of Learning," one can study an inquiry the children made about a large empty space in the Loris Malaguzzi International Center, empty because the center, once a large warehouse and factory for the famous Parmigiano Reggiano cheese, was still begin refurbished. The children found the huge empty space with columns an invitation to run among the columns, intrigued with the number of ways the space could be navigated. They noticed that the columns disappeared into a hole in the ceiling, and they speculated that a creature, in fact, a ladybug, lived there and would come out into this huge space, free to explore, get lost, find her way again.

Teachers in Reggio knew the narrative that was developing about the ladybug would both motivate and mediate the projects for weeks to come, which included

"The computer is like a foreigner, and if you want to talk to it, you have to speak its language."

"Yes, but the computer has to understand how we talk, too, and it has to do what we want it to do." (Drawing and words by children from Diana Preschool).

laying out the itinerary of the ladybug using orange yarn in the actual space, creating a scale model of the space to represent that itinerary, and finally using the alpha channels in Photoshop to animate the ladybug's movement through the space as well as the dynamics of ladybug flight.

The protracted and personal narrative with the ladybug and her habits was nurtured by the teachers, the same way we have seen done in Reggio since we first read of the Zebra coming into the dining hall at the Diana Preschool, or the ants and worms that lived in the 1-meter plot of land cordoned off for study, week after week, in the backyard at La Villetta Preschool. The new media products of the children are so incredibly inventive, nuanced, and varied because of the depth of their relation to their protagonists. The children used Photoshop to represent the ladybug in flight, temporarily squashed, electrified, and revived. The extraordinary renderings came not from the technical skills but from having something to say, from projecting feelings into the ladybug, such as the need to be camouflaged or having antennae to find her way in such a huge space, a space the children themselves had felt, at first, to be overwhelming. The children had a complete narrative about the ladybug. Everything about the huge room that interested the children was folded into this narrative. Again, the educators in Reggio teach us that it is one's personal relation to the subject matter that drives the composition.

The use of the Photoshop helped them create nuance not easily created with markers, paper, and yarn. For example, a photograph of the ladybug's itinerary, laid out in the room with colored yarn, was presented as an image on the computer screen. The children then used Photoshop to add sinuous paths superimposed on the tightly stretched yarn pictured in the photograph. They could also easily swap out different renderings of the lady bug, electrified, smashed, revived, fluttering, flitting as her journey progressed.

The Virtual and the Real

The teachers continually layer the virtual, the real, and the representational codes. In the ladybug's itinerary, the children used touch-sensitive pens on a graphic tablet so they could draw the path of the ladybug on digitized photos on the computer. The images were not generic stock photographs but instead were the actual photographs the children had taken as they marked the itinerary with orange yarn. These personal photographs helped the children remember all of the emotions, conversations, and jokes that previously happened as they were laying out the yarn. The children both remembered and invented as they worked on the computer.

This strategy of putting the children's real world into the virtual world has great merit. We have seen educators in Reggio use this strategy even before they had digital media, such as supporting children to "enter" the projection of an enlarged image of the park fountain, a photograph they had taken (Forman and Gandini, 1992; Piazza, 1995). The slide projector casts the fountain on the children, who then pretend to be the fountain or drink from the fountain or dodge the fountain spray. The compression of the virtual and the real gives new meaning to both.

The children take digital photographs of the space with columns and other landmarks. The teachers ask, "Where were you standing when you took this photograph?" The children are thereby encouraged to "read" the photograph by relating the virtual to the real. Note, however, that the teacher did not say, "Can you find the object in the room that you see in the picture?" The question about perspective is more interesting because it represents the relation between the knower and the known, between the one choosing the angle of the shot and the shot. This relation of the virtual and the real helps children understand the difference. "Reality" is a matter of perspective, of how one frames an experience, even the whole experience. The same columns look crowded, spaced, and hidden depending on where the child was standing.

The integration of the virtual and the real was also used when the children wanted to animate the ladybug, to capture the dynamics of moving wings, using the graphic layers of Photoshop that could be revealed in sequence to simulate movement. The children first made the ladybug as a paper cutout, and through discussion, cutting, trimming, and folding the paper, they constructed the remaining poses to be sequenced for flight. These cutouts were then scanned into Photoshop as separate and numbered layers, organized in the proper sequence, then

The children first made the ladybug as a paper cutout, and by discussion, cutting, trimming, and folding the paper, they constructed the remaining poses to be sequenced for flight. These cutouts were then scanned into Photoshop as separate and numbered layers.

scaled and rotated to render the appearance of one bug flying. The conversion of the paper models into a numbered and precisely positioned sequence gave the children a more generalized knowledge of movement. Movement can be understood as a set of discrete ordinal positions that appear at standard intervals, a concept foundational to the calculus. Yet this more abstract representation is partially "defended" by the intuitive knowledge of the paper models from which it sprang.

The Creation of Codes to Organize Experience

We might remember "The City in the Rain" (one of the themes in "The Hundred Languages of Children" exhibit; Reggio Children (1987/1996/2005). In this project, children recorded the sounds of raindrops hitting car tops, puddles, and the open pavement and the sounds of cars swishing over wet roadways. They translated these sounds into marks, some rows of dots, some coiled swirls, depending on the quality and rhythm of the recorded sound. These cross-modal representations have continued with digital media. Children speak into a computer and see representations of the loudness and frequency presented on the screen (spectrograph). From this real-time, machine-generated representation of their own voices, they create new classes of marks when they work with paper and pen. To quote from *Dialogues With Places* (Vecchi, Filippini, & Giudici, 2008):

> Children learn about the world by creating relationships between different languages. In this research the language [I think they mean the spectrograph] seems to help the children to appropriate [better understand] the "grammar of sound." . . . Rhythm is an essential part of every language, the play of full and empty, sound and pause. We feel that herein lies the passage between the sounds produced by chance by the children and their compositional research. (p. 118)

In other words, the world of raw experience becomes known as a composition, ordered and understood in terms of rhythm motifs, progressions, and repetitions. First the computer generates the correspondence between the analog (the human voice) and the digital (the spectrograph). Then the children use paper and pencil to reinvent some of these regularities to represent sounds in marks. The

Children learn about the world by creating relationships between different languages. A visual representation of sound (the spectograph) helps the children understand the grammar of sound.

children are inventing codes that help them "see" the subtleties of the sounds. Even a careful study of the computer graphics, without this component of invention, would not integrate the digital code with the analog experience. Herein we see a grand example of the constructivist pedagogy in Reggio Emilia. To understand is to invent (Piaget, 1973).

Distorting Reality to Understand It

Digital media, perhaps more than most other media, allow one to create completely new realities—that is, re-presentations of reality. A painting can portray a man as half goat, but a computer can progressively morph Mateo's face into Georgia's face as we watch the transformation over several seconds. At the Diana Preschool, children have been experimenting with this morphing technology. A person, by stages, can look more and more like the trees in the background. The more conventional concept of camouflage morphs by degrees into the invisible. The digital medium gives the child more control over the gradual process of the change: from me, to camouflaged me, to invisible me. The last (the invisible me), of course, is not a stimulus but an inference. You only know it's "me" in the last stage because you have witnessed the progression. Bravo, digital media.

Digital media give the method of distorting reality into the hands of the child. As I have mentioned elsewhere (Forman & Hill, 2010), the child's understanding of the operator, the method of change, is fundamental to a more complete understanding of the physical and social world. What must I do to this image of me to blend with the trees, and then do more of "it" to make my figure so imperceptible that a passerby would not see me at all, even though I know where to look for the telltale vestiges of me? I can't just make my face green. I can't just warp the contour of my body. I have to think more specifically about how the perceiving eye works, how it looks for discontinuities in pattern to isolate one object from another. So in distorting reality using the computer, I am actually learning how reality works. At the same time, I am learning how heretofore discrete categories (full view, camouflage, and invisible) are actually variations on a single operator of change.

The Affordances of Digital Media

Each medium, such as paint, pencil, collage, clay, computer graphic, digital video, when used to tell or explain, possesses a range of referents that the medium can easily and clearly express, at least relative to other media (Forman, 1994). When a child draws a picture to tell others about his sense of what makes a crowd, his pencil can render the anonymous look of the faces. Cutting these figures out as separate objects presents the opportunity (affords) for the child to easily change the orientations of the coming and going people in a crowd (Rinaldi, 1998, pp. 122–125). Indeed, the collection of paper cutouts almost speaks to the children to use the method of varying the orientation. The teachers in Reggio Emilia have long been attuned to the affordances of different media and frequently invite the

Using the graphic features of Photoshop, the children layer the path of a ladybug over four photographs of the spaces they visited in the Loris Malaguzzi International Center. This digital medium allows the children to add purpose and narrative to the corners, columns, and steps in these otherwise empty rooms they visited.

children to discuss which medium would have the best affordance to express what they want to express.

Digital media can be contrasted with other media according to their affordances. A paper cutout can be reoriented in place, but a computer version can be animated to move on its own. Why not just move the paper cutout with your hand? When children, by prior keystrokes or mouse movements, "instruct" the icon to move on the computer screen, they tend to watch the subsequent movement as a shape, an event shape. The computer-generated movement allows (affords) encoding of the event. An encoded event (e.g., "a little up and then down and leveling off") becomes "schematized," a favorite term of Jerome Bruner (1986), a cognitive psychologist. The schematization of experience makes that experience both retrievable for future use and editable in ways that preserve the good and modifies the bad (e.g., "it needs to level off sooner").

Digital media afford the layering of multiple symbol systems to express slightly different aspects of the same phenomenon. In fact, "multimedia" and "digital media" are treated as synonyms. Harking back to the experience of the children animating the ladybug's flight, the text can explain what the animation does not reveal, and the animation can fill in the informational gaps the text has left. Text affords the telling of purpose and failure. The animation affords the telling of timing and change. Close mappings of one symbol form to another improve our ability to understand the relation between theory and practice. Imagine the explanatory power of printed text that contains pop-up video windows. Layered media can present a principle-to-example mapping of the theoretical principle with micro-clips that exemplify and contextualize the theory. The meaning of the text can be seen and thereby shared and even debated by a group of readers. We have in one reading/viewing experience the power of text to present the general and the power of video to present the specific. "Should do" and "how to do" are blended. This close mapping helps us understand the educational value of play, the gradual evolution in the complexity of children's thinking, or the subtle dynamics in a group that might constrain their joy. There are many methods by which educators can use digital presentation formats to juxtapose text explanations with digital video (e.g. Forman & Hall, 2005).

DIGITAL MEDIA AND TEACHERS

The Democratization of Documentation

For years, we have looked at the revealing photographs of children in Reggio Emilia preschools immersed in long-term projects, including moments of intense investigation and joyous turnouts of the whole town for a school event. We see the children's printed words, but we don't actually hear their voices, and we know even less of what was done by the skilled teachers who provide the appropriate tool, word of encouragement, or provocation that enriches the children's day. We have had some video over the years, but by and large, the traveling exhibits, the wall panels of documentation, and many books from Reggio Children have been static print.

Gradually, we are seeing a wider sharing of video, in part because of the ease of distributing digital video across computers. I am sure this delay has little to do with anything other than the care the educators take for the use of any tool. However, there are many advantages that outsiders will realize as this shift to video documentation takes hold. For one, we can better understand the children's accomplished products. Rather than simply being amazed that a 3-year-old can make marks that capture the metaphor of sound, we can now be informed at how the teachers support this way of thinking by a combination of facilitating instruction and helping the child become empathic with the subject. For another, we can understand the terms they use, such as the *pedagogy of listening, revisiting,* or, as in the earlier quote in the section on codes, *compositional research.* So much of our past confusion resulted from supplying our own "moving images" to their terms, not quite knowing how accurate we might be. For a third advantage, we now enter our dialogues with Reggio Emilia with sufficient depth of example and detail to be surprised at what we see, to ask for the rationale behind behavior we both see in the shared referent of the video segment, and to debate one another as co-participants.

This democratization of documentation through digital video will surely accelerate the construction of good practice even as that practice is adapted to other cultures. Perhaps, when our Italian friends give us their preferred answer, "it depends," we can now see in the video on what "it depends."

Returning to the video of the three boys building clay chairs, I would like to explain that this viewing was 1 day after the actual event. Here we were, 70 educators from 20 countries working together to find meaning and to speculate on the children's intentions, even before the local educators had done so, indeed working with the local educators (also see the description of this event in Edwards, Chapter 9, this volume). The video gave us an opportunity that visiting a real classroom never could, even when we visit during a day with full attendance. The video allowed us to relate to the transactions among children and the setup by the teachers, to revisit and rewind. There were three groups looking at the same clip, and then we all convened to give three independent reports on our analyses. Some groups noted how the more skilled workers helped the less skilled workers. Some noted the strategies one child used to ensure the chair would fit under the clay table. Some noted the cleverness of the words the boys chose to define the problem and to propose solutions. Others noticed what caused a rekindling of interest when energy in the project waned during the 90 minutes these boys worked on the clay-building task. The video did give us a shared reference replete with information that we could co-construct into significance, sitting at the table with our Italian colleagues. This was truly a wonderful day.

The Story Power of Digital Video

You may ask, since this chapter is on digital media, if I am speaking of digital video, as opposed to video in general. Yes, digital video as a tool has advantages that analog video does not. Digital video clips can be easily trimmed and edited, can be sent home to the parents, posted on a secure website, tagged for later retrieval in a stored video database, duplicated infinitely, and easily inserted into a page of text that explains the example rather than merely present the example. These are not trivial differences. Imagine the history that any one school can create, the fund of knowledge they can endow, if they index video clips of children and teachers at work and play. How powerful it would be to access those great conversations we may have had several years ago with children on a topic such as crowds. How incredibly useful it would be to have the documentation team at the Loris Malaguzzi International Center create a video data warehouse for practice, both good and not so good. I have seen the beginnings of such an enterprise at the Documentation and Educational Research Center. We do not know the details yet, but we imagine their evolution will recapitulate what is happening worldwide—the use of indexed video to both archive a history and invent a future.

We know that expertise is based on two factors, a large fund of content-based experience and a facility for retrieving the relevant facts and strategies on demand in applied settings. Video stored on a hard drive might represent the experience, but to be transformed into knowledge, it must be indexed, and then those indices must be used with some cleverness to guide practice in the textured context of the physical and social world. We have long used the project titles and mini-story titles from Reggio to "index" our understanding of their practice. I think of "The Story of Laura" (the 1-year-old who puts her ear to the photograph of a wrist watch; Edwards & Rinaldi, 2009); the experience of painting the poppies before and after a visit to the fields (Reggio Children (1987/1996/2005); "What the Ant's and Bird's Eyes See"(an investigation of a 1-meter plot of the yard, conducted at La Villetta in the early 1990s); the Great Debate between Simone and Georgia in "The Amusement Park for Birds" (Forman & Gandini, 1992); and the episode of "The Runner's Handicap" in the Long Jump project (should girls start their run up closer to the line of the jump? recounted in Forman, 1993). These are vignettes that capture some essence of what we want to remember and use as points of reference, not as rote techniques. And we are less likely to apply them as rote techniques for the very reason that they are stories, that they have a narrative structure that could have gone or might go in different directions. The structure of story, captured in a continuous recording on video, facilitates a more useful way to index experience. The index helps you remember the story, and the story opens you to a better application than would some decontextualized principle of practice or carefully worded standard of performance. So in this sense, indexed digital video affords the retrieval of relevant experience in a contextualized form that opens us to the potentials of what we are presently observing and to the actual classroom culture we have established.

The Distributive Power of Digital Media

Many years ago, children remained in the presence of their parents, or at least their mother, until they were old enough for first grade. Now the growing necessity—and desire—for quality early education creates a concomitant increase in our sense of loss. We are losing personal time with our children, and we are almost desperate to know how they spend their day.

I think this sense of loss has been a big reason the American public has grabbed onto documentation as a defining feature of the "Reggio Approach." The panels on the wall, the printed updates going home, fill this void of not knowing what one's child is doing. Yet more than descriptions, the teachers in Reggio explain. Think about how much more satisfied a parent could be when these documents include photographs and video.

North American teachers have begun some initial use of Internet blogs to keep parents up-to-date and invite them to participate, share reactions, and offer information about how something done at school has been continued in the home. However, these innovations are in the early stages and have not yet expanded into a collective or distributed analysis or evaluation of learning moments. Nevertheless, the power of digital media to be distributed to all constituents will surely find a central place in Emilia Romagna, an agrarian region known for its strong sense of community.

REFERENCES

Bruner, J. (1986). *Actual minds, possible worlds*. Cambridge, MA: Harvard University Press.

Edwards, C., & Rinaldi, C. (Eds.). (2009). *The diary of Laura: Perspectives on a Reggio Emilia diary*. St. Paul, MN: Redleaf Press.

Forman, G. E. (1993). Multiple symbolization in the Long Jump project. In C. Edwards, L. Gandini, & G. Forman (Eds.), *The hundred languages of children: The Reggio Emilia approach to early childhood education* (pp. 171–188). Norwood, NJ: Ablex.

Forman, G. E. (1994). Different media, different languages. In L. G. Katz & B. Cesarone (Eds.), *Reflections on the Reggio Emilia approach* (pp. 41–54). Urbana, IL: ERIC Clearinghouse on Elementary and Early Childhood Education.

Forman, G. E. (2010). Documentation and accountability: The shift from numbers to indexed narratives. *Theory Into Practice, 4, 29*–35.

Forman, G. E., & Gandini, L. (1992). *The Amusement Park for Birds* (DVD video). Amherst, MA: Performanetics Press.

Forman, G., & Hall, E. (2005). Wondering with children: The importance of observation in early education. *Early Childhood Research and Practice, 7*(2). Available at http://ecrp.uiuc.edu/v7n2/forman.html.

Forman, G. E., & Hill, F. (2010). *Constructive play: Applying Piaget in the classroom*. Amherst, MA: Videatives. (Available as an e-book at www.videatives.com)

Piaget, J. (1973). *To understand is to invent: A structural foundation for tomorrow's education*. New York: Grossman.

Piazza, G. (Ed.). (1995). *The fountains*. Reggio Emilia, Italy: Reggio Children.

Reggio Children. (1987/1996/2005). *The hundred languages of children: Narrative of the possible* (exhibit catalog). Reggio Emilia, Italy: Preschools and Infant-Toddler Centers, Istituzione of the Municipality of Reggio Emilia and Reggio Children.

Reggio Children (2011). *The wonder of learning: The hundred languages of children* (exhibit catalog). Reggio Emilia, Italy: Preschools and Infant-Toddler Centers, Istituzione of the Municipality of Reggio Emilia and Reggio Children.

Rinaldi, C. (1998). Projected curriculum and documentation. In C. Edwards, L. Gandini, & G. Forman (Eds.), *The hundred languages of children. The Reggio Emilia approach—advanced reflections* (2nd ed., pp. 123–126). Greenwich, CT: Ablex.

Vecchi, V. (2010). *Art and creativity in Reggio Emilia: Exploring the role and potential of ateliers in early childhood education*. New York: Routledge.

Vecchi, V., Filippini, T., & Giudici, C. (Eds.). (2008). *Dialogues with places* (catalog of the exhibit). Reggio Emilia, Italy: Reggio Children.

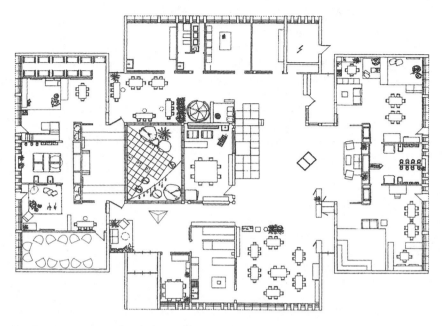

The floor plan of the Arcobaleno Infant-Toddler Center.

have for closeness and nurturing exchanges. Right at the entrance, comfortable wicker chairs invite parents to take time to pause with their infants, meet with one another, or converse with the teachers. There are rooms covered with carpets and pillows where children can crawl safely or snuggle up with a teacher to look at a picture book or listen to a story. There is a large space with equipment appropriate for movement with ramps and rolling carts, built by a parent, that children can enter or push. There is a space for toileting, washing, and changing between the two rooms of the youngest children. One detail, included to invite the child's participation during change, is a mirror hanging over the changing table. But there is also an *atelier* where the children explore with paint, markers, flour, clay, and much more. The glass partitions are used especially in the infant-toddler centers, where children tend to feel a greater sense of separation. There, glass walls are used to allow one to see into the kitchen and into the room where the children's clothes are changed, or to look back and forth between the rooms where children of different age groups play. The ways that very young children come to feel a sense of belonging about their entire infant-toddler center is described in a book, which also provides a floor plan of Nido Arcobaleno and the context of the well-known story of "Laura and the Watch" (Edwards & Rinaldi, 2009).

Similarly, in the preschools, in the classroom of the youngest group, more space is left for play with unstructured materials such as blocks, Legos, toy animals, and recycled materials. The area covered with rugs is larger to allow the children to play on the floor. Furthermore, the housekeeping space is wide and rich with small replicas of pottery and glassware commonly found at home, jars of pasta of different sizes, and beans of different colors.

Entering the mini-*atelier* in the late autumn, one might notice that the children are exploring the properties of three materials: clay, paper, and wire. They spend several weeks on each of these materials. In later months, teachers and children will return to these materials to use their higher level of skills and understanding. Through the year, as they acquire more self-assurance, these children carry out many explorations and projects in the main *atelier* as well.

Space That Documents

According to Loris Malaguzzi, "The walls of our preschools speak and document. The walls are used as spaces for temporary and permanent exhibits of what the children and the adults make come to life" (Chapter 2, this volume).

One of the aspects of space that strikes visitors is indeed the quantity and quality of the children's own work exhibited all around the schools. In fact, this is one of the ways in which children and teachers contribute to shaping the space of their school and to constructing the culture of a particular school. They do it through the mediation of the *atelierista,* who with the teachers selects and prepares the displays with great care. Most of the time, these displays include the teachers' reflections and, next to the children's work, photographs that tell about the process, plus a description of the various steps and evolution of the activity or project. These descriptions are meaningfully completed with the transcription of the children's own remarks and conversation (often tape recorded) that went along with this particular experience. Therefore, the displays, besides being well designed and contributing to the general pleasantness of the space, provide documentation about specific activities, the educational approach, and the steps of its process.

The process of documentation itself, which is done collaboratively through observation, collecting a variety of documents, and interpreting them, gives teachers the opportunity to make informed curricular choices to assess the process and the results of the children's activities. In fact, documentation contributes notably to their professional growth. Of course, it also makes the children aware of the regard adults have for their work. Finally, to document the educational process is a way to make parents, colleagues, and visitors aware of the children's potential, their developing capacities, and what goes on in the school. Malaguzzi commented on documentation:

> Today, we would need other kinds of space. It is clear that where there is an image of the child as being active and productive, the form, distribution, size, and organization of space has to be taken into account. One thing is a school that speaks; another a school that is silent. If it is a school that speaks, we have to consider and help it to

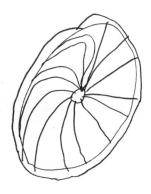

Chapter 20

The Loris Malaguzzi
International Center

Carlina Rinaldi and Sandra Piccinini

We are working in difficult times, ever changing and shifting . . . beyond our ability to predict, for the future has become difficult to govern.

I believe that the challenge facing children today is . . . to think how to interconnect—this is the watchword for the present and the future—a word that we need to understand deeply and in all its forms. We need to do so keeping in mind that we live in a world made not of separate islands but of networks . . . in this metaphor is contained both the construction of children's thought and our own thought construction, . . . which belongs to a wide archipelago where interference, interaction and interdependence are constantly present even when we do not see them. (Loris Malaguzzi, 1993)[1]

HOW THE IDEA WAS BORN

The idea of creating an International Center in Reggio Emilia for giving value to children's, parents', and teachers' culture and creativity had its starting point

357

The Loris Malaguzzi International Center.

in suggestions made by Loris Malaguzzi. The idea was discussed at meetings with various interested parties and began to take shape during the 1990s when the Reggio Emilia municipal administration (*Comune*) made a commitment to the center, and initiatives for public awareness were undertaken for widespread citizen involvement.

At that time, international recognition arrived for Reggio educational services in *Newsweek* magazine (1991) and in the shape of the Kohl Prize (1993). Diana Preschool was chosen to represent the entire Reggio educational system as a symbol of the highly qualified and innovative educational project.

From that moment, we began working in Reggio Emilia to breathe life into an organism capable of responding to international reverberations. Reggio Children was created in 1994 through the wishes of a group of citizens, parents, and workers and the Comune of Reggio Emilia, and it was entrusted with the task of constantly promoting and valuing our educational experiences in suitable ways.

The experience itself is distinguished by its strongly research-oriented nature and by its observation and documentation of children's thinking and work. We wish to encourage further development of national and international relations and exchange through common research projects, and for this reason, in these same years, the idea of the international center for research and future strategic development matured.

THE ARCHITECTURAL AND CULTURAL PROJECT OF THE INTERNATIONAL CENTER

We built the Loris Malaguzzi International Center to value the pedagogical experience that was created and developed in Reggio Emilia. We want to offer a sort of cultural provocation, a necessary element in a center of research.

The initiatives of the International Center will focus on childhood but will also be oriented toward older children and adolescents. The project of the International

Center is designed to value the "hundred languages" and to propose a constantly innovative idea of schools and education. We believe that the International Center is a cultural investment that will produce social and economic development.

Within the work of this center, children and young people are able to learn through exploration and investigation in an environment that combines highly educational experiences with the value of play. The center is a place dedicated to encounters between families and children and young people, and among researchers, scholars, and administrators. The center is open to children and families from Reggio Emilia, from our province and region, from Italy as a whole, and from abroad. Students, teachers, and professionals in education are invited to participate in professional development initiatives at the center, as are administrators from public and private corporations and organizations in Italy and around the world. Scholars and researchers from universities and science institutes have the opportunity to engage in dialogue and study with colleagues at the center.

This project is also a unique opportunity for the innovation and transformation of an important area of the city of Reggio Emilia. The new International Center is located in Santa Croce, the northern part of the city, the first industrial area developed at the beginning of the 20th century. In 1998, the municipality bought the Locatelli buildings, built in 1924, to house the International Center. Once the site of a cheese warehouse, the Locatelli buildings are a good example of industrial architecture. The buildings are in the almost-complete process of being renovated and are located close to the railway station for easy access by train and through pedestrian underpass to the center of the city.

Santa Croce is a neighborhood that reflects the evolution of the city of Reggio Emilia. At one time, it was primarily an industrial neighborhood. Now it is the home of many immigrant families, with a population that is younger than that of the city as a whole and includes more immigrants than the city (primarily from Morocco, China, and Ghana). This changing neighborhood is in the process of finding a new identity. Many of the buildings have been renovated and are being used in new ways. For example, a building that was once a villa is now a public library.

The architectural project of the Loris Malaguzzi International Center was designed by Tullio Zini and his colleagues. The center includes creative areas for multimedia activities, a center for study and spreading pedagogical research produced in the schools, a place for professional development, and the site of a preschool. The center includes a preschool for children aged from 3 to 6 years, as well as primary school classrooms. Within the International Center, there are workshops, *ateliers*/laboratories, and play areas; exhibition areas; and the Documentation and Educational Research Center. Also on site are an information center, bookshop, restaurant and cafeteria, and auditorium.

The International Center is becoming a place of identity for this neighborhood and for the city of Reggio Emilia. The city continues to plan for the future with respect for the memories of the past. In an age of great changes and fear for the future like our own, Loris Malaguzzi's message is even more important: "Children have rights. Children bring culture. On this premise, we can bring a higher level of citizenship to each individual."

THE LORIS MALAGUZZI INTERNATIONAL CENTER: A METAPROJECT

The opening of the Loris Malaguzzi International Center took place in stages, with recognition of the completion of the first phase of construction taking place in 2006. However, the grand opening on February 23, 2009, of the International Center was momentous for the infant-toddler centers and preschools, for the city of Reggio Emilia, and for all the people in Italy and around the world who have hoped for an international center dedicated to Loris Malaguzzi—all those who, through their ideas and actions, have helped to build it.

It is a home for the places that have taken inspiration from the Reggio educational experience but that are looking toward the future, heightening the international and multicultural dimension that has been here since the beginning.

I, Carlina Rinaldi, am one of the lucky people who has had the good fortune and privilege to follow this educational experience from the beginning and with it the construction of this concept of internationality. This experience was born international in its theories. From the beginning, we followed Agazzi, Montessori, and other Italians, but also Piaget, Dewey, and Vygotsky. Those of you who were not with us then—some because you were not yet teaching, others because you maybe were not yet born—need to know that it was incredibly innovative in the 1960s to quote names of this kind. Piaget had only been translated into Italian in 1950, because before this time it was forbidden to do so.

These names manifest our intention for immediate contact and exchange, with the aim of offering children the best that international culture and international thinking—not only pedagogical but other fields—have elaborated. As I said, the experience was born international in its theories, born international in its actions and relations. I would like to remind you how this experience of ours, which dates back formally to 1963 as a *communal,* municipal experience, held its first international conference in 1966. Furthermore, the adventure of "The Hundred Languages" exhibit began—as we often remember—in the '80s, and what we used to call "delegations" and now call "study groups" go back to the '70s with this intention of exchange and reciprocal dialogue.

The experience was born international above all in its aspirations. Thinking on a large scale, thinking big, thinking of ourselves not only in pedagogical terms but also as a cultural experience, as a place producing culture, a place of political action—local, national, international. From the beginning, we felt the responsibility that every gesture, every choice made in this city would have implications

The Marco Gerra Exhibition Hall.

and consequences for other choices and other gestures that would be made or not made in other parts of the world.

Feeling this responsibility is an integral part of our history. It is something we owe our own history, and this is why the center is us, ourselves. In fact, the center is not only a physical place to visit for professional courses and meetings. It is not something "extra," a window to appear in or a reason for working and thinking more. The center is a tool for helping us think better and think *other*.

It is a tool for helping create changes in our teaching, for thinking what we need to do as a city, as world citizens; it is a tool for creating conditions for paradigmatic change, in our way of conceptualizing, of creating relations. In my view, and not only mine, the center is therefore a large metaphor for what we are, for what we have been, and for what we want or would like to be. It is a way of thinking of ourselves differently. It is a *metaproject*.[2] In my view, the center brings the theory of the hundred languages to maturity and fulfillment—not because I hope we will be able to explore this theory more deeply in the center, with the center, and thanks to the center, but because the theory of the hundred languages pertains not only to psychology and pedagogy but is above all a political and cultural theory, a theory exalting the value of plurality and pluralism, of differences and of dialogue between differences. Pluralism as a premise for all discussion on quality and democracy.

Let us remember that it is no coincidence that the theory was born at a time when a small number of languages had cultural dominance over other languages, and therefore a small number of powers over other powers.

To speak of a hundred languages was to speak of the right to give voice and language to those who were not recognized as bearers of even one language. The theory in my view is synonymous with freedom, of the freedom that can guarantee research, the freedom that only research can guarantee.

Research is the connective tissue linking the International Center to the schools, the center to the city, the center to Italy, the center to the world. Another area we can reflect on this year, even more than we have done in the past, is the idea of *research* itself. The word is overused and easy to throw into conversations, but it can quickly generate many misunderstandings. We mean to speak of research as *humus,* as an existential attitude possessed by children and mankind. We also need to understand what types of research to take on and in what areas, with what partners. We have worked on many research projects, and we need to look for others; this will be our contribution to the city, to internationality, to the science of mankind. We will also have occasion to reflect on ethical issues connected to research, to education, to our being an international network. We will need to reflect on how to define our relationship with the university, the world of economy, with young people and families—and not only the families attending our schools.

As we have done before, and hopefully may do even better in the future, we could also think about the narratives we make of ourselves—how we tell our story, how to change, growing richer and enriching ever more through this exchange. We could reflect more and more on this concept of childhood, which United Nation documents define as years 0 to 18, on its places, its languages, and much more besides.

I repeat, the center is nothing if not us. It is us, ourselves, an "us" as big as our city, as big as the world.

NOTES

1. The quotation from Loris Malaguzzi was translated by Lella Gandini and published in *RECHILD: Reggio Children Newsletter,* December 2005, p. 1. "How the Idea Was Born" comes from the same issue, p. 2. "The Architectural and Cultural Project of the International Center" was adapted from a piece with this title by Sandra Piccinini (2005) in *Innovations in Early Education: The International Reggio Exchange, 12*(4), 7–9. The final section, on the International Center as metaproject, is taken from a talk by Carlina Rinaldi given for the opening assembly of the academic year 2006–2007 for staff of the Istituzione Preschools and Infant-Toddler Centers of the Municipality of Reggio Emilia and members of City and Childhood Councils, and published in *RECHILD: Reggio Children Newsletter,* April 2007, pp. 1, 5–7.

2. A *metaproject* is a major project or undertaking containing a set of other projects.

Part V

Conclusion

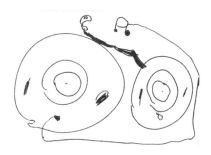

Chapter 21

Final Reflections and Guiding Strategies for Teaching

Carolyn Edwards, Lella Gandini, and George Forman

This book has presented an introduction and overview to the experience of early childhood education in Reggio Emilia. The purpose of the overall educational project, so say the educators, is to produce a *reintegrated child,* capable of constructing his or her own powers of thinking through the synthesis of all the expressive, communicative, and cognitive languages. However, this reintegrated child is not a solitary investigator. On the contrary, the child's senses and mind need help from others in perceiving beauty, order, and goodness and in discovering the meanings of new associations of people, ideas, and things. All young children are *protagonists,* heroic actors on their own community stage of growth and development.

THE VALUE OF COLLABORATION AND COMMUNICATION

This book, like the Reggio Emilia system itself, is the product of many productive collaborations. It is one small result and manifestation of the ongoing and accelerating process of international exchange. Today, the Loris Malaguzzi International

Center provides the physical and institutional embodiment of Reggio Children's international aspirations, their long-term goal to "defend and promote the rights and potential of all children" (Chapter 20, this volume). Study tours and other initiatives bring in international delegations of practitioners and policy makers, as well as scholars, teacher educators, and students from universities and research institutes around the world, for thoughtfully constructed educational experiences. The International Network of Reggio Children contains affiliate groups from Europe, North America, Latin America, Asia, and Oceania.

Yet the most visible work of the international networks takes place in home contexts, where local leaders organize educational opportunities and promote change and innovation in daily work with children and adults. These innovations are steadily gaining in scope, significance, and quality, as can be confirmed by going to sources from many countries: Australia, by Jan Millikan; Korea, by Moonja Oh; Scotland, by Pat Wharton; Sweden, by Harold Göthson; and the United States, by Ronald Lally, in *The Diary of Laura: Perspectives on a Reggio Emilia Diary* (Edwards & Rinaldi, 2009). Other stories of international collaboration are recounted in issues of *Innovations in Early Education* (e.g., Fall 2008, *15*[4]; Fall 2007, *14*[4]; Fall 2003, *10*[4]; Winter 1999, *6*[4]). Collaborations seeded through study tours are particularly powerful starting points for long-term relationships and exploration of teacher growth and change (e.g., Fu, Stremmel, & Hill, 2002).

Furthermore, beyond work with practitioners, research programs with international collaborators draw the increasing energy of Reggio Children. One strong example is the research project undertaken with Harvard Project Zero on individual and group learning among children (Giudici, Rinaldi, & Krechevsky, 2001).

As the international dialogue expands and more people enter, the questions asked become ever more complex, the conversations reverberate farther into more and different kinds of settings and situations, and the process of spread and flow of ideas takes on a life of its own. It is true, as David Hawkins reminds us (Chapter 3, this volume), that importing foreign models wholesale has never worked; each society must solve its own problems. Educational innovations, we know, can never be transplanted from one country to another without extensive translation and adaptation. However, the fact that educational experiences cannot be transplanted intact from one cultural context to another does not mean that educational concepts and practices cannot radiate and spread through "cultural diffusion" (as the exchange and flow of ideas and products is called by anthropologists). Thankfully, cultural diffusion has occurred since the dawn of human history and takes place continually, without direction or premeditation or expert control, indeed whenever human beings of different groups come into contact with one another. Trade goods, tools and technology, scientific discoveries, linguistic patterns, music, games, clothing, and every other kind of cultural practice are constantly on the move. These diffusion processes are the very ordinary and yet also an extraordinary source of endless human vitality and cultural progress.

In the case of experiences and insights springing from Reggio Emilia, therefore, we can expect the ideas to flow as long as they are found to be useful to others and to help people with their own problems and issues. The educators in Reggio Emilia prefer language in which we speak or write of their *experience* (as opposed to their *method* or *model*), and of their experience *entering into dialogue with* (as opposed to *instructing, improving, informing*) educators in other contexts. We agree that this kind of language best conveys genuine partnership and a respect for the knowledge, wisdom, and cultural integrity embedded in the systems of meaning held by those of us educators who live in places outside Reggio who may be *inspired by* (as opposed to *following* or *doing*) the practice of educators in Reggio Emilia.

You may ask, is the international dialogue and exchange worth all of the travel, translation effort, and occasional missteps and misinterpretations that may occur? In reply, we would respond that careful preparation is required, but yes, this kind of cross-cultural exchange appears to be charged with expectation

Children explore the grounds of La Villetta Preschool with a map they are using to situate the amusement park for birds they are constructing.

and reward. It can be rich and multilayered, as a result of the different perspectives brought by "insiders" (those who have grown up in a place and are members of one cultural community) versus "outsiders" (those who have grown up elsewhere as part of a different community), as they talk together about the meaning of actions, words, events, and ideas (e.g., Edwards & Weisner, 2010; Tobin, Hsueh, & Karasawa, 2009). Both cultural insiders and outsiders offer valuable and informative perspectives—complementary interpretations—and from that juxtaposition emerges a more complete "truth-for-now" about the meaning and significance of the Reggio Emilia experience for other contexts.

THE PURSUIT OF INTERDISCIPLINARITY

Beyond collaboration and communication, this book represents a second value we the editors would like to encourage: the interpenetration, or infusion, of the academic disciplines (arts, humanities, and sciences) into the professional discipline of early childhood education. The knowledge base of the arts, humanities, and sciences seem too often used in superficial and uninspired ways in preschool classrooms, perhaps because teachers feel they are not well-enough prepared or

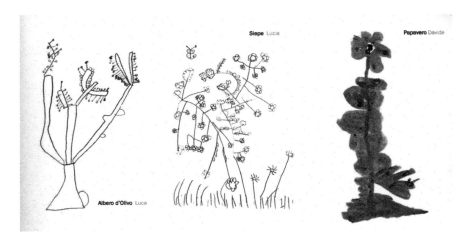

Children's drawings of plants in their park at Martiri di Sessa Preschool.

are "not good at" these subjects. In contrast, the Reggio Emilia experience demonstrates how teachers can, through documentation and teamwork, prepare school environments and activities that awaken in young children powers to perceive, study, and represent the beautiful and orderly worlds of nature and culture surrounding them.

Malaguzzi said, "From the very beginning, curiosity and learning refute that which is simple and isolated. Children yearn to discover the measures and relations of complex situations" (Municipality of Reggio Emilia Infant-Toddler Centers and Preschools, 1996, p. 30). Reggio educators in recent years have been communicating in ever stronger ways their commitment to the aesthetic values of beauty, harmony, and order, as a way of knowing for children and as a *sine qua non* in early childhood environments (e.g., Ceppi & Zini, 1998; Vecchi, 2002, 2010; Vecchi & Giudici, 2004). This emphasis is having a profound effect in North America and elsewhere (e.g., Curtis & Carter, 2003; Gandini, Etheredge, & Hill, 2008; Gandini, Hill, Cadwell, & Schwall, 2005; Cooper, Chapter 16, this volume). As a result, children, through guided exploration, play, and self-expression, are introduced in appropriate ways to the important symbols and knowledge systems of adults, where they absorb values related to aesthetics, as well as to the sciences, mathematics, and other disciplines. Children early gain a deep sense of their history, heritage, and cultural traditions.

NEW QUESTIONS AND DIRECTIONS

So, then, as we asked at the end of the first and second editions of this book, and now need to ask again at the end of this third edition, where do we go from here? The Reggio Emilia experience represents a unique combination of elements, but its basic philosophy and premises about teaching and learning are ones that international early childhood educators have found familiar and sympathetic. For example, despite the heavy emphasis in the United States on the values of autonomy and individualism, many Americans are seeking to promote greater cooperation, community, and democratic participation and to build on our own unique cultural strengths of openness to innovation and change and willingness to form associations and voluntary organizations to solve problems. Even though American educators might find situations in which they prefer to use sequential or behavioral approaches, we are still basically child-centered and holistic. Our common intellectual heritage with Europeans, bestowed by the great philosophers, psychologists, and educational reformers of the past, ensures that many of the same issues resonate on both sides of the Atlantic, and the same hopes and basic goals inspire many of the same kinds of continuing experimentation in early education, child care, and family support systems.

One worthwhile pursuit would be to continue to study in greater depth and critical analysis the educational work that is ongoing in Reggio Emilia. As this volume makes clear, we have begun to understand the ways in which Reggio teachers work together with administrators, parents, citizens, and the children themselves. Nevertheless, additional study is needed of topics that we have raised and addressed in this book but that deserve more critical examination. Such topics include the following:

- The ability of the city to meet public needs and demands for services
- The integration of immigrant children and families into the centers and schools
- The inclusion of young children with special educational needs
- Ways of mentoring new teachers and ongoing professional development
- New forms of family and citizen participation
- Processes of children's transition (e.g., from infant-toddler to preschool, and preschool to primary)
- The sustainability of the educational project within a transforming city

Some questions that Americans ask most frequently about the Reggio Emilia experience ("What happens to the children when they go on to elementary school?" "What does research say about the long-term benefits of the Reggio Emilia experience for children?") cannot be answered on the basis of empirical data. Different concepts of educational accountability prevail in Italy than in the United States. American society, but not Italian society, demands data-driven decision making in the field of education and holds the belief that progress depends on defining problems in terms of researchable hypotheses that are supported or refuted by statistical analyses.

Nevertheless, Reggio educators are interested in pursuing further research in teaching and learning to carry forward their work at older ages. For example, inside the Malaguzzi International Center is a new preschool, as well as a primary school for grades 1, 2, and 3. These classrooms represent an experiment by the Reggio educators to find out how their experience with younger children can be extended to older children. The individual and group learning of these children is being closely followed and documented. Furthermore, the process of transition of preschool children into the municipal elementary schools has been a system-wide focus of discussion and study by the Pedagogical Coordinating Team.

Thus, although the Reggio educators may not be using test scores to measure the "additive benefit" of attending the infant-toddler centers and preschools, they are very eager to evaluate in pragmatic terms whether their experience can have sustainable impact—not at the individual level but instead at the community level. Having tangible effect on the quality of life of the city is the goal. Indeed, the Reggio educators seek to make their work tangible to the community, and they include the wide sweep of the community in their field of concern—for example, through diverse initiatives directed at all ages and backgrounds. Reggio Children encourages the community to hold events—education related or not—in the auditorium of the Malaguzzi International Center. The Istituzione of the Municipality of Reggio Emilia supports initiatives like ReMida Day with broad community outreach. These efforts suggest a civic commitment that extends to all citizen-types, and that may extend or amplify the potential impact of the early childhood services. An important outcome measure will be whether these efforts are appreciated and can be sustained.

Beyond continuing to scrutinize the quality and impact of early childhood services in Reggio Emilia, we should be looking abroad at other Italian and other international successes in education (e.g., Corsaro & Molinari, 2005; Gandini & Edwards, 2001; New & Cochran, 2007). Certainly, Reggio Emilia is not the only interesting site of innovation in Italy, or even in Europe! Societies in Asia are undergoing rapid change in their early childhood systems, with successful and distinctive strategies of introducing the arts, daily exercise, emergent mathematics, and other subjects to children. The societies of Western Europe have long been out in front of North America with regard to publicly supported social services and national family policy, and therefore, North Americans need to become informed about other national experiences as we debate whether and how to finance publicly early childhood care and education, and consider important topics such as environmental design and curriculum planning, different models for grouping children, defining adult roles, and building participation. Many resources are available. For instance, *Children in Europe* (journal published by Children in Scotland) tracks important European conversations on such topics as children's political rights, services for immigrant and underserved groups, young children and science, and the early childhood workforce. *Young Children, Childhood Education International,* and other early childhood journals regularly inform on international developments.

When it comes to making our study of the Reggio Emilia experience worthwhile by "bringing it home," there are many possible directions in which to go. Several leading Reggio-inspired educators have translated their knowledge of Reggio theory and practice into terms that resonate within their own contexts, and this can provide a general orientation (e.g., for Americans, Cadwell, 2003; for Canadians, Fraser & Gestwicki, 2000; for Australians, Millikan, 2003). Specialized books help spread the practice of observation and documentation to childcare providers, classroom teachers, and other practitioners who work with young children. For specialized audiences, thoughtful approaches have been elaborated and refined for using Reggio-inspired strategies in

- elementary schools (e.g., Wein, 2008),
- infant-toddler centers (e.g., Raikes & Edwards, 2009; Smith & Goldhaber, 2004),
- Head Start classrooms (e.g., Scheinfeld, Haigh, & Scheinfeld, 2008), and
- orphanages (e.g., Cotton, Edwards, Zhao, & Gelabert, 2007).

In each case, educators find they must fit the progressive, child-centered vision with response to particular academic demands of an age group. They must consider subject-matter requirements at the elementary level; attachment needs at the infant-toddler level, and the vulnerabilities of each risk category, such as school failure for children living in poverty, or severe developmental delay for abandoned orphan children. This means that the expertise of Reggio Emilia becomes just one part of a multilayered educational and care-giving approach. However, new directions are promising, involving, for instance:

- Emergent curriculum and the arts, combined with rigorous expectations for schoolchildren's learning and achievement
- Relationship-based care promoting continuity, sense of belonging, and connected learning in infant-toddler centers
- Play integrated with a focus on self-regulation and literacy, math, and other school-readiness components in preschool classrooms serving the urban poor
- Daily documentation incorporated into memory books, to help children in welfare institutions build autobiographical memory and sense of self.

Teacher educators, likewise, have made serious steps toward creating preservice education programs that promote constructivist inquiry and the practice of observation and documentation among young aspiring teachers. (For examples, see Broderick & Hong, 2005; Cox Suarez, 2006; Edwards et al., 2007; Hong & Trepanier-Street, 2004; Kaminsky, 2009; Kline, 2008; and Moran & Tegano, 2005). Many of these efforts center around assisting preservice teachers in gaining control of the digital technology tools and the graphic skills for documenting children's learning processes. Other key aspects involve bring students into collaborative teams and fostering a culture of inquiry and intellectual engagement among both adults and children (Goldhaber & Goldhaber, 2007).

Educators focused on social justice and antibias efforts have also commented on common ground with the experience of Reggio Emilia. They find that Reggio educators have helped sensitize all of us to the principles of democratic participation and to the image of teachers as agents for social change (Pelo, 2006). Engaging in pedagogical documentation almost necessarily leads to adult attention on children's rights and greater capacity to hear children's voices, leading to exploration of issues such as fairness and power from the children's point of view (Hall & Rudkin, 2011).

One issue is largely settled. We no longer worry about whether there is a "best" way to proceed in responding to and following up on ideas heard or strategies observed in Reggio Emilia. The ideas, if they are good ones, will spread through exchange and diffusion. Certainly, it is valuable that some educators proceed formally, setting up schools or classrooms that embody as closely as possible all of the important central premises of the Reggio Emilia experience that, indeed, become recognized "reference points" for others wishing to learn about the application of the Reggio experience to that national context. However, it is also productive that other educators proceed informally, seeking to incorporate one or a few insights gleaned from contact with the Reggio experience into their ongoing endeavors in whatever setting or level of education they happen to work. Both approaches can be extremely fruitful.

Indeed, all attempts to incorporate the ideas and approaches of others are bound to be partial and incomplete. Even with all of the money, freedom, and resources wished for, one cannot do everything anew, or import exactly what they do in Reggio; nor would one want to. After all, with over 30 municipal infant-toddler centers and preschools, and additional affiliated cooperatives in Reggio Emilia—each with its own distinct individuality evolving over time—there is no single, static "it" to model upon. Thus, the question becomes simply how ambitious, complex, and far-reaching a project one is able to undertake: what resources and support from stakeholders and colleagues are available, what parts of the current program or system most need to be changed, and how many dimensions to try to consider simultaneously. In all cases, the best (and most sustainable) change processes are those that take place gradually, carefully, and, most of all, collaboratively, with slow but steady assimilation and accommodation rather than wild and sudden lurches from one educational fashion to another.

As insights and knowledge gained from the experiences of Reggio Emilia become shared by other educators, and as they dialogue more among themselves and across national boundaries, we expect that the arguments about their meaning and significance will increase rather than decrease, that there will be less rather than more agreement about what constitutes the Reggio Emilia experience and how to translate from theory to practice.

So the question, "Where do we go from here?" raises infinite possibilities. We hope that your adventures are dense, with moments of confusion and illumination, conflict and progress.

GUIDING STRATEGIES FOR TEACHING

Here we offer a list—certainly incomplete and perhaps oversimplified—of guiding suggestions for teacher–child interaction, as a condensation and synthesis that may be helpful to readers.

1. **Drawing:** The teacher first helps the children establish a relation to the object or event drawn, such as a trip into the field of poppies, a close look at the self in the mirror, or a run through the empty space at the Loris Malaguzzi International Center. The drawing then becomes as expression of the child's relation to the object or event, not simply an observational drawing of what is seen. This relation is often mediated by the use of small living creatures, for example, the ants in a plot of land, a ladybug that lives in the Malaguzzi Center, the birds in the amusement park, or a broken tree branch that misses the mother tree.

2. **Technique in Using Art Media:** Children at a young age have a great deal of opportunity to explore media and materials, and when the teachers see the need, they are taught rather directly how to use the art implements, such as putting small amounts of paint on a brush or how to move the hands to make a snake of clay. Care in the use of art materials derives from Vea Vecchi's emphasis on aesthetics as a form of empathy and sensitivity.

3. **Invented Solutions With Media.** Older children who have mastered the basic techniques are encouraged to invent solutions. The teacher documents the children's solutions and treats the thinking involved as the purpose of the activity. In one case, the teacher discovered four engineering solutions to clay tree trunks that were initially too fragile to hold branches.

4. **Revisiting and Co-construction:** The teacher is more interested in helping children become aware of their choices and assumptions than in teaching children the correct answers or the most efficient procedures. This attitude creates a classroom culture for peer debate and the co-construction of knowledge.

5. **Special Education:** It is understood that teaching children with learning challenges requires particular scaffolding at the beginning of mastering something new, such as learning a correct verb form or remembering other children's names. These didactic moments are embedded in a social context as often as possible. Functional autonomy of the child and improved social strategies define the long-term objective.

6. **The Next Day:** Teachers are more likely to use a documented episode from the previous day as the starting point for the current day, as opposed to referring

to a book of generic activities or lessons. However, before the episode is used, at least two adults confer and agree on the big idea underlying the episode.

7. **The Role of Metaphor:** Teachers note children's metaphoric speech and do not dismiss it as "cute." The teacher assumes that the metaphor comes from an authentic worldview. Metaphoric speech, such as "burglar" for a changing shadow or "lazy" for a gentle breeze, is treated as the child's invented constructions of complex relations and worthy of analysis, revisiting, and extension.

8. **Reinforcement Versus Reflection:** The teacher works to increase the children's awareness of their perspective, theory, assumptions, and rules rather than to reinforce "good behavior." This is done by offering the child ways to revisit their thinking (through drawings, audio and video recording, printed documents of the children's conversations). This mind-set implies a great confidence in the children's ability to reconstruct assumptions that do not work.

9. **Affordances:** The teachers gives children the opportunity to express the same idea in different media (paper, wire, clay, wood) so that they will become aware of the different affordances of each media—the special advantage of using one media over another to capture a particular aspect of that idea. Take *love* as an example. String might capture how tangled love can be, but folded paper might capture the surprises in love.

10. **The Importance of Light:** The teachers prepare the environment to allow light into the room, to flood light from underneath and through objects on the light table, to create shadows on the floor and the wall with an overhead projector. This emphasis comes from a deep understanding of how light calls our attention to changes in color, form, and motion, to personal perspective, and to a ubiquitous and integrative source that brings disparate objects into elegant relations.

11. **Individuality Within the Collective:** Teachers are aware that children desire to reconcile the one within the many without losing either. The children decorate a set of bare columns differently, then treat them as a group to run and weave among. For a project on "the crowd," they make many clay figures that, like the terra-cotta warriors of Xian, have unique faces, yet these figures share in the irregular density that defines a crowd. The myriad sounds of rain in the city have individual graphic representations, but they are all aspects of the rain. The teachers help the children work through the difference between a collection of discrete elements and a group of members with cross-relations.

12. **Plans Before Production:** The teacher will take days and weeks to help children create a plan for what they want to accomplish. Children might make a cardboard model of a room before they redecorate. They might create large graphics of game rules or dance steps to better negotiate changes with the group. They might use computer graphics to render an obstacle course to

check out its complexity. These plans not only reveal mistakes that can be corrected but also provide a shared platform for group discussion.

13. **Thinking Versus Skills:** The teacher works to be consistent with her image of the competent child, rather than to meet achievement milestones. A project that digresses from a study of shadows to finding your way out of the dark would be considered on target if the children were engaged in high-level thinking, carefully crafted representations, quality revisiting, and the consolidation of new ideas.

14. **Wondering:** The teacher realizes content must flow from the child's endogenous worry and wonder. A question answered before a question is formed is an answer without meaning. Without clear wondering at the start, facts remain facts rather than evidence, solutions, or explanations.

15. **Scaffolding Co-construction:** The teacher will write down the comments from the children and look for counterpoints that could generate an interesting debate. She might read back both comments and wonder aloud at their contrariness. The teacher treats debate and conflict as a dialectic that leads to the co-construction of a more complete understanding of content.

16. **Suggesting a Test:** The teacher listens and supports the children's speculations. When a hypothesis emerges, the teacher might ask, "How can we know if [the prediction] will happen?" With the teacher's guidance, for example, children make successive chalk outlines of a changing patch of sunlight to mark the regularity of its advance, place rocks on a shadow to see if it stops, or cut out paper doll figures that can be moved until the arrangement looks like a crowd.

17. **Reframing the Familiar:** The teacher sometimes initiates a project or investigation with a provocative reframing of the familiar. For example, she may suggest that a certain building is in need of "gifts," that the random movements of a ladybug are a sign that she might be "lost," that street sounds are "music," or that an excavated tree lying on the ground has "branches" coming out of both its top and bottom.

18. **The Value of Misconceptions:** The teacher does not treat a child's misconception as something to be summarily replaced but rather as something that derives from an interesting and plausible logic that needs to be understood. The teacher engages in a sort of complicity to make meaning with the child through a process of listening and forming a subjective relationship by wondering with the child.

19. **Group Dialogue:** The teacher establishes classroom routines, furniture arrangements, emotional excitement, and small-group composition that encourage children to talk among themselves. The teacher works not to be the hub of a conversation. She may even suggest leadership to a child with a known and relevant talent. The teacher helps the group become both a competent audience and a set of expressive thinkers. Group dialogues are often

documented and can become starting points for re-launching an exploration or starting a new experience.

20. **Group Composition:** Teachers are not rigid in organizing which students take a turn in the *atelier*. Who works in the *atelier* is determined by the progress of the project.

21. **Emotion and Knowledge:** The teacher understands that an emotional relation to the subject under study is more than a motivator that energizes effort. An emotion represents an implicit question that must form the context of the search. Joy, fear, surprise, and disgust are no less than components of the child's theories about the social and physical world. The teacher works to integrate the implicit assumptions the emotion represents into the project and its solutions. How does the solution yield more joy, less fear, transform disgust, or explain surprise?

REFERENCES

Broderick, J. T., & Hong, S. B. (2005). Inquiry in early childhood teacher education: Reflections on practice. *The Constructivist, 16*(1). Available at http://www.odu.edu/educ/act/journal/vol16no1/index.html.

Cadwell, L. (2003). *Bringing learning to life: The Reggio approach to early childhood education.* New York: Teachers College Press.

Ceppi, G., & Zini, M. (Eds.). (1998). *Children, spaces, relations: Metaproject for an environment for young children.* Reggio Emilia, Italy: Reggio Children.

Corsaro, W. A., & Molinari, L. (2005). *I compagni: Understanding children's transition from preschool to elementary school.* New York: Teachers College Press.

Cotton, J., Edwards, C. P., Zhao, W., & Gelabert, J. M. (2007). Nurturing care for China's orphaned children. *Young Children, 62*(6), 58–62. Available at *Young Children: Beyond the Journal* at http://journal.naeyc.org/btj/200711/pdf/BTJEdwards.pdf.

Cox Suarez, S. (2006). Making learning visible through documentation: Creating a culture of inquiry among pre-service teachers. *The New Educator, 2,* 33–55.

Curtis, D., & Carter, M. (2003). *Designs for living and learning: Transforming early childhood environments.* St. Paul, MN: Redleaf Press.

Edwards, C. P., Churchill, S., Gabriel, M., Heaton, R., Jones-Branch, J., Marvin, C., & Rupiper, M. (2007). Students learn about documentation throughout their training program. *Early Childhood Research and Practice, 10*(2). Available at http://ecrp.uiuc.edu/v9n2/edwards.html.

Edwards, C. P., & Rinaldi, C. (2009). *The diary of Laura: Perspectives on a Reggio Emilia diary.* From a project originally by Arcobaleno Municipal Infant-Toddler Center, Reggio Emilia, Italy, in collaboration with Reggio Children. St. Paul, MN: Redleaf Press.

Edwards, C. P., & Weisner, T. (Guest Eds.). (2010, July). *Journal of Cross Cultural Psychology* (special issue), "The Legacy of Beatrice and John Whiting for Cross Cultural Research," *41*(4).

Fraser, S., & Gestwicki, C. (2000). *Authentic childhood: Experiencing Reggio Emilia in the classroom.* Albany, NY: Delmar.

Fu, V. R., Stremmel, A. J., & Hill, L. T. (2002). *Teaching and learning: Collaborative exploration of the Reggio Emilia approach.* Upper Saddle River, NJ: Merrill Prentice-Hall.

Gandini, L., & Edwards, C. P. (Eds.) (2001). *Bambini: The Italian approach to Infant/ Toddler Care.* New York: Teachers College Press.

Gandini, L., Etheredge, S., & Hill, L. (Eds.). (2008). *Insights and inspirations from Reggio Emilia: Stories of teachers and children from North America.* Worcester, MA: Davis.

Gandini, L., Hill, L., Cadwell, L., & Schwall, C. (Eds.). (2005). *In the spirit of the studio: Learning from the atelier of Reggio Emilia.* New York: Teachers College Press.

Giudici, C., Rinaldi, C., & Krechevsky, M. (2001). *Making learning visible: Children as individual and group learners.* Reggio Emilia, Italy: Reggio Children and Harvard Project Zero.

Goldhaber, D., & Goldhaber, J. (2007). Reggio-inspired teacher education. In R. S. New & M. Cochran (Eds.), *Early childhood education: An international encyclopedia* (Vol. 3, pp. 700–702). Westport, CT: Praeger.

Hall, E. L., & Rudkin, J. K. (2011). *Seen and heard: Children's rights in early childhood education.* New York: Teachers College Press.

Hong, S. B., & Trepanier-Street, M. (2004). Technology: A tool for knowledge construction in a Reggio Emilia inspired teacher education program. *Early Childhood Education Journal, 32,* 87–94.

Kaminsky, J. (2009). Transformation and challenge in Reggio-inspired teacher education programs: An interview with Carol Bersani, John Nimmo, and Andrew Stremmel. *Innovations in Early Education: The International Reggio Exchange,* Part I, *16*(2), 10–18, Part II, *16*(3), 10–19.

Kline, L. S. (2008). Documentation panel: The "Making Learning Visible" project. *Journal of Early Childhood Teacher Education, 29*(1), 70–80.

Millikan, J. (2003). *Reflections: Reggio Emilia principles within Australian contexts.* Castle Hill, Australia: Pademelon Press.

Moran, M. J., & Tegano, D. W. (2005, Spring). Moving toward visual literacy: Photography as a language of teacher inquiry. *Early Childhood Research and Practice, 7*(1). Available at http://ecrp.uiuc.edu/v7n1/moran.html.

Municipality of Reggio Emilia Infant-Toddler Centers and Preschools. (1996). *The hundred languages of children: Narrative of the possible* (catalog of "The Hundred Languages of Children" exhibit). Reggio Emilia, Italy: Reggio Children.

New, R., & Cochran, M. (Eds.). (2007). *Early childhood education: An international encyclopedia. Volume 4: The countries.* Westport, CT: Praeger.

Pelo, A. (2006). At the crossroads: Pedagogical documentation and social justice. In A. Fleet, C. Patterson, & J. Robertson (Eds.), *Insights: Behind early childhood pedagogical documentation* (pp. 173–190). Castle Hill, Australia: Pademelon Press.

Raikes, H., & Edwards, C. P. (2009). *Extending the dance in infant and toddler caregiving: Enhancing attachment and relationships.* Baltimore: Paul H. Brookes.

Reggio Children. (2011). *The wonder of learning* (catalog of the exhibit). Reggio Emilia, Italy: Author.

Scheinfeld, D. R., Haigh, K. M., & Scheinfeld, S. (2008). *We are all explorers: Learning and teaching with Reggio principles in urban settings.* New York: Teachers College Press.

Smith, D., & Goldhaber, J. (2004). *Poking, pinching, and pretending: Documenting toddlers' explorations with clay.* St. Paul, MN: Redleaf Press.

Tobin, J., Hsueh, Y., & Karasawa, M. (2009), *Preschool in three cultures revisited: China, Japan and the United States*. Chicago: University of Chicago Press.

Vecchi, V. (Ed.). (2002). *Theater curtain: The ring of transformations*. Reggio Emilia, Italy: Reggio Children.

Vecchi, V. (2010). *Art and creativity in Reggio Emilia: Exploring the role and potential of ateliers in early childhood education*. New York: Routledge.

Vecchi, V., & Giudici, C. (Eds.). (2004). *Children, art, artists: The expressive languages of children, the artistic language of Alberto Burri*. Reggio Emilia, Italy: Reggio Children.

Wein, C. A. (2008). *Emergent curriculum in the primary classroom: Interpreting the Reggio Emilia approach in schools*. New York: Teachers College Press.

Glossary of Terms Used by Educators in Reggio Emilia

Asilo Nido, **or** *Nido:* Infant-toddler center; full-day program providing education and care to children aged from around 3 months through 3 years.

Assessore: Official, serving under the mayor, in charge of all public education for the city.

Associazione Internazionale Amici di Reggio Children: International Association of the Friends of Reggio Children, a nonprofit association that depends on the work of volunteers to promote and collaborate on many initiatives in conjunction with the infant-toddler centers and preschools and with Reggio Children.

Atelier: A word of French origin referring to the workshops historically used by artists. The term was chosen by Loris Malaguzzi to refer to the school workshop, or studio, furnished with a variety of resource materials and used by all the children and adults in a school. The mini-*atelier* is the space set up in or adjacent to each classroom with the same type of or different materials and as inviting as the central *atelier*. The mini-*atelier* makes it possible for small groups of children to work together and explore materials with or without a teacher.

Atelierista: Educator with a background in the visual or expressive arts, in charge of the *atelier;* supports teachers in curriculum development and documentation; supports and develops children's and adults' expressive languages as part of the complex process of knowledge building.

Centro Internazionale Loris Malaguzzi: The Loris Malaguzzi International Center is located in Reggio Emilia and is dedicated to the encounter of professionals (from anywhere in the world), as well as children, youth, and families, with opportunities for learning and training, study and research. It contains an auditorium, exhibition halls, the Documentation and Education Research Center, *ateliers,* research and innovation spaces, a preschool and primary school, a cafeteria, a bookshop, and offices of Reggio Children.

Comune: Also called *municipio,* municipality; the city government and the building where it is located.

Consigli Infanzia Citta: The City and Childhood Councils, elected committees of parents, citizens, and educators serving a preschool or infant-toddler center as an advisory committee. These councils send representatives to *L'Interconsiglio Cittadino,* the Intercouncil.

Cooperative Early Childhood Program: A legitimate formal organization recognized by law that is formed by a private group to provide early childhood services.

Direttore: Director of Municipal Infant-Toddler Centers and Preschools, a civil service professional who oversees the whole municipal infant-toddler and preschool system and guarantees the quality and integrity of the educational services provided to children and families.

Educatore: Teacher, in a preschool or infant-toddler center.

Federazione Italiana Scuole Materne (FISM): The federation of preschools under the management of the Roman Catholic Church in Italy.

Foundation Reggio Children—Loris Malaguzzi Center: Nonprofit foundation established in September, 2011, in Reggio Emilia, Italy. The foundation is based on the idea of education as an opportunity for social development and the promotion of the rights and potentials of all children and adults. The foundation supports the spread of quality education throughout the world and is an international center of research and study.

Gestione Sociale: Community Management, the system of governance, involving representatives of the different sectors of the local community, used in the Reggio Emilia municipal early childhood system.

Istituzione Preschools and Infant-Toddler Centers of the Municipality of Reggio Emilia: The organization in Reggio Emilia responsible for direct management of the municipal infant-toddler centers and preschools. It is also responsible for relations with affiliated schools (e.g., public–private cooperatives), schools belonging to FISM (Italian Federation of Catholic Preschools), and state (national) preschools.

Officina Educativa: Educational Forum, an initiative of the city of Reggio Emilia to involve all the agencies dedicated to education, serving all age groups and sectors, to discuss issues of educational importance and plan for collaboration.

Pedagogista: Pedagogical Coordinator, acts as consultant, resource person, and curriculum coordinator to the preschools and infant-toddler centers to support the work of teachers, enrich their professional development, support their relationship with families, and facilitate the connections between teachers, administrators, and other stakeholders. In Reggio, the group of *pedagogisti* function together as a Pedagogical Coordinating Team to guarantee the quality of services of the municipal infant-toddler centers and preschools and ensure theoretical and practical integrity.

Progettazione: Derived from the Italian verb, *progettare,* meaning to design, plan, devise, or to project in a technical engineering sense. The noun *progettazione* is used in the educational context to mean flexible planning in which initial hypotheses are made about classroom work (as well as about staff development and relationships with parents and the community) but are subject to modifications and changes of direction as the actual work progresses. The term is used in Reggio in opposition to *programmazione,* which implies planning based on predefined curricula, programs, or stages.

Reggio Children: International Center for the Defense and Promotion of the Rights and Potential of all Children, an organization designed by Loris Malaguzzi and incorporated in 1994. Reggio Children is supported by a majority holding of the Municipality and the Emilia Romagna Region plus public and private shareholders (including parents and teachers). The goals are to promote research and study of the philosophy of Reggio Emilia through seminars, conferences, and study tours; to document, publish, and distribute books, videos, and other media on this subject; and to maintain open channels of communication with other institutions and educators throughout the world.

ReMida: "King Midas," the creative recycling center, supported by the city government and run by volunteers from the International Association of Friends of Reggio Children. This center collects discarded materials from businesses and industries and makes them available to infant-toddler centers, preschools, play centers, sheltered workshops, and so on. It aims to create a relationship between various forces—the worlds of culture, school, and industry—in a synergistic encounter that produces new resources.

Scuola dell'Infanzia Municipale: Municipal preschool, full-day program providing education and care to children aged 3 years to the compulsory school age of 6 years (includes the American kindergarten year).

Scuola dell'Infanzia Statale: State-run (national) preschool, providing education and care to children aged 2.5 years to the compulsory school age of 6 years (includes the American kindergarten year).

Additional Resources

BOOKS

Cadwell, L. (1997). *Bringing Reggio Emilia home: An innovative approach to early childhood education.* New York: Teachers College Press.

Cadwell, L. (2002). *Bringing learning to life: The Reggio approach to early childhood education.* New York: Teachers College Press.

Dahlberg, G., & Moss, P. (2005). *Ethics and politics in early childhood education.* London: Routledge.

Dahlberg, G., Moss, P., & Pence, A. (1999). *Beyond quality in early childhood education and care: Postmodern perspectives.* London: Falmer Press.

Edwards, C., Gandini, L., & Forman, G. (Eds.). (1993). *The hundred languages of children: The Reggio Emilia approach to early childhood education.* Norwood, NJ: Ablex.

Edwards, C., Gandini, L., & Forman, G. (Eds.). (1998). *The hundred languages of children: The Reggio Emilia approach, advanced reflections* (2nd ed.). Greenwich, CT: Ablex.

Edwards, C., & Rinaldi, C. (Eds.). (2009). *The diary of Laura: Perspectives on a Reggio Emilia diary.* St. Paul, MN: Redleaf Press.

Fleet, A., Patterson, C., & Robertson, J. (Eds.). (2006). *Insights: Behind early childhood pedagogical documentation.* Castle Hill, Australia: Pademelon Press.

Fraser, S. (2000). *Authentic childhood: Experiencing Reggio Emilia in the classroom.* Scarborough, Canada: Nelson Thomas Learning.

Fu, V., Hill L., & Stremmel, A. (2001). *Teaching and learning: Collaborative exploration of the Reggio Emilia approach.* Upper Saddle River, NJ: Prentice Hall.

Gandini, L., and Edwards, C. P. (Eds.). (2001). *Bambini: The Italian approach to infant/toddler care.* New York: Teachers College Press. (With accompanying video, available through Learning Materials Workshop.)

Gandini, L., Etheredge, S., & Hill, L. (Eds.). (2008). *Insights and inspirations: Stories of teachers and children from North America.* Worcester, MA: Davis.

Gandini, L., Hill, L., Cadwell, L., & Schwall, C. (Eds.). (2005). *In the spirit of the studio: Learning from the atelier of Reggio Emilia.* New York: Teachers College Press.

Hall, E. L., & Rudkin, J. K. (2011). *Seen and heard: Children's rights in early childhood education.* New York: Teachers College Press.

Hall, K., Horgan, M., Cunningham, D., Ridgway, A., & Murphy, R. (2010). *Loris Malaguzzi and the Reggio Emilia experience.* New York: Continuum International Group.

Hendrick, J. (Ed.). (1997). *First steps toward teaching the Reggio way.* Upper Saddle River, NJ: Prentice Hall.

Hendrick, J. (Ed.). (2003). *Next steps in teaching the Reggio way: Accepting the challenge to change* (2nd ed.). Upper Saddle River, NJ: Pearson Merrill/Prentice Hall.

Hill, L., Stremmel, A., & Fu, V. (2005). *Teaching as inquiry: Rethinking curriculum in early childhood education.* Columbus, OH: Allyn and Bacon.

Katz, L., & Cesarone, B. (Eds.). (1994). *Reflections on the Reggio Emilia approach.* Urbana, IL: ERIC Clearinghouse on Elementary and Early Childhood Education.

Kinney, L., & Wharton, P. (2007). *An encounter with Reggio Emilia: Children's early learning made visible.* London: Routledge.

Lewin, A. (2005). *Possible schools: The Reggio approach to urban education.* New York: Teachers College Press.

Lewin, A. (2008). *Powerful children: Understanding how to teach and learn using the Reggio approach.* New York: Teachers College Press.

Malaguzzi, L. (1995). *Volpino, last of the chicken thieves.* Bergamo, Italy: Edizioni Junior.

Milliken, J. (2003). *Reflections: Reggio Emilia principles within Australian contexts.* Castle Hill, Australia: Pademelon Press.

Pelo, A. (2007). *The language of art: Inquiry-based studio practices in early childhood settings.* St. Paul, MN: Redleaf Press.

Rinaldi, C. (2006). *In dialogue with Reggio Emilia: Listening, researching and learning.* New York: Routledge.

Scheinfeld, D. R., Haigh, K. M., & Scheinfeld, J. P. (2008). *We are all explorers: Learning and teaching with Reggio principles in urban settings.* New York: Teachers College Press.

Smith, D., & Goldhaber, J. (2004). *Poking, pinching and pretending: Documenting toddlers' explorations with clay.* St. Paul, MN: Redleaf Press.

Thornton, L., & Brunton, P. (2007). *Understanding the Reggio approach: Early years education in practice.* London: Routledge.

Vecchi, V. (2010). *Art and creativity in Reggio Emilia: Exploring the role and potential of ateliers in early childhood education.* New York: Routledge.

Wien, C. A. (2008). *Emergent curriculum in the primary classroom.* New York: Teachers College Press.

BOOKS AND AUDIO-VISUAL MATERIALS FROM REGGIO CHILDREN

Many resources for educators are published by Reggio Children: International Center for the Defense and Promotion of the Rights of all Children, Reggio Emilia, Italy: http://zero sei.comune.re.it/inter/rc_publications.htm.

They are also distributed by Learning Materials Workshop, Burlington, VT: http://learning materialswork.com/index.php.

Audio-Visual Materials

The Amusement Park for Birds (1992). DVD.
A Message from Loris Malaguzzi (1993). VHS.
Not Just Anyplace (2008). DVD and VHS.
Landscapes (2009). CD of slide images of infant-toddler centers and preschools.

Books and Print Resources

The hundred languages of children: Narrative of the possible (catalog of "The Hundred Languages of Children" exhibit) (1987/1996/2005).
Children, spaces, relations: Metaproject for an environment for young children (1998).
Everything has a shadow, except ants (1999).
Brick by brick: The history of "XXV Aprile" People's Nursery School of Villa Cella (2000).
Reggio Tutta: A guide to the city by the children (2000).
The future is a lovely day (2001).
Making learning visible: Children as individual and group learners (2001).
Along the levee road (2002).
Theater curtain: The ring of transformations (2002).
Charter of the City and Childhood Councils (2003).
Children, art, artists: The expressive languages of children, the artistic language of Alberto Burri (2004).
REMIDA Day muta . . . menti (edited by the International Association Friends of Loris Malaguzzi) (2005).
Dialogues with places (catalog of the exhibit) (2008).
The languages of food: Recipes, experiences and thoughts (2008).
Browsing through ideas (2009).
The black rubber column (2009).
Indications Preschools and Infant-Toddler Centres of the Municipality of Reggio Emilia (2010).
The Municipal Infant-Toddler Centers and Preschools of Reggio Emilia: Historical notes and general information (2010/2000).
Bikes-lots: An educational, ecological, urbanistic project dedicated to the bicycle (graphic design from the installation Bicitante [Bikes-lots]) (2011).
One city, many children: Memories of a present history (catalog of the exhibit) (2011).
The wonder of learning: The hundred languages of children (catalog of the exhibit) (2011).

Books in the Unheard Voice of Children Series

The fountains (1995).
A journey into the rights of children (1995).
Tenderness (1995).
The little ones of silent movies (1996).
Shoe and meter (1997).
Advisories (2002).

Books in the Coriandoli Series

The park is . . . (2008).
We write shapes that look like a book (2008).

OTHER RESOURCES

The North American Reggio Emilia Alliance (NAREA) contains much information on their website (http://www.reggioalliance.org/index.php) about resources for educators, including information about professional development resources and opportunities for educators interested in the Reggio Emilia philosophy of education. The **Innovations Periodical** pages include information on acquiring CDs of back issues as well as summaries of issues published since 2003 of NAREA's journal, *Innovations in Early Education: The International Reggio Exchange*. In the **Print & Video Resources** section, there is an Articles page and a Buy Now page that list recommended articles, book chapters, and books related to the Reggio Emilia philosophy. The **Schools & Organizations Map** includes information about NAREA member school, centers, universities, and programs in North America. The **Fundamental Workshops** and **Conferences & Initiatives** pages list professional development initiatives related to the Reggio Emilia philosophy in various contexts throughout North America. The **Study Groups** pages include information about opportunities for North American educators to participate in study tours to the municipal infant-toddler centers and preschools in Reggio Emilia, Italy. The **Related Links** page includes a growing list of professional organizations that may be of interest to early childhood educators and teacher educators.

Illustration Credits

The editors and publisher gratefully acknowledge permission for use of the following material:

37	Preschools and Infant-Toddler Centers—Istituzione of the Municipality of Reggio Emilia
42	Preschools and Infant-Toddler Centers—Istituzione of the Municipality of Reggio Emilia
47	Giovanni Piazza
54	Preschools and Infant-Toddler Centers—Istituzione of the Municipality of Reggio Emilia
59	Carolyn Edwards
62	Lella Gandini
68	University of Massachusetts–Amherst
70	Preschools and Infant-Toddler Centers—Istituzione of the Municipality of Reggio Emilia
73	REMIDA—Creative Recycling Centre, Reggio Emilia
74	Preschools and Infant-Toddler Centers—Istituzione of the Municipality of Reggio Emilia
78	Lella Gandini and Ellen Hall
81	REMIDA—Creative Recycling Centre, Reggio Emilia
83	Lella Gandini
86	Lella Gandini
89	Preschools and Infant-Toddler Centers—Istituzione of the Municipality of Reggio Emilia
91	Margie Cooper
96	Preschools and Infant-Toddler Centers—Istituzione of the Municipality of Reggio Emilia
101	REMIDA—Creative Recycling Centre, Reggio Emilia
105	Preschools and Infant-Toddler Centers—Istituzione of the Municipality of Reggio Emilia
117	Preschools and Infant-Toddler Centers—Istituzione of the Municipality of Reggio Emilia
124	Preschools and Infant-Toddler Centers—Istituzione of the Municipality of Reggio Emilia
126	Preschools and Infant-Toddler Centers—Istituzione of the Municipality of Reggio Emilia
135	REMIDA—Creative Recycling Centre, Reggio Emilia
140	Preschools and Infant-Toddler Centers—Istituzione of the Municipality of Reggio Emilia
143	Preschools and Infant-Toddler Centers—Istituzione of the Municipality of Reggio Emilia
147	REMIDA—Creative Recycling Centre, Reggio Emilia
149	Preschools and Infant-Toddler Centers—Istituzione of the Municipality of Reggio Emilia
152	Preschools and Infant-Toddler Centers—Istituzione of the Municipality of Reggio Emilia

Colored photo essay follows page 214. All photos courtesy Preschools and
Infant-Toddler Centers—Istituzione of the Municipality of Reggio Emilia.

Author Index

Subject Index